Revolutionary Law and Order

Revolutionary Law and Order

Politics and Social Change in the USSR

Peter H. Juviler

THE FREE PRESS
A Division of Macmillan Publishing Co., Inc.
NEW YORK

Collier Macmillan Publishers
LONDON

The Free Press
A Division of Macmillan Publishing Co., Inc.
866 Third Avenue, New York, N.Y. 10022

Collier Macmillan Canada, Ltd.

Library of Congress Catalog Card Number: 76-12832

Printed in the United States of America

printing number

1 2 3 4 5 6 7 8 9 10

Library of Congress Cataloging in Publication Data

Juviler, Peter H
Revolutionary law and order.

Bibliography: p.
Includes index.
1. Criminal law--Russia--History. 2. Criminal justice, Administration of--Russia--History. 3. Crime and criminals--Russia--History. I. Title.
Law 364 76-12832
ISBN 0-02-916800-7

To Nina

Contents

List of Abbreviations

BVS	*Byulleten' Verkhovnogo Suda SSSR* (USSR Supreme Court Bulletin)
BVS RSFSR	*Byulleten' Verkhovnogo Suda RSFSR* (RSFSR Supreme Court Bulletin)
CDSP	*Current Digest of the Soviet Press*
GPU	Gosudarstvennoe politicheskoe upravlenie (State Political Administration, the secret police)
GUITU	Glavnoe upravlenie ispravitel'no-trudovykh uchrezhdenii (the Chief Administration of Corrective Labor Institutions)
GULAG	Glavnoe upravlenie lagerei (the Chief Administration of Camps)
IGPAN	Institut gosudarstva i prava Akademii nauk SSSR (Institute of State and Law of the USSR Academy of Sciences)
ITK	Ispravitel'no-trudovaya koloniya (corrective labor colony)
Kriminologiya	A. A. Gertsenzon et al. (eds.), *Kriminologiya* (2nd ed.; Moscow: "Yuridicheskaya literatura," 1968)
MOOP	Ministerstvo okhrany obshchestvennogo poryadka (Ministry for the Preservation of Public Order)
MVD	Ministerstvo vnutrennikh del (Ministry of Internal Affairs, or Ministry of the Interior)
NKVD	Narodnyi komissariat vnutrennikh del (People's Komissariat of Internal Affairs)
OGPU	Ob"edinennoe gosudarstvennoe politicheskoe upravlenie (Unified State Political Administration, the secret police)

Pol. sobr. soch.	V. I. Lenin, *Polnoe sobranie sochinenii* (5th ed.; Moscow: Gos. Izd. Politicheskoi Literatury, 1960–1965) (Lenin's *Works*)
Sbornik zakonov	*Sbornik zakonov SSSR i ukazov prezidiuma Verkhovogo Soveta SSSR 1938–1967; Sbornik zakonov SSSR i ukazov prezidiuma Verkhovnogo Soveta SSSR 1968–1970* (3 vols; Moscow: Izd. "Izvestiya Sovetov deputatov trudyashchikhsya SSSR, 1968, 1971) (Collection of USSR legislation, 1938–1970)
SGP	*Sovetskoe gosudarstvo i pravo* (Soviet State and Law)
SSSR	Soyuz sovetskikh sotsialistichekikh respublik (Union of Soviet Socialist Republics)
SU RSFSR	*Sobranie uzakonenii i rasporyazhenii rabochego i krest'yanskogo pravitel'stva Rossiiskoi Sotsialisticheskoi Federativnoi Sovetskoi Respubliki* (last five words added with *SU RSFSR*, No. 1 (1925) (Collected legislation, RSFSR)
SYu	*Sovetskaya yustitsiya* (Soviet Justice)
SZ	*Sotsialisticheskaya zakonnost'* (Socialist Legality)
SZ SSSR	*Sobranie zakonov i rasporyazhenii rabochekrest'yanskogo pravitel'stva Soyuza Sovetskikh Sotsialisticheskiich Respublik* (Collected legislation, USSR)
UCR	*Uniform Crime Reports for the United States*
UK	*Ugolovnyi kodeks RSFSR: ofitsial'nyi tekst* (RSFSR Criminal Code)
UPK	*Ugolovno-protsessual'nyi kodeks RSFSR: ofitsial'nyi tekst* (RSFSR Code of Criminal Procedure)
Ved	*Vedomosti Verkhovnogo Soveta Soyuza Sovetskikh Sotsialisticheskikh Respublik* (Gazette of the USSR Supreme Soviet)

Acknowledgments

LOOKING BACK at the ten years' work behind this book (though not on it), I realize how much of a joint project it was. Without the help of colleagues here and in the Soviet Union I could not have completed it. Peter H. Solomon, Jr., and Robert Sharlet carefully read an earlier version of this book and made important contributions to it. Yuri Luryi, formerly a leading member of the Leningrad bar, wrote an incisive review of this manuscript and made various writings of his available to me. A conference Sheila Fitzpatrick organized in 1974 on Stalin's cultural revolution encouraged me to retain material on Stalinism I felt to be confirmed by the conference.

I am indebted to Jonathan Harris for his comments on a paper I delivered at the APSA meeting in 1972. Paul Hollander, Henry W. Morton, Rudolf L. Tokes, and Robert C. Tucker organized meetings where as a participant I gained stimulation and insight. Some of the work done for those meetings is in this book. The writings on crime and delinquency in the USSR by Paul Hollander and Walter Connor, whose book *Deviance in Soviet Society* I cite frequently, laid part of the basis for my own work. Helpful suggestions have come from conversations or correspondence with Felice Gaer, H. Kent Geiger, Henry W. Morton, and Michel Meyer of the Institute of Criminology in Paris. I gained from William W. Adams's Ph.D. and post-doctoral research on capital punishment and his co-editing of *Bulletin on Current Research in Soviet and East European Law*. Patricia Jarvis, editorial supervisor at the Free Press and Lionel Dean, copy editor, worked on the difficult task of preparing this manuscript for publication. Charles E. Smith of the Free Press gave unfailing encouragement and guidance.

John N. Hazard pointed the way to using law as a key to social and political change in the USSR. Harold J. Breman's work on tendencies in Soviet legal reforms defined the form for Chapter 4 and, along with the work of Donald Barry, his collaborator in some writing, provided perspectives on Soviet law and the legal profession.

Numerous students have challenged my understanding of Soviet law and politics. Among them several did research for me and I shall be forever grateful to them: Naomi Williams, Tom Parker, Laird Grant, Golda Shabad, and, last but not least, a major helper, Arthur (Randy) Bregman. Martha Bashford brought keen analysis and observation to our collaboration on the proofreading and indexing.

Numerous Soviet judges and lawyers gave me impromptu interviews when I showed up at their courts and offices with my Moscow University *udostoverenie* (identity card). Thanks to the cooperation of such people, as well as of my Soviet colleagues, I could better ask of what I later read, Does this ring true?

My thanks go to the Lenin Library, the library of the Faculty of Law at Moscow University, the Fundamental Library of the Social Sciences, and the libraries of Columbia and Harvard universities and the National Council on Crime and Delinquency. Susan Escoffery, Bruce Escoffery, and Irene Luhn typed parts of this manuscript with superb care. The Inter-University Committee of Travel Grants twice sent me to the Soviet Union, in 1958–1959 and 1964, for three semesters' research, some of which contributed to this book. Barnard College gave me a grant to visit the USSR in the tense summer of 1968. Five other visits, thanks to various scholarly and cultural exchange sources, have helped me to keep in touch with Soviet changes.

I hope that, first, I have left out nobody meriting mention here, second, if I inadvertently do omit somebody, that they will forgive me and, third, that I shall be held responsible, not those mentioned here, for the opinions and the shortcomings in the book.

Chapters 4–6 contain some material originally appearing in Henry W. Morton and Rudolf L. Tokes (eds.), *Soviet Politics and Society in the 1970s* (New York: Free Press, 1974) and Donald D. Barry, William E. Butler, and George Ginsburgs (eds.), *Contemporary Soviet Law: Essays in Honor of John N. Hazard* (The Hague: Martinus Nijhoff, 1974). All the chapters contain something of the matchless patience of Nina, Gregory, and Geoffry.

Revolutionary Law and Order

1

Introduction

It is not so simple . . .

—Earl Warren

THIS BOOK RETRACES the Russians' quest for law and order in the sense of security against crimes, and its effective enforcement, from the tsarist reforms and the first Bolshevik handbills and drumhead tribunals to the elaborate Soviet crime-fighting apparatus as it enters the computer age.[1]

What appear to have been the main trends in crime and responses to it as far as they can be determined?

What social and political changes appear to be related to trends in crime and responses to it in Soviet Russia?

What light do Soviet responses to crime shed on the policy process in Soviet politics?

What do these findings tell us about Soviet successes and failures in eliminating crime?

Answers to these questions help test the validity of existing assumptions about Soviet law and order, and help resolve differences in Soviet and Western assumptions:

1. Soviet comment is mixed on the success of the Soviet attempts at preventing crime and delinquency before 1953. Westerners write almost unanimously that they were successful. To the extent that they go into the earlier Soviet experience at all, the Western assumptions have been that the "totalitarian" controls it brought solved the law-and-order problem for the USSR, even if at a cost in freedom and due process that Westerners—most of them—would not want to pay.[2] For, at a time when Americans' chances of victimization by thieves or violent criminals had almost doubled in ten years, an angry grandmother from Clifton, New Jersey, declared, "If we have to have a police state for law and order, we'll have to have it." [3]

2. About the present Soviet era, the reverse is true. Soviet commentaries are more likely than Western ones to state that the Soviet regime and socialist order have the long-run solution to the crime problem.[4]

3. Picturing how policy is made, some Western sources stress the Party's primacy and the ideological limits on specialists' thought in this area.[5] Other Western sources attribute a primary role to the Party but describe in some detail how specialists participate actively in initiating and formulating at least modest changes in policy and take a large role in drafting and implementing major party decisions.[6] I bring to this book an assumption expressed in 1966, supported in my research on family and criminal policies, that since Stalin, research about social disorganization has shown a greater empiricism and need to know why. This has meant greater feedback of information and expert opinion to the politicians, increased participation in policy debates outside the party elite, with "differences of opinion cutting across lines of occupation and party membership, virtual institutionalization of wide consultation. So far, however, a small party oligarchy retains in its decree power what it has never had absolutely in administrative practice, that is, the last word."[7] Policy studies on interest groups and the professions and the resolution of various issues made in the later 1960s and in the 1970s draw broadly similar conclusions. Some of them stress, as I do, the need to look at trends in opinion cutting across occupational group lines.[8]

The Soviet opinions presented here concern mostly common crimes with unwilling victims, crimes universally at issue—crimes against persons and property, especially the anxiety-causing crimes of theft, robbery, and violence, the crimes highlighted in the well-known 1967 report of the President's Commission on Law Enforcement and Administration of Justice (President's Crime Commission, for short). The fear and anxiety these crimes provoke and their harm to the quality of life belie their small physical toll as compared with the toll of accidents and disease.[9]

At issue also for law and order are white-collar crimes by professionals in positions of trust, mass pilfering of state property by ordinary workers, certain "victimless" crimes (better called crimes without unwilling victims) such as drug offenses and pimping, and political crimes, the response to which becomes relevant at times to general law-and-order issues. Juvenile lawbreaking is a large enough issue to require separate treatment, which I give elsewhere.[10]

Violence and Alternatives

Violence, a frequent companion of social change,[11] defines the basic issue of how to deal with criminals, as the lawmakers of a given country choose to define them.[12] How and when is violence to be used? This issue divides policy makers, Soviet and non-Soviet, into liberalizers espousing a "treatment" emphasis and hard-liners espousing a "punishment" emphasis.[13]

Some Western opinion favors completely eliminating "the crime of punishment." But liberalizing lawyers, though against punishing victimless "morals" offenses, respond that theories of crime still give insufficient guidance to alternative means of prevention and, worse, threaten potentially arbitrary compulsory treatment.[14]

For both treatment and punishment may involve violence,[15] such as forcible detention and administration of drugs or shock therapy as means of "behavior modification." I prefer to call "repression" all responses of compulsory deprivation, including physical compulsion. They include incarceration, compulsory treatment for alcoholism or insanity, and nonpunitive penalties, such as dismissal and other material deprivations. By "prevention" I mean nondepriving measures taken to avert crimes before they occur,[16] such as sports programs, urban planning, voluntary rehabilitation in or out of prison, job training, and warnings to take keys out of car ignitions. Soviet "measures of social influence" like comrades' courts or meetings of workplace collectives to discuss a comrade's conduct as worker or parent straddle prevention and correction. One of the noteworthy aspects of recent Soviet crime fighting has been its intensification of both prevention and correction.

The issues underlying criminal policy, then, add up to this: When should repression be used against criminals, and when should prevention be used? How and when will repression be more effective than are other means of suasion such as education, economic and social reform, censorship, community and youth programs, and economic and social pressures?[17]

Violence is not just an American issue but a universal one,[18] and an issue not only of citizens' disorder from below but also of the uses and limits of "the systematic violence of the state," [19] itself frequently a contributor to lawlessness and disorder, in East and West,[20] but nowhere more massively than under Stalin.

Soviet Policy in Perspective

In sum, crime and responses to it in Soviet Russia provide clues as to the efficacy of violence in the quest for law and order, and as to changes in Soviet politics. Policy studies of responses to challenges restore to its rightful place "purpose as a central element in social and political reality," [21] and also a sense of the sequence of situation and response, of alternatives and choices.

A central Soviet purpose has been, as so often stated, "not only to reduce crime but to eradicate it." But, save for the collapse of the tsarist regime in 1917 and the Bolshevik coup against its short-lived successor, the Provisional Government, nothing in Russia followed the Marxist blueprint of a rapid, almost bloodless withering away of exploitation, the state, crime, and the family during the revolutionary transition to communism.

The family proved indispensable, the need for the state protracted, and the issues of criminal policy perennial. Helping revolutions did not break out in the West as expected but, rather, three years of grim civil war (1918–1920), the period of so-called War Communism. The New Economic Policy, NEP (1921–1928), brought a breathing spell during recovery from war and famine, Lenin's death in 1924, and a fervor of experimentation and research in crime and corrections. Lenin's death at fifty-three opened the way to Stalin and his path of more, not less, coercion as a "lever of change." When Stalin died in 1953, his country was just beginning to feel normalcy, though under the shadow of impending purge.

Under Stalin's successors, "scientific and technological revolution" took increasing precedence over social revolution from above, despite Khrushchev's brief fling at the "full-scale building of communism." Chapters four through six retrace the onset of this postrevolutionary era and describe the trends today in criminal policy and crime and its study.

Pointing to continuity and change in the Bolshevik, Stalinist, and post-Stalinist eras, the book explores as a policy study how the issue of crime prevention is formulated, deliberated at selected times, resolved, and with what apparent results.[22] Hopefully, this will add to the general store of information about the Soviet political process and changes in it,[23] as well as about crime in the USSR.

Crime and direct responses to them are viewed in the setting of (1) the social changes occurring in the USSR, and (2) the political changes brought on by power struggles and the Soviet regime's efforts to carry out revolutionary purposes, defend revolutionary values, and respond to the results of both political and industrial revolution.

Some comparisons are made with Western responses to crime and delinquency. Given what had to be covered here, however, I omitted much of the Western material. But I hope that this narrative will add historical and political dimensions to existing studies of Soviet crime and delinquency. It is meant to bring them up to date and to help others to acquire background on Soviet law enforcement as well as to make their own comparisons with the quest for law and order under the Soviet regime.

Tsarist Reform and Decay

Failure of expected proletarian revolution in the West is only one of many reasons for Bolshevik difficulties with crime after they took power. Some of their difficulties, as we shall see, may be attributed to their own policies.

Others, most likely, originated in the tsarist legacy to the Bolsheviks. Three sides of that legacy seem especially relevant in limiting and shaping Bolshevik choices. Autocratic reforms produced a strange mixture of due process and repression and a distinguished legal profession, its thinking centuries ahead of dying autocracy and most of its subjects, on the rule and role of law. Industrial revolution plus chronic peasant poverty spurred mass migration to cities with their overburdened welfare services and overcrowded slums. Ill-starred foreign adventurism of the last tsar, Nicholas II (1894–1917), hastened war and upheaval, undermining an already precarious law and order.

The courts and bar inherited by the Bolsheviks dated back to the judicial reform promulgated in 1864 by Alexander II (1855–1881), undermined by Alexander III (1881–1894) and Nicholas II, and repaired by the Provisional Government.

Ascending the throne, Alexander II knew of the rot in the tribunals of the land and called for "truth and mercy" in the law courts. During his freeing of the serfs (a reform leaving an embittered, land-hungry, payment-burdened peasantry), Alexander set about reshaping Russia's secret, corrupt, and tortuously complex justice into a court system designed, in theory, for free men in a modern economy.[24]

Commissions of distinguished jurists, who were drafting new laws, eyed watchfully by the Tsar and his bureaucracy, borrowed procedures from reformed Western court systems. They embraced, also, the liberal, classical principles of jurisprudence which underlay the Western procedures. The resulting judicial reform of 1864 embodied classical reform principles first definitively stated a century earlier in 1764 by a young Milanese lawyer, Cesare Bonesana, Marchese di Beccaria, in his book *Dei delitti e delle pene.* It was a manifesto of reform and individual rights against arbitrary justice. At the same time it provided the predictability and equality of justice so necessary for a modern capitalist economy such as was just beginning to emerge in Europe.[25]

Classical theories of crime assume that people are reasonable, that they seek to maximize their own gains at minimum cost to themselves, that they weigh the gains and costs of their behavior. As punishments get milder, beyond a certain point, people will commit more crimes. But too harsh punishment (e.g., hanging for stealing a loaf of bread) encourages more serious crimes since the penalties are the same as for petty crimes. The effectiveness of justice depends, according to the classicists, not on the harshness of justice, but on its inevitability, predictability, and equal application. In its neoclassical form, by the time of the 1864 changes in Russia, this Beccarian school of jurisprudence had incorporated a flexibility by admitting that free will and reason might be absent in children and the mentally ill. They should be relieved of criminal responsibility.

Judges should have leeway in sentencing depending on possible "mitigating circumstances." [26]

Alexander's court reform edict of November 20, 1864, strongly upheld this liberal ideology despite its sources in an intellectual revolt against the sort of absolutist *ancien régime* his autocracy still represented. Then, at the peak of his short-lived reforming enthusiasm, Alexander saw in the judicial reforms the embodiment of his desire "to establish in Russia fast, just, and merciful courts, equal for all Our subjects, to increase judicial power, to give it the necessary independence and, in general, to strengthen in Our people the respect for law without which public prosperity is impossible, and which must serve as a permanent guide for the actions of all and everybody, from the person of highest rank to that of lowest rank." [27]

Draining the judicial bog in one huge operation, the 1864 reforms attacked corruption by putting the courts under public scrutiny in open hearings, and providing juries for many criminal cases. With this new active role for defense lawyers, a professional bar, "a complete innovation for Russia," [28] replaced the courthouse boys—the *stryapchy,* or fixers—who had negotiated their luckless clients' cases through the old bog. Independence of judges was formalized by their irremovability (in the general courts), by the separation of judicial and administrative powers, and by strict requirements of training and experience which greatly raised standards. This was a bold and basic reform stroke, sustained and unified by the imported ideal of equal and independent justice for all.[29]

The 1864 reforms simplified the court system into two parallel tracks: (1) local courts, for reconciliation or punishment where misdemeanors were charged, and for hearing lesser civil disputes, and (2) the general courts, for more important civil and criminal felony cases. Both tracks ended in the Senate, a supreme court with mixed appellate, cassation (review on points of law, not fact), and guidance functions. The Senate served as court of first instance in special cases such as the most serious political ones.

Local courts consisted of the new justices of the peace (*mirovye sudy*) and the old peasant courts for rural districts (*volostnye sudy*). Justices of the peace (magistrates' courts), deliberately informal, had one elected judge trained in the law. Peasant courts heard even lesser cases. Made up of three elected, untrained peasant judges, they had been organized by the emancipation of 1861.

The second track of the reformed courts, the general courts, consisted of 106 circuit courts (*okruzhnye sudy*) and 14 chambers of justice (*sudebnye palaty*), to hear political cases and appeals from circuit courts. Appointed by the Ministry of Justice, judges in these courts heard cases in panels of at least three. Cases of ordinary crime went to the circuit courts, usually to be tried with jury, in which case there was no appeal.

Russia's great reform of justice, like the major Soviet reforms later, were, then, initiated from on high in the name of a set of foreign principles adapted to the nation. Russia's reforms, like the Soviet ones, worked out to a compromise between new ideals, old ways, and political expediency. Keeping special courts in 1864 for peasants (three quarters of the population), disappointed proponents of equal justice for all classes.[30] Much—probably too much—has been made of the ignorance, crudeness, and sometimes venality of the peasant judges and their susceptibility to influence with *vedra* (buckets) of vodka. Peasant judges, however, were tuned to peasant customary law and the life of their villages. To clear up consequences of drunkenness or a brawl, a villager did not have to trudge off far away, sometimes to town. Peasant courts' usefulness in the myriad of petty conflicts brought before them was sufficient to stave off their demise up to 1917 (and to bring their revival—without powers to jail—as comrades' courts in the 1920s and late 1950s).

More seriously, the 1864 reforms left large loopholes for administrative influence in violation of separation of powers. The Minister of Justice was also Prosecutor General (as later in Soviet Russia until 1933). Through his control of the powerful Procuracy (prosecutor's offices), and because the Procuracy was the main avenue to general court judgeships (closed to advocates), the minister had leverage on the courts. The second loophole for ministerial influence lay in control over the judges. They were irremovable, but not immovable. A refractory judge risked transfer to inhospitable regions or a freeze on his promotion. A third loophole for ministerial influence appeared in the system of supposedly independent judicial investigators, like the French *juges d'instruction*. Defendants had no right to counsel during the important pretrial investigation and ways were found to intimidate the investigating magistrate.[31]

Under Alexander III (1881–1894), a reactionary already before his father's assassination, judicial powers became less independent, in 1889 especially, at the expense of the courts closest to the people. A law of July 12, 1889, eliminated elected justices of the peace in the 35 provinces of Russia except for Moscow, St. Petersburg, St. Petersburg region, the territory of the Don Cossack Army, and six other large cities. Powers of the justices of the peace were handed to appointed land captains who were also administrators, to appointed urban judges and to appointed regional representatives of the circuit courts. Justices of the peace returned under the reform law of June 15, 1912 (to 20 provinces by 1917). Part of the reform passed by the Duma (lower, elected chamber established under the 1905 Constitution) was cut by the upper chamber, the State Council. For example, Jews could no longer serve as justices of the peace and chambers of justice went on supervising justices of the peace.

The Russian penal code knew no corporal punishment (save through peasant courts) or death penalty. Leroy-Beaulieu termed the code "probably the mildest code in Europe." [32] Again, there were catches: (1) the rigors of penal servitude in Siberia, (2) the policy of using regular courts and short-cut administrative procedures to repress real or suspected political foes. Governments virtually everywhere seek to use the courts to repress political opponents.[33] Tsarist justice knew flagrant cases of this, such as resort to closed hearings and the courts without juries (courts with class representatives), and military field courts-martial. Field courts handed out death sentences to civilians right and left, especially in 1906–1914, even while capital punishment could not be meted out by civilian courts. In addition to the court repression, the regime frequently used political police channels straight to administrative exile. Political cases, then, opened vast breaches in Russia's rule of law (a phenomenon not confined to Russia but flagrant there).

Russian criminal justice worked more fairly in nonpolitical cases than it did in political ones. But it operated in a swirl of disorder stirred up by huge influxes of peasant migrants seeking jobs and shelter. Russia's cities grew enormously during the spurt of industrialization in the last half century of tsarism. Her urban population nearly tripled (increasing 293 percent) between 1857 and 1897, a period when total population increased by only 74.3 percent. Especially after the emancipation of the serfs in 1861, peasants turned from plough to shovel and lathe. Half the factory workers in 1897 had migrated from the villages.[34] They and their families left the land faster than a new, stable social order could be formed to absorb them in the cities. Youths, especially, lacked the guidance and support of the peasant household and village community. They were more likely to encounter police rather than relatives or neighbors when disorderly. And the incipient urban affluence they found tempted them as a rule more than it offered them the means with which to satisfy their suddenly heightened demands. "The rush of candidates from the village into the large urban centers never ceases," a contemporary of these migrants wrote. "A husky unskilled village youth comes to the city seeking a job or training—and the city gives only street fumes, the glitter of store windows, home brew, cocaine and the cinema." [35]

The migrants swelled the population of already overcrowded and underserviced factory districts of Moscow, Kiev, and St. Petersburg as others had filled the violence-ridden slums of London, Manchester, Glasgow, Paris, New York, and Chicago, with similar effects on crime rates. Appalling conditions of Russian slum life meant wretched tenements and barracks, drunkenness and violence there, and five to eight persons in a tiny room. Many seekers found vocational opportunities. Many also entered a life of broken families, unemployment, drift, and crime, then the revolving door in and out of prison. Small wonder that the slums produced swarms of homeless waifs and other recruits for the criminal underworld.[36] The waifs were only the most disinherited of a generation of Russian children among the poor who had borne the brunt both of industrialization and of political conflict: two disastrous wars and two revolutions in thirteen years, provoked by tsarist adventurism and neglect of the home front. Adding to the upsets of urbanization came the Russo-Japanese War of 1904–1905 and the 1905 revolution bound up with this foreign Russian folly. Ten years later, Russia entered World War I, the last link in the collapse of tsarism. The events of 1904–1905 precipitated increases in total convictions, especially convictions of juvenile criminals ten through sixteen years old. Child crime was increasing all over Europe, but in Russia faster than in any Western European country.[37] After Russia stumbled into World War I, adult convictions dropped, naturally, because of the draft. The number of juvenile defendants, ten through sixteen years old tried by circuit courts increased eleven percent in 1911–1914 but 75 percent in 1914–1916. That year a new adult crime wave began to sweep Russia, feeding on demoralization and growing desertion rates.[38]

Amidst the decay and disorder, and the judicial abuses perpetrated by the tsarist regime, reforms continued in crime fighting even as the old order fell. Russia was a land not only of decay but also of reform, right up to the Bolshevik takeover. A community of exquisitely trained legal scholars remained closely in touch with foreign penology and criminology. Their work was branching out along several paths at once:

1. Criminal lawyers were reforming justice back toward a system more closely fulfilling the ideals of 1864. Political justice abated with the fall of tsarism and the coming of the non-Communist Provisional Government in March 1917. The caretaker regime managed to pass a reform decree of March 21, 1917, admitting women to the bar, ending restrictions on Jews and other non-Christians in the profession, and opening appointive judgeships to lawyers. Also, an eminent commission, A.F. Koni presiding, drew up other reforms including the transfer of all criminal cases to courts with juries. It abolished land captains and urban judges left over from the 1889 changes, completely reviving the principle of elected justices of the peace.[39]

2. Judges, penologists, and welfare organizations were developing children's courts as part of a switch from punishment to treatment for juveniles while slowly improving juvenile corrections.[40]

3. Others than Bolsheviks had gone as far as forecasting an end to criminal punishment. Thus, Professor M.N. Gernet anticipated using less punitive courts for adults as well as children.[41] Gernet, a radical socialist

and distinguished non-Marxist legal scholar, envisaged the withering away of punitive repression. Gallows, prison, corporal punishment, he had written earlier, would "wither away along with the old unjust social relations. With the advent of a new, just socialist order, compulsory rehabilitation with the utmost humanity and respect for the inmates would replace punishment." [42]

4. Community and state agencies were adding social work to crime prevention, so as to try to reach and help potential lawbreakers before they would have to be dragged into the courts.[43]

5. Russian researchers were participating increasingly in the young science of criminology, applying the competing Western theories of crime and punishment, though regarded as subversive by the tsarist government.[44] Unlike classical theories of the individual responsibility of reasonable men, sociological theories of crime depicted it as rooted in social conditions beyond the reach of an individual's reason, in patterns of economic, class, and group relations.[45] An individual's personality may predispose him or her to crime in given situations. But, on a society-wide scale, "individual differences in some sense neutralize each other," in the words of the Belgian statistician and astronomer Quetelet, an early nineteenth century founder of the sociological school, along with his French contemporary Guerry.

The development of the sociological school in Russia has been traced back to 1872 when M.V. Dukhovskii (a teacher of M.N. Gernet, tsarist and Soviet criminologist of note) gave a lecture calling on fellow jurists to study causes of crime. I. Ya. Foinitskii (1847–1913) had an international reputation. A criminal law professor, he served as chief prosecutor of the Governing Senate (high court). E.N. Tarnovskii, also a sociological theorist of crime, worked before and after the revolution as a leading criminal statistician. Russian sociologists, like their European colleagues, did not rule out individual peculiarities among the "factors" causing crime. Their main attention went to factors that were, rather, socioeconomic (unemployment, price rises, slums) and physical (seasons, climate).[47]

Sociological findings face the criticism that they are too expensive and too interventionist in social relations to be practical. By stressing "root causes" rather than the crimes themselves, the critics say, sociological theories miss the point that criminals are responsible members of society with freedom of choice. The result is to neglect relatively cheap, direct means of security and deterrence against criminals.[48]

There has long been a debate on between sociologists who see crime "as a product of society" and biopsychologists of various schools who see crime "as a product or expression of the individual constitution," whether inherited or formed in certain unfavorable environments.[49] Biopsychologists hold that there are discoverable criminal types. They may be throwbacks to primitive men, degenerates, or the feebleminded. Cesare Lombroso, a pet bugaboo of sociologists, especially some Soviet ones, set down his conception of the born criminal in the first edition of his *L'Uomo delinquente* (1876). His school linked crime closely with "anomalies"—physical defects of the skull, face, body, hair, and nervous system. They symptomized rather than caused the criminal predispositions. Later Lombroso greatly modified his theory to stress the play of social influence. Dr. P.N. Tarnovskaya, a member of the strong Lombrosian school in prerevolutionary Russia, found, she said, that women criminals and prostitutes averaged 1.5 centimeters taller than honest women did and their jaws measured 1.5 centimeters longer. The women offenders had abnormally high percentages of peculiar skull shapes, facial asymmetry, and other anomalies.[50]

Lombrosianism has suffered from lack of scientific confirmation. Generally speaking, samples of noncriminals seem to have as many physical and mental peculiarities as criminals do.[51] Psychological theories of crime help deal with individual offenders but do not explain changes in crime rates in a given society and the dramatic results obtained when the environment is radically changed, such as when criminals were deported to Australia or when tough young members of Soviet labor communes could be changed into law-abiding activists without either psychiatric examinations or contemplation of their pasts.

Three sides of the Russian legacy, in sum, appeared especially important for shaping Bolshevik policy and its impact. First, centralized autocratic decision making had fastened a frustrating mixture of reform and repression. Reformers' aspirations for the rule of law in Russia received little support from the last two tsars, or from most of their subjects. Second, industrial revolution, emancipation, and chronic peasant poverty spurred mass migration to cities with their overburdened welfare services, slums and growing underworld. Third, tsarist foreign adventures did not head off discontent but only intensified it in the bitter pangs of defeat. The years 1905–1913 marked a "silver age" for Russian culture. Political parties, trade unions, a lively press, peasant self-help, and credit pools were entering the scene. But both social development and the onset of social disorganization sprang from rapid change that needed the urgent attention of a regime preoccupied with Russian grandeur. War and upheaval further undermined an already precarious law and order.

Russia's wartime crime wave symptomized deteriorating conditions and morale in town and village. The crisis came to a head when hungry working-class women started bread riots in Petrograd* on International Women's Day, March 8, 1917. Riots grew quickly into mass demonstra-

* St. Petersburg, capital of Russia 1712–1918, was renamed Petrograd in 1914 and Leningrad in 1924, after Lenin's death.

tions against the government, and demonstrations into the February Revolution.* When Petrograd regiments refused to fire on demonstrators March 11, the power of the autocracy could be said to have collapsed in Petrograd, vanquished by an unplanned, spontaneous uprising that caught party leaders of all persuasions by surprise. Nicholas' prorogation of the Imperial Duma (the weak parliament created under pressures of the 1905 revolution) became an empty gesture. The next day, March 12, the Duma met in defiance of its suspension and elected a provisional committee of the Duma with a vague mission "to restore order and negotiate with institutions and individuals." On March 15 Nicholas abdicated in favor of his brother. But Grand Duke Michael refused the honor. Authority had passed from the Romanov dynasty, which had reigned for more than three hundred years, to the provisional committee, renamed now Provisional Government, which ruled less than three hundred days.

The stately, columned Tauride Palace in riot-torn Petrograd housed not only the defiant Duma on March 12, but also the Petrograd Soviet (council) of Workers' Deputies, formed by representatives of radical groups and parties which had poured into another part of the palace that same day. Relying on its influence among workers, soldiers, and sailors, the Petrograd Soviet constituted a growing challenge to the Provisional Government during the spring, summer, and fall of 1917.

The Bolsheviks were widely considered a fanatical, ineffective fringe group. But by mid-September they had a majority in the Soviet because of mass support gained by their insistence, as the only antiwar party, on concluding peace, feeding the hungry populace, and turning landowners' land over to the peasants for their use. Under their slogan, "peace, bread, land," led by Lenin and Trotskii, the Bolsheviks gained control through the soviet of most armed units in Petrograd; mobilized their civilian Red Guards under control of local party committees; forestalled a feeble attempt at repression by the Provisional Government, November 6–7, 1917; seized key points in Petrograd; put to flight Premier A.F. Kerenskii of the Provisional Government; took the Winter Palace and arrested Kerenskii's ministers there in the early hours of November 8. That evening the Second All-Russian Congress of Soviets, already in session a day, confirmed an all-Bolshevik cabinet as the "temporary" government of Russia until the convening of the Constituent Assembly. Russia's only free national election, November 24–25, 1917, produced a Constituent Assembly overwhelmingly socialist, but also with a majority of agrarian and Menshevik

* The so-called February Revolution was named after its beginning date, February 23, old style (Julian calendar, which lagged 13 days in the twentieth century behind the Gregorian, or new style, calendar, adopted in Russia February 14—February 1 old style—1918. New style dates are used here unless otherwise noted). The "October Revolution" of the Bolsheviks began October 24 (old style) or November 6 (new style).

(Marxist) socialists willing to support parliamentary, multiparty democracy, and with a Bolshevik minority. When the Constituent Assembly met January 18, 1918, it refused to endorse Soviet power, and the Bolsheviks dissolved it by refusing to let it reconvene the next day. Dissolving the balky Constituent Assembly was child's play in comparison with their ensuing civil war battle to survive, expand control beyond their northwest bastion, and preserve their one-party monopoly of power. This monopoly held, repressively enforced, save for coalition with Left Socialist Revolutionaries (the extremist, terrorist wing of Russian populist, agrarian socialism), December 1917 to March 1918. The remnants of other parties in the Soviets were eventually purged from them.

Such great revolutions as those of 1917 in Russia bring the heady and fearful feeling of a new beginning.[53] Lenin received a tumultuous ovation from the Soviet assemblage November 8, 1917, when he peered out at them and summoned them "to build the socialist order." [54] For enthusiasts in the movement this meant, "Change everything, renew everything," [55] not the least, to bring about a society free of crime and coercion. Yet, today, the Russians continue to grapple with a crime problem of major proportions and exist under a bureaucratic state of coercive power and coercive impact far greater than anything the tsars bequeathed to Russia. It was the tsarist heritage that made Russia one of those states ripest for revolution but least capable of carrying out the time-honored Marxist dream of society without violence.

2
"A Very Simple 'Machine'"

Soviet power is a new type of state in which there is no bureaucracy, no standing army, no police.

—V. I. Lenin, 1917

We are leaving behind the short slogans . . . and are going on to a complicated system of laws.

—D. I. Kurskii, 1921

HANDBILLS OF THE MILITARY REVOLUTIONARY COMMITTEE posted throughout Petrograd, November 6, 1917, the first day of the Bolshevik revolution, carried its first proclamation on law and order. The handbills called on the populace to "detain hooligans and black hundred [radical right pogromist] agitators and bring them to commissars of the Soviet in the nearest military unit. At the first attempt of dark elements to cause confusion, robbery, bloodshed, or shooting on the streets of Petrograd the criminals responsible will be wiped off the face of the earth." In its proclamation of November 10, the victorious Military Revolutionary Committee announced to the people of Petrograd and its suburbs that it "would not tolerate any violations of revolutionary law and order. Thieving, robbery, marauding, attempts at pogroms will be punished immediately. Persons guilty of these crimes will be dealt with mercilessly by the Military Revolutionary Court." [1]

First Steps

"The city was quiet—probably never so quiet in its history, on that night not a single hold-up occurred, not a single robbery." So John Reed described Petrograd the night of November 7–8, 1917. But in the stormed Winter Palace that night there was looting. Several of the women soldiers who had guarded the palace were raped.

By the beginning of December, law and order had broken down in earnest. Soldiers looted the wine cellars of the Winter Palace and any other well stocked caches they could break into. Unable to quell the "wine pogrom" with pleas or threats, the government formed a Committee to Combat Drunken Pogroms [2] and sent Red Guards serving as police to fight pitched battles with rioting soldiers. "Finally," our famous eyewitness reports, "the Military Revolutionary Committee sent out companies of soldiers with machine guns, who fired mercilessly upon the rioters, killing many; and by executive orders the wine cellars were invaded by committees with hatchets who smashed the bottles—or blew them up with dynamite." [3]

All sorts of local tribunals soon sprang up in Russia, spontaneously sometimes, but under the aegis of the new ruling party. Judges and people's assessors (lay judges) of some tribunals were elected by the people, others appointed by local soviets or their executive committees. To promote "widespread participation of the masses," terms of office were short, a month or two or three; trials proceeded before the public, which could question the accused or witnesses and serve as "accusers" or "defenders" without any special qualifications. Sentencing powers of the early tribunals varied considerably.[4] The Provisional Revolutionary Tribunal of the Vyborg District began the practice of sentencing to compulsory, "corrective" work without confinement. [5]

"We Need an Iron Hand"

I

This upheaval, the new tribunals, might never have happened without the return to Russia of Vladimir Ilyich Lenin. Upon his arrival at Petrograd's Finland Station, April 16, 1917, he set about opening Bolsheviks' eyes to the possibility that, although only a minority within the minority Social Democratic movement, by taking a stand against the war and the Provisional Government, they could muster enough popular support to seize power. The Bolsheviks could govern Russia, alone if need be, until the world-wide conflagration destroyed all imperialism [6] through a one-party dictatorship—a prospect abhorrent to some revolutionary Marxists.[7]

Lenin had scant guidelines from Marx and Engels on the nature of the postrevolutionary state and even less on crime and the law-and-order functions of that state.[8] The logic of Marxist economic determinism was, in brief, that crime has no cure under capitalism where it expresses class protest or dire poverty and needs no cure under socialism.[9]

Lenin used the vague models Marx and Engels meant to apply to advanced countries. But he plotted a socialist revolution that was to begin, rather, in backward, developing, disorderly Russia.

By no means could all workers be counted on to support his party or maintain labor discipline. And what workers there were manned bastions of modern industry in a vast rural hinterland. Russia's unschooled and suspicious peasants, its growing corps of merchants, its fading nobility and liberal intelligentsia formed a dubious recruiting ground for supporters of economic collectivism but fertile ground for opposition. Nationalization of Russia's shaky economy seemed to bear very little immediate relationship to liquidating forever the brawling, violence, and thievery in that poor, suffering country. This may help explain the cautious ambivalence underlying Lenin's at-first-glance utopian visions of Russia's postrevolutionary state and law.

Just before the Bolshevik revolution, Lenin, hiding in Finland, grappled with the problem of coercion under the new order he hoped to usher in. His ambivalent contribution was to anticipate and attempt to justify a protracted period of one-party dictatorship applying great state coercion on the way to a distant, classless communism and the withering away of the state with its police and courts, yet also to sketch nonbureaucratic, popular instruments of proletarian justice and repression.

Even during the transition to communism, Lenin thought the elaborate, specialized "bourgeois" bureaucracy of law enforcement and courts could be replaced by "a very simple 'machine'" such as the local Soviet of workers' and soldiers' deputies to maintain law and order.[10] But he never confused simplicity with weakness of the proletarian state. Nor did he interpret "all power to the soviets" to mean lack of elitist, central state and party control over them. "When the state will be proletarian," Lenin wrote virtually on the eve of revolution, "when it will be a machine for proletarian violence against the bourgeoisie, then we are unconditionally for strong state power and centralism." [11]

Lenin's favorite precedents in law enforcement were the simple, informal, and popularly elected tribunals responsive to revolutionary purposes set up by the insurrectionary radical Paris Commune (March 28–May 28, 1871) and by some of those local soviets of workers' deputies that governed briefly here and there in Russia during the 1905 revolution.[12] For Lenin, the guiding principles of justice, infusing his "State and Revolution," were these: smash the old state machine and set up new revolutionary organs of repression; make these tribunals simple, informal, and open to mass popular participation; be sure that law is subordinated to revolutionary goals of the party elite since no law is independent and if it does not serve the Bolshevik purposes it will be serving the purposes of counterrevolutionaries; do not hesitate to use merciless force but look forward also in practice to the eventual "withering away" of coercion. A member of the hereditary nobility because of his father's high civil service rank as inspector and superintendent of schools in Simbirsk Province, Lenin trained for law and practiced it briefly. He displayed brilliant grasp of it, finishing in 1891 with a gold medal at the top of his class, despite adverse conditions. His father, Il'ya Ulyanov, died in 1886. His brother, Alexander, had been executed in 1887 for attempted revolutionary terrorism. Later that year Lenin, a freshman, was expelled from the University of Kazan because he had been present at a student demonstration. He later completed his four years of law school by correspondence in one year, first in his class. Lenin, unlike most lawyers nurtured under the old regime, scorned the very idea of the "rule of law," the goal of liberals in the 1864 reforms and after. When Lenin joined the second Russian generation of Marxists, he came to see rule of law as a cloaking rule by a privileged class.

Lenin's ambivalent forecasts for the state and law expressed the dilemmas of an authoritarian populist revolutionary deeply skeptical about the representativeness of parliaments and the objectivity of any professional state bureaucracy—judicial included. They expressed also the views of a person with great personal influence over all major party decisions but, more than that, of a person who participated actively in all early Bolshevik lawmaking, in close touch with his top officials of justice, even drafting some of the first Soviet decrees himself.[13] Lenin and the other Soviet lawyers, including commissars of justice, G. I. Lomov (1917), P. I. Stuchka (1917 and 1918), I. N. Shteinberg, Left Socialist Revolutionary (1917–1918), D. S. Kurskii (1918–1928), N. Ianson (1928–1931), and N. V. Krylenko (1931–1938), faced, nonetheless, the need for a growing apparatus of law enforcement and justice.

II

From the start Soviet jurists were confronted with the challenge to curb disorder in the struggling new Russian Soviet Republic, where criminals were made more desperate by circumstances worse than those of the disastrous days of 1916–1917, and by causes deeper than "wine pogroms." This was the country that Isaac Babel described where, in the bitter cold of Petrograd, foreigners stood mute, bundled up on street corners, soliciting passing women by marking off slices of black bread with their thumbnails on the loaves clutched under their arms. It was a country where criminals were made by arbitrary arrest just by having the wrong class background or by their opposition to the Bolsheviks; a country where black marketeers almost monopolized food distribution; a country of drifting, demobilized soldiers and hordes of hungry, homeless children, where criminals released from the prisons taken over from the former government swelled the criminal population.[14] Criminal conviction rates had doubled in 1900–1913, but fallen off in 1914–1916, only to rise again in 1916–1917. The increase in crime and convictions continued under the Bolsheviks. The incidence of robbery and murder in Moscow during 1918 rose, it was said, to 10 to 15 times the prewar tsarist level.[15]

Confronting this lawlessness and chaos, influential Bolshevik officials of justice shared Lenin's reluctance to leap forward quickly into a punishment-free utopia. They rejected the view of an official in the Revtribunal system that "the Socialist criminal code must not know punishment as a means of influence on the criminal." [16]

M. Yu. Kozlovskii* expressed what appears to have been the prevailing viewpoint in the Commissariat of Justice. He derided "sentimental means of re-education." During the long time it would take to build socialism, until "remnants of the past, crime and the need for punishment disappear," the regime would have need of decisive surgical measures of terror and isolation." L.A. Savrasov headed the regime's system of concentration camps and prisons as head of the Penal Department of the Commissariat of Justice. Savrasov made it clear that he had only contempt for the hypocritical efforts of bourgeois penologists to 'soften' the regimen in places of confinement." Bolsheviks, he said, could not expect quick results. It was not enough for them to rest on their laurels and wait for socialism to take care of the crime problem.[17] Lenin agreed with his commissars of justice that to stem "increases in crime, hooliganism, bribery, speculation, outrages of all kinds . . . we need time and *we need an iron hand.*" [18] Courts were to be the indispensable arm of the proletarian state. "We would be laughable utopians," Lenin warned, "if we imagined that such a task can be accomplished the day after the fall of the bourgeois regime, that is, in the first stage of the transition from capitalism to socialism, or that it can be accomplished with repression." [19]

III

Decree No. 1 on the court, published December 7, 1917, provided the first form of that coercion. The decree pulled together the experiences of the makeshift tribunals and the sober views of Lenin and the justice officials about the law-and-order problems they faced, and the special political imperatives of the proletarian state in which the health of the revolution was the supreme law and old state machinery of repression was to be smashed. The decree abolished the old system's courts, Procuracy, bar associations. It went for passage to Sovnarkom, the Council of People's Commissars, then all-Bolshevik, rather than to the CEC, the Central Executive Committee of the All-Russian Congress of Soviets, where it faced bitter opposition

* A member of the directing body of the Commissariat of Justice and co-author, with Commissar Pyotr Stuchka, of the 1919 Guiding Principles of Criminal Legislation of the RSFSR (Russian Soviet Federated Socialist Republic).

from those delegates wishing to preserve as much as possible of the old court system.[20]

The simple first new Soviet system of justice had people's courts and revolutionary tribunals.

1. People's courts with limited jurisdiction (criminal cases involving sentences of up to two years, civil cases of disputes over up to 3,000 rubles). They resembled the former justice of the peace courts, save that two temporary lay judges, people's assessors, sat with the full-time judge. Who owned the samovar? What sentence should be passed on a gang of thieves who held up and robbed an old woman at gunpoint? These were the first civil and criminal cases before the Moscow People's Court meeting that December informally in a dingy, stuffy little room of an old wooden house because irate justices of the peace had refused as yet to give up their building.[21]

2. The revolutionary tribunals, explicitly arms of political repression for defense of the revolutionary order, consisted of a judge and six people's assessors. Revtribunals dispensed primitive, severe, sometimes arbitrary justice. There was still room on occasion, however, for the old legal consciousness through the participation of lawyers of the old school as accuser and defender, and room for conflicts of the new revolutionary conscience, at least as of 1919.[22]

By Decree No. 1 of December 7, 1917, local courts were "to be guided in their decisions and sentences by the laws of the overthrown governments." This held, the qualification ran, "only in so far as they had not been repealed by the revolution and did not contradict the revolutionary conscience and revolutionary concept of justice." For awhile, in 1918, the courts, like law and police, harked back increasingly to the pre-Soviet past. During nine months of that year, legislation provided for circuit people's courts whose jurisdiction and procedural laws made them continuators of the circuit courts set up under the judicial reform of 1864.

Was this the way to "smash the bourgeois state machinery"? Maybe not, but two factors seemed to have brought on this retrenchment. First, the higher district courts were needed to process large numbers of complex cases held over from before the revolution—10,000 in Petrograd alone. These cases threatened to swamp the undermanned and underqualified people's courts. Second, apparently there was the influence of the Commissar of Justice, I.N. Shteinberg, and the other Left Socialist Revolutionaries. They remained in coalition with the Bolsheviks from December 23, 1917 until the March 4, 1918 breach over the Peace of Brest Litovsk with the Central Powers. The Left SRs, along with legal scholars, felt that the Bolsheviks had gone too far toward destroying the old judicial system and the old concepts of legality, which they wanted adapted and preserved.

The left SR's proposed basing criminal law on the partially applied[23] tsarist reform code (*Ulozhenie*) of 1903. This found support among Bolshevik officials who reasoned that the Soviet code would have to deal with many of the same crimes that the tsarist one did.[24]

Their departure into opposition as well as some catching up by the courts opened the way for Pavel I. Stuchka, Bolshevik jurist, Shteinberg's predecessor, deputy, and then briefly successor, to lead a return to the simpler system of a single level of people's courts by decrees of July 20 and November 30, 1918. The latter decree, over the signature of Stuchka's successor, D.S. Kurskii, ordered the courts no longer to apply the laws of the overthrown regimes, but only the laws of the Workers' and Peasants' Government, and, where they remained silent, to be guided by revolutionary concepts of justice.[25]

As long, then, as I.N. Shteinberg was Commissar of Justice, and other Left SRs were in the government, legislation nudged the court system back farther toward the forms of the pre-Bolshevik system. After the Left SRs went into opposition, the courts were again simplified. But Soviet justice eventually moved again toward more centralization and complexity, in ordinary and tribunal hierarchies, even before NEP.[26] Decision making and control moved centerward too. Recapitulating Soviet legal histories and the debates covered by John N. Hazard we can trace early Soviet policy-making for criminal justice through several phases:

1. *Grass roots populism.* Between November 7 and December 7, 1917, Russia saw a month of local, rudimentary initatives, and procedures as rough and ready as most of the participants in tribunal hearings.

2. *Central decrees and intraparty debates.* Decree No. 1 on the courts of December 7 and the Cheka decree of December 20 began the shift of policy decisions centerward. Central policymaking featured vigorous debates in the commissariats, Sovnarkom, and CEC.

3. *Bipartisan government and compromises.* Bipartisan coalition with the Left SRs beginning December 20 enlivened debates even further, leaving very much open until the SRs resigned in March 1918 the question of how much of the old system completely to retain.

4. *Continued local self-assertion.* Local initiatives in policy continued after this liveliest period of debate, into 1919. Local court judges in Moscow, Petrograd, and the central provinces themselves expanded jurisdiction of people's courts beyond the bounds of Decree No. 1; that is, of the old justices of the peace. Local officials demanded abolition of the higher circuit courts.[27]

The Moscow general meeting of people's court judges approved on March 30, 1918, a resolution introduced by people's court judge E.B. Pashukanis (elected May 11 one of three permanent members of the seven-person Presidium administering Moscow courts, later still, the eminent theorist), demanding complete autonomy for the courts, after a borough soviet set aside a decision of a people's court.[28]

This recalls the successful hue and cry by the prison garrison after the Ryazan Revolutionary Tribunal sentenced an impressive Tolstoyan C.O. to death.[29]

5. *Growing centralism of policy making and control.* Local judges, distressed with the unregulated advocacy, successfully pressed through the Second All-Russian Conference of Officials of Justice, July 1918, for an organized bar. At the next such conference, June 1920, a minority pushed unsuccessfully to have people's assessors abolished as an unnecessary holdover of "liberalism." The Fourth Conference, in January 1922, had considerable input on matters of bar organization and the Procuracy. Krylenko's proposals for a centralized Procuracy were overruled by anticentralists both in the Commissariat of Justice and in the steering committee of the next session of the CEC in May 1922; they regarded it as a throwback to tsarism and a setback to the withering away of state coercion. Only intervention by Lenin and the Politburo, imposing a procentralist line, saved the proposal.[30]

By then, the old pattern of centralized bureaucracy with specialists was reasserting itself. Other pre-Bolshevik patterns were continuing, like the militia, or returning, like the political police.

The Provisional Government had abolished the tsarist police, gendarmerie, and Okhrana (secret police), replacing them with much curbed state militia. This militia, politically cleansed, continued to function after the Bolshevik revolution under the local soviets, maintaining order alongside the Red Guard. Before the revolution, the Bolsheviks had envisaged a nonprofessional people's militia. Such enforcement by the workers themselves, it appears, never went beyond the paper stage of a decree. Rather, the existing professional militia inherited from the Provisional Government became the Workers' and Peasants' Militia. It operated as a force controlled by the NKVD (People's Commissariat of Internal Affairs), which approved appointments by local soviets, and was defined by increasingly elaborate legislation beginning in August 1918, leading to the Statute on the Workers' and Peasants' Militia of June 10, 1920.[31]

If the Provisional Government ended the secret police, it was the Bolshevik regime which revived it, with new personnel, but elaborating on traditional practices.

The Cheka, so called after the first two initials of its Russian title, Extraordinary Commission for Combatting Counterrevolution and Sabotage, was established on December 20, 1917. Its first head, Feliks Edmundovich Dzerzhinskii, an expatriate Polish aristocrat, had already established a reputation as a political martyr of the Bolshevik underground, fanatical revolutionary, and *de facto* security chief of the regime even before his assignment to the Cheka. The Cheka soon became formally the Vecheka, or All-Russian Extraordinary Commission. Ensconced in Moscow (the capital from March 1918), it oversaw a network of local Chekas (Extraordinary Commissions).[32]

Vecheka controlled the border troops and an elite corps of security troops. It ran an embryonic net of agents carrying out espionage and subversion abroad. It kept a close watch over industry and transport, maintained "special sections" to spy over the armed forces, and became one of the mainstays of Soviet power in reconquered borderlands like the Transcaucasus and the Ukraine. The Vecheka (or, simply, the Cheka) owed its power both to the Bolsheviks' view of law as revolutionary expediency and to their no-quarter fight for survival against huge odds, answering their opponents' terror with a Red Terror of their own, spearheaded by the Cheka and Revolutionary Tribunals.[33]

The Cheka acted as the investigative and punitive arm of this dictatorship. Autonomous, a law unto itself, resorting to arbitrary arrests, shooting hostages, executions, and torture, the Cheka answered in fact only to the party leadership, and not always even to them. Powers of the local prosecutors to check on its investigations, trials by secret *troikas* going back to April 1918, and sentencing remained then as later only on paper. As long as Left SRs remained in the Cheka, until July 1918, they inhibited its use of capital punishment. But, though not formally empowered until September 17, 1918, to mete out death, the Cheka made its philosophy quite clear. In February 1918 it announced that, as it saw the situation, there was "no other way to combat counterrevolutionaries, spies, speculators, burglars, hooligans, saboteurs and other parasites than their merciless annihilation at the scene of the crime." Despite a decree of February 17, 1919, transferring the right to try suspects to the revolutionary tribunals, the Cheka's power to dispose of its prisoners continued largely unlimited. The abolition of its right to execute prisoners decreed January 20, 1920 meant little in actual practice.

Criticism of the Cheka mounted within the Party in 1918–1919. In one attempt to head it off, representatives of the commissariats of justice and interior (ordinary police) were placed on the Vecheka board. So badly were the justice people treated that they walked out, initiating a permanent rupture in relations between Vecheka and the Commissariat of Justice.

Some Bolsheviks worried about the growing power of the Cheka. Its abuses, "insolence," and contempt for the powerless, caused serious disputes within the Bolshevik leadership. Lenin, ambiguously, attacked the scandalous indiscipline of some Cheka agents while he and Trotskii urged it on.[34] "Mass arrests and repressions" prevailed in Cheka policy during the civil war, according to Dzerzhinskii himself. The law of revolutionary justice devoured those "on whom there was not enough information for a court conviction" but whom the Cheka wanted put away: "parasites," former tsarist officials, nobles, capitalists, violators of labor discipline, suspected oppositionists.

Distinctions between common and political crimes, real and imaginary guilt, grew blurred as they did again later under Stalin. Dzerzhinskii and Nikolai Krylenko (who led the Revtribunals during the civil war and became Commissar of Justice in 1931, succeeding Kurskii only to fall a victim of purge violence himself in 1938) later wrote that they knew innocent people were being punished, but that "the need for self-defense was so great that we knowingly permitted such mistakes just as long as the republic was saved." [35] Martin Latsis, a deputy of Dzerzhinskii in the Cheka, enjoined: "Do not seek in your accusations proof of whether the prisoner has rebelled against the soviets with guns or by word. You must ask him, first, what class he belongs to, what his social origin is, what his education was, and his profession. The answers must determine the fate of the accused. That is the meaning of Red Terror." [36]

By the end of War Communism in 1921, the Cheka appeared to be a powerful, ruthless recreation of the tsarist *Okhrana* (political police).[37] In March 1921 the radical rebels of the Kronstadt naval base guarding the approaches to Petrograd assailed the Bolshevik regime for having "brought the workers, instead of freedom, an ever present fear of being dragged into the torture chambers of the Cheka, which exceeds many times in its horrors the gendarmerie administration of the tsarist regime." [38]

Use of capital punishment may be taken as one sign of the intensity of coercion and its underlying philosophy. It, too, like some police and legal institutions, was carried over to the new era. Given the violent and desperate history of War Communism, and prerevolutionary Bolshevik agreement with the use of the death penalty against class enemies,[39] one should not be surprised that the intensity of Bolshevik executions after 1917 far exceeded peak intensities under the tsars, while periods of repeal of capital punishment were much shorter. Torture and whipping could still bring death under the earlier tsars. But *de jure* capital punishment was abolished from Russian codes during the thirteenth and most of the twelfth and fourteenth centuries, under Elizabeth from 1742 to 1754, and up until the 1770s when Catherine II used it against the Pugachev rebels. From then until the execution of the five Decembrist putschists in 1825, nobody was executed for political offenses either. Since 1812 the death penalty applied for some military crimes, but not for common crimes like murder or rape, though this was frequently the case abroad.[40]

Ten days in power, the Provisional Government abolished all capital punishment, later restoring it July 25, 1917, at the front, after the collapse of the July offensive.

When the Second Congress of Soviets abolished the death penalty on

November 7, 1917, Lenin is said to have responded: "This is madness. How can we accomplish a revolution without shooting?" [41] His government formally restored the death penalty in June 1918, abolished it January 17, 1920, but restored it May 4, and then listed it as a "temporary" measure in every major piece of criminal legislation: for example, the RSFSR Criminal Codes, in effect June 1, 1922, January 1, 1927, and January 1, 1961; and the Fundamentals of Criminal Legislation of the USSR and Union Republics, in effect October 31, 1924, and January 1, 1959. Stalin briefly suspended it in 1947–1950, as we shall see. Intensity of use of the death penalty appeared to abate during NEP, especially under the second code, in 1927 and 1928. By the end of 1927, capital punishment applied only to military crimes, state crimes under Article 58, and "banditry." The maximum sentence other than death ran to ten years confinement.

Incomplete tsarist research lists 894 persons shot from 1826 through 1905, 1,310 in 1906 (950 in six months of Stolypin reaction), and only 486 sentenced to death in 1876–1905, years of unrest, revolutionary terism, and massive strikes. Executions came much more often in the civil war. Table 2–1 shows that in 1920 the Revtribunals alone shot 766 persons. Other available incomplete statistics indicate that the Cheka shot 8359 persons at least in 1 1/2 years, 1918–1919 (this does not include persons shot by Revtribunals and simply disposed of by drowning, shooting, etc., without any record). But most of this, as under the tsars, appeared to be for political motivations rather than for common crimes.[42]

The Guiding Principles of Criminal Law of the RSFSR published in 1919,[43] Lenin and the Communist Party Program of 1919 laid great stress on measures of punishment falling short of confinement.[44] The party program, despite the desperate situation in strife-torn Russia, looked ahead to when "the entire working population will participate in administering justice and punishment will be replaced once and for all by educational measures." [45]

In this spirit only about a third of defendants in people's courts in 1920 were sentenced to confinement, including defendants put on probation with suspended sentences (see Table 2–1). Contrary to the deliberate harshness of the Cheka and Revtribunals (see Table 2–1 also on Revtribunal and court measures), with their shootings and high rates of stern punishments, people's courts, which accounted for ninety-seven percent of persons brought to trial by themselves and tribunals, were enjoined under the Guiding Principles of Criminal Law to cause the criminal as little suffering as possible, commensurate with the task of punishment. Punishment was social defense, not expiation of guilt.

Norms of early Soviet justice dealt especially lightly with juveniles. A decree of January 14, 1918, supported by Lenin over hard-line opposition, raised the minimum age of juvenile criminal responsibility from the tsarist minimum of ten to seventeen.[46] Subsequently, a series of revisions and retreat from the policy of "no courts or jails for children" between 1919 and 1923 eventuated in procedures whereby juveniles down to fourteen years old faced criminal liability if found beyond the reach of medical and educational measures by commissions on juvenile affairs, the alternative to courts for juvenile offenders not criminally liable. Shortages of children's correctional facilities forced the authorities to send most fourteen- to seventeen-year-old criminals to adult prisons and camps and to poorly isolated pretrial detention centers. There they were socialized into the criminal underworld.[47]

Mismanagement of child care programs and competition of the health, social welfare, and Cheka agencies concerned played a part in the debacle of the Soviet drive against delinquency and homelessness. So did the young Soviet state's poverty and its preoccupation with fighting the civil war.[48] As that drew to a close in 1921, famine was taking its toll, too, in disorder and lives.[49]

The famine of 1920–1921, plus the long violence of World War I and the civil war, subjected the Russian people to "the most cataclysmic changes since the Mongol invasion in the early thirteenth century." These disasters shattered families, caused fourteen million civilian deaths (in addition to the two million military deaths) [50] and turned homeless children onto the streets, to beg or steal as best they could. A possibly worse fate awaited them in the hastily organized children's homes without warmth or food, than they experienced as *besprizornye* (homeless ones). It needs no special imagination to picture the law-and-order problem posed by hordes of these *besprizornye,* whose number soon reached a peak of seven million, from which it only slowly diminished in the later 1920's.[51] Ravaged by exposure, syphilis, cocaine, the *besprizornye* slept where they could: in empty railroad carriages, flophouses, or giant tar cauldrons still warm from the day's work.

Russia deurbanized in 1917–1920 from 18 to 15 percent town population. Not until six years after the fighting subsided did industrial production and urbanization reach, in 1926, approximately the levels of 1913–1914. Petrograd's population, for example, fell from 1,217,000 in 1918 to 722,000 in 1921. Yet the *besprizornye* flocked to such cities, a major reason why total crimes increased there, and per capita crimes, or chances of victimization, increased much more. Per capita rates of minors charged with crimes in Petrograd rose from 2.0 per 1,000 inhabitants in 1918 to 7.6 per 1,000 in 1921. The scanty statistics of the time show that arrests of adults rose nearly 2.5 times in the Russian republic between the first quarter of 1920 and the first quarter of 1922; arrests of juveniles rose nearly four times in the same period.[52] Dispensing with regular courts and police had to be indefinitely put off, owing both to public disorder and to the requirements of the New Economic Policy which followed the civil war.

Table 2–1. Actions of People's Courts (46 Gubernias) and Revolutionary Tribunals (45 Gubernias), Russian Republic, 1920

	People's Courts		Revolutionary Tribunals	
	Number	*Per-cent*	*Number*	*Per-cent*
Persons Brought to Trial	881,933	—	26,738	—
Exonerated	299,362	35	3,960	14.8
Convicted	582,571	65	22,778	85.2
Including:				
Shot	—	—	766	3.4
Confinement (including suspended sentence)	199,182	34.2	16,107	70.7
Compulsory work without deprivation of freedom	132,835	22.8	1,421	6.2
Fines	172,656	29.6	638	2.8
Public censure	37,678	6.5	623	2.7
Other punishment	40,220	6.9	3,223	14.2

Source: M.N. Gernet, *Prestupnost' za granitsei i v SSSR* (Moscow: "Sovetskoe zakonodatel'stvo," 1931), p. 74.

Legality Means Centralism

During 1920–1921 the last interventionists were expelled, and the last nationalist regimes liquidated in European and Transcaucasian area of the Russian empire regained for Soviet power. Demonstrations of disillusioned and hungry workers had been broken up by troops in March 1921. The related uprising by the radical Kronstadt garrison (once fervent pro-Bolsheviks) guarding the sea approach to Petrograd was mercilessly crushed that month and its appeals for the democratization of the soviets brushed aside. NEP, the New Economic Policy, followed. The NEP years, 1921–1928, brought a breathing spell of reconstruction, relative normalcy concessions to private commerce, and peasant farming.

NEP created the need for detailed and consistent codification in all branches of law—criminal and civil law and procedure, labor law,—and in court statutes. Regulation, mediation, and more precise definitions of crimes and punishments could no longer take second place behind repression and radical social change through law. Order had to be brought into the scattered criminal norms contained in more than four hundred decrees published between 1917 and 1921.[53] As Commissar of Justice Kurskii put it in describing a legal order moving far away from the rudimentary one symbolized by the first Moscow People's Court whose fourth anniversary he was celebrating:

> The old rule that a court shall decide by itself what is criminal and not criminal requires change. We have already worked out a criminal code. The same is true of procedural law. . . . Every citizen must know by what court and for what offense he is being tried and what punishment is possible. . . . We are leaving behind the short slogans in the field of law and are going on to a complicated system of laws in an exceptionally difficult economic and political atmosphere.[54]

Even before the promulgation in 1924 of the Constitution of the Union of Soviet Socialist Republics and all-Union Fundamentals of Criminal Justice, the RSFSR*, and the other constituent Union republics, which had followed its lead, had an increasingly complex, centralized, bureaucratized and permanent system of laws and justice.

Its architects, Lenin and the top jurists, took the theoretical position that the legal order built by them was a temporary bow to the necessities of a social order part socialist but also, more than during the civil war, part capitalist. Law they considered basically a bourgeois phenomenon. "Communism," Stuchka said in 1927, "means not the victory of socialist law, but the victory of socialism over any law, since with the abolition of classes with their antagonistic interests, law will die out altogether." [55]

E.B. Pashukanis, leading legal theorist of the late 1920s and early 1930s, posited that law grew out of the marketplace to regulate exchanges of equivalents in bourgeois society. Even criminal law reflected a marketplace mentality, with its precisely specified "payments" for precisely specified crimes. It, too, must fade when social relations move from those of individuals with class interests, rights, and duties toward an equal collective where everyone works to their utmost capacity for the sake not of payment but of fulfillment in that work.[56]

Even while they engaged in legal system building, then, Bolshevik jurists implied their work was temporary. Moreover, they differed among themselves about just how much elaboration and centralization of justice was necessary or desirable. Their conflicts, already mentioned, over the Procuracy had provided a case in point. News that a legislative majority had come out against the Commissariat of Justice's proposal that "organs of Procuratorial supervision over local affairs be appointed by and responsible only to the center" with the right to protest as illegal decisions of the local authorities prompted the ailing Lenin to intervene in favor of a centralized Procuracy. He feared "bureaucratic centralism" less than he feared local corruption.

Lenin appeared to associate "primitive," "uncultured," and corrupt

* RSFSR—the Russian Soviet Federated Socialist Republic—has been the largest, politically and legally pace-setting Union republic of the USSR, which was formed out of the RSFSR and three other republics (Ukrainian, Belorussian, and Transcaucasian), December 30, 1922. Soviet expansion and new formations on the border areas of the RSFSR raised the total of Union republics. Now there are 15.

behavior with the provinces and enlightened legality with the center, especially when that center, in the Commissariat of Justice, operated under the close control of the Party's Orgburo, Politburo, and Control Committee. They would "immediately correct any errors" in the work of the Commissariat and its Procuracy.[57] Only later in the year did Lenin begin to express doubts about the central apparatus and the "rude" personality and "enormous power" of its leader Stalin.[58] Meanwhile, it was to Stalin that Lenin addressed his support of centralism, and through whom he won a favorable decision in the Politburo supporting the Krylenko position. It then carried the day in the CEC in the form of the decree on the RSFSR Procuracy of May 28, 1922, as in all other major legislation on the legal system, a model for other republics. The RSFSR Prosecutor, appointed by the CEC, served also as Commissar of Justice (D.S. Kurskii). He proposed his own deputies for CEC approval and appointed the provincial prosecutors, as well as their local deputies, on recommendation of the provincial prosecutors. Provincial prosecutors could sit in at all sessions of the provincial soviet executive committees, protest to Moscow the illegality of their decisions as well as decisions of all other agencies including the secret police (a provision of uncertain and later negligible practical effect), and the pretrial investigators under the courts, as well as conduct prosecution of more important criminal cases and, under the Civil Code of July 7, 1923, intervene where necessary to protect state interests in civil cases.[59]

During the ensuing burst of legislative activity in 1922–1924, a court system emerged basically similar to the present one.

1. The three levels of union republic courts—People's courts, provincial courts, RSFSR Supreme Courts—tried over 90 percent of the cases of original jurisdiction. Each court seated a judge or a judge and two people's assessors. Provincial courts replaced both the revolutionary tribunals as court of first instance and higher ordinary courts and the "special sessions" of people's courts. They also heard cases of more serious crimes against the state, persons, and property. As courts of review, provincial courts replaced appellate and cassational functions of the existing councils of people's court judges. As administrative agencies over the lower courts, they replaced provincial departments of justice (abolished until 1939). The RSFSR supreme Court had authority to exercise appellate and guidance functions over the lower courts as well as to act as court of first instance (with people's assessors by decree of July 27, 1923) in comparatively rare cases of "exceptional importance," or crimes involving top officials.

2. The USSR Supreme Court had functions of nationwide guidance, review, and first-instance jurisdiction in cases of all-Union importance such as disputes between republics, judicial review (not exercised) over legislation of republic CECs and councils of people's commissars, and the USSR Council of People's Commissars. The court's Procuracy had no connection

with Union republic procuracies (save for tribunals listed below) until 1933.

3. Special courts were "temporarily" held over. These included (a) military tribunals (also trying civilians accused of such crimes as espionage, refusing military service, and thefts from military stores), (b) military-transport tribunals (abolished November 23, 1923), (c) three-level systems of special labor sessions of people's courts, land commissions, and arbitration commissions to hear cases of material dispute between state organizations.

Russian republic precedents were adapted to the Ukrainian, Belorussian, and Transcaucasian republics. All reflected certain basic guidelines for justice. Trials were to be public. Defense and prosecution were to have equal rights. This was impaired for the defense because the right of the accused to defense (usually an attorney from the local College of Defenders, a form of revived bar association) could be exercised only just before trial, after the conclusion of the pretrial investigation. Proceedings were to be conducted in the language of the given Union or autonomous republic. Persons not understanding the language had the right to interpreters. Professional and lay judges were to have equal votes in decisions of the courts.[60]

In the language the reformers put in the second of Union republic criminal codes, 1926–1928, crimes became "socially dangerous acts," "punishment" became a "means of social defense." Replacing punishment by means of social defense lessened the stigma but, some reformers complained, it left forms of coercion, in practice, basically unchanged over the years.[61] "Everybody is being dragged into court, and in court there is unimaginable red tape, there are an infinite number of instances, controls, appeals, and so on and so forth," a Supreme Court member and eminent Bolshevik complained to the 15th Party Congress in 1927.[62]

The principle of analogy in the codes until 1958 left loopholes for action against possible foes of the regime. If a given socially dangerous act was not listed in the code, it could be punished under provisions of the code listing the act it most resembled.[63] This widened the already broad reach of code articles on political crimes. But there had been efforts to curb the original arbitrariness lurking behind the "withering away" of criminal codes, by making punishments increasingly specific in type and length between the time of the 1919 Guiding Principles of Criminal Law and the Union republic codes of 1926–1928.[64]

Crimes and Criminology

Because of changing policies,[65] conflicting interpretations, and inconsistent statistics,[66] it is hard to get a precise measure of crime trends in the 1920s.

Still, it appears that in the later NEP period, the law-and-order problem grew worse again. Life became easier and more secure for many. But remnants of the once seven million street waifs, *besprizornye*,[67] grew into adult professional criminals, people flocked back to the cities, and urban unemployment grew. Opportunities for graft multiplied in the state apparatus. Indictments and court convictions stepped up in 1925–1927. A million and a half persons were being convicted annually in 1927 for violations of the criminal law, as Table 2–2 shows. With the growth of a large new class of state employees, convictions for white-collar crimes like bribery and embezzlement increased several times over.[68] The large (31 percent) increase in convictions in 1929 reflects the participation of criminal repression in Stalin's new "socialist offensive," to be encountered in Chapter 3.

Table 2–2. Trends in Total Convictions, RSFSR and USSR, 1925–1929[69]

	(1) Convictions per 100,000 Inhabitants	(2) Convictions RSFSR	(3) Index of Convictions 1928 = 100	(4) Convictions USSR (estimated)
1925	1,000	974,000	88	1,420,000
1926		1,030,000	93.5	1,510,000
1927	1,073	1,100,000	99.5	1,602,000
1928		1,106,000	100	1,610,000
1929	1,363	1,450,000	131	2,110,000

As criminals adapted their techniques to NEP, so did the upholders of law and order. They restored legal codes. They opened centers of teaching and research in the law. They published professional journals.[70] And they began collecting criminal statistics.[71] They restored criminology, the study of crime and its causes.

Revolution and the civil war disrupted crime research. Limited research resumed in 1918 through the data gathering of the new commissions on juvenile affairs and children's reception centers. Under the more favorable conditions of NEP, tsarist-trained criminologists and penologists opened up a series of crime study offices in ten cities under provincial courts or health departments, beginning with the Petrograd Office in 1921. Research in these offices centered on the psychopathology of crime and the genetic and social origins of that psychopathology.

A national center for crime research appeared in 1925 under the RSFSR NKVD, the State Institute for the Study of Crime and the Criminal—or here, for short, the Crime Study Institute. Eugene Shirvindt, a penologist, head of the NKVD's Chief Administration of Places of Confinement, directed the institute. The 44 researchers in the Crime Study Institute and the four crime study offices affiliated with it published prolifically—four issues of *Problems of Crime* and 287 works in five years, such as A.A. Piontkovskii's "Murders of Worker and Peasant Newspaper Correspondents." Some works appeared in symposia like "Hooligans and Hooliganism," "Fighting Child Crime," and "Studying the Criminal Personality." The institute had its own statistical bureau set up with the assistance of the chief tsarist criminal statistician, E. Tarnovskii, and headed by V.I. Kufaev, specialist on juvenile lawbreaking and advocate of an end to punishing juveniles. Kufaev's collaborator in this cause, Professor M.N. Gernet, director of the Department of Moral Statistics of the Central Statistical Administration, headed the Socio-Economic Section of four persons including A.A. Piontkovskii, later Professor of Criminal Law, active until his death in 1973. Of the three other sections, the Penitentiary Section was headed by Shirvindt and included B.S. Utevskii. Utevskii was still studying the criminal personality at the time of this writing. There was a bio-psychological section and a criminal statistics section. The institute ran, also, an Experimental-Penitentiary Division and the nursing homes and hospitals of the Moscow Crime Study Office.[72]

Biopsychological theories flourished during NEP in the Biopsychological Section of the Crime Study Institute, in some of the affiliated local crime study offices, and in centers of psychological research. Professor P.G. Bel'skii studied excessive, "atavistic" drives to sexual activity, gambling, violence, and theft, in the Institute of Social Upbringing of Normal and Defective Children. Criminal defectology was investigated by psychiatrists like E.S. Vermel', V.V. Brailovskii, and E.K. Krasnushkin. Krasnushkin believed that once *environmental, economic defects* had done their work during a person's upbringing, his *defects of personality* resulting from these social causes stuck with him, making him a member of a "criminal" group of people. This criminal group was to be found above all among the social derelicts, the unemployed lumpenproletariat of the slums. The implication of Krasnushkin's work was that criminology could not generate effective criminal policy if it relegated the study of the criminal personality to second place behind the study of social conditions. Criminals needed treatment, after all. And no social reforms would work unless theories of crime on which they are based take into account how social conditions work on children and adults and turn them into criminals.

Adherents of the sociological and biopsychological schools carried their dispute on causes of crime from the prerevolutionary into the NEP period.[73] With some notable exceptions like Krasnushkin's synthesis, remedies which should have been seen as reinforcing each other were sometimes put forward as competing for lawmakers' attention, as in the West.[74]

Sociologically oriented Soviet jurists agreed with other European environmentalists like Franz von Liszt that "the best social policy is the best anti-crime policy."[75] Medical people and jurists specializing in criminal psychiatry belived that the best correctional therapy is the best anti-crime policy or, at least, that any social policy of crime prevention must begin with the individual criminal, his personality and his career. Pluralism, not conformity, prevailed among criminologists.

Prisons and Camps

But they joined in opposition to punishment. As Director Shirvindt expressed it, the research of his institute and the trends in Soviet criminal law all pointed toward replacing the idea of punishment with the idea of "social defense" (the Positivists' expression): general prevention, including social amelioration, rehabilitation of lawbreakers, and making it impossible for lawbreakers to commit new crimes by deprivation of freedom (coercion), mitigated where possible by suspended sentences and parole.[76]

Bolshevik law enforcement brain trusters like Krylenko, Pashukanis, Stuchka, and Shirvindt, shared the ideals of all Russian revolutionaries—to do away once and for all with the hated tsarist penal servitude (*katorga*), with Siberian exile, and with the cruelties of Russian prisons.

Eugene Shirvindt, director of the Crime Study Institute, headed the network of correctional institutions run by the NKVD, People's Commissariat of Internal Affairs (not then the secret police). Under him forced labor was officially banned. Prisons became "places of detention" or "corrective labor colonies." Did not the party program demand that prisons be replaced with educational institutions?[77]

The work of correction went on in the old prison buildings. Only now they were embellished with streamers reading, "We are not being punished; we are being corrected." Corrective labor law outlawed all torturing and humiliation of prisoners and forbade "chains, handcuffs, dungeons, strict solitary confinement, deprivation of food, isolation from visitors by means of bars."

Overcrowding because of high conviction rates vitiated such ideals. As Table 2–3 shows, the average prison population of the USSR by 1927 was 198,000—*greater than the tsarist peak:* 183,949 in 1912. The increase is more striking when it is recalled that the Soviet population had shrunk 15 percent below the tsarist population. Even all this understates the increase because the Soviet figures do not include some 30,000 prisoners of the secret police, OGPU* (1928), most of them fitfully doing forced labor in

* The Cheka, an object of criticism and distrust in the party apparatus and Commissariat of Justice, was abolished February 6, 1922. Its trial jurisdiction went to, at that time, the courts and revolutionary tribunals. Most of its functions, including investigations and intelligence, its personnel and its offices including the Moscow HQ, Lubyanka, passed over to its successor police organization, the GPU (Russian

the harsh northern prison camps of SLON, the name for the spreading secret police camp empire formed from the Russian initials for Northern Camps of Special Purpose. OGPU accounted to no judicial authority in many cases of imprisonment. During the early years, political prisoners received preferential treatment because they had shared with the Bolsheviks the lot of radical opponents of the tsars. But OGPU set about reducing politicals' privileges to less than the privileges of common criminals, who victimized the politicals.[78] OGPU's takeover of the remote Solovetskii monastery in June 1923, to be SLON's base camp, turned it from a productive agricultural-fishing retreat into a place of torture and death, despite "Solovki's" propaganda image as a rehabilitative paradise. Later, mass death would come in OGPU camps and the idyllized White Sea Canal and Moscow-Volga canal projects due to exposure, overwork, and near starvation under Stalin in the 1930s and 1940s.[79]

The numbers of prisoners in the colonies and jails of the NKVD more than doubled between 1924 and 1927. They overcrowded the prisons because the regime would not expand prison faculties. Did not the housing needs of workers in city slums come first? And was the Soviet state to build more prisons when crime and coercion were to wither away under it?[80] Table 2–3 shows the result statistically: overcrowding went from 20 percent over the norm in 1924 to 77 percent over by 1926 and higher in 1927. During the last years of tsarism, prisons had been filled at only 80 to 90 percent of capacity, which was about 202,000. Foreign visitors praised Soviet humanitarianism—so many paroles and amnesties. Average terms of confinement were diminishing from 1.25 to 0.72 years. But this had little or nothing to do with any planned withering away of coercion. Rather, it was because of what the NKVD head called, quite frankly, the "prison crisis." There was no other choice. The biggest release of all came with the amnesty on the tenth anniversary of the Bolshevik revolution [81]—again,

initials of its title, Chief Political Administration). Dzerzhinskii headed the GPU and the NKVD, to which the GPU was nominally subordinated. In 1924, after the formation of the USSR, GPU became OGPU (the Unified State Political Administration), formed "in order to unite the revolutionary efforts of the Union republics in the struggle against political and economic counterrevolution, espionage and banditry." Chairman Dzerzhinskii of OGPU was a member of the USSR Council of Ministers with a consultative voice. The real control over OGPU lay not with the government, however, or the Procuracy, but with the party leadership and, eventually, Stalin. Upon Dzerzhinskii's death in 1926, V.R. Menzhinskii, also a Polish aristocrat, took over, but left much of the work to Genrikh Yagoda, his deputy. Simon Wolin and Robert M. Slusser, *The Soviet Secret Police* (New York: Frederick A. Praeger, 1957), pp. 9–13; V.A. Ivanov, "Organizatsiya suda i prokuratury; Puti sozdaniya novogo revolyutsionnogo suda," in O.S. Ioffe et al. (eds.), *Sorok let sovetskogo prava, 1917–1957* (2 vols.; Leningrad: Izd. Leningradskogo universiteta, 1957), vol. 1, p. 589; John N. Hazard, *Settling Disputes in Soviet Society: The Formative Years of Legal Institutions* (New York: Columbia University Press, 1960), pp. 179–180.

Table 2–3. Prisoners in Tsarist and Soviet Places of Detention, Selected Years, 1901–1927

	(1) Number of Prisoners in Tsarist Places of Detention (daily average)	(2) Approximate percent of Prison Capacity	(3) Number of Prisoners in USSR (Jan. 1st of year)	(4) Average Length Sentence RSFSR (years)	(5) Prison Population as percent of Prison Capacity RSFSR
1901	84,632				
1903	96,005				
1905	85,184				
1907	138,501				
1909	175,008				
1911	175,228	87			
1912	183,949	91			
1913	169,367	84			
1914	177,441	88			
1915	156,738				
1916 (First five months)	142,399				
1924			87,800	1.25	120
1925			148,000	0.89	132
1926			155,000	0.72	177
1927			198,000	—	—

Sources:

(1) M.N. Gernet, *Istoriya tsarskoi tyurmy* (3rd ed.; 5 vols.; Moscow: Gosudarstvennoe izd. yuridicheskoi literatury, 1960–1963), pp. 4, 23.

(2) Prison capacity was over 201,774 in last few years before war. Ibid., p. 20.

(3) David J. Dallin and Boris I. Nicolaevsky, *Forced Labor in Soviet Russia* (New Haven: Yale University Press, 1947), p. 160.

(4) V.G. Smirnov and M.D. Shargorodskii, "Ugolovnoe pravo," O.S. Ioffe, et al. (eds.), *Sorok let sovetskogo pravo, 1917–1957* (2 vols.; Leningrad: Izd. Leningradskogo Universiteta, 1957), vol. 1, p. 517.

(5) Ibid., for December 31.

not as a step to communism but simply because jails were stuffed with prisoners suffering from food shortages and epidemics due to unsanitary conditions. This, of course, is not to be simply written off with skepticism. Already the secret police cared little for the overcrowding in *its* camps and took no steps to empty *them*.

Socially useful work, paid at something like trade union rates, and not forced labor lay at the heart of the prison regimen along with cultural means of rehabilitation. But the ideal proved ever more impractical. Funds were lacking for the necessary equipment in many cases. And products of prison labor could hardly hope to find a profitable market and compete in an economy already beset with unemployment. A major Bolshevik innovation was compulsory labor without loss of freedom, meaning work on an assigned job at reduced pay and reporting to the NKVD regularly. But this form of sentence remained unfulfilled, mostly because no jobs could be found. It fell increasingly out of use during NEP.[82]

Conclusions

Revolution and its shock waves dominate the story of changes in law and order during the first Soviet decade. It replaced a faltering reformist coalition with leadership by the most radical socialist fringe. It headed off parliamentary democracy and ushered in the rule of one Party in the name of the toiling masses. Political violence shifted from the war front, not to advanced capitalist countries as expected, but into the heart of Russia, compounding the crime-breeding disarray brought by World War 1.

During their bitter struggle with socialist opposition and counterrevolution, the Bolsheviks led Soviet Russia into a militant period of War Communism, until the spring of 1921. It was a radical era of civil war, foreign intervention, and uncompromising repression. Experiments in economic radicalism, from workers' control to payment in kind, came and went out of both necessity and principle. The government reformed family law in the name of women's liberation, something certain provincial hotheads mistakenly took as a signal to proclaim a short-lived "nationalization of women." [83]

Radicalism, it has been said, yields eventually to a retrenchment that leaves less of a break with the past than revolutionary ideology envisioned or witnesses of the radical period anticipated.[84] This tendency to retrenchment began in Soviet Russia already during War Communism, before the concessions to peasants and private trade which ushered in the New Economic Policy (NEP), beginning March 1921. Thus, legal institutions initially changed more than any other part of the state apparatus carried over into Bolshevism, despite misgivings of the Left SRs and some Bolsheviks. Even during War Communism, though, simplifiers and anticentralists lost ground. Rudimentary justice was beginning to grow into an elaborate, specialized system of law and enforcement. Sharp rises in conviction statistics during the civil war and early NEP period reflected the consequences of the bitter conflicts of 1917–1921 for an already demoralized society. But the increases in convictions originated also in the growing police and judicial power of the Soviet state.

Basically, in its present form, the NEP system of justice was far from Lenin's original dream of "a very simple 'machine.' " "The armed workers themselves" acted for a brief spell during War Communism. Even during that chaotic period, rough and ready grassroots tribunals began to shape into a coherent system with appeals levels. The trend was toward a powerful system of state repression and law enforcement, all in the name of the eventual withering away of the state: the militia carried over and judges, prosecutors, and attorneys were increasingly professionalized. A more centralized network of the Procuracy regained the wide powers of its tsarist predecessor. A correctional system of prisons, labor camps, and reformatories operated in the same buildings, cold Siberian wildernesses, or forbidding monasteries as used by the tsars. It confined more prisoners by 1927 than tsars had. Humanitarianism conflicted with the practical difficulties confronting penologists of the NKVD and with the terror of the OGPU. The Soviet machinery of repression included a brilliantly led army with tsarist-trained officers and NCOs at its core, a powerful secret police, and a four-level court system—people's courts, city courts, Union republic supreme courts, and the USSR Supreme Court.

Like the tsarist judicial reforms, Bolshevik innovations were sweeping and rapid, inspired by an imported and adapted set of guiding principles, but eroded by piecemeal retreats and circumventions.

Alexander II revamped justice in the wake of peasant emancipation. The Bolsheviks revamped justice in the wake of a revolutionary takeover intended to initiate the emancipation of the working class.

In both cases the ideologically inspired renewals had to be adapted to a troubled and authoritarian Russian heritage. In both cases crime rates seemed to reflect not only criminal policy but a series of political decisions about priorities and war and revolutionary strategies. Law-and-order problems resulted from politics as well as from any spontaneous, inherited, or inevitable social processes.

Tsarist legislators never expressed an intention to eliminate repression against common crime (except for a fringe of utopian socialist lawyers and advocates of no repression for children). But they did considerably reduce repression. Bolsheviks intended eventually to eliminate professionalized, police repression and bring order without law and its enforcement. Within five years they had learned to use an "iron hand," and simply replaced one elaborate court system with another, not entirely dissimilar one under the banner of social defense and "revolutionary justice."

Proclaiming rule of law, tsarists partly bypassed and subjugated the courts in political cases. Proclaiming rule above law and by revolutionary conscience alongside decrees, the Bolsheviks came to rule through law and the courts. They also bypassed the regular courts, often in political cases, but in common cases too. Tsarism created a freer profession of lawyers than had existed up to 1864. Bolshevism pointedly eliminated bar associations, but soon recreated them under tighter controls. Specialists trained before the revolution entered the advocacy, the faculty of law schools reappearing with NEP, the apparatus of the Ministry of Justice, and a revived and ideologically pluralist, contentious and vigorously reviving criminology. Again, they upheld liberalization and due process. Paradoxically, they pushed harder for the withering away of coercion than did some of their Marxist mentors.

3

"Revolution From Above": Stalin's Law and Order

We had been talking about it from the time we got there, that men, women and children were enemy soldiers.

—Lieut. William Calley of My Lai

I am an old Bolshevik. I worked in the underground against the Tsar and then I fought in the civil war. Did I do all that in order that I should now surround villages with machine guns and order my men to fire indiscriminately into crowds of peasants?

—An OGPU colonel quoted by Isaac Deutscher

THE FINELY MINTED SOVIET SILVER RUBLE of the NEP period shows a worker in overalls beckoning a bearded muzhik to abandon his horse and plough for a sunnier future in a distant factory. But with production back to prewar levels, how was Russia to feed, house, and train more peasants leaving the land? Where would she get the capital to build and equip new factories for them to work in? How was Russia to resume her once rapid pace of development now that NEP recovery was complete and existing plants were used to capacity? With what was she to replace foreign sources of capital, estranged as she was from much of the West?

The Soviet leadership's answers to these questions had more to do with trends in crime and prevention after NEP than did any other changes in Soviet society and politics. The answers came ultimately from Stalin. Skillfully manipulating factional alliances, the party machinery, and nationalist appeals of "socialism in one country," Stalin emerged as virtual dictator in 1928, within four years of Lenin's death, despite Lenin's warnings against him.[1] The short, pockmarked Georgian, a "grey blur" in 1917,[2] had opposed overthrowing the Provisional Government until Lenin won the Central Committee over to insurrection. Eleven years later, Stalin launched his own great gamble, in its way an insurrection against the more cautious Old Bolsheviks of the Right, a gamble in which he "whipped the country on" to overcome backwardness[3] in seven years of "revolution from above." [4]

Stalin merged tsarist goals of transforming Russia from a "weak" into a "powerful" country with Communist goals of building simultaneously a "socialist society." And he pushed the country along two paths toward those goals. The priority of heavy industrialization over consumer goods would "change from the muzhik horse of poverty to the horse of large scale machine industry." Collectivization, "the transition from individual peasant farming," would make it possible to extract food to sustain and finance that industrialization. Stalin's "great change" unfolded more rapidly and violently than any party factions or even Stalin's maximal plans of 1928–1929 foresaw.[5]

Revitalization and Repression

Unprecedented social mobilization ensued. Spontaneity, already gone from politics, was stamped out of science, culture, social research, and economic decision making during the first two five-year plans (October 1928 through 1932 and 1933–1937). Writers became "shock workers" on the "literary front." Drives against religion gained renewed fervor. The regime pushed technical schools and colleges to turn out more rapidly more practically trained and proletarian "new cadres of red specialists." It set up *rabfacs* (workers' schools) as "firemen's ladders" to the colleges in a short-lived Soviet version of open admissions.[6]

Elementary school enrollments more than doubled, from 10 to 21 million, in five years. Total school enrollment swelled from 12 million in 1928 to 31.5 million in 1938. The number of industrial workers increased 50 percent in three years, 1930–1933. Russia was at last becoming a literate nation with a flourishing mass culture, for all the censorship of creativity. The regime improved social security and urged women to assume the double burden of housewife and worker. But this they did in the the context of formally equal opportunity and wages, improved child care, and—formally, at least—protective labor laws. For those loyal to Stalin, careers opened to talent in all sectors of administration and the economy.[7] For the Young Communists camping alongside the litter of their factories abuilding, the great change betokened a period of storm and struggle that rekindled the proletarian militance of War Communism. Stalin urged his people on as the "shock troops" and "vanguard" of the workers of the world who counted on Soviet power to help emancipate them. Russia,

Stalin told them, had had its fill of backwardness and defeat, and had ten years to make good its fifty- or hundred-year lag "behind the advanced countries . . . or we shall be crushed." But if they wanted to do it, he told his audiences, they could, for "there are no fortresses Bolsheviks cannot capture." [8] What the former grey blur led his country into in 1928–1934 was nothing less than the mass dedication and enthusiasm of a revitalization movement.[9]

To exalting and ever more nationalistic persuasion, to the chances to go to school and better oneself, Stalin added solid incentives to excel, with stratified rewards for managers, record-breaking and rate-busting workers, and his political *apparatchiki* in the party, administrative, and police machinery. There were at least five levels of dining room at Magnitogorsk, the new iron-mining and steel-smelting city in the Urals. They ranged from the well-catered restaurant for top management and foreign VIPs to the canteen serving thin gruel and bread to convict forced laborers.[10]

The forced laborers alongside Komsomol enthusiasts denoted the underside of the revolution from above. Stalinism tapped reserves of dedication, carried out "a vast amount of useful social and educational work," but imposed a system in which "repression and regimentation of every kind became vastly more intense." [11]

Many foreigners from depression-plagued Western countries admired the revitalization and ignored the repression which the regime only too happily hid from them as much as it could. Seemingly humane correctional institutions and the impressive labor communes for youthful and juvenile offenders made an enormous impression on the visitors. Moreover, it seemed to many of them that Stalin had found the key to industrialization without increasing crime. Influential laborites predicted that, as the younger folk left the scene, crime in the Soviet "new civilization" would fade away to "occasional lapses of conduct," [12] as Lenin had foreseen. Crime was no longer a major social problem.[13] Countries with rampant crime, like the United States, had much to learn from the Soviet approach to crime prevention with its "broad social programs," "humane treatment of criminals," and "simplicity of court procedures." [14]

It probably does not take this chapter to point out that the humaneness of Stalin's penology in the early and mid-1930s remained chiefly on paper, for the edification of foreign commentors, except for the juvenile labor communes, which Stalin liquidated late in 1936.[15] Humane penology, such as it was, survived as a remnant of one tendency in NEP justice rather than as any initiative of Stalin's. Across the USSR by the early thirties, an undernation was spreading made up of underfed and diseased camp inmates, army-size forced labor on mammoth projects like the White Sea Canal, deported peasants and their children.[16]

The foreigners—most of them—missed the spirit of the times. But

William Henry Chamberlin caught it, and so did John Scott, an American who worked as welder, foreman, and chemist during five of Magnitogorsk's most heroic years. It was the spirit of all-out war on backwardness and on real and imagined obstacles to a victorious outcome. Scott wrote:

> Ever since 1931 or thereabouts the Soviet Union has been at war. . . . People were wounded and killed, women and children froze to death, millions starved, thousands were court-martialed and shot in the campaigns of collectivization and industrialization. I would wager that Russia's battle of ferrous metallurgy alone involved more casualties than the battle of the Marne. All during the thirties the Russian people were at war. . . .
>
> In Magnitogorsk I was precipitated into a battle. I was deployed on the iron and steel front. Tens of thousands of people were enduring the most intense hardships in order to build blast furnaces, and many of them did it willingly, with boundless enthusiasm, which infected me from the day of my arrival.[17]

The main purpose of this chapter is to test out the assumption prevailing in more recent but scattered commentary that the repressive, totalitarian side of Stalinism secured law and order, if at an unacceptable cost.[18]

Beginning with Stalin's ideological basis for his uses of criminal punishment, I shall explore his system of justice and its extrajudicial accompaniments as well as the state of disorder, both from above and from below.

Class Struggle and Crime

Stalin's law and order received its shape not from the humane, experimental side of NEP policy but from its residual repressiveness and from Stalin's "great break" with individual peasant farming and gradual, evolutionary economic development. His alternative unfolded increasingly as class war in 1928–1929. It decimated the old professional intelligentsia whom Stalin distrusted and used as scapegoats for plan failures.[19] It smashed peasant resistance to leaping tempos of grain extraction and of recruitment to collective farms. It used draconian criminal penalities to regiment the socialized labor force. Ideologically, Stalin prepared the way for repression by revising the Communist theories of class struggle, the withering away of the state, and the causes of crime.

Stalin synthesized an ideological underpinning for his "great break" during months of debate over Russia's future in 1927–1928, more than a year before collectivization swept the land. It prepared the way for Stalin's break with Bukharin and the moderates.[20] It was to color all policy, including crime prevention, by linking criminal law with no-quarter class struggle. "Capitalist encirclement," Stalin warned December 3, 1927, posed continual danger of capitalist attacks from without and intervention through bourgeois class allies inside the USSR.[21] He drove home the point (and simultaneously provided the first scapegoats for possible failures) through the Shakhty affair, the show trial in March 1928 of alleged wreckers among foreign mining engineers in the Donbas region,[22] and through a series of major pronouncements about the need to overcome kulak (rich peasant) grain hoarding so as to feed the towns.[23] Finally, on July 9, 1928, Stalin told a Central Committee meeting that "the advance toward socialism cannot but cause the exploiting elements to resist the advance, and the resistance of the exploiters cannot but lead to the inevitable sharpening of the class struggle."[24]

Such a struggle, very physical during the First Five-Year Plan, 1928–1932, required blood and iron all right. As the Secretary General of the Communist Party, Stalin controlled the repressive power of the state and directed the state violence against real and imaginary enemies. Replacing Lenin's formulation of a gradual withering of an initially strong state apparatus, Stalin called in 1930 for "the highest development of state power so that the state would become the mightiest and strongest" ever, in preparation for the withering away of the state: a contradiction, yes, he said, but a "living" one, part of the dialectic of advance through resolution of contradictions.[25] Great coercive power and decisive leadership no less than economic change became central to Stalin's theory of development. "In order to remake the world," he later told H.G. Wells, "one must have political power as a lever of change."[26]

And the change must appear to be the most beneficial ever, the Soviet socialist state the most omnipotent ever. Under the new Soviet socialism, evils like crime could be only eradicable survivals of a bygone era: a far cry from the explanations prevailing in the flourishing Soviet criminology. At first, Stalinists did not directly attack all the arts and sciences. Often they allowed leftist militants to attack "bourgeois" and "rightist" artists and scholars.[27] Then the Stalinists stepped in and took over control of their professions already weakened by internal purge and dissent. The first attacks on criminology came from "legal nihilists" of the commodity exchange school of law, radical jurists like E.B. Pashukanis, N.V. Krylenko, and P.I. Stuchka.[28] They sought to take over criminology and impose their idea of a proper Marxist approach based on class struggle and the withering of law and crime on the way to socialism.

Criminology first came under leftist attack, as did fields like literature, in 1928. At the First All-Union Conference of Penitentiary Officials, speakers denounced purely biopsychological explanations of crime, as not recognizing the decisive importance of "social and economic causes of crime," and as "opposed to the basic principles of revolutionary Marxism." [29]

During the crucial winter of the moderates' defeat everywhere in 1928–1929, Pashukanis, Krylenko, and Stuchka and their supporters in the Section of Law and the State of the Communist Academy, campaigned against the approaches of the criminologists, most of whom were not Marxists. They authorized a critical article by S. Ya. Bulatov in their journal for January 1929 against the "renaissance of Lombroso in Soviet criminology." [30] Bulatov's diatribe against defectological and psychopathological theories of crime signaled an onslaught which would be followed later by Stalinist policy makers, stopping all crime research. The onslaught began publicly as a debate staged by the Section of Law and the State of the Communist Academy two months after Bulatov's article.

The Communist Academy group and supporters made an attack so broad as to constitute a demand for the end of all empirical criminological research as then conducted.[31] Their threefold critique took criminologists to task for (1) biopsychological explanations of crime when in fact it was, the critics said, a mass social phenomenon and particularly for the genetic explanations by which crime was placed beyond the reach of the new social order; (2) researchers' alleged failure to give practical guidelines to crime fighters; (3) social theories of crimes, guilty of "vulgar positivism" for reducing crime causes to a series of "factors," without a unifying theory of socialist construction, of class struggle, guilty of "sentimental sociologizing" (A.A. Gertsenzon), and guilty of so-called "petty bourgeois sociological deviations" (B.S. Man'kovskii and Bulatov) typified by the "liberal humanitarian approach" of Professor M.N. Gernet, an eminent non-Marxist radical researcher already encountered as an opponent of repression in corrections.[32]

E.B. Pashukanis, main orchestrator of this attack on criminology, was gaining prestige and influence as a prophet of the withering away of state and law.[33] But it took him and his followers two years of siege to capture Shirvindt's Institute for the Study of Crime and the Criminal. As the 1929 discussion revealed, there were biologists like V.A. Vnukov and V.O. Akkerman who stood up for their views linking criminal behavior with certain physical and psychological defects even while other colleagues recanted. The resistance of Shirvindt was crucial.

Shirvindt seemed to try to protect himself and his Institute for the Study of Crime and the Criminal without attacking his subordinates. He had permitted them freedom of research despite his Marxist disagreements with the absence of class analysis in their sociology and biopsychology of crime, and with their failure to realize that their job was not to reduce crime but to eliminate it.[34] If the Rostov Crime Study Office printed an offending article by the sociologist-criminologist Enrico Ferri, Shirvindt said under attack, it was without the institute's approval. His institute's orientation was in fact Marxist. Stingy funding, not any lack of practicality or Marxist spirit, according to Shirvindt, stood in the way of more practical prevention programs. The government, after all, had allotted only 50,000 rubles to run all operations of the institute, but no less than 674,000 rubles for capital repairs of the Communist Academy—a dig at Pashukanis, Krylenko, and other opponents based there.

Shirvindt and his supporters resisted their takeover of criminology until the abolition of the RSFSR NKVD on January 1, 1931 ended Shirvindt's patronage and support. He resigned in February from the directorship of the Institute for the Study of Crime and the Criminal, and eventually "sat" in labor camps from 1936 to 1955.[35] The regional crime study offices were closed in 1931 and the institute transferred to the RSFSR Commissariat of Justice, renamed the Institute for the Study of Crime, its Biopsychological Section shut down and research on the criminal personality stopped.[36]

Shirvindt's Marxist explanation for crimes, propounded without much guidance from Marx and Engels, had depicted three roots in Soviet society: the destructiveness of past revolutionary conflict, "growing pains of development," and "survivals of the overturned order" (the old Marxist formulation for cultural lag).[37] Altogether, Shirvindt's explanation could no longer satisfy a regime with Stalin's activist view of the opposition as "survivals of the overturned order," the omnipotence of the Stalinist state in its struggle with the survival, and the legitimation of Stalin's revolution from above as one removing all the traditional "growing pains" of industrialization, and all the old social strains. Nor could it satisfy the Pashukanis-Krylenko group.

Shirvindt's eventual successor, A.S. Shlyapochnikov, laid down the only acceptable explanations of crime in an address to the purged, reorganized, renamed Institute for the Study of Crime on April 20, 1932. The new explanations of what motivated people to crime in Soviet society made up for Shirvindt's lacks and supported the carefully cultivated image, so widely believed in fact among foreigners, that Stalin and the Party had brought to Russia a "socialist industrialization" vastly superior to any "capitalist industrialization" with its "reserve armies of unemployed and sharp drops in living standards of vast masses of the working people." As mentioned, such a thesis had a credibility in a world where Russia was forging ahead, while the Western countries stagnated with masses on the dole.

Now, the new line went, unlike in capitalist countries, there were no longer any systemic causes of crime in the USSR, no growing pains, no fault of the system, only of "wreckers" or some failing managers. Shirvindt's third factor, "survivals of the past," now became the only explanation of motivations for crime. But no longer were survivals to be pictured only as a passive cultural "lag of consciousness behind economic development." Rather, as Stalin pointed out in 1930, "the radical reorganization of all our social relations" must necessarily "provoke the desperate resistance of the forces of the old world." They might be kulaks, or a worker beating up a mate who approved new lower piece rate payments, or the allegedly ubiquitous wreckers.

Common crimes, so-called "crimes of everyday life" like hooliganism, theft and murder, smacked also of counterrevolution because, though not intended as such, they disrupted socialist construction. Common criminals, said Shlyapochnikov, were not true proletariats but "petty bourgeois elements" among millions of inexperienced and undisciplined new workers who had migrated from the villages to cities during the years of the "great break." "Crime in our country," said Shlyapochnikov, "is a particular form of class struggle by remnants of the old world against a nascent and developing communism; it is acts of class struggle, a class revenge." According to Shlyapochnikov, even the use of the term "crimes of everyday life" was "politically incorrect." "So called 'crimes of everyday life' are also forms of class struggle" by the petty bourgeois peasants and former peasants or by "hidden" class enemies lurking everywhere in the guise of "good" workers or peasants.[38]

Reflecting the regime's punitive inclinations, and Krylenko's demands that the Communist Academy do the theorizing, research gradually shifted from penal policy and causes of crime to studying only current norms of criminal law and trends in sentencing to criminal punishment. In 1933 the institute was transferred to the triple supervision of the RSFSR Commissariat of Justice, USSR Procuracy, and USSR Supreme Court, as the Institute of Criminal Policy. Its emphasis shifted to even more practical research on criminal law and procedure. The transfer left theoretical aspects of crime fighting to the Institute of Soviet Construction and Law, the Section of Law and the State of the Communist Academy, and the Institute of State and Law formed out of their merger. "Criminological studies ceased to appear. Serious course work on crime and the criminal personality was dropped from the curricula of law schools and institutes. Corresponding parts were deleted from textbooks. . . . Trained criminologists left the field. Statistical materials gradually disappeared from print in the early 1930's." The Department of Moral Statistics in the Central Statistical Administration was liquidated, "leaving the country without a center for analyzing and interpreting crime trends." The last national statistics on crime in the USSR appeared in 1935.

When Pashukanis fell from grace after the repudiation of his legal nihilism and commodity exchange theory of law, two sections of his Institute of Soviet Construction and Law were moved in late 1936 to the Institute of Criminal Policy, renamed the All-Union Institute of Juridical

Sciences. Demoted to deputy director, then arrested in 1937, A.S. Shlyapochnikov, a protégé of Krylenko, spent 18 years in prison camp until his release in 1955 and return to the All-Union Institute of Juridical Sciences.[39]

For 25 years, until the post-Stalin thaw, crime could be attributed only to the "lag of consciousness behind economic development," malevolent infusions from the "capitalist encirclement," "enemies of the people," "petty bourgeois elements," and faulty repression of these "survivals" by families, schools, youth organizations, and law enforcers.[40]

On several occasions between 1944 and 1950, jurists like M.N. Gernet, A.A. Gertsenzon, B.N. Khlebnikov, I.T. Goliakov, and I.P. Trainin spoke or wrote in favor of resuming crime research. When Gernet, Gertsenzon, and Khlebnikov joined in an article which called for resuming crime research on the basis of objective statistical data, opposing jurists prevailed. There were no statistics to refute these Stalinists' contention that "obective" causes for crime in the USSR—that is, crime breeding social strains and inequality—had vanished. "Subjective causes" of human failure, moreover, they said, were disappearing.

"In these jurists' opinion all one needed to know about the causes of crime at that time lay in the concept of survivals of the past in people's minds and hostile activities of bourgeoisie from abroad." [41] Had there not been something in the air lending hope to endeavors to revive criminology, the article would not have passed censorship. The Department of Criminal Law at Moscow University would not have expressed support for Trainin's proposals in 1950.[42] But the partisans of criminology "had misjudged the trends; the Stalinist system could end only with Stalin." [43]

Stalin's justice retained a humane, simple side in petty conflicts and disputes. But attributing crime to irreconcilable enemies and their corrupting influence recreated old theological devil theories, opened the door wider to harsh methods of intimidation and vengeance dating back to prereform Russia and preenlightenment Europe[44]—first for adult convicts, then, in 1935, for juvenile violators of law and order.[45] Stalin's devil theory of crime and of class struggle cleared him and the Party of responsibility for disruption and disorder. The economic disruptions could be blamed on criminal disorder, and the criminal disorder, on survivals of the past and "intensification of the class struggle." His theories of class struggle, crime, and the state justified and incited coercive, arbitrary means of social mobilization and control.

Criminal Prosecution

So did revolutionary morality of ends justifying means. Even as the legal nihilists still worked to do away with law, Stalin used criminal law increasingly to work his way as, law lecturers put it, not as a "fetish" of inviolable principles, "but a tool for sweeping away obstacles to socialist construction."[46] Stalin used the law against grain hoarders, thieves, and shirking workers.

Peasant hoarding of grain, holding it back from the urban consumer, prompted part directives for a nonviolent "economic squeeze" and "attack" on the kulaks (rich peasants).[47] But forced requisitioning of grain, civil war style, was not a decision of the Party or the judiciary. Rather, it followed on Stalin's bullying and threats during a circuit of grain-growing areas January 15 to February 6, 1928.

Local party organs objected that courts and prosecutors were unprepared for "emergency measures" of confiscation and prosecution against hoarders and speculators under Article 107 of the RSFSR Criminal Code and the equivalent article in the Ukraine and that this "would only worsen the situation." Stalin retorted with the basic rationale for confiscation (and the later collectivization that broke peasant will and capacity to resist): "We cannot allow our country to be dependent on the caprice of the kulaks."[48]

Aside from a creditable social welfare program for urban and state farm workers, Stalin had little material incentive to offer either workers or peasants.[49] He relied heavily on coercive controls and punishments to drive on low paid and undisciplined new factory workers and expropriated peasants and to nip pilfering and opposition in the bud. All of Russia, free labor included, fell under some form of modified serfdom or corvée. Free villagers, like the woodsmen up in Karelia, felt hardly less compulsion than did the inmates of the labor camps all around them. If they failed to deliver compulsory quotas of timber they faced fines or imprisonment. An old coachman grumbled to his visiting passengers: "This country isn't Karelia any more, it is *Katorga.*"[50]

NEP's tendency toward milder sentences and abolishing capital punishment was reversed. Courts were kept hard at work and the judicial apparatus grew despite the influence of legal nihilists like E.B. Pashukanis and N.V. Krylenko on law, legal education, and legal theory.[51]

Two decrees in 1929, aimed specially at peasants resisting collectivization, ordered stiffer penalties for persons considered "class enemies." The possible length of exile increased from five to ten years, with a minimum of three. Sentences of under one year, which had run as high as 85 percent of all prison terms (1926), disappeared in 1930.[52] That year the government decreed that "class-alien elements" should receive no less than three years' confinement. This helped recruit forced labor for the secret police because, by another ruling that year, convicts serving three or more years went to the labor camps.[53] Convicts receiving lesser sentences went to the corrective labor colonies of the Commissariat of Justice.

Special railroad line and shipping courts were organized in 1933 to provide tighter judicial protection against thievery and damage in transport, a serious bottleneck. This came two years after prison sentences were introduced for violations of labor discipline on the railroads. Also in 1933, the year OGPU received the power to execute, a USSR Procuracy was established, separate now from the USSR Supreme Court, to tighten up law enforcement in the USSR. At the same time courts were sentencing higher proportions of persons found guilty to sentences involving deprivation of freedom.[54]

From then on until post-Stalin reforms, Soviet criminal policy seemed bound to a belief that "rehabilitation and re-education of the criminal was a function only of state corrective labor institutions." [55]

Tomskii's removal from trade union leadership in April 1929 cleared the way for speedups on piece rates, regimentation of labor, and drastic reductions in real wage rates. But skilled labor was short and jobs readily available. Workers therefore job-flitted in search of better pay and housing. In the huge turnover, the industrial work force was changing jobs in 1930 on the average of nearly twice a year. Absenteeism, indiscipline, and thievery plagued production.

Drastic job freeze rules appeared in 1930, naming penalties like loss of ration books and housing for job flitters. Criminal penalties awaited managers not enforcing the new work rules. Individual labor booklets and internal passports (a tsarist control device) came in 1932. To stop what seemed rightly a disruptive menace, the indiscipline, absenteeism, corruption, and negligence, Stalin introduced a whole new list of crimes. Capital offenses multiplied. The death penalty came to threaten many economic criminals, from hoarders of silver coins to railroad workers unintentionally causing wrecks through negligence. Stalin's theory of intensification of the class struggle lent support to a criminal policy marked by an "unjustified increase in punishment for certain crimes and in court practice an unfounded trend toward general increase of repression" to the point that maximum sentences specified for offenses became minimum sentences in practice, and even common crimes of everyday life were often regarded and treated as "counter-revolutionary." [56]

Cases resulting from the intensification of the class struggle jammed the courts; raised conviction rates show it (see Table 3–1). The policy of "squeezing the kulaks" meant high taxes and expulsion from local government and credit and cooperative agencies. This provoked peasant resistance. So did vigorous prosecution, just mentioned, for alleged speculation in grain and concealment of surpluses, under the scrutiny of local prosecutors.[57] Arrests and convictions mounted also during the grain collection campaign of the summer and fall of 1929.

Courts traveled in visiting session to drive home the point of the prosecutions of grain hoarders. Typically, a district center would receive

Table 3–1. Trends in Convictions, RSFSR and USSR, 1928–1938

		(1) Indices (1928 (I) = 100 1928 Year = 100 RSFSR	(2) Court Convictions USSR (est.)	(3) Court Convictions RSFSR
1928	I	100		
	II	104.9		
	Year	100	1,610,000	1,106,000
1929	I	124		
	II	143.9		
	Year	131	2,110,000	1,450,000
1930	I	141		
	II	118		
	Year	126	2,020,000	1,392,000
1931	I	152.7		
	II	138.3		
	Year	142	2,280,000	1,570,000
1933	I	152.2		
	II	143.3		
	Year	144	2,320,000	1,590,000
1934	I	116.8		
	II	101.4		
	Year	107	1,710,000	1,182,000

I = 1st half, II = 2nd half, Year = whole year, 1932 figures not published.

Sources:

(1) A. Shlyapochnikov, "Prestupnost' i repressiya v SSSR (Kratkii obzor)," *Problemy ugolovnoi politiki,* vol. 1 (1935), p. 78; for RSFSR without autonomous republics 1928–1934, and also without autonomous provinces and far eastern territory, 1933–1934.

(2) Estimated from RSFSR figures as for Table 2–3.

(3) Estimated form figures for 1928, 1929, in Table 2–3, and from indices.

word that peasants in a certain village were holding back on grain deliveries. If the center wanted to make a local issue of this, it would send a "judicial-investigative brigade" to the village. After a short investigation, the visiting people's court tried the case before the local peasants assembled presumably to make an example of the hoarders and to try to turn sentiment against them.[58]

As the authorities moved in on grain hoarders, they provoked mounting resistance by whole villages. Kulaks and nonkulaks united together in violent and futile opposition.[59] It was the conflict in the villages that increased conviction rates 30 percent in 1929, to say nothing of the unrecorded administrative sentences meted out by the OGPU.

As the conflict and social purge intensified, the annual number of reported court convictions (of persons sixteen years old and above) rose from about 1.5 million to over 2 million. It is perhaps because convictions rose so high in 1932 that their numbers were not released. Conviction totals would have gone much higher if hundreds of thousands of petty cases of crimes-against-persons cases had not been removed from the courts in 1930 and handed over to nonprofessional comrades' courts in farms, factories, and housing projects.[60] Tables 3–2 and 3–3 record the jumps in convictions for all other main types of crimes.

Counterrevolutionary crime convictions increased eightfold, even though the OGPU was already handling many times the number shown here directly without benefit of court trial. A law of August 7, 1932, treated all theft of public property* as a heinous oppositional act by enemies of the people. It prescribed death by shooting or, in mitigating circumstances, ten years' confinement, then the maximum jail term.[61] Reported convictions under this law in the Russian republic reached a peak of 68,000 in the first half of 1933 and a total of 102,000 for the year (see Tables 3–2 and 3–3). An American visitor to Novinsky Women's Prison noted that one girl already in prison nine times for theft of personal property, had received a sentence of only two years this time. Another girl, sentenced under the law of August 7, 1932, against theft of public property, had received ten years for a small theft from a collective farm. She was a class enemy. The draconian law came to be applied to such nontheft crimes as alleged agricultural wrecking bringing lower harvests, or deliberately breaking tractors and motor vehicles.[62]

Crime in production shaped itself not only according to new penalties but also according to the setting of work. During the summer peasants were picked up for pilfering grain on the stalks in the field. (Ten years for that.)[63] After the harvest arrests for stealing from warehouses replaced field thefts on court dockets. As the bureaucratic apparatus of management and supply grew, so did opportunities for embezzlement, bribery, and the formation of criminal rings of officials on farms and in procurement agencies, plants, even banks, who embezzled funds or channeled food and consumer goods into the black market.[64]

"Misconduct in office" became an even wider means of repression than the better known law of August 7, 1932, against theft of public property. It covered many white-collar crimes, from abuse of office and false reporting to negligence and bribery. The category was a more versatile menu for punishment than the law of August 7, 1932, with a wider range of possible penalties. Tables 3–2 and 3–3 show that, in the Russian re-

* Public property in the USSR is (1) "state" property, i.e., ministerial, most industrial and trade inventory and state farm property; (2) cooperative property, e.g., the property and output of the socialized sector of collective farms. This leaves the "personal" property of citizens: (1) individual possessions; (2) inventory of the jointly owned collective farm peasant household.

Table 3–2. Proportions of Types of Crimes for Which Persons Were Convicted in the RSFSR, 1928–1934 I (first half) and II (second half)

	1928		1929		1932		1933		1934	
	I	II	I	II	I	II	I	II	I	II
Counterrevolutionary	0.1	0.1	0.2	0.6	0.1	0.5	0.6	0.4	0.2	0.3
Theft of public property (law of Aug. 7, 1932)	—	—	—	—	—	1.0	8.3	4.4	2.8	2.5
Against admin. order (mainly hooliganism & moonshining)	49.3	41.3	40.6	44.5	44.0	40.7	39.3	26.1	28.9	33.0
Misconduct in office	8.2	7.3	9.6	12.9	23.1	19.8	21.5	28.7	33.1	28.9
Against property	20.4	20.5	25.4	22.9	27.1	31.3	27.3	36.7	30.6	29.7
Against persons	22.0	30.8	24.0	19.0	5.7	5.4	3.0	3.7	4.4	4.5

Source: Shlyapochnikov, "Prestupnost' i repressiya," p. 78.

Table 3–3. Numbers of Convictions for Categories of Crimes, RSFSR, 1928 and 1933

	1928	1933
Total	1,106,000	1,590,000
Counterrevolutionary	1,100	8,000
Theft of public property (law of August 7, 1932)	—	102,000
Against administrative order	500,000	524,000
Misconduct in office	86,000	398,000
Against property	227,000	508,000
Against persons	292,000	53,000

Note: For a rough approximate estimate of convictions for various crimes in the USSR as a whole, multiply these numbers by 1.46.

Source: Tables 3–1 and 3–2.

public alone, convictions for misconduct in office rose from 86,000 in 1928 to 398,000 in 1933 and from about 7 or 8 percent of all convictions in 1928 to about one out of every four convictions in 1933. Courts in some districts were sentencing between a quarter and a half of all chairmen of kolkhozes and village soviets (councils) for this category of offense. In Moscow Province, 8,847 ordinary kolkhoz (collective farm) peasants were convicted of misconduct in office during 1933 for real or imagined lapses as petty as failing to salt the dinner.[65] Convictions for crimes against property other than those subsumed under the law of August 7, 1932, against theft of public property rose from 227,000 in 1928 to 508,000 in 1933.

Stalin and Molotov called a halt to the "saturnalia of arrests" in a secret letter of May 8, 1933. They ordered the population of houses of detention (for pretrial suspects and petty offenders) to be halved, from 800,000 to 400,000! Followup orders came from the Party to cease "legal repression on an extraordinary scale, which has led everywhere to intolerable overloading of the places of imprisonment, to inordinate burdening of all organs of investigation, the courts and the procuracy." [66] The "prison crisis" of 1924–1927 seems tiny in comparison.

Disorder from Above and Below

Where law and the courts could not cope with the repressive needs of revolution from above, extrajudicial, police, party, army, and vigilante forces were mustered. Policies of the years of social purge, 1928–1934, moved Soviet society back away from law and order—both from above and below.

While prosecutions of grain hoarders went forward, under Article 107 of the Criminal Code, so did "the practice of house-to-house visitations, unlawful searches and . . . other infringements of revolutionary law." [67] Stalin ordered against this, but seemingly more for the record than for practice. The middle and poor peasants also felt the sting of confiscation, ostensibly, despite Stalin's command.[68] And, at Stalin's behest, crash collectivization came unexpectedly and undecreed, at the expense of law and order among both enforcers and victims.

Stalin in 1928 still espoused gradualism[69] and quoted Lenin: "the remaking of the small tiller, the remolding of his whole mentality and habits, is a work of generations" (July 9, 1928).[70] Even as Stalin reemphasized intensification of the class struggle in April 1929, he said middle and poor peasants would play a "predominant part" in food supply "supplemented by the development of collective and state farms." [71]

As grain acquisitions lagged again in the fall, and outside of any special party mandate, Stalin changed policy from gradualism to coerced collectivization as if this were a continuation of existing policy for "the offensive of socialism against capitalist elements of town and country." Exterminating the kulaks as a class, a "folly" in 1928 [72] became policy late in 1929. Stalin demanded it no less than five times on December 27, 1929: "We have passed from the policy of *restricting* the exploiting tendencies of the kulaks to the policy of *eliminating* the kulaks as a class . . . we must smash the kulaks, eliminate them as a class . . . strike at the kulaks, strike so hard as to prevent them from rising to their feet again." War was being waged against not only kulaks but against the peasantry as a whole.[73] Common crime could not be as frightening, depriving, or lethal as were the depredations of the collectivizers.

The initial collectivization targets set at the 16th Party Conference in April 1929 were cautious ones: less than 20 percent of cropland in five years. They were already exceeded three times over in five months, October 1929 to February 1930. Kulaks by state count formed the most prosperous top 5 percent or so. But middle peasants resisted too; they, hardly less than kulaks, felt the brunt of compulsion. "Driving a wedge between kulaks and middle peasants" had somehow been lost sight of in the frenzy.[74] Stalin's "dizziness with success" article of March 2, 1930, called a brief retreat. But the drive soon resumed. By 1933, 84.5 percent of all peasant households were in collective farms tilling 65 percent of cropland.[75] The extreme pace of forcing small private farmers to merge into collective farms provoked desperate peasant resistance, crop burning, and destruction of livestock. Party emissaries and OGPU security troops struck back without mercy in punitive actions and arrests. Theirs was an urgent mandate, for grain was desperately needed to export for foreign currency with which to purchase economic assistance from abroad, and to feed the towns.[76]

"Dekulakized" peasants were divided into three groups. Group I consisted of the "most dangerous" or richest expropriated farmers. They were arrested, tried somehow, had their property confiscated, and were sent to prisons or labor camps. Their families were deported. Group II, somewhat less prosperous farmers, allegedly kulak exploiters of their neighbors, were gathered up and deported with their families, their property confiscated. Group II was twice as large as Group I in the RSFSR. Group III, the remainder of the alleged kulaks, were left some property and resettled in their village but on poor land—eroded, swampy, or marshy. Also, they had to make this land produce and do corvée labor in forests and on highways and railroads in the district on pain of prosecution and confiscation of the rest of their property. Of 3,551 households dekulakized in the Velikie Luki Region, 847 fell into Group I, 1,307 into Group II, the deportees, and 1,297 into Group III, the dispossessed. The rest, the lucky ones, managed to flee.[77]

"Liquidating the kulaks as a class" inflamed the countryside and terrorized nearly three quarters of the Soviet population. Indoctrination in the rightness of their cause plus some sort of mass hysteria of spite and fear prompted local officials with equal enthusiasm to save babies by opening nurseries and kindergartens and to help kill babies by stripping families of everything and then deporting them.[78]

Deportees fared hardly better than peasants shipped to confinement. Many perished in cattle cars and foul holds en route. Many survivors of the journey perished, also, when they lost the battle to survive in the remote wastes of the North, Siberia, and Central Asia where most of them were dumped under NKVD controls. Exposure and strenuous labor drained the deportees faster than their meager rations replaced their dwindling strength. A Volga German exiled with 246 other kulaks early in collectivization to the forests of Vyatka reported later that "Children who had been deported along with their mothers were always hungry and rapidly starved to death. . . . After three years a great many of the original settlers were dead." [79]

At its wildest, dekulakization (expropriation) and its great grab hit all sorts of improbable targets, like former red partisans and a middle peasant's farm at one end of the village while he was expropriating others in a dekulakization detachment at the other end.[80]

Some search-and-destroy missions treated all the populace like military enemies, as in the My Lai–type massacres of Vietnam.[81] Nikolai Bukharin considered the battle of collectivization worse than the carnage of 1919 in that "we were conducting a mass annihilation of completely defenseless men, together with their wives and children." [82] OGPU troops and tribunals led the assault.[83] When Lady Astor asked Stalin in the summer of 1931: "How long are you going to continue killing people?" he shot back, "As long as it is necessary." [84]

Expropriations of individual Soviet peasant farmers merged on occasion into banditry. "Middle" and even "poor" peasants were arrested without grounds. Dekulakization brigades might raid kulaks under another farm's jurisdiction to loot them first, down to eyeglasses, or take bribes to get them off arrest and deportation lists. According to an OGPU report of February 28, 1930, from the Western Province around Smolensk:

> "Certain members of the workers' brigades and officials of lower echelons of the Party-soviet apparatus" deprived members of kulak and middle peasant households of their clothing and warm underwear (directly from the body), confiscated headwear from children's heads, and removed shoes from people's feet. The perpetrators divided the "confiscated" goods among themselves; the food they found was eaten on the spot; the alcohol they uncovered was consumed immediately, resulting in drunken orgies. In one case a worker tore a warm blouse off a woman's back, put it on himself with the words, "you wore it long enough, now I will wear it." The slogan of many of the dekulakization brigades was: "drink, eat—it's all ours." [85]

Wladislaw Gomulka, late leader of Communist Poland (who decollectivized his peasants, incidentally), said of collectivization that it was "the beginning of the process of growing lawlessness, violation of socialist legality, the establishment of an atmosphere of fear, and the growth under these conditions of the personality cult, the cult of Stalin." [86] During collectivization an official of the Commissariat of Foreign Affairs became indignant at the comment aroused in Germany by the plight of ethnic German religious communities of farmers who camped in Moscow suburbs to petition for emigration. Most of the petitioners were resettled back in their ruined villages or sent to labor camps. "They are our citizens aren't they?" said the official. "We can do what we like with them." [87]

More than ten million peasants, it is estimated, perished during collectivization and deportation, in camps and in the manmade famine epidemic of 1932–1933. It was a famine allowed to run its course so that grain might be exported to buy technology, and the peasantry broken once and for all,[88] a famine "without drought and without war." [89] The individual peasantry was smashed. It shrank from 75 percent of the population in 1928 to 15 percent in 1933 and almost zero percent by 1939. Most vital for the grain-hungry state, peasant will to organize resistance had largely disappeared too.

Intensifying the class struggle in such a spirit brought to Soviet people an insecurity as pervasive as any fear of "crime in the streets" could possibly be. Clara Spasova, honest "old Bolshevik" factory worker, a character in Afinogenev's *Fear*, said of the USSR in 1930: "The peasant fears forcible collectivization; the Soviet worker, perpetual purging of the party; the political worker, the accusation of lukewarmness; the scientific worker, the accusation of idealism; the technical worker, the accusation of sabotage. We live in an epoch of great fear." [90]

During that epoch, 1928–1933, the labor camp population increased from 30,000 to 5 million, or over twenty times the prison population before 1917 and in 1928. The Belomor (White Sea–Baltic) Canal project alone had nearly 300,000 convict laborers or 60 percent more than the maximum total tsarist convict and prisoner population of 184,000.[91]

Forced labor on projects like Belomor and in camps formed an ever more important part of the national economic plan. Along with wretched deportees, camp inmates worked on short rations to cut timber, lay railroads, extract gold, dig canals, mine, build, fish, and so on. Crucial labor-intensive endeavors operating at high human but low capital cost created an insatiable demand for new inmates to work where no available inducements could muster enough free labor.[92]

To run its spreading empire, OGPU set up GULAG, the Chief Camp Administration, in 1930 under the energetic Genrikh Yagoda.

The largest group of inmates, perhaps 3.5 million, or seven out of ten in the camps, were peasants. About 15 percent of the inmates were "politicals," the bourgeois "have-beens" and old intellectuals. Another

12 to 15 percent were ordinary criminals, such as white-collar criminals and the "professionals"—nearly three quarters of a million persons convicted of rape, murder, robbery, thievery,[93] as well as hordes of street waifs taken in by the police. Even the ordinary criminals, *ugolovniki* and *bytoviki*, numbered over three times the tsarist and NEP peaks of such inmates.

Law and order broke down from below as well as from above during the "socialist offensive." Files of the Criminal Investigation Department of the Western Oblast around Smolensk record outbreaks of banditry by gangs of armed robbers. Often they murdered their victims, harassing the villagers with burglaries, thefts, and rapes. Some gangs allegedly worked hand in hand with local authorities; some gangs included Komsomol members. More than two such incidents a day were reported in June and July 1934. Negligent arson associated with drunken debauches plagued the farms.[94]

Peasants moved out of the villages as prisoners and deportees but also under labor contracts or as spontaneous in-migrants. The urban population increased at a rate heretofore unequaled anywhere—*two and a half to four times faster* than during peaks of industrialization in the West.[95] Cities and new settlements had to accommodate nearly 2 million peasants a year on the average.[96] Peasants poured in faster than the most strenuous Soviet efforts could adequately house them and establish supervision over their children and the homeless waifs running from famine and family disaster. Another stimulant of disorder was the packed living in urban areas. The in-migrants suddenly found themselves in close contact with each other and with the stealable consumer goods that made life bearable. As a result, a city dweller's chances of victimization by thieves and hooligans increased tremendously, especially when compared with the country, though there, too, they increased. Convictions for theft in Moscow increased 15 percent in nine months between the last quarter of 1930 and the third quarter of 1931. Hooliganism convictions per 100,000 inhabitants of Leningrad Province were 282 in 1928, 444 in 1931.[97]

The steep rise in judicial convictions shown in Tables 3–1 and 3–3 accompanied the swing to coercion. But it reflected also social problems of "recruiting millions of new workers into production."[98] This Soviet comment is supported by interviews with refugees from the USSR. In their recollections of the early thirties, they tell with monotonous regularity in a variety of contexts of the enormous social unrest that accompanied industrialization and collectivization; of the large number of children who were made homeless; of the general inability of parents to maintain effective control over their children in a situation of unparalleled disorganization; and of material want and collapsed moral standards.[99]

Many incidents of hooliganism—70 percent in Moscow—were reported to be petty cases brought on by frictions of everyday life and crowded living quarters that could easily have been referred to comrades' rather than regular courts—jostling a passer-by and fighting with him or tearing a store manager's jacket when ejected at closing time. Hooliganism disrupted public life and production.

> Thus for example one of the residents in a housing cooperative begins yelling and shouting at a tenants' meeting, throws a shoe at the chairman and finally disrupts the meeting. A young worker at the Kolomenskoe factory with three past convictions for hooliganism kicks up a row at the club, disrupting an antireligious evening. Two young Kolomenskoe factory workers run amuck in a dormitory, smashing it up and breaking dozens of windows.[100]

A relative calm descended on Russia in 1934 after the storm of the great change. More governmental attention shifted to the problem of preserving public order. Reports flowed in, still, of armed gangs, acts of vandalism, rampages, dances disrupted, and revelers who resisted the intrusion wounded or killed.[101]

Governmental response included more severe punishment in 1935 for juveniles and for hooliganism—breaches of the public peace—with sentences of up to five years.[102] Courts received orders to deal more firmly with (1) such crimes "bordering on counterrevolution" as beating up "activists" and norm-raising *udarniki* and damaging tools in production, (2) such predatory rowdyism as snatching money and purses from the hands of shoppers in line at the cashier.[103]

"Stability of Laws"

By 1934–1935, class struggle abated as Soviet Russia entered the socialist era. It was an era of class conciliation, of relative educational and social conservatism.[104] A new model charter for collective farms passed in 1935 formally confirmed a peasant household's right to a garden plot, house, some farm animals, and implements.

The "great retreat" toward NEP and prerevolutionary practices caught up with law as well. It turned ideology against Professor Eugene Pashukanis' espousal of "maximum elasticity" of law. Law was in his view only a handmaiden of "proletarian politics" doomed to wither away when those politics had achieved their socialist goals.[105]

Between 1930 and 1935 Pashukanis' version of orthodox Marxism dominated Soviet legal theory and law schools. But by the mid-1930s Stalin had braked the social revolution. "We need stability of laws more than ever," he insisted when introducing the 1936 Constitution. That document formalized the end of legal discrimination and class justice for members of capitalist and other social classes associated with the vanishing old order. By 1937 lawyers and law schools received a new lease on life. Pashukanis, his supporters, and his "wrecking theory of the withering away of the law," already at variance with Stalin's theory and practice of criminal repression, faced extinction. Their attackers like Andrei Vyshinskii distinguished "socialist law" from "bourgeois law." [106] This prepared the way for Stalin's new teaching that Soviet state power would remain even under communism, as long as the "capitalist encirclement did." [107]

Beginning in 1934, the judicial arm of Soviet state power underwent further centralization and restrictions on due process. Special benches of three judges without people's assessors were set up July 10, 1934, to try cases transferred to the courts by the NKVD.[108] A.Y. Vyshinskii led the prosecutors in the direction of aiding, rather than checking, violations of socialist legality. Defense attorneys did not defend in political cases. By statute of August 16, 1939, Colleges of Advocates appeared, running local legal advice offices under the general supervision of republican commissariats of justice. Introducing direct election of people's judges by secret, universal ballot under the Law on the Court System of August 16, 1938, democratized the court system in form, while already a new USSR Commissariat of Justice set up in 1936 had centralized it further in actual administrative controls. By 1939, provincial departments of justice reappeared, taking over supervision of people's courts from the provincial courts. N.V. Krylenko, the harshly militant first USSR Commissar of Justice associated formerly with the liquidated Pashukanis school of law, was replaced in 1938 by N.M. Rychkov,[109] a former military judge with purge trial experience, and shot, it seems, in 1940.[110]

Within the judicial channel of repression, some citizens experienced discrimination in the justice they received. Employees of the railroads and merchant marine went before a USSR system of special RR and water tribunals. Military-judicial tribunals for NKVD troops, it is said, "led to violations of socialist legality in criminal trials." [111] Summary procedures were introduced by a decree of December 1, 1934, the evening of Kirov's murder,* which ordered cases of terrorism to be sped up, death sentences to be carried out at once without appeal.[112] Wrecking and sabotage cases fell under similar summary procedures by decree of September 14, 1937.[113]

The relaxation of 1933 did not last long in ordinary criminal law any more than for terror. A decree of April 7, 1935 lowered to age twelve the onset of juveniles' responsibility for their more serious and frequent crimes against persons and property. A decree of May 31, 1941, lowered from six to fourteen juveniles' age of responsibility for other crimes. All

* See p. 62.

the new crimes and penalties added to criminal law between April 7, 1935, and 1941 are too numerous to list but, omitting essentially white-collar offenses, agricultural crimes and military crimes, the crackdown included:

- melting down coins—up to three years' confinement and confiscation of the metal or a minimum of three years with confiscation of all property if done as a business (April 7, 1935);
- conduct or negligence violating safety in explosives plants—penalties of at least three or five years' confinement (July 17, 1935);
- preparation, possession or advertising pornographic writings, pictures, and other objects and selling them—up to five years loss of freedom and their confiscation (October 17, 1935);
- making, possessing, or selling deadly poisons—up to five years (April 7, 1936);
- performing abortions other than for medical reasons—one to three years in prison (June 27, 1936);
- compelling women to have abortions—two years (June 27, 1936);
- having abortions—social censure, or fine of up to 300 (old) rubles if repeated (June 27, 1936).[114]

Other edicts raised the scale of existing penalties. Two basic forms of confinement existed: milder corrective labor colonies near home for terms of up to three years and harsh corrective labor camps of GULAG, far away in northern Russia and Siberia, for terms of over three years. Prison was defined as the harshest form of punishment by decree of August 8, 1936. Persons could be sentenced to prison by courts, or by the NKVD in the case of inmates of corrective labor camps and corrective labor colonies who violated camp discipline or tried to escape. A decree of October 2, 1937, raised maximum terms, short of shooting, for espionage and wrecking from 10 to 25 years.[115]

As the country went on a war footing, the screws tightened: for quitting a job without permission—two to four months in prison; for absenteeism—correctional labor (dock in pay at workplace of up to 25 percent and loss of time toward seniority, pension, etc.) of up to six months (June 26, 1940), extended to farm machinery operators and other machine tractor station workers (July 17, 1940); theft and petty hooliganism in production—up to one year (August 10, 1940); riding freight trains—up to one year in prison; and unnecessary use of the emergency stop on trains—one to three years (April 9, 1941).[116] Military justice in zones placed under martial law as the Nazis invaded, June 22, 1941, meant loss of some civilian rights, including right of appeal. Persons spreading alarming false rumors received two to five years in prison (as usual, "unless that act did not incur more severe legal penalties") (July 6, 1941). Employees quitting without permission jobs in war industry, evacuated plants, or war-connected production (what was not in those days!) received five to eight years in prison (December 26, 1941, mitigated by amnesty of December 30, 1944). Stealing farm machinery fuel rated three to five years confinement (June 23, 1942). Other possibilities for punishment came with various offenses such as nonpayment of income tax (April 30, 1943), and violation of martial law in inland and ocean shipping (May 9, 1943). Revealing "state secrets" or losing documents containing them meant trial by military tribunal and five to ten years' confinement if in line of duty, up to three years' confinement if by private persons (November 15, 1943).[117] Liberalization of justice proved short lived after the war.

The victory amnesty of July 7, 1945, ignored deportees and gave "politicals" nothing. Only nonpolitical offenders—the casual criminals (*bytoviki*) and the professionals (*blatnye, urki, ugolovnik*)—benefited. The amnesty pardoned offenders sentenced to punishment of less than three years' confinement (and therefore not in labor camps). It halved remaining time for other offenders as long as they were neither politicals (not "sitting" for counterrevolutionary crimes) nor nonpoliticals sentenced for stealing state property (the law of August 7, 1932), counterfeiting, murder, and robbery.[118] Capital punishment was abolished in peacetime (May 26, 1947) but at the same time maximum sentences other than death went up to twenty-five years, a virtual death sentence in GULAG, reminiscent of Tsarina Elizabeth's largesse in pulling down the gallows but leaving the *knut*. Capital punishment was reinstated January 12, 1950, for traitors, spies, and saboteurs,[119] just as labor camp conditions began improving.[120] Criminal penalties for unauthorized absenteeism or quitting were quietly dropped by 1951.[121]

Still, criminal justice showed an ongoing tendency toward greatly increased repression as Stalin's main bulwark against ordinary crime.[122] For theft of personal property the 1926 code imposed light sentences of up to three months' obligatory labor or confinement, or up to one year's confinement at most.[123] The edict of June 4, 1947, virtually disallowed petty theft by setting minimum sentences of *five years,* maximum up to ten years, with from fifteen to twenty years maximum with confiscation of property for armed robbery. Another edict (also June 4, 1947) raised penalties for stealing state and public property, doubling the maximum from ten to twenty years, and setting minimum penalties at seven years for state and five for farm and public property. Edicts of June 9, 1947 set penalties of five to twenty years for revealing "state secrets," four to fifteen for losing documents containing state secrets, and a list making just about any economic, demographic, statistical, and new technical information state secrets, enforced a virtual Soviet isolation from the outside world. Home brewing used to incur up to one year's confinement. It now incurred one to two years if for home consumption, six to seven for the trade (April 7, 1948). Rape brought up to eight years under the 1926 code, ten to twenty under the edict of January 4, 1949. Criminal penalties seemed to be the great backstop for everything from birthrate stimulation to mine safety (six months to ten years for mine safety violations, February 14, 1953).[124]

Relentlessly, then, through the 1930s, the Great Patriotic War, and the postwar recovery, "the legal system was revised to increase strictness of control over behavior." [125] Only in this sense can one understand "stability of law" in the realm of criminal justice. More broadly, stability of laws coexisted with what Khrushchev characterized in 1956 as "the most crude violations of socialist legality and mass repression," [126] egged on by Stalin's formulation of 1937 that sharpening of the class struggle would continue under socialism, against remnants of the old order growing more desperate with every success in socialist construction.[127]

In May 1933, less than two years after Molotov called a halt to the "saturnalia of arrests" and declared "we see our task not in mass repressions," [128] arrests began again. Their immediate pretext was the apparently staged assassination of the popular Leningrad leader, Sergei M. Kirov, a potential replacement for Stalin.

Khrushchev's well-known report to a closed session of the Twentieth Party Congress in February 1956 confirmed the worst suspicions and accounts of the virtual massacre of the party and military apparatus, now all too well detailed, beginning after Kirov's murder, and needing no retelling here.[129] "Mass arrests and deportations of many thousands of people, execution without trial and without normal investigation created conditions of insecurity, fear and even desperation," Khrushchev said in 1956.[130] "Insecurity, fear and even desperation" are what victims of crimes and inhabitants of high-crime areas feel, and that is what millions of Soviet people felt about the arrests, procedural violations, and police brutality.

Khrushchev limited his charges to 1934 and the years following, passing over the illegalities of collectivization. Also, he left the impression that repressions hit only the "honest workers" in the party and state apparatus. But the reach of Article 58 on "counterrevolutionary crimes" and its fourteen parts [131] went right down through society, at least into the late 1940s. Ordinary concepts of "law and order" lose meaning under such conditions.

Ten or more years of labor camp, followed by exile (if one survived until then), usually awaited the following:

- anecdote tellers;
- a person turning off the radio when he or she began reading letters to Stalin;
- Soviet commissars who had fought during the Spanish Civil War;
- the middle classes, intelligentsia, non-Communist politicians of the Baltic states and other occupied areas;

- targets of slanderers' and informers' grudges or opportunism;
- Esperantists and North Caucasus mountaineers;
- possibly, the first person to stop applauding Stalin's name at a meeting;
- Latvian sharpshooters and Chekists who spearheaded the Bolshevik struggle;
- suspected collaborators;
- returning POWs;
- persons who stayed with Stalin in Moscow instead of evacuating during the German attack in 1941;
- entire soviet or party organizations;
- persons who described the horrors of the Leningrad siege or a retreat;
- returning troops who praised the living standards they saw in war-torn Germany and Europe to the West;
- emigrés encountered by Soviet forces;
- the million Soviet slave laborers taken by the Nazis, who had to be forcibly repatriated in 1946–1947;
- whole suspect nationalities carted off into exile;
- Jewish intellectuals;
- the flower of Soviet culture, from director Meyerhold to poet Mandelstam.

The "meat grinder," as Khrushchev put it, chewed up not only "enemies of the people," but, often enough, their hapless wives, children, friends, associates, and students. Russia was a nation of virtual hostages. Even some top leaders around Stalin fell victim, dying under suspicious circumstances, as did Kirov, Ordzhonikidze, and Zhdanov.

Common criminals sometimes found themselves facing political charges and the stiffer penalties under Article 58. For example, a husband killing his wife's lover and a boy driven to shoot a collective farm foreman who brutalized the boy's mother and him faced charges not of murder under mitigating circumstances but of the more serious crime of terrorism (Article 58–8) because the lover was a party member, and the foreman a lower official.[132] A former Chekist Alexander Kalganov recalls that the Tashkent NKVD received a telegram: SEND 200. Ordinary criminals were requalified as counterrevolutionaries, but not enough. So they arrested all males from seventeen to sixty from among gypsies pitching camp in the city square.

Alongside counterrevolutionaries and common criminals labeled as such, the NKVD system had persons arrested, like the Gypsies, entirely without pretext, to fill quotas. A woman went to the Novocherkassk NKVD office to ask what was to be done about a nursing infant left by her neighbor arrested by the NKVD. They kept her waiting two hours for an answer and then arrested her too, to help fill the quota.[133]

Secret police operatives, investigators, informers, and convoy guards accomplished most of this repression. A vast police reorganization in July-October 1934 turned out to be the preparation for it.

A new USSR Commissariat of Internal Affairs—USSR NKVD, or NKVD for short, organized by decree of July 10, 1934—assumed centralized administrative direction of the republic NKVDs and their militia, fire fighting, civil registry, and cartographic functions. OGPU was merged into the NKVD. But, rather than being subordinated to the NKVD, OGPU took the whole commissariat over under the leadership of the redoubtable master poisoner and forced labor organizer, G. Yagoda.*

The NKVD took over all places of confinement from the commissariats of justice, adding them to its GULAG camp empire for convicts with sentences of three or more years' confinement. After this, the NKVD deferred only to Stalin. Its Special Board and local "troikas" decided on punishment secretly, without appeal, with the accused in absentia. But the entire police conduit deprived people of due process: the false arrests, the duress and tortures of investigations, the punishments without trial, and the grim camp conditions.[134]

At least 13 million persons (but possibly 21 million) died in the secret police meat grinder between 1934 and 1950. If the ten million peasant casualties of the collectivization war and famine are added, the total dead in Stalin's onslaughts from 1929 to 1950 came to about twenty-three million, or a toll comparable with that inflicted by the Nazis.[135] How many families could have been untouched one way or another by the "sharpening of the class struggle"?

Legacy of Disorder

The prison population of the USSR reached peaks of ten to fifteen million, by various estimates, or fifty to seventy-five times previous tsarist and NEP peaks, after the war, and some 20 to 30 percent of adult Soviet males left in the country.[136] Stories of military prison camps condition outsiders to think of the camp underground in terms of national or political resistance. No doubt Soviet dissidents found rudimentary ways to communicate. But Stalin's camps were mockeries of law and order. For the dominant underworld in them was that of the professional criminals: the *blatnye, urki,* or *ugolovniki.* A privileged minority, the "professionals" shirked

* Yagoda was replaced by N.I. Yezhov in 1936, arrested in 1937, shot in 1938, the year L.P. Beria replaced N.I. Yezhov (who, no longer useful and a convenient scapegoat for "excesses," slipped into oblivion in 1939 and probable execution). Robert Conquest, *The Great Terror: Stalin's Purge of the Thirties* (rev. ed.; New York: Macmillan, 1973), pp. 622–623.

work. They terrorized other inmates, stealing food and clothing from them. They recruited juvenile inmates to pillage newly arrived prisoners. Members of a durable criminal subculture, many of them hardened repeaters, the professionals and their young assistants preyed almost with impunity on the politicals and peasant prisoners. Camp guards either feared or favored the professionals.[137]

Between the mid-thirties and the mid-forties, "nobody recalls a case when the convoy put a stop to the plundering of the 'political' in his cell, a railroad car or a Black Maria. But they tell of countless cases when the convoy accepted plundered items from the thieves and in exchange brought them vodka, meals (sweeter than the rations) and smokes. This sort of thing became routine." [138] Convoy guards' greed mounted in 1945–1947 when foreigners and returnees passed through with intriguing goods from abroad. Trusties served as bath attendants, tailors, stock clerks, and so on. Also *blatnye,* though camp enemies of the nontrusties, found ways to steal from the politicals. If a political carried a knife, it was "terrorism." If a *blatnoi* carried a knife, it was simply a misconduct growing out of the life style and traditions of people who since the early 1920s were considered "social allies"—apparently despite all the harsh criminal legislation and talk of ordinary crime being, in fact, counterrevolutionary.

Politicals underwent grueling investigation. Most of them would never leave the camps. *Blatnye* underwent swift, painless investigations and trials. Their sentences were lighter than those received by the politicals. There were chances of parole, escape, buying or deceiving one's way out at the expense of an unsuspecting short-term ordinary non-political offender in a transit prison. V.I. Ivanov from Ukhta was sentenced nine times for theft, five times for running away, to thirty-seven years' total confinement. He served five to six years for the whole lot.[139]

How much crime? "Statistics, mute and invisible, said nothing at all. No one even knew whether they still existed." [140] Apparently some sketchy statistics on convictions at least lay somewhere under the seal of "state secret." Post-Stalin reports have it that convictions fell from 144 percent of the 1928 level in 1933 (maybe higher in 1932 but that is not revealed) to 107 in 1934 (a time when a détente in arrests had been called for), to 86.3 percent for 1940, and 76 percent in 1946, or on a plateau in the late 1930s and into the forties and fifties, of roughly 75 to 85 percent of the 1928 level of convictions.[141] This may be an understatement of the level of ordinary crime. It was possible to classify ordinary crimes as counterrevolutionary, leading to processing by the NKVD troikas instead of by the courts.[142] Close reading of Stalinist sources brought out a picture of decay and stagnation in local efforts at law and order.[143] And, as the following chapters show, Stalin's legacy included the unresolved issue of law and order.

Conclusions

Stalin's revolution from above between 1928 and 1934 brought growing industrial power, resurgence of national pride and proletarian militance, full employment, careers open to talent, vastly expanded educational opportunities, showplaces of humane correction such as the labor communes, and the reckless enthusiasm of a vast revitalization movement.

Other aspects of the revitalization were missed by many foreign visitors at the time. Harsh repression and regimentation, coupled with social disorder and a growing bureaucracy, produced a new peak in criminal convictions, under the slogan *intensification of the class struggle.* A social purge of peasants, "NEP men," and "old intelligentsia" under the same slogan swelled the convict population to over twenty times any previous Russian total, and by 1930 to a third of the urban work force.

During a hurricane of violence and demands for awesome self-sacrifice, Stalin successfully evoked ardent support, especially among the young. Cost aside, Stalinism performed great feats of control over peasants, labor, and the intelligentsia alongside its patently terrible—and, likely as not, unnecessary—disruption of Soviet society. To believe more of the regime is to underestimate the feat Stalin did perform and to overestimate the reach and completeness of his controls up to 1934.

If law and order means domestic tranquility and security, then the first seven years of Stalinism rank as probably the most lawless and disorderly in the annals of industrialization.

Stalin's path to development reduced some of the side effects of industrialization, such as unemployment, yet it still created violence and deprivation and criminality on an unprecedented scale. Many of the crimes were committed in the name of authority. But they were crimes nonetheless, changing the quality of life for virtually everyone.

A salient issue of criminal policy is how to increase people's sense of security by stemming crime without making the remedy worse for people than the disease. But the lives, liberty, and property of his citizens were secondary to Stalin, when it came to eliminating real or potential resistance to his authority. Lawlessness from above overshadowed lawlessness from below.

If this first period featured a duality of revitalization and repression, ensuing years under Stalin saw a new duality, that of terror and order, illegality, and "stability of law." Still impelled by the formulation about intensified class struggle, lawlessness from above took the form of arrests on trumped-up charges in millions of "fabricated cases" in a scale which even Khrushchev's stunning report understated. Common crimes were requalified into political crimes. Arbitrary arrests filled quotas for the labor camps. Some NKVD investigators practiced torture, thievery, even rapine.

Punishment for counterrevolutionary crimes came in summary judgment, "extrajudicial repression," mass executions. Camp conditions became so bad that the usual long sentences were virtual death sentences for most inmates.

Conditions for law and order could hardly be worse after World War II. Famine again ravaged the Ukraine. "In a sense it was 1930 all over again, with the peasants being starved to feed the towns."[144] Neither purges nor tough criminal laws solved the law-and-order problem beyond wiping out child vagrancy and the worst forms of gang disorder. Stalin's one-sided preoccupation with crimes against the state and crimes against socialist property and his neglect of preventive measures left society open to disorder and delinquency from below alongside lawlessness from above.[145] His political controls had no equal. But his social controls against ordinary crimes of everyday life turned out flaccid, spiritless, and bumbling.

The experience with Stalin's law and order raises questions as to whether it is not unrealistic to separate out and weigh an imposed law and order against some supposed "cost" of the "police state" repression imposing it. Despite beneficial mediating roles of his courts, Stalin loosed lawlessness on his people which rivaled Nazi aggression in its death toll. Social controls turned out "soft on crooks," the privileged stratum in sharply administered but essentially lawless labor camps. They were schools of crime for juveniles, as the tsarist prisons had been schools of revolution for the luckier politicals of tsarism's last decades. The bureaucratized command economy left a legacy of extensive white collar crime, as we shall see.

The basic point of this chapter is that, under Stalin, new policy did not respond to crime. Policy created crime, especially crime against the populace, so that "the crudest possible violations of legality were widespread and lawless repression was used against perfectly innocent Soviet citizens."[146]

Stalin did "unfetter the police" beyond any dream of U.S. hard-liner foes of "coddling criminals." But there is reason to doubt the widespread Western assumption that therefore Stalin gave citizens more law and order, no matter what the cost in freedom. That case remains unproven. A better case exists for the conclusion that Stalin, rather, "whipped the country on" no matter what the cost in law and order. Soviet people were not respecting the law but obeying out of fear and evading it when they could or when loosened up by drunkenness. Evading or violating rules was the only way for camp staffs to thrive and prisoners to survive. Truly, "if government becomes a law-breaker, it breeds contempt for the law,"[147]—even in a fear-ridden police state.

Hints of détente, of liberalization at war's end, disappointed on the legal as well as on the economic front. Political repressiveness still discouraged judicial reform.[148] Former criminologists tried unsuccessfully to bring back research on crime. Even unsuccessful reform efforts facilitated liberalization of justce and the resumption of crime research after Stalin. Debates on criminal policy and contradictory trends intensifying both prevention and repression showed that among Soviet legal and policy elites the viability of Stalin's law and order remained an open question, something we must label, at best, "not proven."

4

The Quest for Order

The CPSU has condemned the cult of personality and restored Leninist norms of state and party life and has liquidated the lawlessness implanted during the period of the cult of personality.

—Soviet Law Dictionary

THE TACIT DESTALINIZATION OF 1953–1956 began before the late dictator had been laid to rest in the mausoleum on Red Square. Initiatives came from on high at Stalin's funeral service.[1] Ever since then, how to restore legality and what to keep and what to leave in Stalin's legacy have been central Soviet issues and touchstones in reforms of criminal policy, as in all major Soviet reforms of recent years.[2]

Destalinization released a flood of criticism against repressive approaches to crime prevention. The criticism and the reform proposals of the later 1950s reflected grave doubts among legal scholars about the efficacy of Stalin's exclusive reliance on harsh penalties to fight crime.

Debates over legal reform were stirred up especially by the events of the Twentieth Party Congress in February 1956. Mikoyan made the first public attack on "the cult of personality of Stalin" and its deleterious consequences. Khrushchev's even more sensational, secret, but widely leaked speech depicted Stalinist mass repressions and bungling. Khrushchev specifically repudiated Stalin's deadly formulation "that as we march forward toward socialism, class war must allegedly sharpen." [3] For all its carefully drawn limits on frankness and repudiations, Khrushchev's secret speech and his abandonment of the formulation, "intensification of the class struggle," accorded with and encouraged a tendency to deterrorize criminal law and justice.

Have there been internal contradictions in destalinization? Of course there have. Khrushchev's own dedication to legality and liberalization appear questionable if liberalization means relying less on judicial and extrajudicial repression and increasing due process in the quest for law and order. And Brezhnev's coalition turned out to have even more questionable dedication to legality and liberalization.

Full-fledged Stalinist terror and punishment-only crime prevention have been ruled out, however. Soviet crime experts may be the most inhibited and isolated from the non-Communist world of any national group of experts in the Soviet sphere of Eastern Europe. But they are no longer scared into virtual silence publicly, and complaisance with every aspect of criminal justice. Their role in policy making has increased.

Without a strong autocrat at the head of the Soviet regime, without the impetus of revolutionary change, Stalin's successors stopped short of radical innovations in crime fighting like those of Alexander II, the Bolsheviks, and Stalin. Khrushchev came close to radicalizing crime prevention, but failed.

Rather, post-Stalin responses to crime show overlapping, contradictory tendencies[4] toward *liberalization; popularization; harsher penalties; campaigning against disorders* like hooliganism, drug abuse, drunkenness, indiscipline at work, poaching by wily and dangerous backwoodsmen, stealing firearms and explosives; *conscripting labor* of parasites and probationary convicts; *mass legal propaganda; recentralizing law enforcement and justice; reforming and hardening confinement*. Some comparisons and conclusions regarding these tendencies close the chapter.

Liberalization

A current of opposition to the punishment orientation and the chaos in Stalin's criminal laws surfaced soon after Stalin's death. Responding to government initiatives, some influential jurists assisted in bringing proportionate sentencing and order into the criminal codes.

Reform has been for the participating jurists a game of trial and error both technically and politically. But leading legal scholars have left no doubt as to their reservations about Stalin's criminal policy, support for reform, and opposition to restalinizing criminal law. The respected Professor M.D. Shargorodskii has been one of the Soviet legal scholars leading the debate about crime and punishment. It is wrong to believe, he wrote, "that by any one measure (mainly prescription under threat of punishment) one can direct the development of social processes where one wants them to go." Shargorodskii carried into print his insistence that he sees no basis for "simplistic beliefs and forecasts that to diminish crime one must increase punishment, to raise the birthrate—forbid abortions and not produce contraceptives, to curtail alcoholism, forbid the sale of liquor, etc." [5]

Stalinist views die hard in the USSR, as beliefs in harsh punishment die hard anywhere. The big difference from Stalin's day is that this issue of crime and punishment continues to be debated even during the most repressive turns in post-Stalin policy. Questioning purely punitive responses and inflexibly harsh sentencing has come from eminent reformers like Shargorodskii and the late criminal proceduralist I.D. Perlov. Others include G.Z. Anashkin, frequent contributor to the debate while chairman of the Criminal Bench of the USSR Supreme Court; criminologist-jurists like V.N. Kudryavtsev; the late A.A. Gertsenzon; the late A.A. Piontkovskii; the late E.G. Shirvindt; and A.S. Shlyapochnikov (the latter two returning from labor camps). The penologist B.S. Nikiforov, too, has publicly repudiated arguments by proponents of the former single line that "there are no objective reasons for crimes, and if they exist up to now, it is because there are still among us evil people and professors of criminal law who are either simply fools or linked with a criminal milieu . . . criminals should be shot, or better, hanged." His "angry opponents" says Dr. Nikiforov, propagate a "new myth" that in the days of death and long sentences for minor thefts "thieves were wiped out, there were almost none left." "If only it had been so!" Dr. Nikiforov answered them. "If it had, the legislators, being acquainted with available statistics, would not have heeded the advice of jurists and would not have repealed the old laws, as they did, but would have continued to move rapidly in the direction of completely eliminating crime by simple means. *But in fact these means have completely failed.*"[6]

The hasty repeal of many Stalinist measures after his death conveys this impression of failure also, despite later returns to repressiveness as a means of crime fighting. The amnesty of March 27, 1953, three weeks after Stalin's demise, called upon the Ministry of Justice "to revise criminal laws of the USSR and Union Republics so as to replace criminal responsibility for some official, economic and everyday crimes and other less dangerous crimes with administrative and disciplinary sanctions, and to reduce criminal penalties for some crimes.[7]

Between 1953 and 1956 several less serious offenses ceased to be considered crimes, and were treated as lesser infractions or not punished at all. Parole again became possible.[8] Penalties for petty pilfering of state and public property fell from a draconian seven to ten years to more reasonable penalties from six months' "correctional labor" without confinement to three months' confinement for first offenses.[9] Amnesties released thousands of lesser criminals or lowered their sentences and applied also to hardship cases of pregnancy, old age, sickness, and youth (under eighteen in 1953 and under sixteen in 1957).[10]

Justice became more equal owing to the abolition of special water and rail transport courts, summary proceedings in political cases, and the secret police special boards.[11]

Real as well as formal curbs on terror made experts and officials feel that they could draft government-ordered law reforms without fear of denunciation and arrest such as had paralyzed much needed legal reform under Stalin.[12] They also felt that they could debate basic questions about the role of criminal law and punishment and about the rights of parties in criminal and civil cases.[13]

Four years of legal housecleaning and debate touched every facet of criminal justice, with party encouragement.[14] By 1958 a drafting commission of the Council of Ministers had put together reform bills from suggestions streaming in from around the country. In its first version, a bill on criminal procedure explicitly stated that an accused person is presumed innocent until proven guilty and admitted defense counsel much earlier than heretofore. Counsel could enter the case, it was proposed, not just before trial, but from the beginning of the pretrial investigation, the important stage after police inquest when the state prepared its full case against the accused.

But opponents of these concessions to rights of the accused succeeded in blocking them during their final consideration in the Legislative Proposals Commissions of the USSR Supreme Soviet. Implied presumption of innocence remained, though, in several provisions of the 1958 reform and later Union republic codes of criminal procedure based on it.[15] Blocking much earlier right to counsel was, as compared with presumption of innocence, less of a formal compromise and more of a substantial defeat for the reformers. Counsel for nonincapacitated, adult suspects is admitted by right to participate in a criminal case from the time when the accused is informed that the pretrial investigation is completed and the case materials are given to the accused to look over. A suspect's right to counsel goes back earlier in the case only in the minority of situations where the accused is a juvenile, under eighteen, or mentally or physically incapable of exercising his right to defense. Counsel then may enter the case and meet with the accused before the pretrial investigation, when the police inquest has been completed and the case materials collected up to that time given to the accused to look over.[16]

If the accused has been detained, he has had no contact with his counsel up to that time. For all detained accused, this means that during the period of up to seventy-two hours, he may be held as a suspect while the prosecutor decides whether or not to approve continued detention. After this, the detained suspect may be held an additional seven days while the inquest proceeds and a charge is prepared or dropped. Once charged with a crime, the suspect becomes the accused, subject in most serious cases to a pretrial investigation. The accused who is adult and not incapacitated and is still detained may be so held for up to nine months from first detention date without access to a lawyer.[17] In practice, the nine-month limit on detention is exceeded in violation of the law.[18]

Roy Medvedev, neo-Leninist historian and would-be reformer, has expressed what is in fact the view of many legal scholars, judges, and defense attorneys about the deleterious effects of such long isolation on the legal rights of the accused: counsel has less time to prepare a case and less opportunity to explain the accused's rights to him.

> The fatal defect of this system is that in the majority of cases the defense lawyer is deprived of the opportunity to give the accused an explanation of his rights as a person who is presumed to be innocent. The lawyer has no chance of challenging the investigating officials' decision to order the detention of the accused before he is brought into court nor is he able to follow the course of the investigation and prevent possible abuses which unfortunately are by no means infrequent.[19]

The reforms of 1958 did eliminate a long-time loophole for violations of due process, namely, analogy. Criminal codes may no longer be stretched by "analogy" to cover acts not listed there as crimes. Among other changes of 1958, maximum sentences dropped from twenty-five to fifteen years, and maximum exile from ten to five years. Differentiation between adult and juvenile offenders increased. Stricter rules of evidence reflected Soviet repudiations of theories, attributed to the late Procurator General Andrei Vyshinskii, that confession sufficed to prove guilt in many cases and that probability of guilt was sufficient test in all.[20]

The fight is not over for the many legal scholars, judges, and other experts continuing to push, as they did before the 1958 reforms, for trial by jury or at least an expanded bench of people's assessors, a pretrial investigation independent of the Procuracy, greatly increased rights to counsel, safeguards against trial by the press in prejudiced newspaper reports, and restriction on the use of antiparasite procedures.[21] The reformers have failed in most, but not all of their efforts, as we shall see.

The 1958 criminal law reform, the Fundamentals of Criminal Law of the USSR and Union Republics, inched a little back toward the Marxist and sociological formulations of its 1924 predecessor. The 1924 fundamentals of criminal law reflected their drafters' theory that crime was the fault of society, not the individual. They replaced "crime" in criminal laws with "socially dangerous act" and "punishment" with "means of social defense." All through the "revolution from above," as late as the decree establishing criminal liability for homosexuality of December 17, 1933 and March 7, 1934, punishment and "penalty" (*kara*) remained out of the law. Then, in what seemed to be a deliberate policy decision, all criminal decrees beginning with additions to the statute on state crimes, June 8, 1934, began to use punishment (*nakazanie*) and penalty. The 1958 Fundamentals of Criminal Law and subsequent criminal codes retain punishment and penalty. But they recapture a hint of the earlier sociological tinge of the Bolshevik legislation. Judges under the 1958 reforms have greater leeway to set penalties according to mitigating or aggravating sides of the criminal's personality and background. The parole set up in 1954 has been kept (but with some recent restrictions): up to one third time off for adults, up to two-thirds time off for juveniles. Alternatives to punishment have been more or less encouraged in petty cases, as will be shortly described. The minimum age of criminal responsibility for juveniles is back up to fourteen, where it was in the 1920s (it was sixteen in 1929–1935, then twelve). Attention is paid once again to offender's age in corrections, whereas after the mid-thirties juvenile convicts went to the grim adult camps.

Political and economic protection of the socialist state is still unusual by Western standards, though less overwhelmingly stressed than it was in the prereform criminal codes. Elaborate protection remains against theft of public property and "economic crimes" such as substandard production, "private entrepreneurial activity," "buying up bread to feed cattle or poultry."[22] State crimes make up a long list in the new codes. The reach of the law against such crimes, though, is in some ways shorter than it was under the old code. The Law on State Crimes of December 25, 1958, distinguishes more than the old codes did between political and common crime by requiring that murder or assault against an official cannot be treated as a political crime unless committed "with the intention of weakening or subverting the Soviet regime." Anti-Soviet intent is necessary for vandalism of socialist property to be called sabotage. But this restriction is not retroactive. Amnesties have passed by inmates of camps in the early 1960s serving long sentences for "terrorism," though without anti-Soviet intent, imposed under Stalin, such as the farm boy mentioned earlier who shot his brutal foreman. Moreover, camp conditions appear to have worsened in 1961–1962 and the early 1970s.[23]

Popularization

I

Three years earlier, D.S. Polyanskii, then a candidate member of the ruling Presidium of the Party (renamed Politburo in 1966), presented the criminal law reforms of December 1958 to the USSR Supreme Soviet with the comment: "Criminal repression is not the only or chief way to fight crime in the socialist state. More important are preventive and educational measures which eliminate those factors contributing to the appearance of survivals of the past in people's minds." [24]

Enter, then, a new tendency, toward substituting nonjudicial for judicial influences and prevention for punishment. Prevention began with the courts, ordered to bring to light the reasons for the crimes they tried, the immediate circumstances contributing, and to send special findings to places where the defendants worked so as to draw attention to baneful influences there: drunkenness, indiscipline, carelessly guarded stockrooms, antisocial elements among the employees, neglecting problems youth might be having adapting to factory life, and so on.[25] Rates of special findings in criminal cases in the RSFSR rose from 9.9 percent of cases in 1970 to 12.1 percent in 1973.[26]

Two people's assessors (lay judges) sit alongside the professional judge in every criminal trial of first instance—another populist element in justice. Elected for two-year terms, people's assessors serve ten days a year like jurists in many other systems. They have an equal vote on questions of fact and punishment. There are occasional reports of assessors taking an active role in questioning witnesses and even helping exonerate a defendant. More often than not, however, assessors sit mute in court. Efforts to improve legal qualifications and increase the contributions which these representatives of the people make to justice have not moved the assessors out of their usually passive role at trials.[27] For some years now councils of people's assessors have been organizing preventive work by the assessors out in the community. They seem to be more active in youth work than they are in court.[28]

Visiting sessions of the courts are held at workplaces or residences where crimes have been committed. "Public accusers" and "public defenders" appear more frequently in these "show trials" (*pokazatel'nye protsessy*) than they appear in nonvisiting sessions of the courts. Unpaid, nonprofessional supplements to prosecutor and defense lawyers, public accusers, and defenders participate after their "collectives" have petitioned and with the permission of the court.[29] For the sake of driving home a moral, visiting sessions risk sacrificing objectivity. But attorneys may well put up a vigorous defense for their clients, as counsel did in the show trial of a brilliant but kleptomaniacal young surgeon, Dr. Zemlyanikov, before a crowd of about a thousand curious readers, angry staff, and whirring movie cameras at the Lenin Library in Moscow. Zemlyanikov received a two-year sentence for stealing countless books and personal effects of readers. Dr. Zemlyanikov was such a promising gynecological surgeon, his past was one of such heroic and dedicated service in the Arctic waste of Novaya Zemlya, his trial such an awkward place to bring out his motivations, the psychiatric experts were so unpersuasive, his physician wife so shaken, and the description of how he got books past the militiamen at the exit envinced such titters in the audience, that the trial ended with most of the readers apparently on the defendant's side and the object lesson unclear (although the librarians remained hostile). The obvious difficulties and expense of arranging such trials and their dubious psychological impact at times may explain why the share of visiting sessions in all criminal trials dropped in the RSFSR, from a quarter in the mid-1960s to a fifth in 1974.[30]

Where possible, also, courts are to drop cases, suspend sentences, transfer lesser first-offense cases to comrades' courts, or sometimes to remand the defendant to the care of his working collective for reeducation, another practice less in evidence after the late 1950s and early 1960s.[31]

Visiting sessions, entrusting to collectives for reeducation, councils of people's assessors, supplementary findings, and public accusers and defenders forge fragile links between courts and the public. Collectives of neighbors and workmates have formed alternate means of community sanction against deviant behavior ("violation of the rules of socialist living"), supplementing the professional courts and law enforcement agencies.

II

The first step in popularization outside professional law enforcement came with attacks on persons hard to convict for specific crimes but still living in a shadow economy of private speculation, prostitution, handouts from rich parents, vagrancy, and begging. It appeared that Khrushchev was attempting to instill a socialist work ethic and force all available people power into the planned, controlled socialist sector of the economy at the same time.[32] Ideological-moral ends seemed inseparable from more practical ends of social discipline and mobilization. Out of this concern to enforce a beehive model of socialism, where every member brought his share of pollen, first came a law against Gypsy rootlessness (1956).[33] The law did not try to mobilize community sanctions. Then antiparasite laws passed, 1957–1959, in eight of the fifteen Union republics. They did try to mobilize community sanctions. So much has been written about the antiparasite laws that I shall mention only the most salient points here.[34]

Antiparasite proceedings brought in the public through "general assemblies" of neighbors called together with the power to pass sentences of warning or exile from two to five years at compulsory labor on "adult, ablebodied citizens leading an anti-social, parasitic way of life, maliciously avoiding socially useful labor, and likewise living on unearned income." Persons accused of vagrancy and begging were to be tried by people's courts. During their adoption and spread to the other Union republics in

1961, the antiparasite laws stirred debate between their supporters who were generally political activists, governmental officials, and factory workers and their critics who were mainly jurists: legal scholars, advocates, judges, and prosecutors. Jurists reported huge practical difficulties with parasites in exile. They deplored what they saw as violations of socialist legality: vague definitions of parasitism, sanctions outside the regular criminal code in violation of the spirit of the criminal law reforms of 1958, the exclusion of the Procuracy from the early versions of proceedings, the wide punitive powers given to extrajudicial bodies, and evasions in court anti-parasite proceedings of rights of due process for regular criminal cases. Here were proceedings trespassing on jurists' domain of social control and without the protections some of them had been fighting for and all of them had been bound by.

As it turned out in the similar 1961 laws for all fifteen Union republics, claims of "socialist legality" made some advances over "the further extension of Soviet democracy." General meetings of neighbors were almost entirely eliminated. Warning had to precede trial. Cases could be initiated only by prosecutors and the militia. In most republics, able-bodied persons not working and who were living off unearned income were to be tried by the court. Parasites working to cover their (poorly defined) sources of unearned income could be tried either by courts or general meetings where they worked. Neighborhood trial meetings virtually disappeared.

Complaints of abuses and inconsistencies kept piling up and the USSR Supreme Court began to issue rulings on anti-parasite proceedings that further transformed antiparasitism from a social to a judicial campaign. Defendants in anti-parasite cases acquired such regular procedural protections as right to counsel and to call witnesses. Prosecutors participated. General meetings at places of employment appeared more and more to be the exception and court hearings the rule.

But loopholes remained. Undesirables of all sorts passed through court onto prison trains and out to Siberia or Arkhangel for a rigorous exile. Among the parasites on the trains and in the transit prisons one might encounter professional criminals whom the authorities wanted removed but could not convict, alcoholics and drug addicts (who bought drugs from veterinarians out in exile), "speculators," skilled craftsmen like stove builders, prostitutes, playboys, and religious and cultural dissidents.[35]

An edict of the RSFSR effective October 6, 1965, or about a year after Khrushchev's fall, restricted exile proceedings to courts only, completing the move away from community sanctions. It allowed exile outside one's province only from Moscow, Moscow Province, and Leningrad. Elsewhere, local soviets could assign parasites to work near their homes.[36]

These remaining chances for administrative exile remained under jurists' attack,[37] and criminal penalties appeared in 1970 (see p. 92).

III

Khrushchev by 1959 was fostering a "full-scale building of communism." And popularization of sanctions in social control had entered a second phase, beyond antiparasite proceedings. "Volunteer organs for the preservation of public order like people's militia, comrades' courts" were now not only to assist regular law enforcement but even to begin *supplanting* it, as part of the gradual development of "socialist statehood" into "communist popular self-administration." [38]

> Cannot the Soviet public deal with violators of socialist law and order? Of course it can. Our social organizations are no less able and equipped for this than are the militia, courts and Procuracy! Preventive and educational work are the main thing.[39]

Police and the judiciary seemed to be facing obsolescence. Militia staffs had been "sharply" cut, the secret police forces cut even more. The professional law enforcers' role was to be reduced, it appeared, to dealing only with hard-core criminals.[40] Popularization of the quest for safe streets in 1959 meant, then, a transfer of power to party officials, the prime movers of the whole grass roots effort—in particular, the Party's Administrative Organs Departments—at the expense of the power, jobs, and privileges of the militia, Procuracy, and courts.[41] They joined officials of industry and the military (soon it would be of the Party, too) who had reason to resent Khrushchev's innovations.[42]

Comrades' courts, people's detachments, and collective reeducation proliferated under the Bolsheviks but ceased to function in the 1930s.[43] They picked up again after the March 2, 1959, joint decree of the CPSU Central Committee and USSR Council of Ministers, "On the Participation of the Working People in the Maintenance of Public Order." Popularization became a major and lasting reform despite flaws,[44] and the later retreats. Commissions to Protect Socialist Property have tried to stop pilfering in enterprises. Standing Commissions on Socialist Legality under local soviets have enrolled deputies and activists in a range of checkups on law enforcement, putting parasites to work, and so on. Commissions on Everyday Life in workplaces have helped bring homelife into order. There are countless street committees,[45] apartment house committees, parents' committees, Commissions on Juvenile Affairs, posts of people's control. Administrative commissions of the local soviets help enforce ordinances.[46] Photos or caricatures of drunks, rowdies, and thieves advertise them to the populace on billboards or streetcar panels under slogans like "They Shame Our City" or "Do Not Pass This By."

Volunteer people's detachments, numbering about 170,000, enroll 7 million people's guards (*druzhiniki*) to help prevent lawbreaking and preserve public order. People's guards receive instruction in peacekeeping from party lecturers, the militia, the Procuracy, and adult education universities of legal knowledge. They cooperate with the militia and sometimes act together with militiamen.

Criminal law exacts severe penalties on persons resisting or attacking people's guards on the same basis as if the guards were militia. But, unlike their predecessors, the Brigades to Help the Militia, people's detachments organized nationally after experiments in 1957–1958, do not operate as police auxiliaries directly under militia direction. They operate not out of the militia precinct house, but from a headquarters base in a factory, construction site, educational institution, collective farm, or other place of work.[47] The new 1974 Statute on Volunteer People's Detachments for the Preservation of Public Order places them under administrative control of local soviets, the government agencies of cities, boroughs, settlements, rural districts, and villages. Legality of detachment work is supposed to be a concern both of the soviets and of the Procuracy.[48] A secretary of the local party committee is, typically, chief of staff of the area's detachments.[49]

A people's guard may in line of duty (1) order citizens to observe existing rules of public order or stop violating them; (2) ask to see the identification of anyone who is violating public order; (3) write up a report of violations when there is no militiamen around and submit it to the detachment commander; (4) when necessary to stop a violation or to establish a violator's identity, arrest the violator and take him or her to detachment headquarters or a militia station, but not for more than one hour at detachment headquarters; (5) enter clubs, stadiums, and other public places to investigate or prevent a violation, acting with the management's permission; (6) commandeer transport to rush sick or injured people to medical treatment; (7) travel free on all transport except taxis while on duty; (8) see the identification and driver's license of traffic violators and take them to the militia station when they have been driving while intoxicated or without a license.[50]

Some enthusiasts have wanted to give people's detachments police-like powers of sanction and investigation. They have suggested the detachments be empowered also to fine, to search homes and persons, and to issue summonses. These suggestions have been rejected on the grounds that to follow them would mean to bring detachment functions "very close to those of regular militiamen." They would go against the present party line, supposedly enforced by local party and Komsomol committees, that people's detachments enforce public order by "other means of struggle,"[51] and above all social influence and persuasion." [52] M. Portyanko, a secretary of the Chernigov City Party Committee and chief of staff of the voluntary people's detachments, states that one fifth of persons actually taken in to detachment headquarters in recent years are subjected to administrative or criminal penalties. "Most of them realize their guilt in the course of conversation. . . . But if we saw that somebody did not take a sufficiently responsible view of his offense, we sent information about it to his place of work so that the collective in which he worked could bring the proper influence to bear on him." [53]

People's guards, marked by their red armbands, undertake a much wider variety of preventive and peacekeeping activities than auxiliary police or neighbors' patrols do in New York.[54] Press accounts cover people's guards heading off altercations, taking in hooligans at dances and turning them over to the regular militia after drawing up an *akt*, chasing and catching burglars who have just broken into a store, stopping railroad workers on a vodka binge from insulting passers-by and from staggering onto railroad tracks and reporting them to the administration and party organization for disciplining, or visiting on the streets near the factory where the people's guards are recruited.[55]

Aside from crime fighting and prevention, people's guards are supposed to help disaster and accident victims, obey a soviet deputy's call for help in dealing with a lawbreaker, and assist in protecting nature against despoilers and poachers.[56]

While helping the authorities, people's guards create various problems of their own. In the earlier years particularly, it seems, vicious and even criminal types took over some detachments. They used their posts as detachment commanders to terrorize the people they were supposed to protect. They abused their office, raped and humiliated women, and stole public funds. An outside prosecutor and court might have to step in to penetrate the cover provided by local party and soviet officials.[57] Later reports tell of people's guards' crudeness, getting inebriated with the drunk they are escorting home, taking shelter from their winter patrol in a free movie.[58] A Baku conference recently brought out policy problems faced by a borough party committee. Should women serve as people's guards? What should be done about ordering people to patrols as part of their party or Komsomol duties, but in violation of the voluntary principle of service in the people's detachments? Why is it that "despite the fact that the number of militia aides is growing, disturbances of public order are unfortunately still numerous, especially among teenagers? What is to be done about detachments' excessive enthusiasm for raids and patrols and neglect of prevention work to lead erring juveniles back from the brink before they have to be brought in for hooliganism or other crimes?" [59]

The responses to the report of this conference brought out other signs of difficulty with the people's guards patrols. "Why is it some public defenders of order so tactfully avoid the drinking spots and darkened courtyards and doorways where crimes usually occur?" What is to be done about formal, paper victories where, say, 20,000 people's guards are reported in one borough but succeed all year in nothing more than rounding up three drunks? What to do about the fact that half of these ineffectual *druzhiniki* got the additional vacation time that number among *druzhinikis*' rewards? How is the regular militia "that stands at the leading edge of the war against crime" (note the different tone from 1959) to be put in closer cooperation with people's guard detachments, an activity the militia now seems to avoid?[60]

One new try for greater efficiency is to form picked detachments of veteran *druzhiniki*, each detachment specializing in one problem of social order: drunkenness, hooliganism, moonshining, pilfering socialist property, juvenile lawbreaking, or traffic violations.[61]

Auxiliary police in the form of people's detachments, then, have been retained as advantageous to the Soviet regime's program of social control. But they have not proven themselves either safe or effective enough to replace the militia as the main local peacekeeping force. The same is true of those other popular organs, the comrades' courts.

Nearly 300,000 volunteer nonprofessional comrades' courts[62] function under trade union committees and housing offices and under the supervision, in residential areas, of the local soviets. They settle squabbles among apartment dwellers and try cases of petty theft, rowdyism, indiscipline, and petty currency speculation, as well as any other cases the people's courts decide to transfer to them. Three or more members of the court hear a case. Members are selected from a panel elected (without competition) for terms of one year by collectives of their co-workers or co-residents.[63]

Comrades' courts may not sentence to confinement. Their sanctions are (1) to require public apology; (2) comradely warning; (3) social censure; (4) social reprimand which may or may not be published; (5) fines of up to fifty rubles; (6) recommending to the administration transfer of the offender to lower paid or less responsible work or firing offenders working with juveniles or youth or in a job connected with guarding or handing out objects of value; recommending that persons found guilty of petty hooliganism, petty speculation, petty pilfering on the job, petty larceny of personal property, simple assault, and inflicting minor injuries be shifted for fifteen days to unskilled manual work at correspondingly lower pay; (7) recommending the eviction of persons impossible to live with or destructive of their housing. (8) In addition to the above sanctions, the comrades' courts may require that an offender make good damages up to fifty rubles and compensate fully for stolen state or cooperative property, and that the state confiscate items traded in petty speculation.[64]

Soviet and trade union officials have felt pressure on them since late in 1969 to bring comrades' courts into the drive against shirkers, truants, lazybones, and drunkards at work.[65] Apparently, comrades' courts, though formally existing, operate infrequently, lapsing into inactivity until prodded to meet in one of the periodic local campaigns of the Party for grass roots prevention.[66] This is a long-standing pattern. The comrades' court met in the spring of 1964 at Moscow University's Law Faculty only for the second time that year. Yet I understood from students then that other cases came up lending themselves to comrades' court hearings that year. The case I attended involved a law student in his twenties. He worked as a procuracy official during the day and studied evenings. An alleged hooligan, he faced the charge that while intoxicated he became so violent that he frightened his wife and baby out of their home, knocked down a door, and cursed a neighbor and the police officer other neighbors had called to take him in. As is customary in such trials, the audience added its comments pro and con. His classmates vouched for him as a sober, conscientious student. His woman neighbor and law students in other classes clamored for punishment. The court reprimanded him and posted its findings. They put the law faculty officially on notice about his misconduct and raised with the faculty the question: Should such an irresponsible person be considered worthy of being a prosecutor? We heard of no further action in the case.

Inertia and indifference account in part for the spasmodic functioning of comrades' courts. One suspects, however, that they are not pushed harder to take on cases because they tend to be ineffective and to violate people's legal rights. Ineffectiveness and dangers of abuses probably account for a toning down of both people's detachments and comrades' courts. These shortcomings and abuses spring from the low level of legal education of the volunteer law enforcers and the generally low level of legal consciousness among the populace.[67]

Harsher Penalties

I

Khrushchev's enthusiasm for popularizing justice soon gave way to anger about disorder and to pressures for a harder line.[68] He made it clear at the Twenty-second Party Congress in October 1961 that the transition from state repression to public suasion did not outdate firm, professional government enforcement of law and order. The new party program he presented, more conservative than the 1919 program it replaced, moved to the distant future the time when "criminal punishment will be replaced with measures of public influence and education." The new program called meanwhile for "stern measures of punishment against criminals and parasites."[69] The militia, judges, prosecutors, and jurists faced obsolescence in 1959. Then they were admonished to play down "the role of state repression." By 1961–1962 they were resolving not to "underestimate" it.[70]

The repressive impact of comrades' courts and people's guards is debatable.[71] After two years of boosting them, Soviet policy makers turned also to toughening criminal law. Their major revision of it in 1961 and 1962 added new crimes and new penalties. Recidivism prompted changes making it more likely that a repeater will become an "especially dangerous recidivist," subject to more than normal punishment and less than normal parole. Parole became shorter or impossible for a longer list of serious crimes. The death penalty was extended to sixteen existing or newly listed crimes.[72]

Death penalties figured prominently for leading culprits in Khrushchev's campaign against crimes in the economy like bribery, theft of state property, and currency speculation. The large number of Jewish names and the anti-Semitic stereotypes gave the campaign overtones of an official pogrom. Jan Rokotov and Vladislav Faibishenko achieved a sort of fame in the thieves' underworld and through the strident reports in the Soviet press for their gang's currency and gold coin speculations grossing some 2 million (current) rubles. They inspired press stereotypes of "dirty, slovenly old" Jews, and greed in the synagogues.

> Of course Crafty Jan had no intention of salting away the currency and gold he had bought from his stilyagi [lit., "style chasers" —P.J.] agents. He kept none of the currency or coin. There were still bigger vultures in the night world who took gold and currency from him wholesale, no questions asked.
>
> One Adel Bikkulov bought 500,000 rubles' worth of valuables from him. Then certain shady characters put him in contact with those dirty, slovenly old men Ber Yakovlevich Shnitser, Ilya Yulianovich Dubershtein and Semyon Davidovich Yefraimovich. These ancients, who were apparently sunk in poverty, had actually been dealing in the resale of gold since the time of the New Economic Policy. Untold wealth passed through their hands. They were miserly and careful. Crafty Jan brought gold coins directly to them in their synagogue where, to the doleful words of prayers intoned by the rabbi, the speculative deals were made.[73]

This and similar reports about the case showed that Rokotov, Faibishenko, and others involved enjoyed no presumption of innocence. They were virtually tried in the press. Their case showed also that the Khrushchev regime did not hesitate to violate socialist legality in the trial procedures and sentencing. The original sentences of Rokotov and Faibishenko in Moscow City Court were higher than the maximum specified when they committed their crimes. Then, quite probably pressured by Khrushchev, the Prosecutor General himself had the black marketeers retried on his appeal and the two of them were sentenced to death. Not only were both their sentences illegal, but they involved three separate retroactive violations.[74] The press in June 1961 featured report after report on death sentences handed out right and left before even the July 1, 1961 edict made currency speculation a capital offense. This meant, in effect, shooting by analogy. Many of the other high sentences mentioned probably involved retroactive violations as well.[75]

In the wake of the various extensions of the death penalty, an estimated 700 to 1,000 criminals are shot every year—two or three a day—"on a wide variety of charges ranging from homicide with aggravating circumstances to the 'theft of state property on an especially large scale,' prohibited currency operations and other charges unfamiliar to Western law." [76]

Khrushchev, it has been said, once believed "any working or peasant community to be quite capable of finding its own bad elements without the need for lawyers and their law." [77] The lawyers resisted him in this, though divided on issues of how regular justice should be used.

Khrushchev's formulations reflected the ambivalence about state coercion in Soviet Marxism going back to Lenin.[78] Lenin and Khrushchev regarded state coercion through criminal law as a holding operation that would lead, through social development of the new man, to no state coercion at all. Stalin regarded state coercion as something to push to the physical limit before it could wither away. Brezhnev moved step by step toward a synthesis of past approaches (before sponsoring some innovations). This synthesis he developed through anticrime campaigns and the continual rethinking in their wake.

II

Brezhnev had already assumed a central role in the quest for law and order by 1964 before Khrushchev's fall,[79] while national meetings[80] of crime fighters looked for ways out of an impasse on the crime front. They heard a harder line against "liberalism" from a segment of legal opinion headed by L.N. Smirnov, then head of the Russian Republic (RSFSR) Supreme Court, and V.S. Tikunov, then head of the RSFSR Ministry for Public Order (MOOP), the most important regular police official since Khrushchev abolished the USSR MVD in 1962 and renamed its republic branches the ministries of public order. Like advocates elsewhere of "strengthening the peace forces against the criminal forces," such officials blamed crime not on any social causes but on lack of moral fiber, hooliganism, drunkenness, courts' "sentimentality," permissiveness, lax communal controls, not living up to potentials, and too easy paroles. And they called for realism in place of whitewashing the crime picture with loosely doctored statistics.[81]

Conference participants and the public were regaled with stories of a permissive climate of public opinion. Crowds pressured militiamen to release suspects or treat them with kid gloves. Detachments seemingly ignored the rowdies swarming the streets after being drafted for service willy-nilly by shop chiefs trying to meet formal quotas. Comrades' courts met now and then, ineffectually and in the lunch break amidst sandwiches, beer, and the click of dominoes. Management, trade union and Komsomol officials, and working collectives ignored workers' hooliganish misdeeds or petitioned courts for leniency. Culprits remanded by court for reeducation by the collective received nothing of the kind and went on new rampages.[82] Big bulges in numbers of teen-agers and their crimes added new urgency to the quest for order in the 1960s. Khrushchev's limits on alcohol sales in 1958 had not cured public drunkenness and crimes associated with it.[83] Another argument of leading "practical workers" for direct action was that criminology (then a decade into its post-Stalin revival) had not come up with any workable programs for crime prevention.[84] So they pushed courts and prosecutors to crack down harder on lawbreakers.[85]

Some dissatisfied participants in the law-and-order debates pushed extreme measures in policy discussion: "retribution," no parole, no suspended sentences and no mitigated sentences, and prisons that "not only educate criminals but also frighten them." Unscientific, retorted the future director of the Institute of Crime Study, citing "empirical social science research" to the effect that laws were strict enough.[86] A prevailing group of policy makers did not argue. They launched a vigorous campaign against hooligans and drunkards in mid-1966.

Campaigning against Disorder

I

Campaign principles appeared in a decree of July 23, 1966. It was approved by a joint session of the Central Committee of the CPSU, Presidium of the Supreme Soviet, and Council of Ministers, to show its supreme importance for the regime, and entitled[87] "On Measures More Intensively to Combat Violations of Public Order." Four edicts of the Supreme Soviet Presidium elaborated the decree on July 26, 1966,[88] and received billing as a "battle on many fronts launched against lawbreaking, using the resources of all state and social organizations. . . . A climate of intolerance of all anti-social manifestations must be created at every enterprise and collective farm, in city and countryside."[89]

The drive was a victory above all for the MVD (then MOOP). Virtually every suggestion militia leaders had made at an April crime prevention meeting the Russian republic MOOP sponsored in Moscow, just after Brezhnev's call for more law and order, appeared in the campaign edicts.[90] The militia received new equipment for motorized patrols and new powers to conduct summary inquests of hooligans, to take over pretrial investigations from under control of the Procuracy in cases of malicious hooliganism without a weapon, to fine public drunks three to ten rubles, to summon rowdies for warning and registration, and to keep administrative surveillance over released habitual criminals. Central control and a central voice for the militia was restored through the reappearance of the USSR Ministry for Public Order, MOOP. The USSR MOOP and the republic MOOPs resumed the formerly used name of MVD in 1968.[91]

A sentence of seven years maximum was added alongside the existing five-year maximum for malicious hooligans when they used a weapon, under the new rubric "especially malicious hooliganism,"[92] duly added to the list of crimes for which juveniles fourteen and over were liable in court.[93] Community involvement in law enforcement through comrades' courts and people's detachments was to be stepped up and encouraged by awards and by protection from legal penalties for injuring a suspect. Managers received the right to penalize employees for hooliganism reported to them by the militia, depriving the culprits of bonuses, their place on the apartment waiting list, and discount vacation package trips. A new social service for juveniles to help prevent such sentences appeared in the form of volunteer "social counselors," big brothers or big sisters to youngsters in trouble.

II

It was characteristic of Brezhnev's cautious pragmatism that, unlike the flamboyant Khrushchev, he made no sweeping ideological changes to mark the policies he approved. Rather, there was an adjustment. Theorists kept the term "state of the whole people," but no longer spoke of the dictatorship of the proletariat as unnecessary in that state as Khrushchev did in 1961. At a time of repressing hooligans and dissidents, counterposing the "socialist state" or the "dictatorship of the proletariat" to "state of the whole people" were clearly deemed inappropriate.[94] Just before the 1966 campaign, high legal authority noted that whereas Stalinism "overstressed government channels, administrative processes, coercion," Soviet law enforcement later—that is, under Khrushchev—had gone "to the other extreme" of overemphasizing "the role of the community in strengthening law and order. . . . This has caused us to underestimate the role of organs of state coercion in educating the new man, in the fight against survivals of the past." [95] Just too many incorrigibles had been turned over to their "collectives" for reeducation and spared criminal punishment. The threat of those "organs of state coercion" from "subjectivism" and "premature voluntarist conclusions" [96] was over.

III

Party and police administrators tried vigorously to push the anti-crime measures of 1966,[97] down to the local level of the distant Siberian village, where the militia took up nightsticks.[98] Monthly conviction rates almost doubled in the hectic early months,[99] filling labor colonies to overflowing,[100] until the 1967 amnesty provided relief, as the 1926 drive against hooliganism had filled prisons forty years earlier, until the amnesty of 1927, also on a revolutionary anniversary.[101] All sorts of deviants from prostitutes to persons frequenting with foreigners to traffic violators were charged wrongly with hooliganism. Or relatively harmless rowdies found themselves bundled off to long prison terms as "malicious hooligans." [102] Sometimes citizens abused their fortified rights of self-defense.[103] And some police and judges took the campaign sweep and new simplified procedures for hooligans as signals for "nihilistic, contemptuous attitudes toward rules of criminal procedure," despite court warning against illegalities and the pleas of legal scholars like the late Dr. I.D. Perlov, consultant to the USSR Supreme Court, and Justice G.Z. Anashkin, chairman of its Criminal Bench and an unsuccessful opponent of reliance on harsher penalties to restore public order.[104]

IV

Optimistic reports on the vigorous drive's results do not square with sober second thoughts that serious crimes had risen in some republics, January to June 1967,[105] and that the "poor results of the struggle against serious crimes are cause for grave concern." [106] Serious crimes may have seemed to decrease, the Procuracy said, but only because, in their overemphasis on hooliganism as the root of other crimes, law enforcers neglected other felonies. Also they drove hooligans off the streets, out of parks and stadiums into courtyards and communal apartments, where it was harder to catch them and to distinguish hooliganism from family quarrels or simple assault.[107]

Thus the campaign against rowdyism in public places attacked a symptom of social disorder, filled correctional institutions, and caused widespread procedural illegalities, but produced dubious results. It caused neglect of more serious crimes and scattered the hooligans without entirely repressing them. Alcohol abuse and conflict of interest hampered police efforts.

Managers failed to exercise their rights to penalize workers the militia reported to them for drunkenness or hooliganism because the managers did not want to hurt production by souring or losing members of their labor force.[108] State trading outlets violated liquor sales restrictions to increase business. Kiosks labeled "dumplings" sold nothing of the kind, only vodka, at forbidden hours, to juveniles under sixteen and in forbidden places, including enterprise, mine and office canteens, and even school buffets.[109]

V

As with Russia's North European neighbors (and quite a few other milieu), drinking is of the heavy determined kind.

Tsar Alexei, on Patriarch Nikon's advice, ordered taverns in 1652 to serve only one cup of vodka to a customer.[110] Nicholas II unsuccessfully decreed prohibition during World War I. Khrushchev limited vodka to 100 grams a customer in 1958, and banned vodka sales before 10:00 A.M. He turned to shaming too. Cartoons, photographs, and workplace meetings publicly ridiculed drunks. But sales pressures of plan-fulfilling kiosks, stores, and restaurants overcame social pressures.[111] And cleanup women winked at drinking from bottles spirited into ice cream parlors because of the tidy extra income from deposits on bottles the drinkers left behind.

Besides bans and shaming, the regime tried education. The Russian Republic Ministry of Public Health published over a million antialcoholism pamphlets (1960–1965) and organized thousands of lectures on the evils and hazards of alcohol. According to the head of Education and Hygiene for the Russian republic, the campaign brought "negligible results" largely because such campaigns try to teach people *not* to drink rather than *how* to drink.[112]

Whether drinking would have been more or less without the various halfhearted campaigns, we cannot know. But we do know that sales of alcoholic beverages by state and cooperative stores and public catering, down by 1950 to 75 percent of the 1940 level due to the war, have risen more than fivefold over the 1940 level, sevenfold over the 1950 level: 2.7 times between 1950 and 1960, 57 percent between 1960 and 1966, the year the antihooliganism campaign began, and another 12 percent between 1966 and 1967, 23 percent more by 1970 (439 percent of the 1940 level), another 22 percent in 1970–1973 (to 534 percent of the 1940 level and 712 percent of the 1950 level!).[113] Between 1967 and 1973, alone, sales of alcoholic beverages increased by 50 percent, despite a whole series of antidrunkenness restrictions.

In 1967 the regime launched a drive against alcohol abuse. It restricted sales, imposed stiffer sanctions, and extended compulsory treatment. Intoxication while committing a crime became an aggravating circumstance, making the punishment more than normally severe.[114]

No longer did an alcoholic have to commit a crime to be liable to compulsory treatment. Effective September 1, 1967, "habitual drunkards (alcoholics) who regularly misuse alcoholic beverages, shun voluntary treatment or continue to drink to excess after treatment and who violate labor discipline, public order and the rules of the socialist community, in spite of public or administrative measures taken against them, are subject to be sent (by decision of a People's Court) to treatment-labor medical institutions for compulsory medical treatment and labor re-education for a period of one to two years."[115] This took on some of the aspects of criminal punishment without crime.[116] Families of persons abusing alcohol or drugs but not sentenced to confinement (in a provision widely welcomed) could seek to be protected financially through court powers to restrict the legal competence of the alcoholics or addicts, and establish guardianship over them, and turn their pay straight over to their families.

Liquor sale bans in Moscow and Leningrad before 11:00 A.M. and after 8:00 P.M., introduced in 1970, preluded a nationwide sales restriction drive in 1972.[117] The regime had so far ignored pleas for more research and therapy or for a new discipline of "narcology." Instead it issued orders in 1972 for more drastic action such as tighter restrictions on places for alcohol sales and limited the hours that package stores were open from 11:00 A.M. to 7:00 P.M.[118] These restrictions were backed by many new administrative and criminal sanctions against liquor law violators:

- persons speculating in vodka (taxi drivers, door keepers of restaurants, etc., are being apprehended for profiteering);[119]
- moonshiners (let off lightly in past practice);
- persons drinking in public outside permitted spots;
- persons coming to work drunk or drinking on the job and superiors ignoring this;
- those inducing minors to get drunk, and parents of juvenile offenders;
- drunken drivers.

Commissions for Combatting Drunkenness were ordered set up under the soviets to coordinate the drive against problem drinking—a drive in which community sanctions play little part.[120] Criminal and administrative law have been mobilized to direct state compulsion against the symptoms, if not the cause, of alcoholism and drunkenness. So have communal suasion, medical therapy plus work, and antialcoholism propaganda.

The Soviet Union is one of the many countries so far spared a major epidemic of drug abuse such as plagues the United States. But the government has been concerned enough with drug abuse to resort to several recent repressive measures: sentences increased in 1962 from one to ten years maximum for possessing or selling narcotics (defined in the USSR as opium, cocaine, morphine, heroin, hashish, and marijuana) and for cultivating the opium poppy or hemp without permission.[121]

A Supreme Court directive to the lower courts in 1966 complained that courts "underestimate the social danger of spreading narcotics among the populace," cultivating poppies and hemp, and violating rules governing producing, storing, and issuing narcotic, strong-acting, and poisonous substances. The directive ordered the lower courts to pay more attention to all sides of the problem of drug abuse. Inducing minors to take drugs[122] or to get drunk [123] was declared a crime, punishment by up to five years' confinement in 1965.

Five years after the particularly punitive 1967 decree for compulsory treatment of alcoholics guilty of no crime, a similar decree appeared ordering compulsory treatment of drug addicts who refuse voluntary treatment or persistently create disorder.[124] By 1972, then, the courts applied (1) code provisions for compulsory treatment of alcoholics and addicts who had committed crimes; (2) their authority under the 1967 edict to commit to compulsory cure addicts even when not in connection with a crime; (3) the edict of July 23, 1971, empowering the judges by their own initiative, without a petition to them, to commit alcoholics for compulsory treatment; and (4) the 1972 edict authorizing judges to commit drug addicts also even when no crime was involved.

Prosecutorial supervision has uncovered serious lapses such as commitment of the alcoholic without required examination by a three-person medical commission. Also, the possibility of protecting families by limiting the legal competence of alcoholics or addicts is rarely used. Whether for shortage of room or other reasons is not clear, but court practice seems to lean on criminal punishment, neglecting the treatment side prescribed by law.[125] "Many crimes are committed because of drunkenness and drug addiction. Nevertheless, compulsory medical treatment for chronic alcoholics and drug addicts who have committed crimes is rarely used in the Uzbek, Kirgiz, Georgian, Armenian, Kazakh Union Republics and not at all in the Moldavian and Tadzhik Republics." Kirgiz republic courts have found many addicts among drug offenders but applied compulsory cure to only *one* of them. Carrying out its function of checkup on legality, the

Procuracy has uncovered cases where persons are sent to "Medical-Labor Prophylactoria" of the MVD on the basis of false denunciations by their spouses, relatives, and acquaintances, despite evidence clearly disproving their addiction. Addicts and alcoholics have been sent to Medical-Labor Prophylactoria with illnesses dangerous for themselves or others—TB in an infectious stage, venereal disease, kidney ailments. Sometimes commitment is decided without the addict or alcoholic present, or without carefully reasoned and worded decisions. "Some courts draw up and duplicate standard texts of decrees on which they leave spaces for entering names of judges, defendants and length of treatment decided." [126]

An edict, "On Intensifying the Struggle with Drug Addiction," of April 25, 1974,[127] extraordinary in its length and differentiations, marked a second time since 1962 that the government stepped up punitive measures against drug abuse. Containing ten subtypes of offense and altogether twenty-five degrees of liability, this may be the longest Soviet edict ever published on a single category of criminal offense: drug thieves and pushers get up to fifteen years, plus property confiscation; growers of opium poppies or marijuana hemps, up to 8 years; proprietors of drug dens, five to ten years with or without property confiscation. Other penalties extend to such offenses as covering up or not reporting drug offenses. Drug *users* face lesser penalties, use of narcotics without doctor's prescription—fine of up to fifty rubles levied administratively, by the precinct militia captain or his deputy, unless union republic codes provide for criminal punishment. Parents of juvenile abusers are accountable to the Commissions on Juvenile Affairs. The commissions process all apprehended juvenile delinquents under fourteen and those over fourteen not criminally prosecuted and tried in court.

The 1974 edict gave drug addicts the choice: either submit to treatment in "medical-prophylactic institutions of the public health agencies" or, face compulsory treatment in Medical-Labor Prophylactoria of the MVD upon court order for a term of six months to two years.

These penalties are not severe by the standards of U.S. justice. But detailed comparison would spot the more specific U.S. differentiation among forbidden drugs: from hallucinogens to LSD, speed, marijuana, narcotic drugs, stimulants, and so on, while Soviet practice lumps everything under "narcotics" and "narcomania."

Penalties for alcohol and drug abuse have brought to over thirty the number of offenses newly listed as crimes under Brezhnev between 1964 and the mid-1970s—a policy softened little by the 1975 amnesty. Newly listed crimes range from the misdemeanor of revealing the secret of an adoption against the adopter's wishes (social censure, fine up to fifty rubles, or up to one year's correctional labor) to knowingly spreading

VD, if a repeated offense or infecting two or more persons or a minor (up to five years' confinement); stealing firearms, military supplies, or explosives, a crime entailing penalties of up to fifteen years' confinement if by armed robbery or an especially dangerous recidivist.[128] This type of offender has been subjected to increasingly severe punishment.[129] Violating hunting and trapping rules, subject to a maximum one-year sentence, has brought a tripled maximum sentence of up to three years since December 1972.[130] Maximum sentence nearly tripled, up to five years for illegal carrying, possession, or making or sale of arms and explosives in 1974.[131] When some Jewish alleged hijackers received death sentences in 1970 (subsequently commuted), no law existed specifically penalizing aerial hijacking this way. That loophole was closed by an edict in 1973 during the worldwide furor over terrorism in the airways.[132] Since early 1974 polluters of seas and rivers face fines or labor camp.[133]

Conscripting Labor

Like Anglo-American vagrancy laws,[134] Soviet measures against vagrancy serve two apparent purposes: to send away undesirables and to put all available able-bodied people to work in times of labor shortages.

Parasites—that is, able-bodied men eighteen to fifty years old, and able-bodied women eighteen to fifty-five years old "refusing to perform socially useful work and leading an anti-social parasitic way of life"—received warnings from the militia and work orders from the local soviets required under the edicts of 1961 and 1965. Beginning in 1970, alleged parasites ignoring the warnings and orders no longer faced administrative exile or work assignment but possible criminal punishment of up to a year's deprivation of freedom, or two years if repeaters.[135]

"Parasite" was a term vague enough to cover any person regularly receiving substantial "unearned income," that is, making money in ways contrary to the law or to "norms of Communist morality:"—prostitutes, gamblers, fortune tellers, petty black marketeers and people "working only for appearances sake, but where their basic means of support is unearned income,"[136] or dissidents first fired or denied work and then harassed with charges of parasitism.[137] Edicts of August 7, 1975 seemed to de-emphasize the drive against non-vagrant parasites holding approved jobs, apparently directing repression mainly against drifters at the edges of the community and the underworld and still, possibly, dissidents.[138]

There is no reason to believe the 1975 measures solve the problems posed by militia laxity on parasitism and the militia's losing track of local loafers and shady types who go to work for show and then quit.[139] The new measures will continue to create a revolving door for released convicts whom nobody will hire and who end up, therefore, as parasites,[140] the same sort of revolving door trapping U.S. ex-cons too.[141] Only, the Soviet correctional system is better geared to take ex-cons back in and find assigned work for them in or out of labor colonies.

During the late sixties and the fervor of the drive for public order, criminalists could be heard cautioning that camp sentences, particularly if too long or unfounded, overcrowd labor colonies and hurt rehabilitation,[142] and that labor colony sentences can waste skilled labor—only 40 percent of which is used in colonies.[143] Conceivably, arguments like this brought about the 1970 legislation on suspended sentences with obligation to work.

According to an edict of June 12, 1970, able-bodied persons eighteen to sixty years old, if men, and eighteen to fifty-five years old, if women, sentenced to one to three years' confinement, may be given suspended sentences or paroled from confinement with the obligation to work wherever the militia sent them on construction sites or in factories, without being isolated from society, and with prospects of having their convictions erased under administrative surveillance of the militia.[144]

While antiparasite measures of 1970 brought parasites under criminal law, the work-release measure of 1970 brought to persons sentenced for all lesser criminal offenses including parasitism the possibility of being sent to work in exile. They were to be treated as parasites had been under the legislation of 1961, save that the 1970 measure appeared to rule out work on collective farms.

The work-release measure has potential for a more humane and effective rehabilitation of criminals by saving them from camps and the stigma of a criminal record. It provides ways to draft deviants and dropouts to help fulfill national economic plans, in places unattractive to free labor, without exposing them to criminal elements in labor colonies (except in transit to the place of work exile). As one authority on corrections put it: "First of all, people do not end up in places of confinement, which means they have less chance of picking up the lifestyle, outlook and skills of the criminals. Secondly, the state is enabled to have working hands where they are especially needed."[145]

The same authority, I.I. Karpets, pointed out that shorter term offenders tend to be less habitual criminals and constitute an able-bodied and valuable working resource. About 50 percent of persons deprived of freedom serve up to two-year sentences. Of these, according to the sample, 63 percent are first offenders, 92 percent were performing socially useful labor at the time they were charged, 65 percent have a work record of more than three years, 50 percent have families, 90 percent are able bodied, and 60 percent are under 30. According to Karpets, these figures show that work release (with compulsory recruitment to work in an assigned region) is practical and of value to the economy. If living conditions are tolerable so that workers do not run away, with supervision well organized and work set up to make use of the available skills, then "the social and economic benefits to the state from that measure are obvious." [146]

The 1970 provision for suspended sentence with recruitment to work will soften punishment for those who would otherwise have been sent away not just to fixed residence and assigned work under militia surveillance, but to a corrective labor colony of general regime (the mildest of four colony regimes and two severe prison regimes).[147] But how many persons will be recruited to this work-exile status who might otherwise have been simple suspended sentences?

Apparently, the courts are having trouble deciding whom to include. Their guideline is that they should include only able-bodied men eighteen to fifty-nine and women eighteen to fifty-four, as mentioned; that these persons do not merit straight suspended sentences, and would otherwise serve from one to three years in confinement; and, generally, that they do seem to merit a chance at rehabilitation in the work recruitment program.[148] Thus the other side of the 1970 measure is that it smacks of forced labor when convicted persons, through judges' errors, are recruited although in ill health, or where they should have received lesser penalties, such as simple suspended sentences, corrective work, fines.

Authorities must cope with misconduct among persons sent to compulsory labor, "who refuse to work or who persistenely or maliciously violate labor discipline, public order or residence rules established for them." [149] But there is as yet no sign that the government has lost enthusiasm for suspended sentences with obligation to work. The measure promised to replenish labor-short construction projects in faraway places with "a considerable part" of all lawbreakers.[150] Its conscript labor aspect dovetailed with existing programs for utilizing "volunteer" and temporarily impressed labor, such as the work of schoolchildren and college students or persons giving up a Saturday of work contributed to the state.[151]

Mass Legal Propaganda

By 1970 the only liberalizing innovation in principles of crime fighting under Brezhnev had been the new program of giving suspended sentences with obligatory recruitment to work. Whether this is really a liberalizing step will depend on how widely it is applied and to whom.

That same year, 1970, it began to look as if the regime had abandoned in practice the formula that prevention should be the main way to fight crime. But the onrush of disciplinary and criminal crackdowns on the labor force should not obscure two other approaches that overshadow the work recruiting program in scope. One approach is the expansion of crime research into new areas. I shall deal with this in the next chapters. The other innovation was to take the existing, low-key effort at mass legal education and turn it into a vast campaign pushed ahead by Brezhnev himself in 1970.

For Brezhnev and his officers of justice, social discipline and law and order needed for efficient production and more rapid development rested on the public's understanding and internalizing Soviet laws passed to regulate commercial, administrative, and social relations and to deter crime.[152] "Now knowledge of what the law means is not enough," according to the USSR Minister of Justice, V. Terebilov. "Its commands must take deep root in the conscience, behavior and habits of every citizen."[153] "People," said Terebilov's first deputy, "must come to believe in the utility and social justice of Soviet laws and of conscientiously carrying them out."[154] This is a legal culture of obedience and social rights, though not of civil rights.

Coordinated down to the local level by the ministries of justice,[155] the legal education campaign moves on three wheels: (1) a good example by officials (easier said than done, given the lapses of said officials),[156] (2) dissemination of information, and (3) studying public opinion.

The *Znanie* society for adult mass education, jurists, the MVD, educators, radio, television, and the press are all called on to make the program successful. Jurists, long the most important source of volunteers, help give the 1,300,000 public lectures on law a year and teach the 249,000 part-time students at the 1,586 evening People's Universities of Legal Knowledge and their 106 branches. The authorities are well aware of how ineffectual merely hortative or dryly technical lectures can be and of how hard it is to check up on what participants have learned, or to get needed textbooks and supplies—even in Moscow, despite the cooperation of *Znanie,* Moscow University, the people's detachment headquarters, and law enforcement agencies.[157]

The legal department of the Podol'sk Machine Building Plant runs a "Faculty of Legal Knowledge" with a biweekly lecture series on labor and family law, comrades' courts, the Labor Conflict Commission, bonuses, pensions, how to calculate work seniority, "strengthening labor discipline," and "instilling respect for the law." For the management, the factory legal office sends out an information letter to keep them up to date on everything from "Privileges for Women," to "The Work of Youth," "Labor Discipline," and "Privileges for Those Studying While

They Work." Outsiders come in to lecture like the city prosecutor who spoke on "Socialist Legality and Law and Order in the City of Podol'sk."[158]

Yet another grass roots agency cropped up during this campaign, prophylaxis committees, different from committees to help the family and the school and other community volunteer agencies because jurists sit on them, they are under close guidance of local party organizations, and they have a single special purpose, to work with persons "inclined to law-breaking."

Organized teaching and social work is backed up by mass media: over 1,200 articles on legal themes in the Moscow press in 1972; a lively pocket-sized tabloid, *People and the Law,* begun in January 1972, its circulation now up to over 3,000,000; radio and TV programs of the same name; law journals with circulations of 120,000 (*Soviet Justice*), 216,000 (*Socialist Legality*), and 35,000 (*Soviet State and Law*), which run regular columns to guide lecturers and discuss frequently asked questions on crime prevention and on various rights and duties under the law. Youth comes in for special attention as elective courses on law are developed for students down to the eighth grade and in vocational schools.[159]

Extracurricular Schools of the Young Lawyer, sponsored by law faculties and *Znanie,* mix films, excursions, court visits, lectures, and essay competitions. Sample questions might include: "By what juridical act was the formation of the USSR confirmed? What forms of legal influence are applied against violators of public order? How would you act if somebody in your social gathering started a fight? What would you do if a friend committed a crime and brought the stolen goods to the home of one of your other friends?"

A School of the Young Lawyer under the Moscow Palace of Pioneers and Schoolchildren, has its academic part run by the Institute of Crime Study and Prevention of the USSR Procuracy, a one-year course for students in grades eight–ten (secondary school is ten grades in the USSR starting at age seven). The program of the school gives a flavor of what the regime is trying to put across, and how:

1. "The jurist, who is he?" (meeting with jurists—scholars and practitioners).
2. "I am a citizen of the Soviet Union" (meeting with journalists, people who have become Soviet citizens, and officials responsible for formalizing citizenship).
3. "The right to work and obligations of the toilers" (meeting with veteran workers, movie).

4. "Law and the family" (lecture and seminar on questions of marriage and the family, duties and rights of spouses, obligations in raising children, obligations of children toward their parents).
5. "Civil law and the citizen" (meeting with jurists, showing and discussion of movies).
6. "Conscience and the law" (discussion on the question: May an action, though legal, be immoral? Is law always just? Leninist principles of socialist morality).
7. "The law protects nature" (meeting with experts, showing of documentary films).
8. "Space and the law" (meeting with experts on international and space law, with cosmonauts, portions of movies).
9. "Law protects the person" (lecture and seminar).
10. "Soviet law in the defense of peace and humanity" (meeting with participants in the Nuremberg trial, Chekists).
11. "Socialist property is sacred and inviolable" (meeting with officials of the Department of Combatting Thefts of Socialist Property, portions of movies).
12. "The fight against lawbreaking is our common cause" (meeting with officials of the militia, People's Guards, portions of movies).
13. "Able to enforce the law" (meeting with officials of the court, Procuracy, People's Control, Executive Committee of the Soviet).
14. "Science in the struggle with crime" (meeting with criminalists and other experts, investigators, detectives).
15. Concluding meeting (summing up results, awarding certificates of completing the school).[160]

As one of its sponsors views the campaign for mass legal education in the Soviet Union, it is not simply a step up in the number of lectures, articles, and so on, but a program of "universal national legal education, of a qualitatively new approach to forming legal consciousness of all Soviet groups and strata, of protracted, systematic work, based on the findings of science." Under the "directing influence" of party organizations, that use of science is to uncover the key to unlocking the public consciousness.

The third pillar of the campaign is studying public opinion so as more effectively to mold the "new Soviet man." After the twenty-fourth Party Congress and the ensuing decree of the Central Committee of the CPSU "On Ways to Improve the Legal Education of the Working People," special sections for related research appeared in the All-Union Scientific Research Institute of Soviet Legislation (under the Ministry of Justice), the All-Union Institute of Crime Study and Prevention (under the Procuracy) and the Institute of State and Law (of the Academy of Sciences).[161]

There is a long way to go. Less scientific studies of public opinion show that much. Stores operate under the control of fourteen public organizations containing several million people. But only a little over 6 percent of criminal cases originate in "signals" from the public.[162] One study showed that only 15 percent of persons apprehended for petty pilfering of state and public property were detained on the spot by management or people's guards; the others were uncovered by MVD operatives.[163]

Still reports come in of comrades' courts meeting regularly to try drunkards, while their shiftmates watch genially, even sympathetically. Nobody seems yet to have stopped the loss of time due to slackers who gossip for a half an hour before turning to work or fail to deliver parts and blueprints to machinists.[164]

The trade union has organized 10,000 social-legal consultations in 3,500 enterprises as they look for a way to reshape deviant informal associations where "instead of severe public condemnation of drunks, absentees, loafers, sometimes one finds good natured indulgence," and rowdies carrying on without the various penalties in pay and vacation passes.[165]

The Coordinating-Methodological Council of Legal Education in a rural area of Tambov Province consists of thirteen soviet, party, judicial, and prosecutorial officials. It conducted a poll of grades eight–ten and found extensive indifference to and ignorance of the Soviet legal order:

31 percent know what petty hooliganism is
13.9 percent know which agencies are specially authorized to fight crime
34.2 percent know which public organizations are supposed to prevent crime.

As a stopgap, visits of lawyers (social legal counselors) are being arranged so that people on collective and state farms may receive legal assistance. *Znanie* is setting up lectures. Competitions proceed for the title of "Village of Exemplary Public Order." [166]

The public's scant legal consciousness prompted this mass campaign. Is it promising? The first pillar of success, I said, is that officials should set a good example of legality. Soviet problems with official corruption aired in these chapters could well undo the effects of thousands of lectures about law and order. The former chairman of *Znanie's* legal section in the Sverdlov and Vasilevostrov boroughs of Leningrad and a practicing attorney in the Leningrad bar for twenty-five years concludes from his experience in the mass legal education drive that "this campaign has more propagandistic than real effect." [167] The campaign outruns all apparent means of measuring its success or failure. Secrecy and sensitivity over crime rates shroud the results. In any event, the results will be hard to estimate.

Recentralizing Law Enforcement and Justice

Harsher penalties and popularization of crime fighting began before Brezhnev. Recentralization is but a return to structures dismantled under Khrushchev. It marks the reappearance of powerful Union republic agencies of police and justice (USSR ministries with branch ministries in the Union republics are accountable to both republic and central governments), alongside republic and all-Union agencies.

1. *Republic agencies.* People's courts of boroughs, towns and rural districts try 98 percent of criminal cases and 99 percent of civil cases.[168] State crimes, economic crimes, murder, and aggravated rape cases go to middle-level courts of provinces, territories, autonomous republics, and cities, or to republic supreme courts. The latter try cases only of exceptional importance or complexity, and they hear appeals and protests from decisions of the middle-level courts or, where no provincial subdivisions exist, as, say, in Estonia, then directly from the people's courts. Appeals are by parties to a still open case. Protests, by the Procuracy or court chairman, reopen completed cases. This makes possible double jeopardy but also unexpected vindication.[169]

Among the principles of Soviet justice, such as public participation, publicity, equality before the law, and collegiality of the bench, the most crucial politically is "the independence of judges and their subordination only to law." [170] As in jurisdictions worldwide, this principle evokes the ongoing and unavoidable conflict between judicial autonomy and outside influence, especially, but not only, in political cases.[171] Cleaning up after Stalin, the Party Central Committee warned local party organs to stop violating the constitutional principle of judicial independence, to stop interfering with the courts.[172] Interference in specific decisions in non-political cases is generally ruled out. Guidance over court practice is not.

> Guidance by the Communist Party surpasses all political and judicial means of assuring that the courts observe socialist legality in their actions. . . . The task of the local Party organization is, while not interfering in the judicial process, actively to influence courts to improve their work, to instill in officers of the court a high sense of responsibility, to take steps to strengthen discipline, fulfill Party and government decisions.[173]

It is not unusual for local party committees to form inter-agency administrative committees in party organizations, bringing together Communists from the courts, Procuracy, militia, and the KGB to coordinate law enforcement.[174] People's court judges are popularly elected for five-year terms and people's assessors, for two years. The Party takes much care in guiding election of the judges and people's assessors (in practice screening one candidate for each post).[175]

Political influence over court practice is heightened because the people's assessors replace the juries introduced for more serious nonpolitical cases under the 1864 reform. Juries exercised in their decisions "a certain portion of the legislative power of which the people as a whole was deprived."[176] On the other hand, party control is undermined by "family groupings"—cliques of local officials.[177]

2. *All-Union agencies. Organs of state security* have had their wings clipped. Their in-house recruiter for the labor camps, the Special Board, went in 1953.[178] Labor camp administration lodges not in the KGB but in the MVD. But, given the KGB's role investigating and repressing dissidence,[179] one may presume a powerful KGB (Committee of State Security) presence in the camps. Since 1958 ordinary crimes are more clearly distinguished from political ones. Party leadership is a coalition wherein the KGB chairman, Andropov, became a full member of the Politburo in 1973, and the military, once burned by the secret police, sat watchfully in the Politburo too.

The Procuracy has functioned, since its emergence in final form by 1936, as a separate centralized guardian of legality, charged with prosecutions and, under Article 113 of the USSR Constitution, with "supreme supervision over the precise obedience of laws by all ministries and agencies under them, all officials and citizens of the USSR."[180] In its centralization, the Procuracy harks back to the Procuracy set up by Peter the Great in 1722 and operating until the Judicial Reform of 1864.[181] Procuratorial intervention in criminal justice seems confined largely to nonpolitical cases. Much of our information on abuses of the 1966 campaign and commitment to compulsory medical treatment of alcoholics and addicts, for example, came from the work of the Procuracy. It has been known to intervene in at least one case of criminal significance—to free Andrei Amalrik from the remainder of his work-exile sentence as a "parasite."[182] But it should not be expected to take an independent stand in political justice. Prosecutors seldom do anywhere, unless endowed with special authority or character and in the Soviet system the Procuracy, "like all state organs in the USSR, acts under the guidance of the Party, fulfilling its directives."[183]

The USSR Supreme Court sits rarely in original jurisdiction. It heard only three cases of first instance in fifteen years: the espionage trial of U-2 pilot Francis Gary Powers in 1960,[184] the espionage trial of Soviet citizen Oleg V. Penkovskii in 1963,[185] and the trial in 1974 for violation of safety regulations by those held responsible for the terrible explosion in the TV cabinet shop of the Minsk radio plant.[186]

The USSR Supreme Court had a mouthpiece reputation during past show trials. It has no right of judicial review. Given the central controls through Party, Procuracy, Ministry of Justice, and KGB, its role might seem negligible. But the USSR Supreme Court is also an enforcer of more uniform and predictable justice. And, as touched on later, the court is a central clearing house of legal opinion and a channel of influence from the legal profession.

Sitting in plenary session, the Supreme Court consists of its chairman, vice chairman, member judges from the civil, criminal, and military benches, and the chairmen of the supreme courts of the Union republics, *ex-officio*. The Procurator General must attend, and the Minister of Justice usually does, along with other visitors such as chairmen of some provincial or city courts. The Plenary session, or plenum, hears protests of the chairmen or Procurator General against directives of Union republic supreme courts to the lower courts, on the basis that they contravene all-Union legislation or harm the interests of other Union republics.

The plenum hear also protests of the chairman, deputy chairmen, or Procurator General against Union republic supreme court decisions in specific cases, as well as protests against decisions of the USSR Supreme Court Benches. Finally, the plenum hears reports about court practice in the Union republics, and issues decrees, called "Guiding Clarifications," to correct court practice.[187]

Its plenum's Guiding Clarifications are the USSR Supreme Court's highest ranked signal to lower courts. Some explain the implications of important turnabouts such as the decrees of May 14, July 31, and December 3, 1962, instituting a series of harsher criminal penalties. The import of the decrees: courts were "to combine severe measures of punishment provided by law for dangerous criminals with measures of social influence for less serious first time offenders."[188]

Guiding Clarifications frequently tell the courts how to apply a given edict, with prominent examples of cautions against excesses, as in court decrees in the wake of the antihooliganism edicts of 1966, or the edict of June 12, 1970, "on suspended sentence with obligatory recruitment to work,"[189] where the Supreme Court ordered people's courts not to send into work exile persons who otherwise would receive simply suspended sentence, fine, or corrective labor: pregnant women, women with children up to two years old, women over fifty-four and men over fifty-nine, disabled persons or persons already convicted but whose conviction later was expunged. During the unfavorable reaction of many jurists to antiparasite laws in 1957–1965, the USSR Supreme Court investigated antiparasite proceedings and helped bring them closer to regular trial guarantees.[190] The USSR Supreme Court is not supposed to be a source of law.

But it frequently interprets existing points of law which create difficulties for court practice, for example, the tricky question of what use of force exceeds "necessary self-defense," or what is assault, hooliganism or homicide.[191]

A recent *Bulletin* of the USSR Supreme Court informed its 87,500 subscribers about, among other things, the decisions on court practice in criminal cases adopted after reports and discussion at the latest week-long plenum. Guiding Clarifications covered court practice in cases involving enticing juveniles to commit crime, applying the edict of June 12, 1970 "On Suspended Sentence with Obligatory Recruitment to Work," on thefts of state and public property, and on infecting with venereal disease.

The bulletin contained review articles on court practice in violations of work safety rules and on the Seventh International Congress of Criminologists.

The same issue of the bulletin printed directives (*opredeleniya*) of the Criminal Bench based on specific cases. A directive of July 9, 1973, in the case of M.A. Lavrent'ev, came nearly six years after a decision of the Kirgiz Supreme Court Criminal Bench sentenced Lavrent'ev to 15 years for intentional homicide out of hooliganist motivations. The directive pointed out that Lavrent'ev was awakened in the night by outside noise, his dog barking and stones being thrown into his garden. He fired a warning shot in the air, at which time someone knocked the gate open and shouted "Come out" followed by some foul language. Scared, Lavrent'ev fired a second shot toward the gate and killed one of two rowdies, both of whom had been intoxicated. Because the victim's "improper actions" provided some motivation, the homicide, though ruled intentional, should not, the court said, be treated as a motiveless manifestation of sheer hooliganism. It lowered the sentence from fifteen to ten years.[192]

The USSR Supreme Court combines the British role of "mouthpiece of the law" with the specifically Soviet role of being, as Lenin put it, a "lever" or "transmission belt" of party policy.

3. *Union republic agencies.* The years 1954 to 1963 brought some decentralization of appeals and administration. Ministerial management of the courts ended with the abolition of the USSR Ministry of Justice in 1956 and republic ministries of justice in 1956–1963. Autonomy and status of the courts was further boosted by the elimination of all-Union agencies like the special boards of the secret police and the railroad and shipping courts.

After the abolition of the USSR Ministry of Justice in 1956 and the USSR MVD in 1962, no Union republic law enforcement agencies existed. Their return marked a reinforcement of centralized administrative over justice and a partial reversal of the decentralizing measures of 1954 to 1963. It is probably no coincidence that each ministry reappeared at a time of exasperation with lawbreaking. The USSR MVD was reestablished during the 1966 drive for public order. Its main preoccupation is law enforcement, but it also administers mapmaking and firefighting, penal institutions, and convoy and security troops.

First named the USSR Ministry for the Preservation of Public Order, like its existing branch ministries in the Union republics, it was renamed the USSR MVD in 1968 during an upgrading of operations, training, and equipment.[193] From then on the militia (the ordinary police under the MVD) was supposed to recruit heavily from working people's collectives, with the participation of trade union and Party and Komsomol organizations. Party and Komsomol officials moved laterally into high posts in the militia and parent ministries of the interior.[194]

The militia operates through a patrol service of uniformed police, a Department for Combatting Theft of Socialist Property, and a Criminal Investigation Department.[195] The great increases in its power began with the administration of the antiparasite laws in 1957–1961, then a new right to conduct pretrial investigations in 1963.[196] New responsibilities to fine drunkards, maintain administrative supervision over released and paroled convicts, and process hooligans came in 1966. Other penalties and restrictions later—for example, on liquor sales in 1970–1972—further added to the powers (and headaches) of the militia, and the channels of recruitment into the labor colonies run by another part of the MVD. In late 1969, concerned by a drop in industrial growth and labor productivity, Brezhnev and the Party started yet another campaign, this time against slackness and indiscipline, drunkenness, economic crimes, and pilfering in production,[197] with some of the penalties already noted. Pressure mounted on law enforcement and some allegedly lax MVD officials lost their jobs.[198]

As a result of its added duties, the MVD's operatives now have powers to fine offenders on the spot or at the precinct house; conduct administrative supervision over released convicts and exiles; uncover and warn parasites and vagrants; run jails, the internal passport system, and the external passport and visa system; issue residence permits; operate reception lockups for derelicts and beggars before sending them to trial or to homes for the aged;[199] and maintain sobering-up stations. The MVD itself, as we shall see, has played an active role in crime research, as well as in correctional policy generally.

There have been some signs of interservice rivalry between the militia, on the one hand, and the KGB and Procuracy, on the other. The militia operated with surprising autonomy under N.A. Shchelokov, a former party colleague of Brezhnev and not a policeman.[200] Thus the Procuracy, supposedly the legal watchdog over all agencies including the police, has experienced difficulties in obtaining case materials from the militia's Criminal Investigation Department at the local level, even while

MVD investigators in the same ministry easily obtained these materials. Prosecutors have found it imposisble sometimes to verify whether steps they recommended to the Criminal Investigation Department have been carried out, and hardly less difficult to discover and prevent illegal means of keeping down crime statistics such as lumping several complaints under one investigation.[201] Law enforcement is as centralized and politically directed as ever, but far from monolithic.

The USSR Ministry of Justice was abolished in 1956 and ministries of justice of the Union republics were also abolished in 1956–1963. Supervision of colleges of advocates and legislative drafting was taken over by restoration of the USSR and Union republic ministries of justice. The given increased supervisory powers in 1967.[203] During the crackdown on indiscipline and thefts of socialist property beginning in 1969–1970, the authorities found that "there is still not a sufficiently energetic struggle against crimes such as theft of state and public property and crimes against public order, and several other crimes." [204] Complaints abounded about deficient courts. The courts failed to analyze crimes and their causes. They conducted clumsy and counterproductive visiting sessions. They neglected comrades' courts and people's detachments. They only feebly propagandized legal knowledge. They shrugged off citizens' grievances.

Such complaints built up to the decree of the Party Central Committee and USSR Council of Ministers of July 30, 1970, on measures to improve the work of the courts and the Procuracy. The decree ordered restoration of the USSR and Union republic ministries of justice. The restored Ministry of Justice regained supervision of court staffing and operations, judges' conduct in court, budgeting, colleges of advocates, legislative drafting services, and the campaign for mass legal education.[205]

Court structure returned to its Stalinist form. But the extrajudicial secret police special boards and the special railroad and shipping courts had been abolished. The political context of justice changed from one of mass terror and legalism to a much more complex mix of policies and trends.

Reforming and Hardening Confinement

Creating the USSR MVD tightened central control over the elaborate Soviet system of restraints on deviant persons. As executors of punishment and parole procedures, the USSR MVD and the MVDs of the Union republics, along with their regional administrations of justice in the local soviets, had charge of:

I. Militia supervision of exile and banishment. Exile is expulsion to a place; banishment is expulsion from a place or places. Exile and banishment are eliminated for juveniles. The militia also supervises parolees and certain other prisoners released from confinement.

II. Noncorrectional places of detention.
   1. Cells for temporary detention in police (militia) stations.
   2. Houses of detention during investigation and trial and the wait for transfer.
   3. Military brigs and stockades.
   4. Transit prisons.

III. Corrective labor institutions.
   Corrective labor institutions operate under GULAG's successor, GUITU, the Chief Administration of Corrective Labor Institutions of the MVD.
   1. Educational labor colonies (VTKs) for juveniles 14 through 17 years old.
   2. Corrective labor colonies (ITKs) for adults over seventeen. First offenders convicted of less serious crimes go to colonies of ordinary regime. Depending on the number and seriousness of previous convictions, the rest of the convicts sent to colonies go to colonies of increasingly rigorous regimes: colonies of firm regime, colonies of strict regime (where political prisoners convicted of serious state crimes usually go, in zones apart from ordinary criminals), and colonies of special regime. Women serve out their sentences only in colonies of ordinary or strict regime. The more severe the regime, the lower the food rations, maximum allowable purchase of food from the commissary, visit and mail privileges, and the harder the work.
   3. Prisons are the most severe form of confinement. They hold a small percentage of adult prisoners. Prisoners receive less food and fewer mail, visit, and food purchase privileges than do the colony inmates. As in colonies of special regime, prisoners are housed in cells. There are two regimes, both considered more severe than in colonies: ordinary and strict. Prisoners are sent from colonies to prisons as punishment for indiscipline. Also, one may serve all or part of one's regular sentence in prison.
   4. Colony settlements have operated since 1963. Open residential and work areas, nonpenal in appearance, colony settlements are intended to adapt long-term but reformed prisoners to life as free persons. A colony settler works under normal wage and union guarantees and may have his family with him.[206]

Pardons, rehabilitations, and the end of police justice, summary proceedings, and mass purges drastically reduced the Soviet prison population and shrank GULAG's camp empire after Stalin. But Soviet prisoners of all kinds still number at least 1 million by minimum, conservative estimates. The total prisoner population could run as high as 1.5 million or more. Somewhere in the order of 10,000 of these are political prisoners, or what Amnesty International calls "prisoners of conscience" because they are nonviolent nonconformists sentenced for their political, cultural, ethnic, or religious dissidence. Though this number of political prisoners seems high, it is nowhere near the top of the world list in per capita terms.[207] Using a minimum estimate of 1 million Soviet prisoners, one discovers, as shown in Table 4–1, a relatively high ratio of prisoners to population in the USSR. The prisoner-to-population ratio is roughly two or three times higher in the Soviet Union than it is in the United States and roughly eight to fourteen times higher in the Soviet Union than it is in Sweden.

Post-Stalin reforms restored a significant differentiation between colonies for juveniles and colonies for adults. They annulled, too, other Stalinist revisions from the years 1935–1941 which had virtually eliminated differential treatment of juveniles.[208] Soviet statutes and legal codes between 1953 and 1969, already reviewed, appeared to create new safeguards for the protection of prisoners' rights against arbitrary acts by police and correctional officials. The anti-crime drive of 1966 produced a USSR MVD to give nationally centralized control of correctional institu-

Table 4–1. Estimated Prisoners, Population, and Prisoners per 10,000 Population (USSR, U.S., and Sweden, 1970s)

	(1) USSR (1975)	(2) U.S. (1970)	(3) SWEDEN (1975)
Prisoners, all facilities	1–1.5 mln.	0.37 mln.	3.700
Population	253.3 mln.	204.9 mln.	8.17 mln.
Prisoners/10,000 inhab. (estimated)	40–60	18	4.5

Sources:

(1) Amnesty International, *Prisoners of Conscience in the USSR: Their Treatment and Conditions* (London: Amnesty International Publications, 1975), pp. 51, 53; Andrei Sakharov, *My Country and the World* (New York: Vintage Books, 1975), p. 12, lists 1.5 million while Amnesty International estimates 1 million min. *SSSR v tsifrakh v 1974 godu* (Moscow: Statistika, 1975), p. 7.

(2) U.S. Department of Justice. Law Enforcement Assistance Administration, *National Jail Census 1970* (Washington, D.C.: U.S. Government Printing Office, 1970), p. 1; Congressional Quarterly Service, *Crime and the Law* (Washington, D.C.: Congressional Quarterly Service, 1971), p. 11.

(3) Tom Wicker, "Judging the Judges," *New York Times*, February 6, 1976; *Encyclopedia Britannica Book of the Year, 1975,* p. 648; *Narodnoe khozyaistvo SSSR v 1973 godu* (Moscow: "Statistika," 1974), p. 803 (1975 population is estimated).

tions. Soviet jurists told an Amnesty International delegation that the first national Soviet corrective labor statute, the Fundamentals of Corrective Labor Legislation of the USSR and the Union Republics of 1969, included guarantees of prisoners' rights going beyond the United Nations standard minimum rules for the treatment of prisoners. These rights were spelled out even more explicitly in the Corrective Labor Codes of the Union republics.[209] If so, then Soviet corrections had moved closer to and even surpassed many Western correction policies in attention to prisoners' rights and humane treatment. But de-Stalinization in corrections turned out by the mid-seventies to be apparent as well as real. An irrefutably consistent flood of prisoners' statements and *samizdat* reports point to severe setbacks in correctional reform, even retrogression, during the 1960s and 1970s.[210]

Article 1 of the Fundamentals of Corrective Labor Legislation and of the Corrective Labor Codes based on it states that "the execution of punishment does not aim at inflicting physical suffering or degrading human dignity." Suffering and degradation are not the stated *aim* of punishment in the USSR. But nowhere do the codes rule out suffering and degradation as a *means* to deterrence, reform, and correctional discipline. Hunger and faulty medical care stand out among all the complaints of prisoners and are signs of suffering inflicted as fundamental policy.

There is more than probable cause to believe that Soviet codes and regulations institutionalize hunger as the main way to pressure, control, and punish prisoners. MVD regulations set diets meaning creeping malnutrition even in the mildest regime colonies. The available food is deficient in vitamins, minerals, and calories. This is true even counting allowances of food parcels and food purchases. In prisons—and, even more, in PKTs (punishment cells) and SHIZOs (punishment isolators)—diets mean various speeds of starvation.[211] Amnesty International concludes, from data covering the sixties and mid-seventies, that

> not only the law itself but governmental decrees and the policy of colony and prison administrations ensure that prisoners remain hungry as a basic condition of their imprisonment. Though not acknowledged formally, the punitive intention of this policy has been affirmed orally many times by officials. For example, when the Ukrainian prisoner Valentyn Moroz complained to the deputy procurator of the Mordovian camp administration that prisoners seriously ill with stomach ulcers were being kept on a starvation diet, the offical replied: "That's just what the punishment consists of—hitting the stomach." [212]

Hunger, bad food, heavy labor, and cold turn some prisoners into invalids. But medical care for them is so bad that, according to one *samizdat* report from the Perm region, "many sick prisoners who are in serious condition do not want to go to the hospital." Reports multiplied in the 1970s of incompetent or willfully negligent care and the lack of medicines. A 1966 regulation barred the import of medicines into labor colonies even when a prisoner's life might depend on it. Other reports told of permanent physical damage, loss of limbs, and deaths needlessly inflicted by indifference and neglect or even flashes of cruel hostility on the part of some MVD medical staff.[213]

At the time of publication of this work, procuratorial supervision and the public observation commissions give little or no protection to prisoners' rights. Prisoners' regimes are changed without court order. The withholding of privileges, like visits, sometimes takes the form of humiliating and costly refusals after a spouse or relative has arrived at camp after a long journey. The vague wording of codes leaves details of food and medical care up to the MVD and camp administrations to set by regulation. The MVD perpetuates countless abuses either by omission, leaving local authorities with a free hand, or commission. It issues a number of unpublished administrative regulations or instructions. They tend to circumvent the already shaky Corrective Labor Codes. History repeated itself after Stalin as before him. Codes were rendered increasingly inoperative by such instructions.

Secret instructions appear to have worsened conditions for prisoners in 1960–1961 under Khrushchev and in 1966–1972 under Brezhnev.[214] This may have had something to do with Khrushchev's campaigns against economic and other "especially dangerous crimes" in the early 1960s and Brezhnev's conflicts with dissidents beginning in the mid-1960s. The MVD Instruction No. 020 of January 14, 1972, and ensuing regulations increased maximum possible confinement in SHIZOs (punishment isolators) beyond the existing fifteen-day limit; restricted the types of food prisoners may purchase in their places of confinement; added grounds for censoring mail; reduced the number of books permitted a prisoner to five, secretly ordered suppliers of Soviet books and periodicals not to send them to prisoners; mandate the wearing of surname and serial number on prisoners' clothing; required new respectful salutations:

> When meeting a member of the camp personnel or other person visiting the camp in an official capacity the convict must greet them by standing up and, in the warm seasons of the year, taking off his cap. The convict must use the polite form of address to the camp personnel and call them "citizen" or "citizeness" followed by their rank and official position.[215]

A Russian republic decree issued also in 1972, shortly before MVD Instruction No. 020, put new limits on the kinds of food which may be taken into corrective labor institutions. This worsened the rigors of the hunger regimes and occasioned humiliating body search procedures for wives and other visitors.[216]

Correctional reforms, then, ended some abuses but left survivals of others within or without the framework of "socialist legality." Hunger, cold, faulty medical care, and discrimination against cultural and religious dissidents in favor of compliant former Nazi collaborators and common criminals remained hallmarks of Soviet correctional policy in the 1970s. It anything, conditions worsened in 1972.

Some suffering and degradation inflicted on Soviet prisoners calls to mind similar practices in U.S. prisons. I am referring to the "adjustment centers" and other coercive U.S. means of controlling defiant prisoners. They parallel Soviet SHIZOs and the psychiatric prison hospitals I shall discuss shortly. I refer also to prisoner informers and provocateurs, exploitation of prison labor, and correctional officers' punishment of self-assertion and rewarding of subservience among prisoners. Correctional institutions in the United States tend less to build in cold and hunger deliberately than Soviet correctional institutions do. But the U.S. lockups abound in other hazards, including those of homosexual assault. Poor and minority prisoners are likely now to be at the center of articulate prisoner resistance in the United States. Cultural and national minority dissidents from the intelligentsia are more likely to be at the center of prisoner resistance in the Soviet Union. A strong criminal subculture persists in the correctional institutions of both countries. Sometimes the criminal subculture sucks in and corrupts the guards.

U.S. prison medical care leaves something to be desired. But the worst medical abuses today seem to be those perpetrated on willing victims, prisoner volunteers in drug-testing experiments. According to the summarized testimony of the president of the Pharmaceutical Manufacturers Association, "eighty-five percent of the initial tests on people to determine the effects of new prescription drugs are made on prisoners." Safeguards for the prisoner subjects are inadequate. As a result there are relatively high rates of painful side effects, permanent injury, and death among the prison volunteers. Their pay is low and the doctors conducting the experiments and the drug companies whose products are tested reap handsome profits from such procedures.

A special problem for U.S. prisoners in some states is the practice of giving indeterminate sentences. Indeterminate sentences are under fire and may be on their way out. Soviet correctional institutions discriminate against political prisoners and house them in facilities of relatively severe regimes when they are convicted of serious state crimes. U.S. correctional institutions tend to house political prisoners in facilities of less severe regime and to discriminate against poor and minority prisoners.

Soviet courts support rather than limit Soviet correctional authorities. U.S. courts since the 1960s have begun to intervene extensively on behalf of prisoners' rights and prison reform.[217] Reform is underway in the Soviet Union as well.

A loose, uncoordinated prison reform movement has emerged in the USSR. The rudimentary movement, though barely more than a tendency in opinion, would have been impossible under the old terror. Waves of arrests in the 1960s and 1970s put thousands of outspoken dissidents (*inakomyslyashchie*) into the Soviet system of labor colonies and prisons. But the regime putting the dissidents away was not so repressive as to block the writing and circulation of prisoners' memoirs, diaries, reports, and petitions. *Samizdat* picked them up and spread their texts at home and abroad. An inhibited but persistent above-ground wing of the reform movement consists of critics among jurists and officials. It operates within the bounds of party tolerance. Foreign petitions and criticism support the underground and above-ground wings of the prison reform movement within the USSR. Perhaps one day pressures from below and above ground will prompt a new Soviet leadership team to reinterpret socialist legality and "socialist humanism." Perhaps these pressures will persuade an eventual Soviet leadership to reduce or eliminate the "degradation and suffering" which are not supposed to be the aim of Soviet corrections although they are an integral part of those corrections. This will require overcoming the biggest obstacle of all, the resistance of MVD and KGB functionaries and their "inertia of style."[218]

Codes of Soviet justice today also embody the principle of Western legal systems: punishment shall be for no crimes except those specified by law and shall be applied in no way except by sentence of court. Soviet justice has its own particular—and familiar—ways of departing from this principle in political cases. An unrecanting dissident, though non-violent, may be framed with charges of a common crime like hooliganism or parasitism.[219] Drug offenses and assaults on prison guards (who provoked them in the first place, if they occurred at all) provide convenient grounds for a frameup in the U.S. context. Witness these cases of "prisoners of conscience" adopted by Amnesty International. Martin Sostre, U.S. ex-convict and militant, owned a radical bookstore. His part in protest was interrupted by a charge of a fifteen-dollar drug transaction, for which he was put away for thirty–forty years. Intercession by Amnesty International, Andrei Sakharov from the USSR (his human rights advocacy is not confined to Soviet victims of arbitrariness), and other prominent people prompted New York State Governor Carey to pardon Sostre on Christmas Day, 1975, after he had spent twenty of the last twenty-three years of his life in jails, seven of them under a charge in which, according to Amnesty International, Sostre "was falsely implicated because of his political activities."[220] An active protester in prison, Sostre spent four of his years there in solitary confinement and sustained many beatings.[221] Soviet citizen Alexander Feldman, a Ukrainian Jew and a stoker by trade, had his emigration blocked because, authorities said, Feldman knew "military secrets" from his service four years earlier. Police harassment after his emigration application in 1972 was followed by three fifteen-day administrative sentences (probably for petty hooliganism or some such charge) during a time when he persisted in protesting and petitioning. He was tried and convicted, finally, of malicious hooliganism and sentenced to three and a half years' deprivation of freedom. Amnesty International concluded that Feldman's trial was a "frameup," accompanied, as in other cases of dissidents, by procedural lapses gravely prejudicial to the accused.[222]

Without resorting to charges of ordinary nonpolitical crime, there are many ways to apply Soviet criminal codes against nonviolent religious and cultural dissenters.[223] The Nobel Prize ceremonial provided a setting for Sakharov's protest against the political crimes prosecutions. They mean that

> in the Soviet Union today many thousands of people are persecuted because of their convictions, both by judicial and nonjudicial organs, for the sake of their religious beliefs and for their desire to bring up their children in the spirit of religion, for reading and disseminating, often only to a few acquaintances, literature that is unwelcome to the state . . . and for attempts to leave the country.[224]

Compared with the millions of victims in the old days, criminal charges against religious sectarians, national minority activists, litterateurs, human rights advocates, and extreme right Russian chauvinists today produce only thousands of victims. At least Madam Sakharov could get to Oslo to read her husband's Nobel Prize address. Foreign Communists now condemn Soviet repression from time to time. Soviet responses, from releasing prisoners to touchy editorial articles, show a sensitivity to foreign opinion. Criminal punishment may no longer be meted out unless cases go to court. The court hearings, even when illegally closed, provide an occasion for some publicity.[225]

Confining dissidents in psychiatric prison hospitals reentered Soviet practice about 1961 as an alternative to criminal punishment.

Any defiance of authority might bring commitment as insane. The offending behavior did not have to be religious, cultural, or political dissent. Nondissidents could be committed psychiatrically for confronting authority by refusing an investigator's demand to corroborate a murder charge against his friend by false testimony, or by making a fuss when petitioning at government or party reception offices.[226]

Dissidents, however, provided most of the tens or hundreds of recruits for psychiatric hospitals. There are worse and larger scale infringements of human rights in the world—sometimes in Western-supported countries of the "free world" as torture surveys show.[227] Still, the practice of confining dissidents in psychiatric hospitals poses serious human rights issues, to say nothing of the suffering inflicted on those committed. Such "compulsory psychiatric treatments" could make for telling comparisons of how law and medicine may be put to repressive purposes in various countries.[228] The treatments continue at the time of writing so I shall use the present tense. But, given the attacks on such treatments from inside and outside the USSR, they may conceivably be called off for use against dissidents within the next few months or years.

One is committed to compulsory psychiatric treatment in the USSR by civil procedure, juridical procedure (more common), and juridical procedure along with transfer from a correctional institution. Civil commitment rests on unpublished 1961 USSR Ministry of Health directives. Desiring to dispense with criminal indictment, the KGB then informs a local health agency that it holds an apparently mentally ill suspect, or has one under investigation. The health agency sends a psychiatrist to examine the suspect at home, work, or in detention. If the psychiatrist finds the suspect constitutes "a clear danger to those around him or to himself" under the 1961 directives, "the health organs have the right (by way of immediate psychiatric assistance) to place him in a psychiatric hospital without the consent of the person who is ill or his relatives or guardians." [229] This doctor's order must be confirmed by a panel of three psychiatrists within twenty-four hours of the suspect's arrival at the psychiatric institution,[230] and his closest relatives informed of his hospitalization.[231] Vague criteria for finding "social danger" include "hypochondriacal delusional conditions causing an irregular and aggressive attitude in the patient." Doctors' leeway for cooperating with investigative organs is broadened by clauses in the directive to the effect that "morbid conditions" such as these may be covered up by "externally correct behavior and dissimulation." Also, the directives say, its list of "immediate indications for hospitalization" is not exhaustive.[232]

Court commitment of the insane to compulsory treatment instead of punishment provides a humane alternative urged in their time by psychiatrists of many countries including Russia's Bekhterev and Serbskii. Ironically, it is the Institute of Forensic Psychiatry named after Serbskii which has headed the use of psychiatric commitment procedures, civil and juridical, in violation of humanism and human rights.[233]

Declaring dissidents insane rather than trying them, subjects of such commitment say, has several advantages. Psychiatric commitment

> conveniently enables the authorities to deprive persons of their freedom for an unlimited length of time, keep them in strict isolation, and use psychopharmacological means of "reeducation." It hampers the struggle for open court proceedings [committal hearings are closed and without the suspect present, though his counsel may participate —P.J.], and for such persons' release since even the most objective persons will, if not personally acquainted with such a patient, always have doubts about the patient's mental health; it deprives the victims of those few rights a prisoner enjoys, sets the stage for discrediting ideas and actions of dissidents and induces feelings of fear, dismay, hopeless powerlessness among dissidents.[234]

Soviet psychiatric confinement for political reasons dates back to the late 1930s.[235] An eminent committee of inquiry after Stalin confirmed the protests of a Central Committee official. But the commission report was shelved after minor changes. Moving the Serbskii Institute of Forensic Psychiatry from police jurisdiction to the Ministry of Health meant nothing. The veteran party official and war hero who initiated the 1955–1956 commission of inquiry found that "the principal officers of the institute from the personality cult era . . . stay on in their former jobs and assiduously continue the evil practices of that era." [236] These officers included as of the mid 1970s, Dr. G.V. Morozov, institute director, and Professor D.R. Lunts, prominent also in writing and commission psychiatric examinations related to the commitment of dissidents suffering from "creeping schizophrenia" and other forms of political psychopathology. Morozov, Lunts, and others appear to take their orders from the KGB. The hospitals to which they send dissidents are run by the MVD, virtually as prisons. The institute officials train young psychiatrists to carry on their work. No official concerned, within the institute or the Procuracy, has ever been punished for his part in the abuse of Soviet criminal law and medicine.[237]

After a lull of legality in the mid-1950s, psychiatric confinements of dissidents resumed under Khrushchev in 1961. That same year the new Russian republic Code of Criminal Procedure appeared, shorn of the old Article 148.[238] The old article had made it a crime to commit normal persons on false pretenses. By eliminating that article, the Soviet legislators of the new code at once removed the threat of penalty from psychiatrists cooperating with the KGB and Procuracy and ended court remedies for friends and relatives of the alleged insane, forcing them to go up the chain of command of the Ministry of Health.[239]

Psychiatric repression first came to public attention in the West through the confinement of writer Valery Tarsis.[240] According to his *Ward 7*, "there were neither patients nor doctors but only jailers in charge of inconvenient citizens" in the psychiatric wards and hospitals.[241] Commitment rates picked up in 1966 after the Daniel-Sinyavskii trial stirred up support for them. Commitment rates increased even more in 1969–1970 after a special order of March 15, 1969. It urged more use of the 1961 directive, "to prevent dangerous actions by mentally ill persons." Commitment, heretofore reactive, could now be preventive.[242] Either way it is covered formally by the codes of criminal procedure. They allow commitment either to an ordinary psychiatric hospital or to the prison psychiatric hospitals—"psychiatric hospitals of a special type"—run by the MVD.[243] Permissive though they are, even these regulations have been violated frequently.[244]

The third path to psychiatric hospitals leads also via court commitment, but from corrective labor institutions. Article 100 of the Corrective Labor Code permits release of seriously ill persons from criminal sentence. No dissident was known to have gained freedom this way as of the mid-1970s. Article 100 has been used, however, to transfer troublesome dissidents declared "mentally ill" to psychiatric prison hospitals.[245] Bad as labor colony conditions are, prisoners deem conditions in the psychiatric prison hospitals to be worse. Transfer there is used as a threat.[246] Prisoners most fear in the hospital routine the administration of strong chemicals causing pain, sickness, disorientation, and apparently permanent injury in some "patients." Also feared is confinement with the criminally insane, staff brutality, or any number of punishments such as being wrapped in wet canvas (which contracts painfully when drying) or being strapped to one's bed for several days without sanitary facilities.[247]

Major General P.G. Grigorenko was the much decorated head of the Department of Cybernetics of the Frunze Military Academy. His protests and organization of dissident groupings brought transfers and demotions. After he founded the "Union of the Struggle of the Revolution of Lenin," Grigorenko was arrested in 1964 on charges of anti-Soviet agitation. Rather than try Grigorenko, the authorities had him committed to psychiatric hospitals of the special type until his release in 1965. Also he was demoted to the ranks and expelled from the Party. Supporting the Crimean Tatar bid to return from exile to the Crimea ended for Grigorenko in 1969 with arrest and a charge of "disseminating fabrications known to be false which defame the Soviet state and social system."[248] A commission of psychiatrists in Tashkent found Grigorenko sane after a careful four-hour examination. (Not all psychiatrists cooperate with the police and prosecutors.) But an investigator may order as many examinations as he deems necessary and select the finding he wants.[249] Grigorenko was sent to Moscow. After Grigorenko had spent a few days at the Serbskii Institute, a panel, headed by the institute director Dr. Morozov, conducted a desultory twenty minute examination. The examining commission found Grigorenko insane. On the basis of its findings, the Tashkent City Court committed him. His counsel's vigorous appeal was denied by the Uzbek Supreme Court. Two unidentified visitors suggested to Grigorenko in the Chernyakhovsk special psychiatric hospital of the MVD that he change his views. He refused. His regime then worsened. After many appeals from inside and outside the USSR, and transfer to an ordinary psychiatric hopsital in September 1963, Grigorenko was released on June 26, 1974. He had been declared sane in May without renouncing his views. Grigorenko's pivotal case points up the schisms in the psychiatric profession over political psychiatric commitments. It points to the courage and possibilities of a spirited defense though the suspect is banned from the court hearing. The case also points to court complicity, veiled by the legal basis of an expert finding[250] of diseases like "creeping schizophrenia," "paranoid development of the personality," "reformist delusions," or "persecution mania." Serbskii Institute psychiatrists have linked political protest to mental illness. "Ideas of truth and justice," they write, "most frequently arise in personalities with a paranoid structure."[251]

Normal people are supposed to acquiesce, to conform to politically approved limits of criticism. It was not normal for Pyotr Grigorenko to be willing to give up his 800-ruble-a-month post at the Frunze Academy. What did he lack, a woman psychiatrist asked Grigorenko at his preliminary Serbskii Institute interview? "You won't understand—I couldn't breathe." At this answer, the examining psychiatrist was convinced "that before her sat a crazy lunatic. . . . It is only a person who bows submissively before any arbitrary act of the bureaucrats who is considered a normal Soviet person."[252] Only renouncing their views will bring dissidents their release, they are told.[253] But the leadership of the 1960s and 1970s bowed sometimes to pressure and released dissidents still silent or unrelenting.[254] The vigorous defenses by counsel and the balkiness of some psychiatric commissions are departures from an old conformity. Perhaps a future leadership will take the next step and end commitments for political reasons.

After all, there are means other than criminal punishment or psychiatric commitment available to use against dissidents and their supporters. The government is virtually the only employer. It is easy for the government "to put pressure on individuals who may be totally competent professionally but insufficiently 'loyal' in the view of some functionary or other."[255] Such deviant individuals may be fired. They may be prevented from finding anything but temporary physical labor. They or their children may be expelled from school.[256] A slight misstep may foreclose any travel abroad, no matter how valuable that travel might be for the specialist involved and for Soviet society.

When they abolished secret police tribunals, Soviet policy makers left themselves with a sharper issue of how and when to use the remaining means of penalizing dissent just reviewed: criminal trial, psychiatric commitment, and extrajudicial deprivations. Brezhnev's coalition continued and extended these three means of penalizing dissent. The regime's grip reached out to put dissident writers on trial. But political penalization touched thousands, not millions, as in Stalin's time. Though camp conditions were not appreciably better than they had been in 1953 when Stalin died, there were signs of concessions and wavering in camp[257] and out. The authorities released prisoners after pressures at home and abroad. Condemnation from foreign Communists in the West would have been inconceivable under Stalin's cult of personality. Balky psychiatric commissions found dissidents sane. Defense lawyers responded to Brezhnev's indictments often with spirited representation of their clients' interests despite the risks and frustrations. Limitations on a lawyer's fight for his client's rights and vindication occur somehow in many foreign jurisdictions. But it is the Soviet limitations and how they compare with Western legal systems that I shall use to close this chapter.

Comparisons and Conclusions

I

Defense lawyers practice not privately but through legal aid offices accountable administratively to regional and city colleges of advocates and the republic Ministry of Justice and accountable politically to the Party.[258] The administrative intervention and the open-ballot selection of collegium leadership erodes defense lawyers' autonomy.

> By depriving the profession of so elementary a principle of democracy as the secret ballot in election of the presidium of the defense counsels' collegium; by giving the executive committees [of soviets] the right to nullify the decisions made by the collegium presidiums and to present demands concerning the admission or expulsion of collegium members [an intervention now exercised by the Ministry of Justice —P.J.] thereby turning the defense counsel into a *chinovnik* [a low-level official or clerk in the bureaucracy —Transl.] —the new regulations adopted in some republics essentially hinder the defense from becoming an independent side in criminal proceedings.[259]

Defense lawyers are the most independent minded practitioners of the law. Many defense lawyers chaff at being *chinovniks*. Acting otherwise, though, in political cases brings the risk that the Party or KGB will demand their total disbarment, forced retirement, expulsion from the Party, or at least loss of clearance (*dopusk*) to participate in political and other sensitive cases.[260] Such clearance, duly formalized in a document, is not required by Soviet codes and not mentioned in commentary. The need for clearance contravenes the accused's right to choose a defense lawyer. An accused in Leningrad has the choice of 500 defense lawyers in ordinary criminal cases. In political cases that choice is narrowed to the twenty defense lawyers with clearance. Clearance used to be required under Stalin only in political cases or cases under special regime of secrecy. Other highly sensitive cases including those involving police officials' crimes in line of duty, did not require clearance. Defense lawyers have no access at all to cases tried in the unlisted special courts for persons doing secret work. State-paid attorneys conduct the defense in special courts.[261] Nor do defense lawyers have access to hearings in cases reopened upon protest, though half the changes or annulments of decisions by higher courts occur as a result of protest (by the Procuracy or higher court leaders).[262] In sum, a too vigorous defense can bring, at least, deprivation of the right to participate in the "big" cases—the political ones and the especially sensitive nonpolitical ones.

Even where clearance is not required, the defense lawyer is barred from participating in cases involving twenty-three articles of the criminal code, and crimes ranging from petty theft of state and public property and ordinary or malicious hooliganism to malicious refusal to obey assignments to work and to end a parasitic way of life. These are lesser crimes involving maximum penalties of up to five years' confinement. Criminal proceedings for prosecuting such crimes include only a police inquest (*doznanie*) and not a full-fledged pretrial investigation save where juveniles and incapacitated suspects are involved. Defense lawyers are barred from a *doznanie*. So in these *doznanie*-only cases, defense lawyers do not participate until the cases have been sent to court.[263]

A majority of crimes still involve pretrial investigations. Unlike the continental practice, Soviet investigators are not independent. They work under the supervision of the Procuracy, MVD, or KGB, depending on which agency receives jurisdiction.[264] As a result of a 1970 reform and a partial retraction of it in 1972: (1) defense lawyers *may* enter a case before the pretrial investigation if the prosecutor permits, a relatively rare occurrence; (2) participation of defense lawyers is obligatory in capital cases; (3) participation of defense lawyers is obligatory in cases where the accused does not speak the language of the proceedings (a 1972 provision replacing the 1970 rule that such accused may have counsel at the conclusion of the inquest, before the pretrial investigation).[265]

These rights to counsel may be vitiated. Investigators are known to have failed to explain to the accused their right to counsel. Sometimes investigators persuade the accused to agree that a defense lawyer is not necessary. Jurist critics find other evasions and legal loopholes in procedure. Investigators are known to abridge counsel's right to unlimited meetings with the accused, to careful study of case materials,[266] to appeal from investigator's denial of defense motions, to early admission in special cases (juveniles, etc.), and to deny counsel permission to participate actively in the very extra inquiries counsel initiated.[267]

Advance knowledge is an advantage in Soviet and continental criminal procedure. The accused and defense lawyer know ahead of the trial who will be the witnesses. They know what evidence will be used against them. Unlike witnesses, the accused may refuse to answer questions, though at risk this will count against him or her.[268] Because lawyers fees are low, and there are no private Soviet law firms, rich and poor clients have almost equal access to available legal talent. As for the little time the defense lawyer has to prepare the defense before trial, a part-time American public defender concludes that

> this is not very different from the situation in most offices of public advocacy [in the United States]. My experiences as a volunteer at the Philadelphia Public Defenders, which handles about 80 percent of the city's criminal defense work, brought me in contact with attorneys who, despite their participation from the outset of the investigations, were so overburdened as to be unable to provide an adequate defense.[269]

Once Soviet defense lawyers enter cases, they work in a context closer to that of continental than of Anglo-American legal systems. The pretrial investigation in the USSR not only establishes cause to indict and try an accused but also gathers the prosecutor's evidence for conviction at the trial. A Soviet defense lawyer's role in court is mainly a dialogue with defendant, witnesses, and judge over the meaning of the evidence, not a contest with the prosecutor over the admissibility of evidence as well as its meaning. The Soviet judge, flanked by two taciturn people's assessors, has an inquisitorial role rather than a refereeing role. This is an attribute of continental legal systems. Actively questioning judges play a large part in developing the case in court. Judges have been more active than prosecutors at the scores of trials I attended in the USSR. I have rarely seen an inactive defense. Even in political cases, defense lawyers do not necessarily carry part of the prosecution as they once did.

As in continental legal systems, Soviet criminal trials may also try an accompanying civil damage suit. Even when the defendant admits guilt during the pretrial investigation or the trial, the trial must go on. Uncorroborated confession does not suffice in Soviet law to prove guilt. Besides, the court is obligated to explore carefully all mitigating and aggravating sides of the crime and the defendant's character, as well as circumstances contributing to the crime.[270] Moreover, in line with the paternal, educational side of Soviet law,[271] the case must go forward so as to provide an object lesson to the onlookers and the public. At trial's end, the Soviet judge and people's assessors decide questions both of fact (guilt) and law (sentence).

Soviet judges and people's assessors are decreed "independent and subject only to law." They must decide cases "on the basis of the law and in accordance with their socialist legal consciousness under conditions excluding outside pressure on them."[272] Judges actually free of "outside pressures" are a rarity in the world. Soviet judges operate under multiple pressures. Their disposition of cases—acquittal or conviction—is entered on a statistical form. This record keeping produces a tendency to convict and to leave the acquitting to higher courts hearing appeals and protests, according to one experienced insider's view.[273] Campaigns to popularize justice seemed to have influenced judges to drop more criminal cases than they would have otherwise. Later campaigns against specific crimes like hooliganism generated illegalities owing to eagerness to comply with the crackdowns. "Whether or not the Party interfers in particular cases, there is no doubt that it exerts a very important influence on the course of judicial decisions by its frequent 'campaigns' against various forms of illegal activity. . . . Under the influence of such campaigns, courts have convicted men who were later shown to be innocent."[274] Courts are all the more pliable for lack of a jury or enlarged panel of people's assessors voting on a two-thirds or three-fourths rule as reformers wanted.[275]

The Party tends to step in directly in individual cases when party officials' innocence or its political interests are on the line[276]—but virtually always in political cases. Party and KGB agencies instruct the judges from the center and in advance in major cases, or by local ongoing contact during minor cases.[277] "Sometimes during the actual consideration of a verdict or in the intervals between court sessions judges even call the district party committee or some other nonjudicial body to ask for advice or for approval of a particular verdict."[278] As of the mid-1970s there were no known acquittals in Soviet political cases, and many procedural violations in their conduct, from closing or packing the courtroom to stacking the list of witnesses and violating presumption of innocence in the press and in the courtroom.[279]

This account of criminal procedure is not meant to imply that limitations on the effectiveness of defense lawyers exist only or particularly flagrantly in the USSR. Administrative controls, limitations on defense lawyers in criminal procedure and violations of it, and judicial partisanship under various pressures and influences are almost universal. But the 100 percent Soviet conviction rates in political cases, the campaigning and the political guidance of the courts, all point to significant departures from the continental legal systems on which the Soviet legal system is modeled.

II

Criminal policy shows a delicate balance of conservatism and reformism, as in Soviet politics and society. Considerations of effectiveness yield in part to oligarchical coalition politics and bureaucrats' "inertia of style." Unlike Stalin, his successors preserved many results of liberalization and popularization when they intensified the punitive, prosecutorial side of policy. Also, they resorted to massive experiments in consciousness raising through grass roots suasion and mass legal education. Time will tell whether the impressive legal education campaign produces a verifiable antidote, more wholly effective than grass roots suasion has been, to public cynicism and ignorance about the law, and to crime-breeding deviance like alcohol abuse.

Paradoxes have abounded. It was Stalinist sycophant and cruel purger, police chief Beria, who spoke out first for legality—at Stalin's funeral, no less. He, of course, perished somewhat mysteriously later that year in the general grab for power. Though not often seen that way, more liberalization had occurred before 1958 than during and since the legal reforms of that year. Reform went tacitly and bit by bit. Then Khrushchev gave it new thrust with his secret speech. But, again paradoxically, that speech and its debunking of Stalin and "the intensification of class struggle," set in train upheavals in the socialist countries that came close to upsetting the legal reforms, and certainly hampered them.

By late 1958 reformers were pasting together their final drafts of various criminal and judicial code principles, not under the sure encouragement of a destalinizing regime, but amidst troubling signals in the press, at legal conferences. There had been the Pasternak Nobel Prize affair and attacks on *Doctor Zhivago* in October. The year before, in the wake of demonstrations of support for Hungary, political arrests and secret trials once again hit the intelligentsia—especially among university students and teachers—as almost anyone at a Soviet university could tell you in those days. Conflict was raging with Yugoslav "reformism." And how do you put defense attorneys into the hitherto sacrosanct pretrial proceedings, and presumption of innocence into the criminal law when you are supposed to be fighting dangerous "revisionism" in Yugoslav programs and laws, with the Chinese scorning you for not being militant enough?

Criminal policy, as suggested at the beginning of this book, cannot but reflect its political and social setting. It did so in the great drives against dangerous crime in 1961–1962, public disorder in 1966–1968, labor indiscipline and pilfering of socialist property since 1969 (the laws under all these drives accumulating penalties on the books), and the recentralization of the police and court administration.

Yet another paradox: Khrushchev, the populizer and theorizer in

1959 about bypassing the courts and militia and in 1961 about the All-People's State, ended up invoking the courts and militia with a sharp turn back to harsher penalties including an unprecedented legal extension of the death penalty for nonpolitical crimes, far outdoing Stalin on that. Khrushchev had tolerated liberalization. In 1961 and 1962 he belied his liberality by the first of several Soviet retreats to criminal law as a means of social defense. If statistics hold up (see Chapter Five), then criminal convictions numbered about 2,800,000 in the three years 1961–1963. They totaled less—about 2,760,000—during the equivalent Brezhnev drive for public order, 1966–1968, the first three years Brezhnev used more severe penalties extensively.

Again, a paradox: Khrushchev no sooner intensified enforcement against bribers, thieves of socialist property, gang rapists, labor camp disrupters, attackers of policemen, and so on, then he turned around and abolished the USSR MVD, the central militia agency. Brezhnev was more consistent. During each campaign against areas of social indiscipline, he increased bureaucratic means of law enforcement, with the USSR MVD, then the USSR and Union republic ministries of justice.

Another paradox: Stalin's grass roots social controls were flaccid and listless despite his totalitarianism. There was no community, even a pushed-together, mobilized one. Everyone tucked his or her head under a wing, except for a few discreet and not insistent reformers here and there after World War II, and rambunctious people like Khrushchev around Stalin. It was Khrushchev and Brezhnev who re-introduced a pervasive structure for social control with the popularization of justice and the push for grass roots influence on deviants.

Khrushchev and his successors have left some basic Stalinist features in Soviet law, including its inclusiveness and a primary role, "to discipline, guide, train and educate Soviet citizens to be dedicated members of a collectivized and mobilized social order," [280] but with personal twists. Khrushchev sought ideological grandeur. Brezhnev preferred the grandeur of administered campaigns. Khrushchev's penchant for ideologizing change and making sweeping innovations contrasts with Brezhnev's reluctance to make ideological pronouncements on state and law and the relentless, pragmatic cautiousness of his creeping drive for social discipline after the first flush of the antihooliganism drive. Perhaps the least pragmatic side of policy under Brezhnev was the reliance on massive arrays of criminal and administrative sanctions like the restrictions on alcohol production and sales. For a time, three or four new offenses, plus several longer sentences, were added annually to the criminal code.

As under Stalin in the 1930s, specialists in crime fighting first faced planned obsolescence and then were spared. There is no more convincing evidence of their renewed indispensability than the post-Stalin increase in legislative action, police debates, and powers and tasks of law enforcement bureaucracies. I have alluded, for example, to the reappearance of the USSR Ministry of Justice, the reemphasis on professional over popular law enforcement, and the reentry of the USSR MVD as central social monitor and supervisor of forced labor inside places of confinement as well as over the exiled parolees and parasites outside them. Judges, prosecutors, and policemen are likely to be supplemented, but not supplanted, in the Soviet mix of repression and prevention as means to law and order.

Mass legal education for children and adults grew to an unprecedented scale in the early 1970s, urged on by some disturbing data on the Soviet people's knowledge of and respect for the law—and professional law enforcers. We have yet to see whether there are any ascertainable results, and whether the campaign becomes a major part of crime fighting alongside the system of justice, social influence (to which it is closely linked), and research into the rates, nature, and causes of crime—our closing topics.

5

Crime and Its Study

Under socialism crime prevention is becoming a part of the general system of directing social processes. . . . Crime prevention in its broadest sense includes the entire complex of political, economic, social, ideological, and legal measures for eradicating causes of crime.

—*Soviet Justice* editorial

DESTALINIZATION OF SOVIET JUSTICE left a longer than ever list of deviances subject to repression—to punishment or compulsory rehabilitation. But destalinization also reintroduced prevention into crime fighting. "Recently more severe liability was established for some kinds of lawbreaking. But besides punishments provided by law, a growing concern is becoming apparent for averting crimes and lawbreaking and bringing the community into it." [1]

"Concrete social research" entered crime prevention in the late 1950s as the regime began encouraging study of social processes it wished to control, rather than simply smothering them with decrees. By restoring criminology, the Party has reopened several issues of policy to be touched on here. (1) Criminologists do not work in a vacuum. They depend upon other specialists on crime—officials and scholars—who gather data and provide administrative and financial support and political guidance. Criminology, then, touches on the general issue: How should the participation of experts be structured so as to contribute to policy making, but in a way compatible with the leading political and ideological role of the Party? This is taken up in the section *Consulting Experts.* (2) How is crime to be recorded and how much of the record is to be divulged? This is taken up in the sections, *Crime Research Resumes* and *Measuring Crime.* (3) How is crime to be accounted for in a way that will reaffirm party claims for the superiority of one-party socialism yet give useful guidance for prevention programs? What is the proper mix of "red" and "expert?" (4) How are statistics and theories of crime to be applied to bring about the sort of policing and social changes which will prevent crime? These last two questions are taken up in the next chapter.

Consulting Experts

Crime fighting is everywhere both professionalized and politicized. In the Soviet case, no major change occurs in either repression or prevention without the approval of the Communist Party, which "defines the basic scope of action by State and social organizations including those agencies responsible for crime fighting." [2]

Few lawyers—few crime fighters of any specialization, for that matter—hold high political office in Party and state, relative to the representation of other professionals including secret police and military. Lawyers lack a national bar association. Efforts to form one failed in 1958–1959.[3] This may be a blessing because professional unions can be instruments of party control as well as protective and influential guilds.[4]

Moreover, party officials have accepted inputs of advice and initative from experts on crime more extensively in recent years: witness the process of legal reform already sketched, the greater prestige of and demand for lawyers since the mid-sixties, and the changes in studying—measuring and explaining—crime touched on in this and in the next chapter.

A Soviet natural scientist once asserted to me that "lawyers talk a lot but do nothing." It seemed that Khrushchev shared this skepticism. He complained about "an overproduction of jurists." Stalin, ironically, had rescued the profession from possible oblivion with his "stability of laws." Even Krushchev, after beginning to supplant law enforcers, had to tolerate steps under a Central Committee decree of June 14, 1964 (before Krushchev's resignation) to produce more jurists and better ones to meet current demands for them.[5] The legal profession has outlived the various abortive projects for the "withering away of law" and has grown from 15,000 jurists in 1928 to more than 150,000 in the mid-seventies.[6] When I told an eminent Soviet law professor what the Soviet scientist had said about lawyers talking a lot and doing little, he shot back, "Good, let them think that!"

The Party's current policy is to place increasing reliance on lawyers and their professional expertise to smooth the course of transition to orderly modernity.[7] A Central Committee decree of improving legal services in the national economy was followed by the ultimate accolade delivered by President Podgornyi on the occasion of the fiftieth anniversary of the formation of the USSR in 1972. "Now the jurist is no less important for production and our society than, say, the engineer, agronomist or economist." [8] Numbers of college law school graduates working as jurists increased from 106,000 to 127,000, or twenty percent, in only three years, 1970–1973. A major governmental effort in 1973–1974, involving officials from many branches of administration and law enforcement as well as law school deans and scholars, has put into effect reform in legal education so as to raise by 50 percent the graduation of specialists directly for legal service, upgrade the quality of their training, and introduce law courses for nonlawyers.

Secondary school law courses are being reintroduced. When abolished in 1957, secondary training was a stopgap source of people's court judges, prosecutors, and investigators. Now it provides a necessary legal minimum for the staffs of law enforcement apparatuses, welfare and civil registry offices, local soviets, notaries, court secretaries, and bailiffs as well as technical specialists needing some background in the law. More jurists are being supplied to state and collective farm organizations, now desperately short of legal counsel.[9]

Of law school graduates staying in legal and administrative work, about 4 percent are legal scholars; [10] 45 to 55 percent are officials or on legal staffs of political agencies such as courts, the state commercial arbitration tribunals, procuracies, MVD, KGB, soviets, ministries, and trade unions; and the rest are attorneys. About one out of four attorneys works as an "advocate" in legal aid offices under regional colleges of advocates, supervised by the USSR and republic ministries of justice.[11] The remainder work as *jurisconsulty*—that is, legal counsel—to institutions, enterprises, and farms.

The striking aspect of jurists' participation in making the laws generally and criminal policy in particular is not the absence of access channels to the party decisionmakers, but their variety, and the elaborate opinion gathering procedures. Given the research that has been done and is being done on this subject,[12] I shall stick to a short outline here.

The Communist Party has two formal channels of interchange with jurists and at the same time surveillance over them: (1) The Department of Science and Educational Institutions of the Central Committee and its local branches, for years under a reputed conservative, S.P. Trapeznikov,[13] is, as I gather from high scientific authority, both a conduit of suggestions and information to the party leadership and a device to enforce the party line, something that *Soviet State and Law* conveyed as "party mindedness," "a class analysis of social phenomena," and a "vigorous struggle against bourgeois ideology." [14] (2) The other party channel for both sensing and surveillance is the Department of Administrative Organs of the Central Committee and its local branches.[15]

The Department of Administrative Organs watches over the KGB, the Ministry of Justice, the MVD, courts, soviets, colleges of advocates, and the Procuracy. N.R. Mironov, its head from 1959 until his death in a plane crash in Yugoslavia in October 1964, served in the security apparatus of the KGB from 1951 to 1959. Nevertheless, Mironov "became, presumably by virtue of the requirements of his party post, a vigorous public proponent of restoration of party control over the security agencies, the Procuracy, and the courts." [16] Only four years after his death—in 1968—did a replacement appear for Mironov. It was N.I. Savinkin, an official without apparent personal prestige like Mironov's, a former political commissar, Central Committee official, and first deputy head of the Department of Administrative Organs.[17] Savinkin or a deputy head of the Department of Administrative Organs turns up at virtually every top-level meeting on law and crime, presumably to observe and convey an impression of the proceedings back to the Central Committee Secretariat.[18]

The Party may arbitrarily "turn off" advice or protest. Still jurists, as other professionals, gained greater access to policy makers after Stalin.[19] Jurists' expectations of greater participation [20] in policy making through professional channels have been at least partly fulfilled. We saw that soon after Stalin's demise the regime turned to the Ministry of Justice to draft reforms in criminal law.[21] Piecemeal liberalization turned later into a major effort at liberalizing justice as part of an ongoing recodification in all law, from pension reforms in 1956 to environmental protection in 1972.

Liberalizing justice developed a life of its own beyond ministerial confines through broad consultation and debate across the country among theorists, officials, and attorneys in the pages of the press, law faculty meetings, sessions at research institutes and agencies, regional law conferences on socialist legality, public discussions of drafts and the detailed work of the last stages in consultative and working groups in the Presidium of the USSR Supreme Soviet, the sub-commissions of the legislative proposals commissions of the USSR Supreme Soviet and republic supreme soviets.

Jurists' professional chains of command and channels of access in administration run through the MVD, the Ministry of Justice and Presidium of the USSR Supreme Soviet, standing commissions of the USSR Supreme Soviet, the Procuracy, and the Supreme Court.

The USSR Supreme Court chairman L.N. Smirnov, recorded, "permitted violations of socialist legality as did other judicial organs," under Stalin [22]—and, it may be said, permitted violations of socialist legality in political trials after Stalin, involving Smirnov too, though rarely in the rehearsed confessionals of the Stalin show trial type.[23] Two judges, Sergei Bannikov and Nikolai Chestyakov, were former KGB generals.[24]

Most Supreme Court activity, however, concerns nonpolitical cases, "cases of general jurisdiction." Here the Supreme Court acts as a channel of advice and suggestions from jurists, rather than as an instrument of political repression.

Five changes after Stalin fostered closer Supreme Court links with legal opinion: (1) curbing terror; (2) long delayed legal reform and the growing need for scholars to help sort out legislation and summarize court practice under the rush of new laws; (3) granting of legislative initiative to the USSR Supreme Court and its use of same under its 1957 statute; (4) restriction of the USSR Supreme Court's review-protest powers only to decisions of the Union republic supreme courts, freeing it of a mass of detailed followup and red tape in reviewing provincial and people's court work; and (5) establishment of a permanent Scientific Advisory Council under the USSR Supreme Court.[25]

To help its study and guidance of court practice, the USSR Supreme Court keeps up close and active ties with legal scholars. Members of the court serve on scholarly councils of law schools and institutes. Supreme Court judges visit department meetings in the Moscow University Law Faculty to talk over a draft Guiding Clarification informally with the law professors, as with well acquainted colleagues.

Under an edict of December 3, 1962, the USSR Supreme Court has had a Scientific Advisory Council made up of leading scholars and "practice workers." Members of the Scientific Advisory Council take part in analyzing court practice, drafting Guiding Clarifications, lecturing to officials of the Supreme Court, helping to organize, and speaking at large conferences on court work. Legal scholars are in touch, through the Supreme Court, with copious information on how laws work out in practice and with judges throughout the court system.

Apart from participation in drafting Guiding Clarifications and in plenary discussions, outside jurists take a more direct hand in policy via working on the USSR Supreme Court's responses to the USSR Supreme Soviet Presidium's requests for opinions on draft laws (300 requests from October 1967 to June 1972); drafting texts on edicts about court practice and penalties upon requests of the USSR Supreme Soviet Presidium (on such matters as pretrial detention, parole, and new court proceedings on divorce) and new legislation. After an initiative of the USSR Supreme Court and ministerial parleys, the USSR Supreme Soviet Presidium issued an edict of June 25, 1973, ordering that persons found guilty of violent crime should compensate the state for any hospital expenses incurred in treating the injuries of victims of their criminal acts.[26]

The scholarly, as opposed to judicial and administrative, base of jurists' influence rests in thirty-three university law faculties;[27] the law institutes (separate law schools) of Khar'hov, Sverdlov, and Saratov; the All-Union Correspondence Juridical Institute,[28] departments and sections (not counting institutions of the KGB, the Military Law Faculty of the Military-Political Academy, and any other such agencies), a council in the USSR Academy of Sciences, and research institutes.

The Scientific Council on Principles of State, Administration and Law of the USSR Academy of Sciences. No lawyers have been full members of the academy since Andrei Vyshinskii was forced on the academy. There are several jurist corresponding members. They deliberate on this rarely publicized council about broad directions of legal research [29] and crime prevention.[30]

The Institute of State and Law of the USSR Academy of Sciences. In 1930 law research institutes were absorbed into the Institute of Soviet Construction and Law of the Communist Academy, a Marxist center. By 1936 the Academy of Sciences proper had been sufficiently politicized and law given a sufficiently permanent lease on life that the Institute of Soviet Construction and Law could be transferred to the USSR Academy of Science, along with other institutes. In 1938 it became the Institute of Law and in 1960 the Institute of State and Law, IGPAN, publisher of the journal *Soviet State and Law* and many law books, and the leading Soviet center of theoretical research on most legal topics outside crime and criminal justice. Research on crime and criminal justice proceeds under academies of science of the non-Russian republics.[31]

The All-Union Research Institute of Soviet Legislation of the USSR Ministry of Justice helps that agency in codification and publishes its scholarly notes, mainly on civil law matters. Up to 1963 it was the All-Union Institute of Legal Sciences, successor to the Institute of Criminal Policy in 1936 (see Chapter 3). That year its experts on crime and justice, along with those at IGPAN (including A.A. Gertsenzon's group of criminologists who went to IGPAN from the Procuracy's Institute of Criminalistics in 1960), moved to the newly formed and soon-to-be discussed Institute for Crime Study and Prevention.

The All-Union Research Institute of the MVD has groups working on criminological aspects of crime prevention and forecasting (see Chapter 6). With some 250 researchers, it is larger than the Procuracy's institute but, it appears, concentrates mainly on non-criminological work related to automobile accident prevention and other MVD activities.[32]

Whether researchers or officials, neither crime fighters generally, nor the jurists among them, nor criminologists in particular are united on issues of crime and punishment. They form no single coherent "interest group" despite the sense of being in one profession that their training or legal calling may give them. Any potential effect due to crime fighters' professional access is necessarily reduced because they are no more in agreement, no less divided into cross-cutting opinion groupings than crime fighters are anywhere else.

Only when professional crime fighters tried to head off Khrushchev's extremes in popularizing justice via anti-parasite assemblies, comrades' courts, and volunteer police did crime fighters come close to unanimity of opinion. They were defending their professional role, their administrative power, and their careers against being supplanted by amateurs and *ap-*

paratchiki. Their opposition to amateurs transcended their differences over criminal policy.

Outside the muted confrontation between jurists and Khrushchev, no one theory of crime or punishment, no single working, middle-range ideology or theory of crime causation prevails among crime fighters. Stalin's conformity was forced, more apparent and surface than real. Crime fighters today openly divide between reformists and hard-liners, sociological and psychological explanations of crime. They disagree even within those groupings.[33]

Such differences over causes and prevention of crimes limit the impact of expertise. They contribute to the piecemeal and contradictory nature of Soviet criminal policy. But they enliven the Soviet quest for law and order. Contrast the recent diversity of views with the apparent but imposed near-unity of Stalin's day.

Unbelievable though it was to this observer at the national law conference in 1958, most of the audience drowned out with foot stamping the speech of their top scholar-jurist, P.S. Romashkin, director of the Institute of State and Law, while a minority sat in stony silence. Romashkin had attacked some Soviet jurists for finding common ground between "bourgeois law" and "socialist law." Had they not heard of party strictures against "peaceful coexistence in ideology"? Much of that same audience in the classic auditorium of Moscow University's downtown campus cheered when a young colleague went up to reproach Romashkin for "the polemics and methods of criticism I thought we had left behind us."

Romashkin spoke for a trend of thinking at the conference seeking to preserve a certain isolation from the "bourgeois" West and from "revisionist" trends in socialist countries.[34] His adversaries sought to bring Soviet law back out of its isolation, for practical reasons they too felt to be in the national interest.

Socialist chauvinism like Romashkin's, perhaps a response to a felt threat to political stability and political authority, remains as a survival of the Stalinist past. Romashkin appeared to embody the conflict between ideological defensiveness and empirical innovation, between red and expert. In June 1958 Romashkin himself urged research into causes of crime beyond "capitalist encirclement and survivals of capitalism in people's minds." For these formulations, Romashkin said, did not explain "why crimes are committed for example, by fifteen to seventeen year-old youths who grew up when a socialist society had already been built in our country."[35] So other causes had to be found with meaning for policy but within the framework of socialist superiority. Romashkin's advocacy of and opposition to legal reform showed that contradictions may exist not only between viewpoints of different individuals, but also within individual outlooks. Further progress in criminology, as elsewhere, will continue to depend on how and when Stalinist ideological survivals lose their restrictive force. Persistent secrecy about crime rates was one manifestation of such Stalinist survivals, a rough spot on criminology's road to recovery.

Crime Research Resumes

Criminological research, paralyzed under Stalin, resumed by 1955 in sample surveys of its labor camp inmates conducted for the MVD by the late E.G. Shirvindt, newly released from labor camp.[36] Attacks on scholarly dogmatism and the devastating influences of the "cult of personality" of Stalin at the Twentieth Party Congress (1956), and clear party encouragement to legal sciences including criminology to catch up with "the needs of life" encouraged the few criminologists surviving from the 1920s and 1930s, like A.A. Gertsenzon, B.S. Utevskii, and E.G. Shirvindt, director of the Institute for the Study of Crime and the Criminal, before his defeat and eventual labor camp sentence, to promote as best they could the restoration of their shattered discipline. By 1963 criminologists achieved a long-sought goal, the establishment of a national crime study center, the All-Union Institute of Crime Study and Prevention under the USSR Procuracy.[37]

The Institute of Crime Study and Prevention absorbed the Procuracy's own Institute of Criminalistics, where crime studies had been under way. Also it recruited researchers from the Institute of State and Law and from the All-Union Institute of Juridical Sciences (then renamed the All-Union Institute of Soviet Legislation). The Institute of Crime Study and Prevention has no monopoly. Crime study proceeds also in the law faculties and institutes of the Ministry of Higher and Specialized Secondary Education, the Ministry of Justice, and in the MVD.

Studies relevant to crime prevention go on also wherever sociologists, educators, and psychiatrists explore problems of upbringing, the family, youth, labor, and deviance.[38]

Not only does the Institute of Crime Study and Prevention have no monopoly on crime research, it does little in practice to control and coordinate Soviet crime research.[39]

Measuring Crime

The start had been encouraging. Specialists, and the USSR Procurator General himself, publicly recognized after the Twentieth Party Congress that criminology should move from vignettes to statistics and that statistics should be freed from plagues of amateurishness and secrecy.[40] The militia,

Procuracy, and courts joined with remaining statisticians like S.S. Ostroumov to begin modernizing and standardizing the gathering of information on crimes, criminals, and court work.[41] This participation by all the law enforcement agencies created the possibility of collecting crime statistics superior to the limited and therefore dubious data from police reports being gathered elsewhere.[42] As time went by the courts as well as other guardians of law and order, such as the Procuracy, began compiling data cards on persons convicted and on persons under investigation, that were supposed to contribute to regional and national analysis under categories proposed by the criminologists: "incitements to committing illegal acts" (family difficulties, conflict with the victim, etc.), "circumstances facilitating the achievement of a criminal result" (e.g., selling liquor to minors, sloppy security for stockrooms), and "causes" of crime (educational shortcomings, social, cultural, and economic changes and problems, the age, sex, occupation, and background of the offender).[43]

The Central Statistical Administration, which had issued crime and other "moral statistics" before the blackout under Stalin, maintained that blackout. Beginning in 1956 it began to issue more and more sensitive data on hitherto secret subjects like harvests, industrial production, birthrates, and divorces despite ideologically unfavorable trends showing up in the data. Yet years after Prosecutor General Rudenko demanded an end to secrecy and despite experts' later pleas for openness,[44] national crime statistics remain unpublished state secrets even harder to unravel than are the carefully screened Soviet military budgets.[45] The only published clues to national trends are the optimistic statements appearing from time to time, as in Ostroumov's *Soviet Criminal Statistics,* pointing to a tendency for criminal convictions to drop in contrast to horrendous upsurges in U.S. convictions. For example, "If we take the number of persons convicted in 1928 in the USSR as 100, then in 1955 it went down to 63, although the population during that time grew from 147 to 200 million people, or by 30.5%. This decrease of crime continues today."[46] By estimating the convictions for 1928 and piecing together scattered statements like Ostroumov's, one gets a series on criminal *convictions* (not reported, even less actual crime) since 1928, as in Table 5–1. Court convictions for crimes appear to run close to 900,000 a year.

Because of changes in criminal policy, police effectiveness, and types of crimes, I have added indices only for the most comparable recent years: (a) after the criminal law reforms of 1958 and (b) after the major code revisions of 1961–1962. With registered divorce rates doubling and birthrates halving in the 1950s and 1960s, what was so wrong with the crime trends shown in Table 5–1? Conviction rates dropped over the long run from Khrushchev to Brezhnev even in absolute totals. During the same period, in the United States, national crime indices soared. So, then, why

Table 5–1. Criminal Court Convictions, USSR, 1928, 1940–1971; Trends in Convictions and Convictions per capita Population, 1959–1971 (approximate estimates)[47]

Year	(1) Convictions		(2) Trends in Convictions (a) (1959 = 100)	(2) Trends in Convictions (b) (1963 = 100)	(3) Trends in Convictions per Capita (a) (1959 = 100)	(3) Trends in Convictions per Capita (b) (1963 = 100)
1928	1,610,000					
1940	1,390,000					
1946	>1,220,000					
1955	1,015,000					
1958	1,421,000	Khrushchev				
1959	>1,130,000	Is	100		100	
1960	<942,000	First	<83		<82	
1961	825,000	Secretary	73		70	
1962	1,080,000		96		91	
1963	905,000		80	100	75	100
1964	<815,000		<72	<90	<67	<89
1965	755,000	Brezhnev	67	83	61	82
1966	998,000	Is	89	111	80	107
1967	>835,000	First	>74	>93	>68	>91
1968	922,000	Secretary	82	103	72	96
1971	>870,000		>77	>96	>66	>88

Note: > = more than, < = less than

was secrecy imposed for so long on absolute conviction rates and on other data such as reported crimes and arrests? I can only guess at three possible contributing factors, finding none of them entirely convincing:

1. *The small number of experts needing crime statistics.* Criminologists number a few hundred, judging from their participation in forecasting, described later. These experts could be serviced with closed, unpublished statistics. But this does not square with real Soviet needs for, "on the contrary," according to an eminent source, "a considerable number of specialists—criminologists, sociologists, pedagogues, generally a considerable portion of the intelligentsia badly needs criminological statistics." [48]

2. *The defects of available statistics.* Perhaps Soviet crime statistics are too unreliable to publish. After all, experts who *have* seen them criticize the statistics for being inconsistent and inaccurate,[49] in some ways inferior to tsarist criminal statistics, [50] compiled locally without the usual computers or calculators by busy court secretaries,[51] subject to errors by unskilled agency staffs,[52] "closed," and scattered among various agencies,[53] based on poorly devised classifications of crimes and criminals' traits.[54]

Add to these defects the difficulties of comparison over time created by changing criminal policy, legislation, and efficiency of enforcement.[55] It is risky, for example, to use the conviction numbers in Table 5–1 as precise indices of trends in real crime. Convictions rose after 1953, according to the Soviet text, because the liberal 1953 amnesty released too many unreformed criminals. Convictions dropped in 1959–1961 because criminal punishment was deemphasized and then rose because of the crackdowns in 1962 and 1966. Surprisingly, they rose, it seems, slightly higher under Khrushchev in 1961–1963 than under Brezhnev in 1966–1968.[56]

Yet incomparability alone does not bar other statistics. Many policy changes lurked behind the ups and downs in Soviet divorce statistics of 1.1 per 1,000 inhabitants in 1940, 0.4 in 1950, and 2.7 in 1973.[57]

Although difficulties and defects reduce the usefulness of crime statistics, the defects should not necessarily prompt their "closed character." Statistics do exist on "all registered crimes, persons charged with crimes, persons subjected to measures of social influence and persons convicted." The government agencies and criminologists use them.[58] And if they were published and Soviet arguments for open publication held, publication would only improve them.[59]

3. *Unsatisfying and ideologically embarrassing crime trends revealed in secret data.* The benefit of publication might be just what the regime wanted to avoid. Either the statements used in Table 5–1, despite their internal consistency, are more optimistic than other information in state hands, or publication would spur statistical reforms which certain officials would rather not see. Both statements may be true. Conviction statistics have been criticized in print as unreliable. The chairman of the RSFSR Su-

preme Court (later, in 1972, chairman of the USSR Supreme Court) appraised conviction rate data as "superficial" measures of the "real state of crime and convictions," "frequently contradicting it."[60] Behind the scenes, many local police officials "fix" crime figures and arrest proceedings to conceal the "real state of affairs" and "embellish" crime statistics in their precincts. To cover up, they ignore reports of crime, list murder victims as missing persons, book suspects for crimes less serious than those actually committed, and improperly report crimes as less serious "administrative infractions." To make matters worse, prosecutors connive in this local whitewashing.[61] Militia, courts, and prosecutors are motivated to understate in crime statistics because a tradition hangs on stubbornly, in administrative practice, of regarding levels and trends in crime and lawbreaking as directly measuring how well the militia, courts, and Procuracy work, despite the theory that crime is a "complex social occurrence," with some still unknown causes, "difficult to eradicate."

> This fosters in these agencies a tendency, difficult to overcome and almost uncontrollable, to "achieve a steady decrease" in a number of indicators, i.e., simply not to register some citizens' reports about crimes, unfoundedly to refuse to initiate a criminal case.[62]

Another reason to believe that the "real state of crime and convictions" is improving more slowly than conviction totals show is the fact that because of the 1958 reforms, the share of all criminal cases based on private complaints sent for criminal investigation had dropped in 1967 to one quarter of the share of cases based upon private complaints sent for investigation in 1958 before the criminal law reforms. In constant terms, conviction totals should be raised 14 percent for this reason alone in 1967, if they are to be compared with conviction totals for 1958 and earlier postwar years.[63]

Plotted on a graph, the conviction totals in Table 5–1 for 1959–1971 show fluctuations in convictions, with peaks at the time of the crackdowns in 1961–1962 and 1966, then a leveling off in absolute terms, but a long-term decrease in per capita convictions. Perhaps the decrease is not fast enough or has stopped, as shown if one takes as a basis not 1959 but 1963, after the deliberalization of 1961–1962. Perhaps the regime is not yet sure that the decrease will continue after it releases crime statistics. If trend indices in Table 5–1 were to turn out erroneous, corrections could prove embarrassing.

Weighed with all their weaknesses, the explanations add up to this: A prevailing group of leaders and officials has so far prevented open publication of crime rate statistics because it feels the benefits of that publication would not outweigh the possible disadvantages in shaking the basic ideological tenet that crime is "alien to socialist society" and slated to disappear.[64] Those blocking the publication of statistics must fear that the data will not help to live up to Lenin's summons to statisticians "to confirm the theoretical conclusions of Marxism and make them unassailable." [65] Even if experts could explain away a high plateau in conviction rates on the basis of new criminal penalties added under Brezhnev—for example, against "parasites" in 1970—questions might arise as to why new penalties were necessary.

Pressing for an end to the state secret approach to crime data, a sociologist versed in law and criminal statistics has written what may be a retort to conversative arguments against publication. "Open, official publication of moral statistics (including, of course, criminal statistics)," he says, is "one of the most acute questions." The present secrecy he considered "an anachronism, which does no real good but on the contrary a lot of harm." Statistical methods and the results of using these methods, G.A. Zlobin said, are the only way to overcome impediments of time and distance separating the "many scholars" whose concerted efforts are essential to improving criminal statistics.

> Doubtless, the present still far from perfect system (or more precisely, systems) of criminal statistics never would have reached even its present level had it been established by "closed" methods. . . . Only a solid, official publication will provide visibility, preservation, real comparability of statistical data and will reliably protect them from any distortion, whether intentional or accidental.[66]

Against secrecy about national crime rates, then, the argument is being advanced that secrecy does in fact make statistics less useful, impedes the quest for law and order, averts much needed criticism of statistical methods, and leaves statistics open either to misuse by unskilled operators or to abuse by coverup and understatement of crimes.

The Impact and Types of Crime

Whatever may be the Soviet motivations for statistical secrecy, criminologists and other observers do not take lightly the "real state of crime," as it filters out from piecemeal reports in the Soviet press. Despite secrecy on national crime rates, these reports, as Walter Connor says, are "exceedingly informative and valuable in gauging the significance of problems of deviance in the USSR." [67] Take the state of affairs in Moscow. A New Yorker is likely to find Moscow streets much safer than New York's. Professor Kuznetsova and her Moscow University law students have drawn a dramatic contrast between the disorderly and dangerous Moscow of 1923 and the safe Moscow of 1968–1969.[68] Per capita convictions there have fallen several times over, especially for the most dangerous crimes like murder. Robbery by gangs of armed bandits is all but wiped out. So is much of the once notoriously overdeveloped Moscow underworld of professional criminals. And all this has occurred despite the huge population increase since 1923.

Moscow, however, was always an extraordinary case, one way or the other. Moscow in 1923 as a major railroad hub was extraordinarily ravaged by transient vagrancy and child vagabondage in the aftermath of war and famine. Moscow in the years after World War II was extraordinarily controlled as to residence permits, population in-migration, and criminal deviance. Yet even in contemporary Moscow thieves plague wealthier residents with well planned burglaries. It is not uncommon for people living in an apartment house to have keys to the elevator, equip apartment doors with peephole and double locks, chip in for someone to run the elevator and lock and guard the door by 1:00 A.M.[69] And Moscow has not been spared juvenile violence.[70]

Worst reports on crime come from the fastest growing, most rapidly industrializing parts of the USSR, the new industrial settlements and the provincial towns, such as Dzhambul, Kazakhstan. (Dzhambul's population has tripled since 1939 while Moscow's has increased 60 percent;) [71] Citizens' lives in Dzhambul have been turned upside down because of their widespread fear of violent crime in its streets. Apparently, many crimes known to the authorities never enter crime registers. A visiting reporter found nine people recovering in hospitals from injuries inflicted by hooligans. *But not one of the people involved was reported in the log of the militia's HQ, the city department of Internal Affairs.*[72] Dzhambul, where people try to stay off the streets at night, is closer in atmosphere to many fear-ridden American cities than are most places foreign tourists reach in the USSR. Perhaps the average crime picture for the USSR lies somewhere in between James Reston's glowing depiction of a Moscow that is a "policeman's paradise" [73] and troubled Dzhambul, where sometimes one's spouse or relative, out late, may not get home at all but end up in the clinic or the morgue.

Soviet car owners remove windshields from their machines except when driving in the rain. They keep kids off the streets as much as possible, especially after amnesties, such as the prisoner release in 1967. They carefully watch their baggage when traveling.[74] Gates on many a high garden fence carry a sign, ZLAYA SOBAKA (Beware of the Dog). Some homeowners go to the extent of sleeping outdoors with shotguns or stringing up electrified fences when their fruit and vegetables are temptingly ripe, with fatal results to intended and unintended young victims.[75] Residents in factory barracks and distant collective farm villages become accustomed to thieving, violence, and drunkenness among the young and not so young, and try to protect themselves accordingly.[76]

Saratov is a Volga River manufacturing town of some 773,000 inhabitants; its population more than doubled since 1939.[77] Researchers there asked a sample of 827 male blue-and white-collar workers in the mid-1960s about their experiences with crime. And they did get results published. One out of three respondents said they had been victims or witnesses of crime. Most crimes involved were serious: 45 percent violent crimes against individuals and hooliganism, a crime usually involving violence and defined as "intentional acts crudely violating public order, and expressing flagrant disrespect for society." The other 55 percent of crimes experienced or witnessed by the Saratov informants were those against socialist (state and cooperative) property and personal property.[78] National data such as listed in Table 5–2 show similar high proportions of crimes likely to be most felt by individual citizens or by persons responsible for guarding socialist property against theft.

According to the statistics from the late 1960s grouped in Table 5–2 by title of the criminal code chapters, crimes victimizing private citizens with theft, violence, or indignities accounted for nearly 57 percent of the total convictions. Of these, nearly 46 percent in the overall total were convictions for crimes associated with violence: hooliganism, homicide, rape, assault, robbery, snatching, and arson.

Hooliganism is an age-old offense containing elements of crime against the person and the public order. It persists as the leading cause of convictions despite periodic drives against it.[79] Hooliganism accounts for up to 40 percent of convictions in some urban courts.[80] Convictions for crimes against persons and their property are said to have dropped off sharply after World War II, but seem to have leveled off in the 1960s. At best, there were mixed progress reports after the various anticrime campaigns.[81]

Breaches of law and order generally cited by state officials in terms such as "most dangerous and widespread" are theft of state and cooperative (socialist) property, hooliganism, economic crimes, crimes committed by juveniles, recidivist crimes, and the offenses of alcohol abuse (see below) which they link with many crimes.[82] Crimes against state and cooperative property fell off since World War II but remain widespread,[83] harder to detect than most other leading catgories of crimes, more likely to be "latent" (that is, unreported), and quite possibly the most frequent crime in actuality, far outstripping hooliganism, though Table 5–2 does not show it.

Drug offenses have prompted increasing coverage in the law journals and press, and two severe criminal law crackdowns in 1972 and 1974.[84] Traffic offenses climb as more cars go to long-waiting Soviet purchasers. Compounded by drunkenness [85] and obviously ill-marked highways, negligence on the road is evoking a vigorous militia response. Jaywalkers are in-

Table 5–2. Proportions of Crimes for Which Persons Were Convicted, USSR, c. 1967 (percent, estimated)[86]

	PERCENT
Crimes against public safety, order, and health	
Hooliganism	24
Traffic offenses	5
Other (including drug abuse)	over 4.3
Crimes against life, health, freedom, and dignity of persons (homicide, rape, assault, infecting with VD, homosexuality, libel, slander, etc.)	17
Crimes against socialist (state and cooperative) property	17
Crimes against personal property	
Larceny, burglary, fraud, blackmail, vandalism, arson	11.2
Snatching (*grabezh*) and robbery (*razboi*)	4.8
Economic crimes (substandard production, speculation, home brewing, forging stamps and railroad tickets, poaching, violating veterinary and plant health rules, falsifying statistics, etc.)	5
Crimes against administrative order (slandering Soviet system; public disorders; disobeying peace officers; violating rules governing passports, residence, miltary draft, parasitism, etc)	4
Malfeasance in office (abuses, carelessness, bribery, etc.)	4
Crimes against justice (by judicial personnel, inmates escaping, etc.)	1.5
Crimes against political and labor rights of citizens	0.5
Crimes which are survivals of local customs (feuds, paying bride price, forcing women to marry or marrying person under legal age, bigamy, polygamy—where such acts are survivals of local minority customs)	0.4
Other crimes (state crimes, military crimes)	less than 1.3

cluded. A young researcher who stopped for a drink on the way home took a short cut across the street when alighting from his bus, and caused an accident with four injuries. He received two years deprivation of freedom in a labor colony of strict regime [87] plus a fine of 1,500 rubles to compensate for damages to a trolleybus, parked car [88] and to a taxi, which had swerved to avoid him.

Dissent also caused rising state concern, despite the near disappearance of violent political crimes after World War II.[89] Convictions for political crimes are lumped in Table 5–2 with those for military crimes. Political convictions numbered probably under 1 percent of all convictions. There were approximately 10,000 political prisoners in the USSR out of a total prison population of 1 to 1.5 million prisoners.[90] These political prisoners

Table 5–3. Convictions and Conviction Rates per 100,000 Inhabitants (rough estimates), U.S. and USSR, 1971

	U.S.	USSR	Ratio of Rates, U.S./USSR
A. For crimes against persons	276,400	298,460	
Per 100,000 inhabitants	133	163	0.8
B. For crimes against property	580,900	245,300	
Per 100,00 inhabitants	280	101	2.8
C. For crimes against public health, safety, and morals	294,388	80,910	
Per 100,000 inhabitants	142	33.2	4.3
Robbery per 100,000 inhabitants	10.7	17.1	0.63

A = for USSR "crimes against life, health, freedom, and dignity of citizens + hooliganism + robbery and snatching of personal property"; for U.S. = criminal homicide, forcible rape, aggravated assault, other assault. Categories match within the approximations of this rough estimate.

B = for USSR "crimes against personal property" and "crimes against socialist property" minus robbery and snatching (*grabezh*) of personal property (robbery and snatching of socialist property are unlisted in data, so are omitted in A, making the Soviet total in A slightly more conservative and this total slightly overstated). For U.S. B = larceny, burglary, arson, fraud, embezzlement, and vandalism.

C = for USSR "crimes against public safety, order, and health" and for U.S. = auto theft (to match Soviet listing here), weapons violations, prostitution and commercialized vice, sex offenses, violation of narcotic drug laws, driving under the influence, vagrancy, gambling, a rough match of the Soviet listings in Chapter X of the RSFSR Criminal Code, except that prostitution is not a crime in the USSR, save when subsumed under parasitism.

Source: U.S. Department of Justice, Federal Bureau of Investigation, *UCR, 1971* (Washington, D.C.: U.S. Government Printing Office, 1972), p. 110 (Disposition of Persons Formally Charged by the Police). I use totals of convictions both for offense listed and for lesser offense, as I think this introduces the least error. Method of estimation will be supplied on request. U.S. population for 1971 est. at 207,180,000. Conviction data corrected to convert from sample of 63,269,000 population to base of 207,180,000, by multiplying by 3.274. Est. for USSR based on Table 5–2 and population of 244,000,000. Date 1971 used as the latest in Table 5–1 from which total Soviet conviction figure of 870,000 is taken.

do not include prisoners in psychiatric prison hospitals and religious dissenters sentenced under code articles not listed as political crimes.[91]

Most of the other 12 percent of convictions are for crimes against the administrative order—for example, attacks on fish, game, and forest wardens by poachers,[92] or crimes of malfeasance in office. Few Soviet parents wishing their children to go to college can be unaware that they might possibly have to deal with a ring of bribe-taking officials who fix entrance into higher educational institutions.[93] But what about U.S.–Soviet comparisons?

Even if statistics were available on the Soviet side, differences in crime classification, social structures, and police methods would make comparisons of limited value. Soviet secrecy all but rules out comparison. But with misgivings, I have estimated some comparative totals and rates of conviction in the United States and USSR for: A. crimes against persons (violent crimes); B. crimes against property; and C. crimes against public health, safety, and morals, a category including the so-called victimless crimes like drug abuse, gambling, and vice. I emphasize that these figures are convictions and not crime rates, and do not necessarily reflect equivalent crimes. But they do point up the prominence of violent crime convictions in the USSR and of convictions for stealing, possession of narcotics, and drunken driving in the United States. The high violent crime conviction rates may well reflect the Soviet problem with violent drinking. U.S. conviction rates are higher than Soviet rates by a substantial margin for crimes against property and relatively higher yet for category C, the category with the huge contributions from convictions for drug abuse and driving under the influence. If actual crime rates followed anywhere near these conviction rates, then Table 5–3 shows that one would be safer from violent crime in the United States. I am suspicious about the ratios for crimes in category B. For, there is much "socialist property" to steal in the USSR; thefts by officials and ordinary citizens are often not reported.

Conclusions

Crime experts expect and exert more influence in policy making since Stalin. Party leaders are willing to permit debate and innovation. But their reliance on campaigning—a response useful in very specific types of crime—is of unproven value in massive anticrime drives and often goes against expert advice. Statistical secrecy testifies, I must conclude, both to the incompleteness of destalinization and to the gravity of crime and alcoholism in the USSR.[94] Even the conviction trend data pieced together in Table 5–1 seem harder to come by recently, though this could always change.

No reasons for the continued secrecy seem valid except that available statistics labeled "secret" or "for official use" show crime rate trends contrary to the Soviet goal of gradually eliminating crime. Soviet sources of as yet unimpeachable accuracy write of "the almost continuous growth of alcoholism and crime, not least among young people," [95] of "the spreading epidemic of senseless, brutal hooliganism and crime," [96] of the fact that far from "being eliminated, bribery and corruption increased, particularly in the work of many economic and trade organizations, in institutions of higher learning, in various state organizations and enterprises, and even within the party."[97] To the extent that Soviet secret crime statistics show such ominous trends, the statistics do not invite Soviet publication. Statistics will appear either when the crime situation improves or when the leadership becomes convinced that statistics should be published for practical reasons outweighing ideological ones. By ideological reasons, I mean concern for the image of Soviet society and its leadership.

6

Explaining Crime

Survivals of the past in people's minds themselves need an explanation.

—Professor A. A. Piontkovskii

Red and Expert

AFTER YEARS OF DOGGED STRUGGLE away from the paralysis of the Stalin era, Soviet criminologists find themselves part way back to the freedom and diversity of the twenties. They are hampered as well as helped by their government's patronage. Often, in a country where academic and scientific work brings high formal prestige, they are humiliated by the residue of Stalinist isolation, secrecy, and political tutelage surrounding their work of explaining crime trends and persistence in the Soviet Union.

Criminologists feel, as do other social scientists, the strains of their regime's cross-purposes. For the regime is torn between a craving for "red" interpretations and its need for expert practicality (and, I think, a genuine excitement with the "scientific and technological revolution").

By red I mean ideologically orthodox, legitimizing because supporting the Party's claim that it has found a superior path of development that the Soviet, "socialist system creates preconditions for eliminating crime. Crime is inherent in capitalism but alien to socialism by its very nature." By "expert" I mean based on empirical research and oriented toward "applied scientific means of social prophylaxis,"[1] let the chips fall where they may.

How in criminology are experts and mentors resolving the issue of red and expert? Is progress now blocked? I would say no. Rather, it seems, expert explanations of crime have been slowly gaining, though with setbacks, over red explanations such as "class struggle," "influence of the imperialist camp," and "survivals of the past." Strikingly, some of the clearest tendencies toward more latitude for explanations of crime came under Brezhnev's coalition even while cultural orthodoxy became more narrowly and repressively defined. That there are still political limits in explaining crime reflects the ideological tension in Soviet party policy between commitment to the "scientific and technological revolution" and attachment to rearguard conservatism in the ideology of social and cultural change.

The limits to, and yet progress in, criminology reflect also contradictions in the organization and funding of research. State funding of criminological research provides needed resources but adds budgetary rigidity in the USSR as elsewhere.[2] State patronage of Soviet criminology through research institutes, publications, and law faculties gives advantages of access to funds, agency cooperation, and crime data collected by government agencies. Among the disadvantages are the tutelage and secrecy stemming from the same patronage.

But the extent of tutelage and secrecy depends on the political context. During the Brezhnev era, as we saw, opponents of "liberalism" and "coddling" criminals made further headway. The hard-liners saw no unavoidable pressures to commit crimes in the USSR. They blamed crimes on their perpetrators' lack of character.[3] Legislation increased the severity and reach of criminal penalties. Political repression cast a darker shadow over Soviet life. When Stalin resorted to repression, totalitarian logic demanded that criminology cease. Unlike Stalin's day, however, proponents of repression win only partial victories; researchers keep their institutes and their access and a chance to argue back publicly.[4] For, instead of intensifying repression alone, as Stalin did after the relative liberalism of 1926–1928, leaders after Stalin have given something to both sides. They have intensified both repression and prevention to fight crime. Criminologists meanwhile have contended with technical and political obstacles, rapidly increasing their participation as consultants and more slowly gaining the autonomy many of them continue to seek, within the system and through channels.[5]

Khrushchev's repudiation in 1956 of the "sharpening of the class struggle" [6] and of mass terror took away one obstacle. This left the task of adopting and supplementing the theory of "survivals" and of morally subversive bourgeois influences.

The Party's expert tendency since 1956 has been to encourage "concrete social research." The Party's red tendency leads it still to endorse from on high the thesis that crime is a survival of the past.[7] Survivals is still part of official ideology (defining ideology as a stated set of beliefs and preferences oriented to evaluating, guiding, or justifying political action). The formulation persists despite some withering of obligatory ideology in the USSR, because it supports the irreducible core of doctrine: the need for the Party's leading role in society and the legitimizing purpose of that role; its "historic mission" to build the best society the world has seen.[8] If crime is a stubborn but "diminishing" survival of the previous social order, then its survival in the USSR does not blemish party achievements, does not belie the doctrine that only the guidance of a single "Marxist-Leninist" party and planned socialism can eliminate the evil side effects of industrialization.[9]

Survivals theory, however orthodox, has been open to ridicule in the Soviet Union. It is a standing joke among many criminologists to ask, "where do survivals of the past come from in the mind of a youth in his twenties born in the fourth or fifth decade of Soviet power?"[10]

Criminologists may still include formulations attributing crime to "survivals of the past in the minds of certain people and the influence of the imperialist camp," but appear virtually united in the belief that to say this alone about crime "means not to explain it at all." Crime researchers now spell out survivals in terms of specific factors they find associated with crime. They go beyond human failings to cite deep-seated material problems of development.

> Research studies have drawn attention to such reasons for crime as trouble in the family, the absence of a regular healthy influence of older people on the younger generation, shortcomings in schooling, difficulties in the job placement of youth, drunkenness, unfavorable housing conditions, material difficulties of the lower paid strata of the working people, deficiencies in recreational facilities for the working people, slipshod accounting of materials in state and public organizations, badly organized protection of socialist property, shortcomings in the work of corrective labor institutions, etc.[11]

Texts and statistical studies in the USSR classify crime-breeding aspects of society into *objective reasons* and *subjective reasons* for crime.[12] As objective reasons they mention "difficulties" and "nonantagonistic contradictions" of development such as are associated with fallout of the harm done during the Great Patriotic War, international political dangers (of imperialism, it is said) necessitating the diversion of funds for defense, baneful "influences of so called 'Western culture,'" and temporary economic shortages and difficulties. Dire poverty is out as an "objective" cause. Nonantagonistic contradictions inherent in Soviet socialist development involve the question of social stratification owing to "the inadequate living standards of part of the population, the lower level of culture, and the lack of social consciousness of a segment of the working people."[13] But work on social stratification remains at a tentative stage.

Soviet criminologists have progressed far into practical research on *circumstances and inducements* contributing to the achievement of a criminal result; have collected more data than theory in the more ticklish area of criminal *subcultures and gangs;* study criminals' *personality and biology* but with inhibitions springing from suspicions of "biologizing" research. They have begun ambitious pilot projects in *forecasting and planning,* reinforcing a tendency to come to grips with social inequality and strain.

Circumstances and Inducements

Criminologists have researched in detail the short-run causes of crime: (1) conditions or "circumstances contributing to the achievement of a criminal result," such as, in the above quote, "slipshod accounting of materials in state and public organizations, badly organized protection of socialist property," and (2) "inducements to commit a crime."

One such project of the Institute of Crime Study and Prevention has used court cases and other research to draw up recommendations for stopping thefts by truckers. About eighty percent of all Soviet freight goes by trucks, hired out to enterprises by trucking agencies. "Circumstances contributing to the achievement of criminal result" abound.

The project uncovered many ways find to rip off the state. Outsiders have ready access to bills of lading on dispatchers' boards. Using the stolen papers, they can make off with cargoes. Delivering cargoes late in the day, when regular checkers have gone home, truckers find it easy to hoodwink semiliterate and untrained watchmen into receiving short cargoes. Drivers switch less valuable loads for more valuable ones or overload, taking the difference, by packing more boxes on the bottom than the top row, hiding cargo in specially prepared caches right on the truck. The loose checking allowing this also makes it possible for truckers off-loading loose cargo like coal, cement, lumber, and other construction materials to skim off a portion for themselves, especially since many railroad depots lack truck weighing scales, or to make off with a whole truckload, hoping it will not be missed among many coming from a train. Or, even if a truck is weighed, there are possibilities to conceal brick or metal scrap on the empty dump truck or to put water in spare fuel tanks; and then to have the empty truck weighed with this extra "cargo." Then there are opportunities to slip this extra weight off and have the truck loaded with official cargo and weighed. Before reaching the destination, the driver can skim off for himself cargo weighing the amount of the bricks, water, or scrap. There are also ways to get seals put on trucks or crates after the theft, or to break some seals undetected. And of course it helps to have accomplices at the shipping or receiving end.

After a study like this it is normal for the institute team to submit a list of recommendations for "special measures of crime prevention"—the direct preventive measures applied to security or criminals or potential lawbreakers—as opposed to "general measures of crime prevention" getting at the sort of broad social "reasons" (*prichiny*) for crime just outlined. Take better care of documents and verify them, the researchers say; check cargoes more carefully, both leaving depots and while *en route,* change sealing means and procedures, improve trucks and cargo measuring, and so forth.[14]

Practical studies like the trucking inquiry rate higher in Soviet research priorities than they do in America. American criminology has in fact encountered criticism for neglecting to deal with "symptoms," about which something at least can be done, and fruitlessly chasing after untouchable "root causes." A serious policy analysis of crime, by contrast, would place heavy emphasis on the manipulation of objective conditions, not necessarily because of a belief that the causes of crime are thereby being eradicated, but because behavior is easier to change than attitudes, and because, as James Q. Wilson puts it, the only instruments society has for altering behavior in the short run require it to assume that people act in response to the costs and benefits of alternate courses of action.[15] The trucking study and studies of the ingenious devices for stealing from railroad cargoes [16] are just the sort of "policy analysis" Wilson had in mind. Without such practically oriented emphasis on "special means of crime prevention," it is hard to see how the Soviet regime would be willing to support research into social processes and personality formation, clues to broader reasons for crime.

"Incitements to commit a crime" or "the concrete life situation" are immediate causes of a criminal act, from incidence of drunkenness at the time, to types of provocation, a family quarrel, or provocation by the victim. Researchers of the Institute of Crime Study and Prevention concluded from a sample of 338 cases of homicide, assault, and rape involving 411 convicted persons that these crimes occur typically among persons who are related, friends, or acquaintances.[17]

The policy side of this study recommended criminal code reform that would reflect present court practice by counting as mitigating circumstances various forms of "illegal or immoral" (*nepravomernoe ili beznravstvennoe*) behavior on the part of the victim.

According to an institute researcher, 29 percent of crimes in her sample were accompanied by "illegal or immoral behavior" on the part of the victim. Among the victims, 38.8 percent were drunk at the time they were victimized, over half of them were under 25, 28.6 percent were under eighteen—physically and mentally healthy, though often with bad references from work or place of residence. Among the victims, 25.5 percent had used force before being victimized, 23.5 percent had attempted to use force or had insulted the offender or threatened force against the perpetrator or his or her family, or the damage or destruction of property, 27 percent helped create conditions arousing sexual desire, 7.4 percent started the quarrel, 2.9 percent had been unfaithful, 9.2 percent made unfounded material demands on the victim, 14.5 percent had behaved provocatively in various other ways. "Very often," Minskaya concluded, "it is a matter of chance who will become victims in such a situation," and difficult to decide sometimes who is the victim and who is the criminal.

Problems abound in the methodology, at least in the published results. Personality traits are listed: for example, 12.2 percent of the victims were characterized as "aggressive." What is aggressive? Do some traits prominent among rapists or murderers also characterize high achievers among noncriminals? And was there a control group with which to compare this sample of victims? Are the general population more or less aggressive?"[18] In Minskaya's analysis of women's conduct or reputation before rape, there is an evident moralistic propensity to give some benefit of the doubt to the rapist, a double standard.[19] I am not arguing against ever giving benefit of the doubt, but I am pointing to the evidence of bias tinging the empirical research here. One is always likely to find some bias in this morally and psychologically sensitive policy area.

Subcultures and Gangs

Criminologists working on the broader causes, the social and economic reasons of crime are inching toward the analysis of affluence and sources of crime-breeding subcultures.

Because there is more stealing among lower income groups and more violent crime among persons with lower educational attainments, it is widely assumed that stealing must automatically diminish as living standards rise and that violent crimes must automatically diminish as educational attainments rise. Unpublished statistics, says Dr. A.M. Yakovlev, deputy director of the All-Union Research Institute of Soviet Legislation, do not show this direct relationship.[20] Crime does not go down, he says, simply because living standards and education go up. "The roots of criminal behavior lie in the unwritten laws and customs" of informal groups. People become lawbreakers when "socially beneficial" values lose out to "antisocial" values in the "conflict of norms." This is Sutherland's theory of differential association.[21] Crime may get worse, then, while life gets better, unless group influences are effectively controlled to support law and order.

Subcultures harboring antisocial values crop up among prisoners, juveniles,[22] drug addicts, various dissenters, and the unemployed, among others.

Persons not working made up 27 percent of those convicted for acquisitive property crimes in Moscow in the first quarters of 1968 and 1969 and 13 percent of those convicted of murder. "There is no unemployment in the USSR," it is often said, and indeed there is a labor shortage, not a glut. The state of being unemployed is often loosely called "parasitism," regarded with suspicion which is only confirmed by such statistics as these, and called "an extremely dangerous pre-criminal state which is very likely to end in crime." A community of hoboes resists extinction. Vagrancy and passport rule violations, separately listed crimes, naturally go together. So deeply rooted are they that together they are fourth highest on the list of recidivism for all types of crimes.[23] But I shall concentrate here on other subcultures of crime: those involved with alcoholism, pilfering, women in crime, gangs, private enterprise, and white-collar criminality.

Alcoholism and alcohol abuse are so rampant that drinking may be called a "*sub*culture" only in that the rulers deplore and disapprove. They single out alcohol as a "direct 'accomplice' of the convicted in a majority of cases." [24] Observers in America, where there are more than nine million problem drinkers and an annual social cost of alcohol abuse [25] of fifteen billion dollars may wish to follow closely in coming years the results of an almost continual stream of punitive, therapeutic, and restrictive Soviet directives poured out by party, government, and courts since 1966 to treat and prevent drunkenness.[26]

Soviet surveys associating drunkenness and crimes may not exactly tally but two recent studies, A and B, record that over 50 percent of criminals committing crimes were intoxicated, and 68 to 74 percent in A and B, respectively, were drunk during murder; 69 and 73.4 percent during rape; over 85 and over 90 percent during criminal hooliganism; 76 percent (A) during robbery and snatching; 75 percent (A) during aggravated assault.[27]

Curbing drunkenness is complicated not only by ignorance as to its social causes but also by public tolerance and social custom. In "no other case or deviance is the gap between official and unofficial or public attitudes so great as in that of drunkenness." [28]

An eminent Soviet criminal law expert, asked when he thought the Soviet Union would solve its law-and-order problems, replied that because of alcohol abuse he was not sure that his country could ever solve those problems.

Pilfering of socialist property—about three quarters of all cases,—occurs on the job. According to a sample survey in the Lithuanian republic, 21 to 22 percent of public property thefts occurred in factories, 9 to 15 percent in offices handling funds, 15 to 23 percent in construction organizations, and 20 to 25 percent in state farms. Most of the thefts were by stealing, embezzling, and misappropriation rather than by robbery or snatching (*grabezh*).[29]

An institute research team explored court cases and interviewed people on the spot to find out why they rip off the state. They discovered, that sloppy management (lax controls, excessive hoarded stock inventories, and poorly guarded stocks, extravagance, and waste) was one of the factors contributing to high theft rates.

A second contribution to the climate encouraging lawlessness is managerial lawbreaking, such as toleration of drunkenness on the job, misappropriations report padding, and other examples of malfeasance in office.[30]

Employees pilfer, also, because they feel no qualms in taking material from the impersonal "state." Zh., convicted for theft of socialist property, had been a bookkeeper in a large electric machinery factory plagued with thefts, contract nonfulfillment, disorder, and drunkenness. Zh. was asked, "Do you consider yourself on a par morally with criminals who burglarize apartments or pick people's pockets?" "What are you saying!" she answered. "I never in my whole life would take anything not mine from pockets or apartments." When she was told that, although she does not consider herself a thief, she had taken state money, she answered: "Well that's another matter. The factory has lots of money." Zh.'s friend and accomplice said that "to steal from citizens is a low thing to do, but the state is big, it will not get poor if we take a little." [31] "Probably you know people," the USSR Minister of Justice has written, "to whom you would entrust the keys to your apartment with complete peace of mind knowing they would not take a pencil, but who have no inhibitions against 'helping themselves from production,' . . . rationalizing that the state won't miss it." [32]

Pilfering public property is a crime likely to be understated in the percentages and higher than the 15 to 18 percent reported for recent years because many people tolerate it or turn away when they see it, often because they steal themselves when they get the chance.[33]

According to the Institute's report, when the Central Urals Constuction Organization put into effect nineteen proposals for plant security, personnel selection, and wage setting worked out by the Institute of Crime Study and Prevention on the basis of such findings, losses from theft fell to 4 percent in two years. After the party committee of Zh.'s electrical machinery plant, local people's court, militia Department for Protecting Against the Stealing of Socialist Property, comrades' courts, People's Guards, bookkeepers, and other agencies cooperated in a prevention drive, convictions for theft from that plant, it was said, went down to 15 percent in four years.[34]

Women make up only one in ten convicts. More intuitive than substantiated explanations for women's low share in convictions point to social norms which frown on women's drunkenness or fighting to resolve conflicts as boys and men will, and sex role differentiated since early childhood which keeps girls under tighter control, more bound up as girls in running the home. Criminology today gives social-psychological explanations for women's special role in crime rather than the biopsychological theories about women as the "weaker sex" propounded by some criminologists in the twenties.[35]

A Moscow study found in 1968 that various forms of larceny and burglary predominated in women's crimes. The share of convictions of women for stealing socialist property had greatly increased since 1923 because of the inrush of women into outside employment. Like men convicted for property crimes, convicted women are distinguished by "low educational attainment, lack of interest in their work, parasitism, immoral conduct in everyday life." But, unlike men, women steal more often for economic reasons, for example, to help feed their families or make up for the wages their husbands drink away.

Relatively liberated though Soviet women are, they provide the Institute for Crime Study and Prevention with reason to link some of their crimes with a dependence on or subordination to lovers or husbands. Taken into court for stealing or defrauding, they may blame "family reasons" which an indignant publicist declares should have been left behind as vanished remnants of the past. A long and happily married woman takes to drink and petty thievery after her husband leaves her for someone else. A state farm bookkeeper embezzles ever larger sums to meet the needs of her lover and his dying wife. Sentenced to seven years in a labor colony, she gets not even one letter from him. A saleswoman was in that colony for cheating customers (the number of convictions for that crime recently doubled) in order to support her two children because her husband drinks away his support. R. killed her chronically ill mother because the hospital would not take her and her husband threatened to leave her. Kuznetsova wonders, "Can we say seriously that there is no way out because 'he stopped loving me,' 'deceived me,' 'left me,' or 'I wanted to support him but he craved a Zhiguli [Soviet Fiat] so I began to steal?' "[36]

Women figure prominently among pilferers. Women account for 25 percent of persons convicted for stealing socialist property, 60 percent of persons convicted for speculation, and 70 percent of persons convicted for defrauding customers (they make up 70 to 80 percent of salespersons).

Female thieves of personal property interviewed in two labor camps included a large number of single women without family ties—typically, professional thieves, vagabonds, or beggars. Former alcoholics, drug addicts stealing to support their habits, and prostitutes who had robbed clients abounded among them. Females serving time for stealing personal property usually had lived off sailors in port cities.[37] The Moscow study found that in the 1.5 percent of cases where women participated in robberies and snatchings, it was to practice "*khipestnichestvo*," to act as lures to help their men when thieving yields lean pickings. They pick up men and entice them into courtyards and apartments where male accomplices can rob or mug them.[38]

Women's criminality is much lower than that of men, especially in violent forms of crime. But they commit a substantial share of thefts of personal and socialist property. As with men, criminality among women has fallen off since the twenties, if convictions are any indication.

Gangs. Old-time criminal haunts—flophouses, dens, old markets teeming with pickpockets, thieves, and street waifs—have been all but eliminated in the USSR. Russian cities once had large dangerous bands, but never anywhere near the power and wealth commanded by U.S. organized crime. Since the twenties and thirties, property and violent crimes have become extensively "deprofessionalized," much more casual, and in some places have dropped off sharply, in reports of the early seventies.

Professional criminals now operate in fragmented groups with nowhere near the membership and cohesion and elaborate techniques and differentiations by trade characterizing crime in the twenties.[39] But this criminal underworld is constantly replenished from the ranks of juvenile lawbreakers. Its remnants crop up in statistics of the Institute of Crime Study. According to the Institute, 38 percent of adult thieves have no legitimate occupation, 72 percent are repeaters. Among the repeaters 53 percent have no legitimate occupation and 25 percent have no permanent place of residence but drift across the country at the edge of organized society. Only 20 percent of robberies and snatching (*grabezh*) are committed by criminals acting alone. Nearly 40 percent of the robberies and snatchings are committed by permanently organized gangs or groups of at least two people.

Recidivists make up 47 percent of all those convicted of robbery or snatching. Likely as not, these criminals began their careers in childhood or adolescence. For 60 to 70 percent of recidivists began their criminal careers before reaching the age of 18.[40] They get further trained to crime in corrective labor colonies.[41] When they come out, they tend to seek the company of former criminals, according to an MVD general, head of the Moscow Province Department of the Interior. "It was noted a long time ago that almost everyone who has served a time in a colony tends for some time after his release to keep company with persons similar to himself. They are less demanding about his behavior, he hears no reproaches about the past, there are always common topics of conversation." [42] The former convict also may be able to obtain a homemade pistol, fountain pen gun, or knife, despite the insignificant use of guns to murder in Moscow.[43]

The doings of a gang of bank robbers in Rostov-on-the-Don who shot their way into death sentences or long prison terms [44] pales beside the exploits of a criminal gang of seventeen Georgians. *Soviet Justice* devoted part of three issues to reporting on their trial. The trial consolidated sixty cases and lasted six months. (Felony trials are usually over in a day or two.) Working in twos and threes, the crooks committed sixty-seven known robberies, thefts, and swindles in two years in more than a dozen cities, and with takes running into hundreds of thousands of rubles. They would gain a victim's confidence, play on his desire for scarce black market items, and then defraud him, or more often, rob him using a gun or knife or their favorite means—wine drugged with narcotic sleeping pills—from which three of their victims died through overdose. They used mistresses' flats as home bases and relied on the gullibility of victims and their readiness to drink. Hotels rented rooms to the crooks after seeing their forged passports or none at all. Private renters taking high payments failed to register them with the police, then regretted this when they discovered other tenants drugged and robbed. Savings banks honored stolen passbooks on the basis of false identification to the tune of 170,000 rubles. The gang even managed to get a well-known writer to let them use his country retreat in the literary colony of Peredelkino.[45]

The Soviet criminal underworld, then, still breeds some gangs with cohesiveness, permanence, and huge takes.[46] As a rule, though, such traits better describe the white-collar groups, soon to be discussed, that enrich themselves by speculation, larceny, and fraud through their regular employment in a branch of the Soviet economy, administration, or in the Communist party itself. The white collar criminals, though, are simply the front runners in a shadow economy of barter and black marketeering.

"Private enterprise," "speculation," and "trading" are economic crimes created by Articles 153 and 154 of the RSFSR Criminal Code. They have negative connotations ideologically as "survivals of capitalism and private property mentality." And they divert income from the state, incite theft of socialist property and even violence. But they have a function—getting scarce goods and services to acquisitive and impatient Soviet consumers whom the rigid legal Soviet economy has neglected. Countless Soviet citizens supplement their incomes by trading *"na levo,"* under the table.[47]

A resourceful free-lancer manages to set up an illegal printing plant for posters, to the delight of the Estonian state farm hosting him with whom he shares the 134,000 rubles profit, and of the government officials whose cooperation he assures by generous fees for make-up and "editorial" work. This happens in a country where a private citizen may not operate even a mimeograph machine [48] and every printed item, even posters, bears the censor's mark. Car owners pay well for spare parts stolen from the state, as well as for maintenance services otherwise practically unobtainable. [49] Many times the statistical handbooks' fraction of a percent of the labor force is actually engaged full or part time in private enterprise, from renting dachas and beds to vacationers, to raising profitable crops of cucumbers, a much-loved vegetable in Russia.[50] Truck drivers going north from the fruitful Caucasus conceal delectable loads of tangerines and melons from the procurement cooperative inspectors in cargoes of gravel or chopped fish chicken feed.[51] A night stoker receives twelve years, deprivation of freedom for passing on his factory's hairpins and costume jewelry to his wife (7 years' sentence), her store manager (3 years), and a salesperson (4 years).[52] A group of poachers on the Kazakh steppe sell illegally bagged game to a lead factory canteen at ten times the legal price.[53] Bagging the poachers themselves can be a dangerous, even fatal business.[54]

An institute study of two years of court cases in a northwest Russian province found the most frequently traded black market items to be articles of clothing, buttons and bows, wines and vodka, iceboxes, honey, fish, and jewelry. The state lags in getting early fruits and vegetables on sale? That lag is made up privately. State cattle procurement agencies neglect to go far out into the boondocks to buy livestock? The peasants are happy to sell them to speculators for a little under procurement prices to save the trouble of travel and transportation. The enterprising middlemen take the difference. In half the cases investigated speculated foods actually were bought at retail; 62 percent of the goods were sold in cities; 30 percent to collective farm markets; 62 percent to individuals at home and at work; 8 percent to trade and procurement organizations. Where the speculated item was not in short supply, bad distribution served as another spur to the black market.[55]

Organized black marketeers and middlemen are, typically, not full-time professional entrepreneurs, but persons moonlighting as such or using their legitimate employment to cover or assist the speculation.[56] Many of them are white-collar criminals or work with such. Bound up with the large governing bureaucracy, white collar crimes are the main Soviet manifestation of organized crime.

White-collar criminality. White-collar crimes were defined by the late Edwin H. Sutherland as "crimes committed by persons of respectability and high social status in the course of their occupations." [57] Without calling it such, singling out such a concept, Soviet sources give white-collar criminality a prominent place.

In place of U.S. price fixers, the USSR knows wholesale suppliers, thieves, and stores that sell off scarce items at above fixed prices. In place of financial and market frauds, there is, in the USSR, report padding to avoid reprimands and wangle fat unearned bonuses on a large scale. Building contractors do not have to bribe officials to get work. On the contrary, it is the state building contractors who get bribes for illegal services and sales of material. In place of key money, there is the practice of bribing officials to get apartments ahead of others on the waiting list.[58] Beyond thefts and negligent damage of property, criminality of the white-collared costs the state dear at the hands of "executives" who "tolerate the production of substandard goods," who unlawfully fire workers and office employees, or "motivated by careerist or self-seeking considerations, permit report-padding and other deceptions of the state." [59]

This glimpse at Soviet white-collar criminality brings out the close links between theft of socialist property, economic crimes, and malfeasance in office. Together they account for about a quarter of all convictions for white collar crime (see Table 5–2).

A flagrant example of such a web of white-collar criminality has come to light in a scandal rocking the Georgian republic, sending First Secretary V.P. Mzhvanadze of the Georgian Communist Party into retirement.[60] Housecleaning of sorts under his crime-busting successor, First Secretary

E.A. Shevardnadze, former Minister of Internal Affairs, took several years. It revealed an administrative structure rotted out by white-collar termites at all levels of the Party and administrative apparatus. It involved smashing huge black market rings and jailing their kingpins who once enjoyed complete party protection under Mzhvanadze. Below them, ordinary workers and farmers, too, have been stealing from and hoodwinking the state.

Luxurious homes sprang up illegally. Thefts ran into "several million rubles" in the Ministry of Local Industry alone. Officials in it passed desirable goods in short supply on to "shady dealers" and became their "obedient servants." The rector and party secretary of the Tiflis Medical Institute saw to it that entrance exam graders flunked worthy applicants and raised "unsatisfactory" marks of others to passing because they had "someone 'pulling wires' " for them in "so-called top circles." This corruption illustrates how "many of the bribetakers, schemers, and other criminal elements spread wirepulling through the system, sucking in many executives up to and including responsible officials of the Party." The party officials became merely "appendages" and "shadows" of the administrators they were supposed to control, drawn into the general "egoism, money grubbing, the cult of gain, bribery, extortion, and careerism," the flaunting of "diamonds and dachas," before the cleanup.[61] Corruption in Georgia—but not in Georgia alone—spread, for better or for worse, into the very apparatus of cross-checks and controls, both party and state, which were supposed to guard against it.[62] Soviet white-collar criminality may well be higher than the criminality of the poor, as it may be elsewhere.[63]

Thefts of socialist property linked with economic crimes and abuse of office, the various alliances of embezzlers, bribe-takers, and thieves with the apparatus of administration and rule betoken a pervasive Soviet pattern of group crime. It includes conspiracies to enrich, conceal, and defraud cutting horizontally across occupations and vertically from top organizers to accomplices at the bottom or thieves at the bottom to accomplices at the top, from conspiracies of dispatchers and truck drivers [64] to rings of admissions peddlers and black marketeers.

Soviet criminologists, however, have yet to publish theories of white-collar criminal motivation and of the functions of Soviet white-collar crime.

Personality and Biology

Research on the criminal personality led off the criminological revival in the USSR.[65] Soon, however, it fell behind, snagged on the question of how inherited biological and psychological traits related to criminal behavior. Criminologists who had the most to do with reviving criminology were the most adamantly opposed to biopsychological research. For social theorists like Gertsenzon, this controversy reopened the old sores of the disputes in the twenties and conjured up the specter of "the renaissance of Lombrosianism." [66] Reiterations of their adversaries, psychiatrists and lawyers, that "man is not born a criminal," failed to end objections to biopsychological research on the causes of crime.[67] No matter how moderate their opponents' thesis might be, the social theorists rejected biopsychological explanations for allegedly "begging the question of differences between socio-economic systems, between capitalism and socialism," and in effect asserting that "the task of eradicating crime posed by Marxism on the basis of its analysis of social development is impossible."[68]

This dispute between advocates and opponents of research on genetic factors has cut across professional lines, dividing jurists. It has evoked memories of similar disputes in the twenties and the sociological-biological debate in Western criminology. As always in such disputes, it is impossible to tell whether the attackers care only about doctrinal correctness or act also out of professional competitiveness, just as when they insisted that criminology be centered in their discipline of criminal law, alone, of the social sciences, with the other social sciences like psychology and sociology being merely auxiliary.[69] Social theorists have not been mollified by one of their main opponents' efforts to assure them that biopsychological research will not displace the sociology of law but will only "broaden the front" of crime prevention.[70] Ideology appeared for a while to hold progress in criminology to a standstill.[71]

If a pause in the progress of criminology did occur, it was brief. By the early seventies, the generation of the twenties who led the restoration of criminology was leaving the scene. A new middle generation, uninvolved in the disputes of the twenties over biological *versus* social roots of crime, was taking over. Other factors favored a resolution of ideological deadlocks: (1) the social psychology of criminals and their typology had engaged capable scholars for years, accorded with the political line that "stateways" can indoctrinate new "folkways," that is, "mold the new Soviet man;" (2) this research produced some experimental results; (3) the psychopathology of criminals and their typology received new support from jurist sociologists.

1. Research on the criminal personality received such prestigious support that it could hardly be stalled any more. From the supportive remarks of two successive directors of the Institute of Crime Study and the deputy director,[72] and from the organization of the institute,[73] however, it appears that the sponsorship is not for biopsychological but for social psychological research: [74] "moral-psychological characteristics, social psychological aspects of the personality, the mechanism of anti-social behavior, the scientific classification of criminal personality types, etc." [75]

2. A limited, practical application of social psychological pressures on lawbreakers compared attitudes toward the law in a sample of lawbreakers and a control group of citizens without a record. Lawbreakers, it was found, knew as much about the law as nonlawbreakers but respected it less. Asked whether they would report a crime, committed or in preparation, 3 percent of the nonlawbreakers said no, compared to 25 percent of the lawbreakers, a ratio of more than eight to one. Five percent of nonlawbreakers said they had no goal in life, compared to 25 percent of the lawbreakers. This prompted a recommendation that the campaign of mass legal education already described should especially emphasize ways to instill respect for law and legality. A campaign based on disseminating legal knowledge alone would fail.[76] It remains to be seen over the years whether public opinion study and psychologically based techniques will help the campaign of legal education, described in Chapter 4, to give tangible results.

3. Proponents of biopsychological studies of the criminal [77] look to colleagues like embattled penologist I.S. Noi in the Saratov Juridical Institute and his collaborators L.G. Krakhmal'nik, V.V. Shabalin, and Yu. A. Demidov and to the psychiatrist O.E. Freierov in the ill famed Serbskii Institute of Forensic Psychiatry for support. They have also gained support in the findings of a Moscow University Law Faculty research group, headed by N.F. Kuznetsova.

Moscow's crime rates dropped as social chaos disappeared. Crime there has been at once deprofessionalized and psychologized. Particular traits of character and temperament moved to the fore as motivators of crime in specific situations. Clinic enrollments of patients with neurotic disorders shot up in the 1960s. This indicates to Kuznetsova a need for work on such criminal traits as frustration and aggression, neurotic and more severe psychic disorders, rediscovering lost ways of psychological testing, exploring "the connection between the social and the biological in criminology." [78] A veteran criminologist and labor camp survivor has publicly supported proposals for reopening the Moscow Crime Study Office, closed in 1931, as a place for psychological and physical testing of convicted criminals.[79]

Progress is slow in the study of the criminal personality. It is still hampered by delays in developing approaches for research on "individual psychological peculiarities and biologically pre-determined traits, which play an important part in the mechanism of human behavior, in particular, the mechanism of criminal acts," without falling into the error of "psychologizing and biologizing reasons for committing crimes." [80] The question of "the connection between the social and the biological in criminology" continues to present ideological difficulties. Meanwhile ground has been broken for new approaches.

Forecasting and Planning

Delayed on the biopsychological front, Soviet criminology surged ahead in "general social prevention." Overwhelmingly, in the sixties and early seventies, expert recommendations for change came in response to existing crises of law and order, as in a textile region near Moscow. It had been a region of lonely women and serious lawlessness.

> The region's chief industry, textiles, created a noticeable surplus of women due to its traditionally high concentration on female labor. Among the bad social consequences of this imbalance was the influx of various anti-social elements (drunkards, parasites, released convicts who did not want to do approved work, etc.), who had no trouble moving in with single women. As a result the region's moral climate deteriorated; rates of crime and other anti-social behavior went up. General social measures such as building large enterprises depending mainly on "men's work" were taken to correct this situation. And they were taken with the existing criminological situation in mind.[81]

The very success of social engineering in simple cases like this one provided incentives to retool crime study so as to make it a reliable source of recommendations. Criminology was still a long way from separating out effects of changes in law enforcement, and of various types of social change, on the rates of various crimes in specific regions.[82] By the mid-seventies, revamping methods and techniques claimed attention alongside problems posed by political tutelage and ideological imperatives. Sampling and questionnaires remained crude.[83] Aspirations of crime experts continued to outrun the quality of their statistics [84] and training programs.[85] Above all, criminologists confronted the challenge of converting their science from a means of delayed prevention through response to past crimes, into a science of anticipatory prevention based on forecast of probable future crime trends.

Economic development placed a twofold demand on Soviet criminologists. Their political and administrative superiors expected that, in return for all the support and patronage they received, they should come up with effective ways to head off criminal side effects of the scientific and technological revolution, which made crime rates in some regions four or five times higher than in others. Simultaneously, criminologists were expected to press into service "the achievements of science and technology: computers, advanced techniques of information gathering and processing, cybernetics and systems analysis," so as to end "the constantly growing disproportion between needs for information and the actual level of information available to state organs and research centers." [86]

From the late fifties into the seventies: (1) *Cybernetics and systems approached* remained enormously fascinating to the Party as a possible means of retaining centralized economic control while achieving a much needed boost in the productivity of labor and material. (2) *Forecasting* based on these approaches eventually moved criminology into a new stage of development. (3) *The First Tests of the new forecasting approaches* began in the early 1970's. (4) *Legal cybernetics* meant that all phases of crime prevention, not only criminology, faced drastic overhauling.

1. *Cybernetics and systems approaches.* Cybernetics is the science of control in complex systems through feedback—that is, through commands based on past performance. Feedback devices range from thermostats and the simple speed governor on Watt's steam engine to nervous systems and the economic and crime sensors of the modern state.

Cybernetics is a synthesis of existing information, systems, and probability theories. It grew out of urgent World War II needs for better firepower control. By 1943 an international group of natural scientists, mathematicians, engineers, and logicians became "aware of the essential unity of the set of problems centering about communications, control and statistical mechanics, whether in the machine or living issue." By 1947 they had named their new science "cybernetics," after the Greek word, *khubernetis* (steersman). Cyberneticists like Norbert Wiener espied common mathematical properties of all control processes, whether in machines, living organisms, or animal and human society.[87]

Overwhelmed with undigested information from their centrally directed economy, choking on their own paperwork, Soviet policy makers quickly reconciled cybernetics with Marxism-Leninism. It stirred hopes of central drive and local initiative through adequate flow. Within ten years after Norbert Wiener's *Cybernetics* came out in 1948, Soviet economists and mathematicians were moving to apply cybernetics to economic management, planning, and automation. A veritable intoxication with cybernetics swept through the Soviet elite.[88]

Cybernetics is a special, feedback-and control-oriented variety of systems analysis. Systems approaches conceive of natural and social processes in terms of sets of interdependent parts—systems.[89]

Strongly encouraged by Brezhnev and the Party,[90] planners and managers picked up cybernetics and systems approaches. Party and government decrees in 1966 ordered practical applications of cybernetic and systems analysis to forecasting, long-term planning, and the first so-called ASUs (automated systems of administration). By the mid-seventies, "ASU" had become as fashionable and ubiquitous as cybernetics, despite formidable technical and administrative difficulties encountered in applying ASUs, and productivity increases from ASUs generally below expectations.[91]

"Cybernetics is called upon above all to provide a technical base for the administration of social processes by the Communist Party and the Soviet state." [92] As Brezhnev presented them to the Party, mathematical models, the "complex approach" of systems analysis, and computer networks would make possible realistic long-term plans resting on "scientific forecasting of our economic possibilities, on an exhaustive analysis and appraisal of various possible alternative decisions and their immediate and long-range consequences." [93] By that time, forecasting was underway in leading Soviet scientific and technical centers.[94]

2. *Forecasting* caught on outside economics as a means of anticipating the impact of the "scientific and technological revolution" as it "involves all spheres of Soviet social activity." [95] Proponents of forecasting in crime prevention saw it as a way to "gain time." [96] Again, as in economics some crime specialists expected that a broad "systems" approach, calling on interdisciplinary expertise, and correcting programs continually on the basis of past results, would bring a higher level of effectiveness to their profession.

The first criminological work using feedback and forecasting concepts appeared in 1968. Its eminent author, director of the Institute of Crime Study, lost no time following up Brezhnev's call for forecasting by one of his own.[97] Rationalization through cybernetics and computers took on a sustained quality lacking in past anticrime drives.[98] Criminology became the first of the legal sciences to apply cybernetics and computers to forecasting.[99] Under its minister N.A. Shchelokov, a former close associate of Brezhnev in the provinces before Brezhnev appointed him to the MVD, this ministry emerged as the first Soviet center working on criminological forecasting. An MVD jurist, A.G. Avanesov, headed a pilot forecasting project in the Group for Forecasting and Long Term Planning within the Organization and Research Department of the MVD. It sponsored a groundbreaking national Seminar on Forecasting and Long Term Planning, May 14–18, 1970, an occasion for professional support for the idea of short-range and long-range forecasting to gain time and head off crime. An expert commission of eminent consultants was organized to meet at MVD headquarters periodically to discuss and evaluate its forecasting. By 1970 the MVD had produced a first middle-range crime forecast, for 1971–1975, region by region, based on a combination of extrapolation, expert forecasting, and a simulation model.

The MVD forecasters began with questionnaires to about one-hundred experts—jurists, psychologists, pedagogues, sociologists, and economists—at a crime conference the MVD sponsored October 6–8, 1970, asking the experts what factors influenced crime rates, structure, and trends. Then the MVD researchers questioned 150 criminologists on a nationwide scale, probably all the recognized criminologists in the USSR. What factors bred crime? Inhibited crime? How intensively did these factors influence the roles of various specific crimes? The answers formed matrices of 250 factors. Matrices then went out to 100 experts asked to anticipate whether each factor's influence would rise, drop, or stay the same over five years, five to ten years, and later. On the basis of this expert opinion about factors, Avanesov and his team built and ran off "multi-factor forecasting models," compared the results with those from extrapolation and estimating, and drew up a final forecast for 1971–1975.

The forecast contained three parts: (1) a description of crime rates and trends in 1962–1970; (2) forecasts of relevant social, economic, and demographic changes in 1971–1975 (factor forecasts); and (3) forecasts in broad terms of specific and total crimes in 1971–1975, in minimum, maximum, and intermediate variants.[100] Unfortunately, these crime statistics and forecasts, of enormous comparative interest, remained state secrets, along with the many working documents and conference proceedings.

Forecasting increased, at least temporarily, the influence and access of criminologists in planning decisions affecting crime prevention. How long this state of affairs lasts will depend on whether there is an appearance of success and enough state support for forecasting to continue. In a country where published policy studies are virtually unknown, it is striking that Kudryavtsev urged criminologists also to study how decisions affecting crime prevention are made so as to be able to lobby more effectively for their proposals.[101] Research institutes of the MVD, Procuracy, Academy of Sciences, and Central Statistical Administration began cooperating to improve the quality of forecasting based on simulation models suggested by the Economic-Mathematical Institute of the Academy of Sciences.[102]

A.G. Avanesov's prestige was probably increased by the publication of his *Basic Principles of Criminological Forecasting,* hailed as the first work "in a new scientific direction." [103] His minister, Shchelokov, and V. Klochkov, the new director of the Institute of Crime Study, backed "scientific prognostication," that is, forecasting.[104] Klochkov replaced Kudryavtsev in 1973 when Kudryavtsev became director of the Institute of State and Law. Kudryavtsev's promotion marked the first time a professional criminologist enjoyed the honor, and a boost to criminology's input into policy. It did not hurt that Kudryavtsev's deputy director of the Institute of State and Law, Yu. Tikhomirov, had an ongoing interest in the sociology of law, cybernetics, and forecasting.

3. *The First Practice Tests.* To enlist the cooperation of local law enforcement officials, the Institute of Crime Study and Prevention runs a special section devoted to implementing anticrime measures recommended by the criminologists.[105] In principle at least, the approach is now broadly cybernetic. For it means combining central data storage, planning, and coordination with localized data gathering and planning, corrected in the light of past results.[106]

Entering the "new stage" is by no means a smooth process. Skepticism and indifference increase away from the center. When the head of the Donetsk Province Internal Affairs Administration of the MVD wanted funds, and permission to train local police officials in information theory and computer programming, he experienced difficulties convincing both his superiors and his assistant that the new program for local crime forecasting would serve an essential purpose. Once he did, the provincial militia agencies began to chart the geography and calendar of specific crimes, alcohol consumption, and other possibly relevant behavior and compare them with plots of social trends like migration, to help prepare forecasts and plan crime prevention in a way more closely tied in than before with known and probable crime trends.[107] Local forecasting may be spotty and hard to put through. Without it, however, central forecasting would lose essential channels of feedback and implementation, and fade away altogether from the new juridical subdiscipline of legal cybernetics.

4. *Legal cybernetics* was, by 1973–1974, the fastest growing program to guard social legality and law and order. It is "an interdisciplinary, applied science of the optimal and goal oriented control of complex juridical systems."[108] As in economic management, legal cybernetics treats the gathering, storage processing, and feedback of information.

Jurists joined formally in cybernetic work by April 1958 in the membership of the USSR Academy of Science's new Scientific Council in Cybernetics, under academician A.I. Berg.[109] By 1960 lawyers like the prescient D.A. Kerimov, impressed by foreign trends in computer techniques, were urging work on legal cybernetics and anticipating the technical challenges of coding and programming it would entail.[110] Practical work on a "thesaurus" of standard terms in information language, encoding, and use of manually and mechanically sorted perforated cards, then 80-column punch cards and computers, began in 1965 in Estonia. It proceeded ahead of other known work in the USSR in the Criminological Laboratory of Tartu University and the Section of Law of the Institute of Economics of the Estonian Academy of Sciences.[111]

The Estonian trial run turned into a larger central effort after orders from the Central Committee and Council of Ministers, December 23, 1970, "to apply up to date science and techniques" to set up a central legal information service for all governmental agencies.[112] Legal cybernetics acquired new urgency upon the government's undertaking to publish eventually a multivolume collection of current legislation of the USSR.[113] Better equipped than the Procuracy and the Ministry of Justice, the police in the MVD already had, for several years by 1974, an operating computer center and an expanding net of local computer centers. Organizing ASUs for all their legal activities proceeded in the research institutes of the MVD, Procuracy, and Ministry of Justice.[114] The latter's Research Laboratory of Legal Information Service in the All-Union Institute of Soviet Legislation, benefitting from the Estonians' work, had a coding system ready for use by 1973. It could put the legislative information from 300,000 file cards in the Ministry of Justice on three reels of computer tape, and could keep all stored information updated as laws, directives, and criminal codes were revised.[115]

Legal information for proper administration and legislative drafting only began the list of expected uses of OASUs—branch ASUs in the various law enforcement agencies. OASUs were expected to help forecast the impact of projected criminal and civil legislation; collate suggestions for reform; guide researchers to the published materials on law and crime; keep track of crime and other deviant behavior like drunkenness, juvenile lawbreaking, and administrative violations (from jaywalking to petty hooliganism); register convictions and economic and demographic changes; check up on the speed and disposition of case work in every stage of civil and criminal procedure and of commercial arbitration.[116]

It was expected that legal cybernetics and the ASUs set up according to its principles would provide, in short, more complete information more rapidly to close the feedback loop in making, applying, and interpreting rules of law. "Use of the ASU's will contribute to a significant improvement in law-enforcing activities . . . will create an informational base for long-term planning of crime fighting and systematize the introduction of research findings and path breaking experiments into practice. Creating automatic systems of information retrieval will be also a step forward to deeper knowledge of the dynamics, prevention and eradication of crime in a society building communism." [117]

As work proceeded, it brought not only great expectations but, as in economic cybernetics,[118] a growing realization that ASU could be only as good as the level of data, personnel, and administrative procedures they worked with. Automation did not mean automatic miracles. Machines would be using criminal statistics which "may not always show the real growth of crime," may "wrongly indicate a drop in crime," and which depend on the skill and honesty of local law enforcers. And "the so-called 'latent' (hidden, undiscovered) crime is possibly such a serious part of the iceberg that its measured tip gives no realistic idea of the actual national rates of crimes." Are forecasted factors "positive" or "negative"? How does one untangle demographic processes? [119] Quantitative meaning and accuracy depend on all this. Also, as an interdisciplinary science, legal cybernetics will greatly expand the circle of experts who must use the now secret statistics.[120] Legal cybernetics has indeed made the question of secrecy (as well as that of techniques) an "urgent" one.

Statistics aside, innovators have to contend with "the indifference and misunderstanding of some practical workers and legal scholars." Party leadership in legal matters is sometimes so distantly political as to leave unresolved the matter of coordinating efforts and practices across departmental lines of the Procuracy, MVD, arbitration, courts, and specialists in various disciplines. Also unresolved is a single, standard system for legislative information, statistics, and criminological information. With the best possible statistics and interagency cooperation, how may qualitative, sometimes creative, legal information be converted into mathematical formulas without distortion?[121] ASUs are unlikely to run themselves, as some jurists seem to believe. Where are the trained and reliable personnel to come from? Law faculties and institutes are only beginning to follow the lead of Kiev University. It started courses on legal cybernetics in 1968–1969.[122]

Even with accurate data and trained operators, ASUs will still require that results be interpreted. What significance do the computer readouts have for administrative reforms? Changing the codes? Social and economic planning? A long period of trial and error, of correcting through feedback from ASUs, still lies ahead. This says nothing about the legal problems of defining the rights and duties of consumers and providers of computer services and the responsibility for decisions turning out to be erroneous. No wonder ASU building will go "step by step and gradually." And it should mean a thorough stock taking of every point of crime prevention.[123]

Criminology, and therefore all crime prevention, entered a "new stage"[124] in the early seventies, cautiously testing out the use of cybernetics and systems analysis. Simple factor analysis began to yield to the "complex" analysis of behavior, social change, and law enforcement. Broader proposals for social planning based on criminological forecasts were replacing piecemeal proposals. Limited manual and mechanical information processing began to be replaced by computers and ASUs. If ASUs prove successful in the economy generally, then their prospects for use in crime prevention improve, and so do prospects for programs of crime prevention that require an accurate and timely feedback of past results.

What then? (1) Because of the difficulties enumerated, ASUs may significantly alter nothing. *If* ASUs do prove successful in crime prevention, then either (2) the police and criminal justice begin to wither, or (3) a subtle and sinister shift in criminal justice brings closer the total states of Zamyatin's *We* or Orwell's *1984,* or (4) the USSR becomes the first modern state to resemble the less brutal but still somehow sinister conditioned society of Skinner's *Walden Two,* as the Soviet planning for "forming the new man" in school, family, and "working collectives" bears fruit.[125]

I did not include as a fifth possible outcome that, in the event ASUs are successful, "expert" will prevail over "red," and party controls will erode. This is not impossible. Also, legal cybernetics may well increase both the influence of criminologists and their elbow room in research on social strains and crime.

Red does clash with and limit expert in biopsychological crime research treatment of social inequality and in the matter of publishing statistics. Red elements in party policy dictate also that criminologists may borrow "bourgeois" social science techniques and approaches, from cybernetics and systems analysis to structural functionalism.[126] But red elements also dictate that criminologists "struggle against" bourgeois premises about the universality and inevitably of crime or increasing crime during the "scientific and technological revolution." It must always be concluded that crime "gradually diminishes" under socialism and will disappear under communism.[127] Red clashes with expert also in the close monitoring of experts' foreign contacts and arbitrarily limited foreign travel. This irksome and disheartening isolation cannot but impede research, including that in criminology.

Beyond this, the "party-mindedness" and all embracing control one reads about [128] is little but a formula (whose practical meaning must be explored in each case), and an impetus not only to curb but to reduce crime. Soviet legal studies betray ideological biases like a commitment to social planning, which would be tabu in many Western societies, or to reducing crime. This does not doom legal cybernetics to be less objective than Western behavioralism which assumes opposite premises. It is extremely doubtful that purely objective behavioral research exists. Purely "objective" research is little but a myth. Value preferences shape what is chosen for research and how results are interpreted.[129] Professors in the Soviet Union who lecture about the *sturm und drang* of the "struggle for communism" get ticked off from within the Central Committee's Academy of Social Sciences, a stronghold of orthodoxy. They are told that the USSR is now in an era of "scientific management of Soviet society and scientific management of building communism." Biased empiricism *is* different from purely intuitive "struggle." [130] But both Soviet and Western theorists are probably right when they point to the impossibility of stripping social scientific research of an orientation to some set of values or another.[131]

The system approach is not novel, but the self-conscious emphasis on it is.[132] For all its shortcomings, the systems approach discourages facile, politically convenient correlations taken out of context. Systems approaches predispose their users to see (1) interrelationships within a system which make it more than the mere sum of its parts, (2) subsystems in the system, and (3) a chain of higher systems of which a given system is a part. Some Soviet criminologists, for example, may start like David Easton [133] with the biological organism, and trace the hierarchy of systems up through the human personality, small groups, larger institutions, and so on.[134] Other Soviet criminologists may, because of their premises, exclude the biological system altogether and treat crime as a purely social occurrence.[135] But Soviet users of the systems approach agree that the causes of crime are complex. Lawbreaking, politics (policy), and social processes each are complex systems interacting with the others. Crime can be prevented, therefore, only by a "scientifically sound complex of economic, ideological, social psychological and legal measures." [136] This is a basic principle of cybernetics: to control complex phenomena both feedback and response (commands) must have variety.

I think what is happening is that red, the party orthodox and supportive line, is itself becoming more expert. Red and expert are partially fusing in an ongoing dialectic just as, once upon a time, "revolutionary internationalism" and national interest fused (witness Soviet Russia "firstism," and the national counterclaims in the Sino-Soviet dispute). Rather than slink off the scene, leaving it to cyberneticists and other rationalizers, the Party is busily coopting them. "Information has become the symbol of our era along with the atom," [137] with party blessing and party retooling deep into the Party's own inner information and training processes.[138]

Under party guidance, policy has moved from Khrushchev's neo-Leninist ideological grandeur of full-scale building of communism, to the post-Krushchev coalition's neorationalist ideological grandeur of "the scientific and technological revolution." [139] Dangerous, damaging isolation and ideological suspicion, and cultural repression hang on. Meanwhile, ASUs create hopes and problems, for everything from Leningrad's communal economy to Lithuania's public health services and Soviet enterprises.[140] Computerized feedback and forecasts are devised to help steer economic and social change and deal with their consequences.[141]

From their speedy and wide adoption, one may assume that party policy makers regard cybernetics and systems analysis as tools, not threats, and find them in accord, not in conflict, with Marxism and its rationalist traditions. These traditions go back to the French and Greek enlightenment. According to these traditions, scientific insight into basic laws governing nature and society makes it possible to steer social economic development along a path of steady progress.[142]

Conclusions

Leaps forward and methodological difficulties, reasonable requests for better statistics and unfathomable refusals, frankness and secrecy, favoring social over biopsychological research, redness and expertness add up to the picture of an effort at crime study and prevention which slowly lurches forward and, occasionally, backward. Innovation is impelled by state support and the enthusiasm with new methods from the "scientific and technological revolution." But it is also inhibited by intraprofessional rivalries, controversies over method, and survivals of Stalinism in the minds of men.

Despite what I call "political tutelage" in crime studies, the mix in them of red and expert elements and the contradictory directions in some sectors point to a looser party reign recently giving more play to professional interests and competition among the jurists which cut across the legal profession and other concerned disciplines.

Forecasting and other legal cybernetics opened new prospects for the prevention tendency in crime fighting. Forecasting is experimental. It faces huge technical obstacles and no fewer political ones if crime fighters ever get around to proposing elaborate and costly plans for social engineering in competition with established interest groupings in industry, agriculture, defense, health, education, and welfare. But at last the Party is aiming to give Soviet growth the "organized, planned and scientifically based character" to which it lays claim in its statutes. Crime prevention is to be included in the new rationalism.

Trends in crime study since the first version of this part was written [143] support its suggestion that Soviet criminology "has entered another new and maybe critical phase of rethinking." Even if all the difficulties listed are overcome, a basic informational bottleneck remains. Society's flux, Norbert Wiener pointed out, makes "long statistical runs under essentially constant conditions" impossible.[144] Also, information feedback tends to be distorted by its communicators' self-interest. Hence, the social sciences "can never furnish us with a quantity of verifiable, significant information which begins to compare with what we have learned to expect in the natural sciences. We cannot afford to neglect them, neither should we build exaggerated expectations of their possibilities." [145]

Communications problems aside, party policy will weigh in the scales too. It has been noted here and elsewhere that political tutelage brings support as well as interference, access as well as controls.[146] How successful forecasting becomes in the USSR will depend not only on its internal problems, but also in part on how the Party treats informational policy on crime and social statistics. Elsewhere, systems analysis has been the experts' point of support against interference by the politicians.[147] It remains to be seen whether this will happen in the USSR. As of now, criminologists' enthusiastic turn to cybernetics and forecasting seems to have increased their prestige and access. Chances are that Soviet policy making will continue in its delicate balance between expertise to counter "subjectivism" and "voluntarist decision-making," and vigilance against any expert "discrediting of the people's revolutionary accomplishments." [148] Crime, in this delicate balance, must be precisely recorded and analyzed, along with social and economic trends, but in the context of its "gradual decrease."

For all this ambivalence and motivational conflict in crime prevention, one detects in Soviet responses to crime an erosion of ideology about crime under socialism but not the end of ideology, only the possible end of some chauvinist red aspects and their gradual replacement with an ideological impetus closer to the original spirit of Marxist hubris and rationalism, with its faith in the human ability to liberate ourselves through our command of nature and technology and thereby to end violence and crime.

7

Conclusions

Crimes and Responses

DESPITE PERIODS OF CONFLICT AND REVOLUTIONARY VIOLENCE, Soviet cities and villages on the whole seem safer, more orderly places to live in than they were when the Bolsheviks took over. But Soviet enforcement, statistics, and laws have changed enough to rule out any long-range comparison of social order and crime rates, even if we had figures on reported crime for the bulk of the period, which we do not, given statistical flaws of the early confused years and the changes and secrecy today. Also fluctuations and legal differences call for care in interpreting trends in one region or nationwide.

Among nonpolitical crimes, offenses like hooliganism, moonshining, and all sorts of crimes of theft and violence egged on by the desire for drink or consumer goods and by drunkenness have gained in prominence, while crimes committed for survival, out of "dire poverty," have faded. The crimes of survival were particularly dangerous and poignant during the waves of child homelessness. Drug and traffic offenses, conversely, seem on the way up. Organized crime survives in small groups of a professional criminal underworld. It has grown among corrupt officials engaging in "economic crimes," "official crimes," and "crimes against socialist property" in groups reaching from high party and ministerial levels down to factories, farms, construction outfits, and shop storerooms and counters. Pilfering state property is widespread among the populace.

Ordinary crimes causing policy makers the most concern are (1) juvenile crimes, (2) crimes in the national economy ranging from bribery and report padding to larceny, and black marketeering, and (3) crimes against persons and property connected with alcohol abuse.

Obviously, revolutionary law and order must be charted in terms other than those of simply crime and response. For, in eras of political conflict and forced social change, many crimes are themselves responses to government policy, or simply the change of once legal behavior into illegal behavior through assaults on private trade, such as in 1918 and in 1928–1933.

The Provisional Government had time only to institute reforms moving Russian justice back to the original ideals of 1864 and eliminating the dreaded Okhrana. Ambivalent about state coercion, trying the impossible task of both increasing and popularizing repression, the Bolsheviks intended to leave "not a stone on stone" of the old system of enforcement and justice. But they held over and converted the ordinary police. They revived the secret police. They could not do without the courts and the Procuracy. But they made the Procuracy as centralized as it had been before the 1864 reforms. In a regime divided over how and when to end professional lawkeeping, those Bolsheviks prevailed who stood for greatest centralization of justice and for not retaining a reformed tsarist criminal code.

Lawyers most consistently against repressiveness were not the Marxists, despite their doctrine of the withering away of the state. They were the non-Marxists like M.N. Gernet, and, during his short service as People's Commissar of Justice, I.N. Shteinberg, the Left Socialist Revolutionary. Most Bolsheviks supported terror when the ends justified it. Those like Bukharin who later became moderates did so too late. Also, the leading Bolsheviks, with few exceptions, shared Lenin's ambivalence about the need for state force after the revolution. The goal of its eventual withering away even justified its interim use and, for Stalin, its intensification to unprecedented levels. By dragging their feet on land reform and insisting on staying in the war, the Provisional Government only made this more possible. By deciding on violent opposition to the Bolsheviks, their opponents and the allies only made it more likely.

Two contradictory trends preceeded in the 1920s during the active experimentation of NEP. Theory and penology moved away from criminal law repression and legal regulation in general. Yet law enforcement practice saw a steady building of court and prosecutional institutions as well as a separate Cheka camp system. Not counting the Cheka's 30,000 prisoners, the prison population by 1927 exceeded the tsarist prison population at its peak. Under Stalin, it went on to more than twenty times that peak by 1933 and fifty times by 1938. Even during the greatest influence of the "legal nihilists," headed by Pashukanis, Stalin was making more and more use of all repression, including legal. I shall not detail it again except to recall that the first shot in Stalin's civil war was Article 107 of the (RSFSR) criminal code against grain hoarding. Alongside the NKVD dragnet, many criminal code articles and additions of 1929–1935 were used to help regiment the populace even before the famous 1936 change supporting law and legal education. Conviction figures confirm this.

Crime study flourished quite freely in the 1920s, expired in 1931–1936, and never recovered under Stalin, in spite of movements to restore it. Socialism, it seemed, made superfluous the study of the causes of crime in the USSR.

Bolsheviks gave juveniles and proletarians preferential treatment in court on the theory that they were victims of bourgeois injustice, a supposition with some basis to it. Stalin cut out the preferential treament for juveniles (after extending it in 1929) in 1935 when criminal responsibility for many serious crimes began at age twelve and late 1936 when he liquidated the famous juvenile labor communes. (His practice of preferential treatment for common criminals over political prisoners never stopped to this day.)

Legal reform, liberalizing criminal law, and curbing the secret police appeared among the first policy changes signaled after Stalin. He died early in the 1950s, Russia's first decade in this century without new mass political violence. Russia felt the aftereffects of war still, in the broken and incomplete families, the delayed shock of an unplanned-for birthrate bulge. As conflict faded from the foreground, the long-range problem of dealing with side effects of industrialization and migration to the towns took its place. Urbanization challenged planners and controllers' capability to hold the line against crime.

Khrushchev's secret speech provided a lasting boost to social and criminological research. But it did not initiate legal reform any more than it initiated the cultural thaw. Before that speech penalties had been removed for a substantial number of offenses, reduced for others; the secret police purge organs, the special boards, were abolished; parole was reestablished; a large amnesty was proclaimed and recodification of criminal law, procedure, and laws governing the courts was initiated. After the secret speech, measures against Gypsy rootlessness spread to others outside the socialized work force in the first antiparasite laws. Tremors in the Communist movement after the speech prompted in turn a Soviet backlash against "revisionism" including revisionism in law. This helped the conservatives and truncated some of the liberals' reform proposals, as far as I can gather from the course of events, Soviet writings, and observations and informal conversations in Moscow in late 1958. I look forward to some better informed opinion on this point.

Popularization of justice is too mixed a response to place with certainty on the spectrum between prevention and repression, between liberal measures (moving away from reliance on repression for its own sake) and illiberal measures (reflecting the opinion that the more repression, the better). The most active remnant of popularization has been the institution of the people's guards. There can be no question about the wholesale revisions of the criminal codes, begun five years after the secret speech, and detailed in Chapter 4. Even without Brezhnev's extensive additions, the revisions of 1961–1962 amounted to a major change in criminal law. They introduced the widest extension of the death penalty in Soviet history.

Responses to crime before the secret speech, save for the reintroduction of capital punishment for aggravated murder, took a liberal course. After the secret speech, though for reasons lying outside of any directives in the speech, the pattern of Soviet responses to crime became a skein of threads woven in piecemeal: popularization of crime prevention; harsher penalties; drives for public order and social discipline, including the lost cause of restricting alcohol consumption; speeding the revival of criminological research; greater centralization in the court system; conscripting drifters and parolees into the labor force; and mass legal education. This amounted to an intensification of both prevention and repression. It blended, not always too smoothly, tsarist, Bolshevik, and Stalinist responses with the first applications of cybernetics and forecasting to crime fighting. The same MVD fostering this new experiment was mired in regressive correctional practices and abetting the KGB's political repression, though on a modest scale compared with earlier purges.

Politics and Social Change

Law and order in Russia's revolutionary era, the first half of the twentieth century, supports the contention of Soviet texts and of Western analysts like Hollander and Fyvel that social upheaval reflects not simply industrialization in itself but how a country industrializes. As Ralf Dahrendorf has said, industrialization is not "an irresistible steamroller."

Political decisions, priorities, and conflicts during industrialization are of incalculable importance in shaping it and the social side effects.[1] Tsarism left a particularly unsettling legacy of autocracy tempered frustratingly with grudging reform, of retrograde social policy, and of wasteful and demoralizing foreign adventures. It left a legacy also of an exquisitely trained profession and many theoretical moves toward reforms in criminal policy which were picked up and accelerated under the fleeting Provisional Government. But decay outraced reform, and misdirected violence in disastrous wars helped bring down the whole structure.

Crime waves followed the conflict in 1904–1905 and 1914–1917, and so did revolution. War took away fathers, sharpened hardships, nullified gains in justice, distracted attention from the migrations, the inequalities, and the violence-breeding squalor of tenement living. Annual increases in juvenile convictions were *nine* times greater in 1914–1916 than they had been before the war in 1911–1914.[2]

Soviet law-and-order problems, too, intensified during and after episodes of strife—War Communism and the early 1920s, collectivization and the Great Patriotic War. Each of these conflicts produced great disorder and hordes of homeless street waifs. Echoes of these episodes resounded for years after, into the present day. Like industrialization, violence has an effect which depends on how it is handled. War's effects depend on how it strikes.[3] Domestic political violence may directly breed crime, as in 1917–1921 and 1929–1933. Or it may have only indirect effects—hard to gauge, as during the periods of purge which produced no new waves of homeless children but crippled social prevention and legal research, and provided millions of trapped victims for the common criminals who made up the supreme faction among camp inmates.

When centralized politics rides the saddle as it did in the wake of the Bolshevik revolution, the personal factor and chance loom large. Single events like Lenin's return to Russia in 1917 and his premature death in 1924 have untold effects on crime because of their momentous political consequences. Lenin's death cleared the way for Stalin's eventual takeover. Stalin changed force from a measure of social defense and retribution to a "lever of change" for his "revolution from above."

Attempts to relate crime trends to crime prevention efforts in the Soviet experience encounter difficulties due to insufficient statistical data, the impossibility of separating cause and effect in crimes and justice, and of separating the effects of criminal policy, political change, and social change. Thus, when crime rates seem to drop, it is impossible to separate effects of criminal policy or socialist transformations from effects of normalization, as in the 1920s during the recovery from fighting and famine, the 1930s during the recovery from collectivization and famine, and the 1940s during the recovery from the Great Patriotic War and famine.

Success and Failure

This interplay of crime, setting, and criminal policy, plus statistical vagaries, makes statements about "success" and "failure" risky ventures, especially in turbulent times. During the settling out after them crime-reducing effects of political order and social calm are easily mistaken for crime-reducing effects of criminal policy. NEP produced several experiments of note in penology and prevention amidst overwhelming practical difficulties of administration, scarce funds, and unemployment.

Stalin coped decisively with child vagrancy before, during, and after World War II. He packed millions of real or suspected common criminals to labor camps. But, first he unleashed devastating crimes affecting perhaps three quarters of the population between 1928 and 1938 alone. Later, criminal law became not merely stable but a hodgepodge of partly obsolescent provisions, as stagnant as prevention generally.

Soviet accounts now deplore "crimes and violations of socialist legality" during the "period of the cult of personality." However, they date the crime too late, after collectivization with some exceptions. Clearly crimes by instruments of the state against persons and property began during collectivization, after earlier Bolshevik forerunners of governmental terror. As earlier suggested, Stalin's one-sided preoccupation with crimes against the state and crimes against socialist property and his neglect of preventive measures left society open to disorder and delinquency from below, alongside lawlessness from above. Waifs and criminal gangs made the easiest targets and were in fact cleared off the streets. Organized crime shifted partly into the labor camps and the state and party apparatus, breeding there corruption and arbitrary violence and theft.

Judging from Soviet reform proposals since Stalin and the evidence of the Stalin era, it seems not proven, even dubious, that Stalin gave citizens more law and order by his methods, as compared with less repressive ones. He brought beneficent effects of full employment in the camps and out, social welfare, school expansion, and, in the 1930s, a cause for youth to follow, and determined police action against the often criminal street waifs. Beyond that, a better case exists and has been made, essentially within the USSR by liberalizers, that Stalin drove the country on no matter what cost in legality and law and order.

Stalinism provides a flagrant illustration of the general principle that authorities entrusted with upholding law and order may themselves infringe it at the cost of people's lives, limbs, or property. Stalinism underlines the point that violent crime can be fearsome, whether by civilians or by persons acting in the name of law and order. One thinks of authoritative violence in Berlin, 1919; Soviet villages undergoing collectivization; North and Latin American Indian villages undergoing expulsion; the violence during the labor camp rebellions at Norilsk in May 1953; Vorkuta in July 1953, and Attica in September 1971; shootings of college students; Chile after the military coup of 1973; and the extraordinary repressions of dissenters in countless countries including the USSR. The overwhelming share of threat to societal security, for certain groups, in such instances, has been inflicted by those acting in the name of central or local political authority.[4]

The results of intensifying repression and prevention after Stalin lie obscured by an astounding secrecy about crime trends beyond vague statements about percentage changes in convictions, wrongly equated with "crime." Stated conviction trends were favorable as compared with trends in some European countries, and especially in the United States, and unfavorable as compared with trends in others. Crime trends in the USSR are still not favorable enough to censorship and their party superiors to show that crime is "steadily diminishing," is alien to socialism, and will eventually disappear as programmed in revolutionary Marxist and Marxist-Leninist ideology.[5]

Secrecy about statistics and many exasperated statements of leading officials indicate the continuing sensitivity and difficulty of the crime problem in the Soviet Union.[6] First Deputy Prosecutor of the USSR M.P. Malyarov told the editors of *Pravda* that "despite certain successes, the state of affairs in the struggle against lawbreaking rightly evokes concern among Soviet people." Malyarov seemed to find common crime as stubborn a problem as he did dealing with defiant dissidents like the physicist Andrei Sakharov.[7] Sometimes in dealing with dissidents by applying to them criminal law on hooliganism or parasitism, the authorities increase common crime statistics—a fact very significant for the dissidents concerned and for human rights but not for overall crime statistics. Results of all recent drives for social discipline—against hooliganism, drunkenness, crimes in the economy, pilfering, juvenile crime—remain clouded in equivocal summaries, the Procuracy's doubts, local coverup by law enforcement agencies, and contradictory reports of success and failure.

In sum, law and order appears to be closer to realization now than under Stalin (all verdicts still open and unproven on his era), but has still been sufficiently insecure to push successive leaders to maintain secrecy and to grasp periodically at new ways to fight crime. The resultant policy is not yet a whole, a reflection of a penological principle such as under Stalin. Rather, policy is an accretion of piecemeal approaches growing out of Soviet bureaucratic policy making.

Policy Making

Centralized under Lenin, near paralyzed under Stalin, innovation in crime fighting returned after Stalin. His successors turned to a wide circle of consultants. The variety and freedom of 1920s research has not yet fully returned. It moved slowly forward against ideological obstacles in the 1960s.[8] It continues to move forward into biopsychological research and considerations of inequality and disadvantage. Criminology's progress illustrates the contrary directions of policy possible in social controls—on the one hand, the repression and psychiatric imprisonment of dissidents, on the other hand, new departures in research to guide the judiciary in dealing with common crime.

This progress illustrates also how criminology is affected both by the political climate and by findings in other fields such as labor studies, cybernetics, systems theory of which cybernetics is a part, and computer technology.

Criminologists won over top administrators like the head of the USSR MVD to the view that crime fighting is multidimensional or, as a leading criminal lawyer puts it, crime fighting includes "planned implementation of social and economic change; the influence of ideas, traditions and all means of upbringing; the legal regulation of social relations and law enforcement . . . an organic part of the system of steering social processes."[9]

By now one can see the limits on the principle that our assumptions about crimes determines what we do about them,[10] and that criminology not only reflects but also influences those assumptions. First, under any circumstances this depends on channels of access from experts to policy makers, and on available resources for prisons, police, alternative programs, child care, and social amelioration and education, as the difficulties of the 1920s in the USSR and penal reforms everywhere point up. Second, policy depends on other priorities for funds, be they foreign adventures, revolutionary subversion, consumption, or capital repairs on the Communist Academy. They took more funds than did the entire prison system of the USSR in 1928 and fourteen times the funds allotted to the Crime Study Institute. It was from this same Communist Academy that Pashukanis and Krylenko launched their attacks on the institute and on all criminology. Third, policy reflects time-honored attitudes toward crime, as well as social values of various participants in making it. A fourth limitation on the principle that criminal policy reflects assumptions and, in part, the influences of criminology, applies especially to revolutionary law and order. Criminal policy at the beginning of revolutionary rule is likely to reflect ideological, nonempirical assumptions about the path to the new order, as in the populist, anticentralist side of Bolshevik thinking during War Communism. Criminal policy during Stalin's revolution from above, again, reflected an ideological teaching, the "intensification of the class struggle." But this teaching of Stalin's reflected, in turn, the mix of Stalin's economic and political goals.

Soviet criminologists work under bureaucratic controls of their superiors in the Procuracy, Supreme Court, MVD, Ministry of Justice, institutes, faculties, party committees. But channels of state and party controls are also channels of expert *access*. The regime cares about what its experts are uncovering in more ways than one. Controls are a backhanded compliment to the importance of experts in the scientific and technological revolution.

Criminologists' findings are to be of practical value, hence based solidly on the recording of real conditions and trends. On the other hand, the criminologists' work must not conflict with basic ideological tenets of

Marxism-Leninism about diminishing crime in socialist society, and it must not be politically embarrassing to the regime.[11] These ideological and practical requirements tend to clash.

The Communist Party steers crime fighting through the hierarchies of party organizations, courts, police, and procuracy, through legal aid offices, people's detachments, the Komsomol, soviets, comrades' courts, commissions on juvenile affairs, numerous volunteer committees, and commissions at the grass roots.

Centralism like this, though less pervasive, made possible the tsarists' foreign-inspired "series of revolutions effected peacefully by the autocratic power," [12] among them, the judicial reform of 1864. Under less peaceful auspices, the Bolsheviks and Stalin made radical changes in law and justice. Like tsarist reforms, the Communist ones were inspired by an ideology adapted from abroad and giving impetus and justification, drafted by bureaucratic and expert elites, implemented rapidly on a sweeping scale, vitiated or modified in adjustments and retreats, and followed by a turn to more piecemeal, empirical, and contradictory policy making.

Since Stalin, the Party still reserves the right to redefine what legality is at any stage, that is, to reorder justice in terms of its changing political needs.[13] Khrushchev attempted another radical change from above in justice, education, property rights, and administrative structures, under the slogan launched in 1958 of the "full-scale building of communism." His new revolution from above proved abortive. But institutions associated with his popularization of justice survived, alongside the regular system they were originally supposed to supplant.

With some oversimplification, it may be pointed out that the Party is not a monolithic abstraction but a complex hierarchy headed in the Secretariat and Politburo by an interlocking directorate working interdependently with various segments of their governing apparatus. The twenty-five or so oligarchs must represent and balance competing regional,[14] institutional, and economic interests.[15] These interests can unite, but never more formally than when in defense of the status quo, as Khrushchev's fall revealed.[16]

The Soviet oligarchy has lacked the unity and drive essential for any new radical social change or reordering of justice, though fully capable of sponsoring an imposing series of separate legal reforms in many fields. First, autocratic power eroded in Russia, then dictatorial power of one party secretary, then the force of one ideological vision. For Soviet leaders seem today to be "driven and guided by circumstances more than by ideology." [17]

Ideology in Daniel Bell's sense of an officially codified consensus on values has a core of doctrine which upholds the Party's tutelage and mission. Today, however, it is not inspiring an immediate agenda of radical change. Since Stalin the inspirational and coercive sides of ideology as an official doctrine have been fading, leaving its rationalizing function more exposed. The repression of dissidents is not a product of mission but of defensive fear for legitimacy. Jerry Hough's detailed study of party officials leads him to believe that "to speak of 'the retention of the essentially dogmatic character of the ideology' and to state that the years since 1964 have seen movement away from 'an ideologically more tolerant system' is to overlook the crucial fact that on all but the most central questions, party ideology is less and less incorporated into clear-cut, undebatable 'ideology,' with a consequent widening of the areas open to public discussion. In almost every policy sphere, ideology is ambiguous and ill-defined."[18]

One of these policy spheres turns out to be crime fighting. This does not necessarily augur an "end of ideology," except in Bell's sense of official, codified doctrine. For, as I mentioned earlier, there are many signs that even the most "objective" social research is influenced by the researchers' preconceptions. These preconceptions may be called ideology too in a broader, less elitist sense than Bell's, of ideology not only as codified doctrine but also as a set of beliefs and resulting preferences oriented to evaluating, guiding, or justifying behavior.

In that sense, there is no end of ideology among Soviet social engineers and experts on crime. Rather, there is a decline in the force of an official ideology as it touches crime fighting among other spheres of Soviet life. Ideological innovation and initiatives are very slowly diffusing down among the experts. Their formulations still internalize a party essential about the superiority of socialism in dealing with crime. But they modify this central proposition with their own interpretations of how this applies to their own work. Now, as compared with the NEP era and its ideals of the benevolent utopians and child-centered progressivists, current self-ideologies of the experts are tinged with the materialism of the computer age. It remains to be seen whether the computers will make crime fighters either as all-molding or as sensitively responsible to social change as their ideology requires. An interplay of control and response without complete takeover of either is a likely outcome.

Notes

Chapter 1

1. I use law and order, a subjective term with many connotations, in the Soviet sense of *pravoporyadok:* the condition of societal security against crime and the governmental means of enforcing it. John N. Sutherland and Michael S. Werthman, *Comparative Concepts of Law and Order* (Glenview, Ill.: Scott, Foresman, 1971); V.M. Chkhikvadze et al., (eds.). *Entsiklopedicheskii slovar' pravovykh znanii (sovetskoe pravo)* (Moscow: "Sovetskaya entsiklopediya," 1965), pp. 350–351.

2. T.R. Fyvel, *Troublemakers: Rebellious Youth in an Affluent Society* (New York: Schocken Books, 1964), pp. 264, 286–310; Paul Hollander, *American and Soviet Society: A Reader in Comparative Sociology and Perception* (Englewood Cliffs, N.J.: Prentice-Hall, 1969), p. 280; L.J. MacFarlane, *Violence and the State* (London: Nelson, 1974), pp. 70–71; Toby Jackson, "Affluence and Adolescent Crime," *The President's Commission on Law Enforcement and Administration of Justice, Task Force Report: Juvenile Delinquency and Youth Crime,* (Washington, D.C.: U.S. Government Printing Office, 1967), pp. 71, 144; Marvin E. Wolfgang, "The Culture of Youth," Ibid., p. 152.

3. U.S. Department of Justice. Federal Bureau of Investigation. *Uniform Crime Reports for the United States* (hereinafter UCR), *1968* (Washington, D.C.: U.S. Government Printing Office, 1969), pp. 31–50, 94, 98–99, assuming chances of victimization change proportionally with per capita crime rates. The rise continues—*UCR, 1973* (1974), pp. 1–5; Ray Reed, "The North Finds the North Has As Much Appetite for Violence as the South," *New York Times,* October 9, 1968.

4. See Chapter 6 for Soviet interpretations. For a variety of Western impressions see, e.g., Bernard Gwertzman, "Soviet Awareness of Crime Problems Rising," *New York Times,* September 8, 1969; James Reston on Moscow as a "policeman's paradise," in ibid., November 20, 1968; Clark P. Walace, "Killing of Two Women on Moscow Streets Officially Reported," ibid., November 4, 1974; Walter D. Connor, *Deviance in Soviet Society* (New York: Columbia University Press, 1972), pp. 147–228.

5. See, e.g., Ivo Lapenna, *Soviet Penal Policy* (London: Bodley Head, 1968).

6. Peter H. Solomon, Jr., "Specialists in Soviet Policy-Making: Criminologists and Criminal Policy in the 1960s" (Ph.D. dissertation, Faculty of Political Science, Columbia University, 1973), note 56.

7. "Family Reforms on the Road to Communism," in Peter H. Juviler and Henry W. Morton (eds.), *Soviet Policy-Making: Studies of Communism in Transition* (New York: Frederick A. Praeger, 1967), pp. 29–36; "Crime and Its Study," in Henry W. Morton and Rudolf L. Tokes (eds.), *Soviet Politics and Society in the 1970s* (New York: Free Press, 1974), pp. 200–237; "Social Disorganization: The Debates over Remedies," Paper prepared for Princeton University Conference on Conflict and Change in Soviet Society, March 3–4, 1966.

8. Case studies of conflicts in the Soviet leadership appear, e.g., in R. Conquest, *Power and Policy in the USSR: The Study of Soviet Dynasties* (New York: St. Martins Press, 1961); Michel Tatu, *Power in the Kremlin: From Khrushchev to Kosygin* (New York: Viking Press, 1969); Sidney I. Ploss, *Conflict and Decision-Making in Soviet Russia: A Case Study of Agricultural Policy* (Princeton, N.J.: Princeton University Press, 1965); Arnold Horelick, "The Cuban Missile Crisis: An Analysis of Soviet Calculations and Behavior," *World Politics,* vol. 16 (1964), pp. 363–389, repr. in Erik P. Hoffmann and Frederick J. Fleron, Jr. (eds.), *The Conduct of Soviet Foreign Policy* (Chicago–New York: Aldine-Atherton, 1971), pp. 346–370. Policy studies dealing with occupational segments of society like the military, administrators, and specialists appear in, e.g., H. Gordon Skilling and Franklyn Griffiths (eds.), *Interest Groups in Soviet Politics* (Princeton, N.J.: Princeton University Press, 1971); Joel J. Schwartz and William R. Keech, "Public Influence and Educational Policy in the Soviet Union," in Roger Kanet (ed.), *The Behavioral Revolution and Communist Studies* (New York: Free Press, 1971).

9. President's Commission on Law Enforcement and Administration of Justice, *The Challenge of Crime in a Free Society: A Report by the President's Commission on Law Enforcement and Administration of Justice* (Washington, D.C.: U.S. Government Printing Office, 1967) (hereinafter, *Challenge of Crime*), pp. v, 1–15, 17–53.

As many workers are killed annually in their factories as people of all ages and occupations are murdered. The annual death toll in work-connected accidents in mid-1970 was reported to be about 14,000. There were 13,648 reported cases of murder and non-negligent manslaughter in 1968. "Industry-Labor Battle Line is Emerging Over Pending Job-Safety Legislation," *New York Times,* July 13, 1970.

Autos—their defects and accidents and pollution—kill and maim many times the number of crime victims. Nearly two million Americans have died in auto accidents (more than twice as many as in all America's foreign wars). J. Robert Moskin, "Life and Death in Your Automobile," *World,* March 13, 1973, p. 14. But it means little to people at home behind police-locked doors and barred windows that "one is" five times more likely to die in an auto accident than to be criminally slain, one hundred times more likely to be injured in a home accident than in a serious assault.

"[To] suffer a deliberate violence is different from experiencing an accident, illness, or other misfortune." Violent crime means terrifying attacks by other people. The victim feels the "fear of the hunted in the presence of the hunter." One feels in control (perhaps wrongly) when using cars or appliances. Our sense of control is threatened by crime and mass protest, which seem to lap irresistibly at personal security and foundations of civil authority. *Challenge of Crime,* p. 34.

10. *The Soviet Experience with Delinquency,* a monograph in preparation.

11. Charles Tilly, "Collective Violence in European Perspective," in Hugh Davis Graham and Ted Robert Gurr (eds.), *Violence in America: Historical and Comparative Perspectives. A Report to the National Commission on the Causes and Prevention of Violence, June 1969* (New York: New American Library, Signet Books, 1969), pp. 4–41.

12. On criminal law as an expression of social values, see Lapenna, *Soviet Penal Policy,* p. 9. On importance of knowing *who* makes the laws, and their preferences, see Howard S. Becker, *Outsiders: Studies in the Sociology of Deviance* (New York: Free Press, 1963), pp. 1–18, 121–176. On varieties and relativities in the definition of crime, see, e.g., Hermann Mannheim, *Comparative Criminology* (2 vols.; London: Routledge and Kegan Paul, 1965), vol. 1, pp. 22–67.

13. Edwin H. Sutherland and Donald R. Cressey, *Principles of Criminolgy* (7th ed.; New York: J.B. Lippincott, 1966), p. 365. For examples of hawks' opinions, see J. Edgar Hoover, as quoted at length in ibid., pp. 36–53; excerpts from the American Independent Platform, *New York Times,* October 14, 1968; "Transcripts of Acceptance Speeches by Nixon and Agnew to the G.O.P. Convention," *New York Times,* August 9, 1968; Governor Reagan on "the decline of law and order and the rise of crime," quoted in *Newsweek,* October 9, 1967, p. 27; President's Commission on Law Enforcement and Administration of Justice, *Task Force Report: Crime and Its Impact* (Washington, D.C.: U.S. Government Printing Office, 1967), pp. 50, 85–87.

For an example of a contrasting reaction, read James Vorenberg: "The best hope of crime control lies not in better police, more convictions, longer sentences, better prisons. It lies in job training; jobs and the assurance of adequate income; schools that respond to the needs of their students; the resources and help to plan a family and hold it together; a decent place to live, and an opportunity to guide one's own life and to participate in guiding the life of the community." (Professor Vorenberg of the Harvard Law School was executive director of the President's Commission on Law Enforcement and Administration of Justice, whose report of 1967 is cited here.) James Vorenberg and James Q. Wilson, "Is the Court Handcuffing the Cops?" *New York Times Magazine,* May 11, 1969, p. 134.

14. See contrasting views in (1) Herbert L. Packer, *The Limits of Criminal Sanction* (Stanford, Calif.: Stanford University Press, 1968), and Nicholas N. Kittrie, *The Right to Be Different: Deviance and Enforced Therapy* (Balti-

more: Penguin Books, 1973); and (2) Karl Menninger, *The Crime of Punishment* (New York: Viking Press, 1968).

15. By "violence" I mean "the threat or use of force that results, or is intended to result, in the injury, or forcible restraint or intimidation of persons, or the destruction or forcible seizure of property." *Progress Report of the National Commission on the Causes and Prevention of Violence, January 9, 1969* (Washington, D.C.: U.S. Government Printing Office, 1969), p. 3.

16. Lapenna, *Soviet Penal Policy,* p. 10, makes a somewhat different but also useful distinction between prevention and repression.

17. *Violent Crime: Homicide, Assault, Rape, Robbery; The Report of the National Commission on the Causes and Prevention of Violence* (New York: George Brazilier, 1969), p. 34.

18. "Violence is as American as Cherry Pie," according to H. Rapp Brown, quoted in *Crime and Justice in America* (2nd ed.; Washington, D.C.: Congressional Quarterly Service, 1968), p. 6. On its universality, see note 11 and *Progress Report of the National Commission on the Causes and Prevention of Violence,* pp. A-6, A-7.

19. Aleksandr I. Solzhenitsyn, "Peace and Violence," *New York Times,* September 15, 1973. See also Chapter 6.

20. Jerome H. Skolnick, *The Politics of Protest* (New York: Ballantine Books, 1969), pp. 1–8, 210–326; J. Roland Pennock and John W. Chapman, *Coercion* (Chicago: Aldine Atherton, 1972)

"Since crime and social unrest have both increased over the past decade, Richard M. Nixon and his running mate, Gov. Spiro T. Agnew, have made the restoration of 'law and order' the chief theme of their campaign." From an editorial in *New York Times,* September 26, 1968; Richard Harris, *Justice: The Crisis of Law, Order and Freedom in America* (New York: E.P. Dutton, 1970), p. 13. Once in office, President Nixon declared "war against the criminal elements" and sent thirteen controversial crime-fighting measures to Congress. *The State of the Union: An Address by Richard Nixon, President of the United States, January 22, 1970* (undated pamphlet), p. 8. Four years later Agnew, Nixon, and their administration had fallen amidst America's greatest scandal over crimes in high office.

21. Dankwart A. Rustow, "Communism and Change," in Chalmers Johnson (ed.), *Change in Communist Systems* (Stanford, Calif.: Stanford University Press, 1970), p. 355.

22. Herbert J. Spiro, "An valuation of Systems Theory," in James C. Charlesworth (ed.), *Contemporary Political Analysis* (New York: Free Press, 1967), p. 172.

23. "Learning by cases . . . leads to an understanding of how people behaved in the past in given circumstances, and encourages reflection on what kinds of conditions induce what types of behavior." Harold Stein, *Public Administration and Policy Development* (New York: Harcourt Brace and World, 1952), cited in James B. Christoph (ed.), *Cases in Comparative Politics* (Boston: Little, Brown, 1965), p. viii. This book contains useful case studies, so does Gwendolin H. Carter and Alan F. Westin (eds.), *Politics in Europe:*

5 Cases in European Government (New York: Harcourt Brace and World, 1965); and William P. Andrews, *French Politics and Algeria: The Process of Policy Formation* (New York: Appleton-Century-Crofts, 1962).

24. Unless otherwise stated, this description and appraisal of the 1864 judicial reforms and their antecedents is based on K.P. Zmirlov (ed.), *Uchrezhdenie sudebnykh ustanovlenii* (rev. and enl. ed.; St. Petersburg: Izd. Yurdicheskago knizhnago sklada "Pravo," 1913), *passim;* N.N. Rosin, *Ugolovnoe sudoproizvodstvo* (2nd ed., rev. and enl.; St. Petersburg: Izd. Yuridicheskago knizhnago sklada "Pravo," 1913), pp. 162–197; Donald Mackenzie Wallace, *Russia: On the Eve of War and Revolution,* ed. and intro. by Cyril E. Black (New York: Vintage Books, 1961), pp. 67–91; Anatole Leroy-Beaulieu, *The Empire of the Tsars and the Russians* (3 vols.; New York and London: G.P. Putnam's Sons, 1894), vol. 2, 252–425; N.P. Eroshkin, *Ocherki istorii gosudarstvennykh uchrezhdenii dorevolyutsionnoi Rossii* (Moscow: Gosudarstvennoe uchebnopedagogicheskoe izd. Min. prosveshcheniya RSFSR, 1960), pp. 305–312, 364; S.V. Yushkov, *Istoriya gosudarstva i prava SSSR. Chast' I* (4th ed.; Gosudarstvennoe izd. yuridicheskoi literatury, 1961), pp. 547–556; Samuel Kucherov, *Courts, Lawyers, and Trials under the Last Three Tsars* (New York: Frederick A. Praeger, 1953), *passim;* Chapter 2, notes 39–41.

25. For a brief summary of *ancien régime* justice before the classical reforms as well as the classical liberal reforms, see Leon Radzinowicz, *Ideology and Crime* (New York: Columbia University Press, 1966), pp. 1–28.

26. Sutherland and Cressey, *Principles of Criminology,* pp. 305–333; Radzinowicz, *Ideology and Crime,* pp. 5–28.

27. Quoted in Kucherov, *Courts, Lawyers, and Trials under the Last Three Tsars,* p. 26.

28. Ibid., p. 43.

29. Leroy-Beaulieu, *Empire of Tsars and Russians,* vol. 2, pp. 253, 266–277.

30. A. Vorms and A. Parenago, "Krest'yanskii sud i sudebnoadministrativnyya uchrezhdeniya," in N.V. Davidov and N.N. Polyanski (eds.), *Sudebnaya reforma* (2 vols.; Moscow: Knizhnoe izd. "Ob'edinenie," 1915), pp. 120–121, 161–165.

31. Judicial investigators were irremovable, like the judges, but only when moved from probationary to permanent status. By postponing promotion to full status, the Procuracy effectively kept most judicial investigators—and hence the important pretrial investigation—under its thumb.

32. Leroy-Beaulieu, *Empire of Tsars and Russians,* vol. 2, p. 395.

33. Otto Kircheimer, *Political Justice: The Use of Legal Procedures for Political Ends* (Princeton, N.J.: Princeton University Press, 1961), pp. 3–172, 419–431.

34. Peter I. Lyashchenko, *History of the National Economy of Russia to the 1917 Revolution,* transl. by L.M. Herman (New York: Macmillan, 1949), pp. 503, 544–555.

35. L.M. Vasilevskii, *Detskaya prestupnost' i detskii sud* (Tver': Izd. "Oktyabr'," 1923), p. 38.

36. Aaron Zak, "Kharakteristiki detskoi prestupnosti," in M.N. Gernet (ed.), *Deti-prestupniki* (Moscow: "V.I. Znamenskii i Ko.," 1912), pp. 88–89; N. Mankovskii, "Sotsial'no-ekonomicheskie faktory detskoi prestupnosti v Moskve," *Ibid.*, pp. 252–257; N.I. Ozeretskii, "Nischenstvo i besprizornost' nesovershennoletnikh," in E.K. Krasnushkin et al. (eds.), *Nishchenstvo i besprizornost'* (Moscow: Izd. Moszravotdela, 1929), pp. 116–124. This source points out that child vagrancy goes far back into Russia's past.

37. E. Tarnovskii, "Dvizhenie chisla nesovershennoletnikh, osuzhdennykh v Rossii za 1901–1910 gg," *Zhurnal ministerstva yustitsii,* No. 10 (1913), pp. 45, 48–49, cited in S.S. Ostroumov, *Prestupnost' i ee prichiny v dorevolyutsionnoi Rossii* (Moscow: Izd. Moskovskogo universiteta, 1960), p. 194.

38. E. Tarnovskii, "Voina i dvizhenie prestupnosti," *Sbornik statei po proletarskoi revolyutsii i pravu,* Nos. 1–4 (1918), p. 113, cited in Ostroumov, *Prestupnost' i ee prichiny,* p. 199; A.A. Gertsenzon, *Bor'ba s prestupnost'yu v RSFSR: Po materialam obsledovaniya NK RKI SSSR* (Moscow: Yurid. Izd. NKYu RSFSR, 1928), pp. 13–16.

39. Kucherov, *Courts, Lawyers, and Trials under Last Three Tsars,* pp. 296–307.

40. P. Vsesvyatskii, "Nesovershennoletnie v tyur'me," in Gernet, *Deti-prestupniki,* pp. 420–421; Yu Bocharov, "Pervye detskie sudy po delam o maloletnikh v Rossii," *ibid.,* pp. 525–532, 536–540.

41. M.N. Gernet, intro. to *Deti-prestupniki,* p. 6.

42. M.N. Gernet, *Obshchestvennyya prichiny prestupnosti: sotsialisticheskoe napravlenie v nauke ugolovnogo prava* (Moscow: Izd. S. Slirmunta, 1906), pp. 204–208.

43. A.M. Rubasheva, "Ocherk sistemy bor'by s detskoi zabroshennost'yu i prestupnost'yu v Amerike i Zapadnoi Evrope," in Gernet, *Deti-prestupniki,* pp. 483–524.

44. Peter H. Solomon, Jr., "Soviet Criminology: Its Demise and Rebirth," *Soviet Union,* vol. 1, No. 2 (1974), pp. 122–140; note 42.

45. Edwin M. Schur, *Our Criminal Society* (Englewood Cliffs, N.J.: Prentice-Hall, 1969), pp. 12–21; Sutherland and Cressey, *Principles of Criminology,* p. 34. For the view that psychotherapy can rehabilitate the individual but only a "better social order" can prevent crime from flourishing, see, e.g., Hyman Rodman and Paul Grams, "Juvenile Delinquency and the Family: A Review and Discussion," President's Commission on Law Enforcement and Administration of Justice, *Task Force Report: Juvenile Delinquency and Youth Crime,* p. 215.

46. Quoted in Radzinowicz, *Ideology and Crime,* p. 37.

47. For a summary of prerevolutionary Russian criminology, see Ostroumov, *Prestupnost' i ee prichiny,* pp. 229–336.

48. James Q. Wilson, "Crime and the Criminologists," *Commentary,* No. 1 (July 1974), pp. 47–53.

49. Radzinowicz, *Ideology and Crime,* p. 30; Sutherland and Cressey, *Principles of Criminology,* pp. 53–76, 311–313.

50. Ostroumov, *Prestupnost' i ee prichiny,* pp. 302–304.

51. Sutherland and Cressey, *Principles of Criminology,* p. 51.

52. Leon Trotsky, *The History of the Russian Revolution,* transl. by Max Eastman (3 vols. in one; Ann Arbor: University of Michigan Press by arrangement with Simon and Schuster which published the work in three vols. in 1932); William Henry Chamberlin, *The Russian Revolution, 1917–1921* (2 vols.; New York: Macmillan, 1952); Leonard Schapiro, *The Origin of the Communist Autocracy: Political Opposition in the Soviet State—First Phase, 1917–1922* (Cambridge: Harvard University Press, 1955); *Merle Fainsod, How Russia Is Ruled,* 2nd ed. (Cambridge: Harvard University Press, 1963), pp. 3–86, giving a fine shorter introduction to the origins of Bolshevism and its road to power.

53. Hannah Arendt, *On Revolution* (New York: Viking Press, 1963), p. 28.

54. John Reed, *Ten Days That Shook the World* (New York: Boni and Liveright, 1919), pp. 125–126.

55. Alexander Blok, quoted in I.N. Steinberg, *In the Workshop of the Revolution* (New York: Rinehart, 1953), p. 12.

Chapter 2

1. Proclamations are reprinted in V.G. Smirnov and M.G. Shargorodskii, "Ugolovnoe pravo," in O.S. Ioffe, et al. (eds.), *Sorok let sovetskogo prava, 1917–1957* (2 vols.; Leningrad: Izd. Leningradskogo universiteta, 1957), vol. 1, pp. 479–481.

2. V.P. Portnov and M.M. Slavin, "Nekotorye voprosy istorii sovetskoi militsii (1917–198g.)," Institut gosudarstvo i pravo Akademii nauk SSSR. *Problemy gosudarstva i pravo na sovremennom etape.* Vyp. 7 (1973), p. 86.

3. John Reed, *Ten Days That Shook the World* (New York: Boni and Liveright, 1919), pp. 100–102, 106, 205, 277–278, 336–337. Reed shared the Bolsheviks' belief that the wine rioters were egged on by "counterrevolutionaries who distributed plans among the regiments showing the location of stores of liquor," ibid., pp. 277–279, and p. 94.

4. B.A. Galkin (ed.), *Organizatsiya suda i prokuratury v SSSR* (Moscow: Izd. "Yuridicheskaya literatura," 1967), pp. 67–68, 71; V.A. Ivanov, "Organizatsiya suda i prokuratury: Puti sozdaniya novogo revolyutsionnogo suda," in Ioffe, *Sorok let sovetskogo prava, 1917–1957,* vol. 1, pp. 566–567; Ivo Lapenna, *Soviet Penal Policy* (London: Bodley Head, 1968), pp. 28–30.

5. Ibid., p. 29.

6. Leon Trotsky, *The History of the Russian Revolution,* transl. by Max Eastman (Ann Arbor: University of Michigan Press, by arrangement with Simon and Schuster which published it in 1932), pp. 328–330; N. Sukhanov,

The Russian Revolution 1917: A Personal Record, ed., abridged, and transl. by Joel Carmichael (New York: Oxford University Press, 1955), pp. 272–325, 380.

7. Rosa Luxemburg, "The Russian Revolution," in *The Russian Revolution and Leninism or Marxism,* with new introduction by Bertram D. Wolfe (Ann Arbor: University of Michigan Press, 1961), pp. 25–80.

8. John N. Hazard, "Introduction," in Hugh W. Babb and John N. Hazard (eds.), *Soviet Legal Philosophy* (Cambridge: Harvard University Press, 1951), p. xvii.

9. Karl Marx and Frederick Engels, *Selected Works* (New York: International Publishers, 1968), pp. 35–53, 62–63, 182–183, 331, 430, 589; Lapenna, *Soviet Penal Policy,* pp. 13–22; Harold J. Berman, *Justice in the USSR* (rev. and enl. ed.; (New York: Vintage Books, 1963), pp. 13–24; Leon Radzinowicz, *Ideology and Crime,* (New York: Columbia University Press, 1966), pp. 42–46; A.A. Gertsenzon et al., *Kriminologiya* (2nd ed.; Moscow: "Yuridicheskaya literatura," 1968)—hereinafter *Kriminologiya*—pp. 102–104.

10. V.I. Lenin, "Gosudarstvo i revolyutsiya." *Polnoe sobranie sochinenii* (5th ed.; Moscow: Gos. Izd. Politicheskoi Literatury, 1917,) (hereinafter written *Pol. sobr. soch.*), vol. 33, pp. 89–91.

11. V.I. Lenin, "Uderzhat li bol'sheviki gosudarstvennuyu vlast'?" (end of September – October 1, 1917), *Pol. sobr. soch.,* vol. 34, pp. 313, 315, 318.

12. Ivanov, "Organizatsiya suda i prokuratury," pp. 561–562; Lenin, "Gosudarstvo i revolyutsiya," *seriatim.*

13. Ivo Lapenna, "Lenin, Law, and Legality," in Leonard Schapiro and Peter Reddaway (eds.), *Lenin: The Man, The Theorist, The Leader: A Reappraisal* (New York: Frederick A. Praeger, 1967), pp. 249–250; his *Soviet Penal Policy,* p. 42.

14. A.A. Gertsenzon, *Bor'ba s prestupnost'yu v RSFSR: po materialam obsledovaniya NK RKI SSSR* (Moscow: Yurid. Izd. NKYu RSFSR, 1928), pp. 14–19.

15. E. Tarnovskii, "Voina i dvizhenie prestupnosti," *Sbornik statei po proletarskoi revolyutsii i pravu,* Nos. 1–4 (1918), p. 113, cited in Ostroumov, *Prestupnost' i ee prichiny,* p. 113; A.A. Gertsenzon, "Osnovnye tendentsii dinamiki prestupnosti za desyat' let," *Sovetskoe pravo,* No. 1 (1928), pp. 70, 71. This must be only a rough estimate given the statistical chaos and changes in law enforcement.

16. Yakob Berman, "Nakazanie ili ispravlenie? (po povodu stat'i L.A. Savrasova, 'Prestuplenie i nakazanie v tekushchii perekhodnyi period,')," *Proletarkaya revolyutsiya i pravo,* Nos. 8–9–10 (1918), pp. 46–51.

17. M. Kozlovskii, "Proletarskaya revolyutsiya i ugolovnoe pravo," *Proletarskaya revolyutsiya i pravo,* No. 1 (August 1918), pp. 26–28; L.A. Savrasov, "Prestuplenie i nakazanie v tekushchii perekhodnyi period," ibid., Nos. 5–6 (October 1–15, 1918), pp. 21–27; L.A. Savrasov, "Kvoprosu o nakazanii," ibid., Nos. 2–4 (1919), pp. 74–82.

18. V.I. Lenin, "Ocherednye zadachy sovetskoi vlasti" (April 13–26, 1918), *Pol. sobr. soch.*, vol. 36, p. 195.

19. V.I. Lenin, "Variant stat'i 'Ocherednye zadachi sovetskoi vlasti" (March 23–28, 1918), ibid., p. 163.

20. Ivanov, "Organizatsiya suda i prokuratury," pp. 568–580; Galkin, *Organizatsiya suda i prokuratury v SSSR*, pp. 71–76; and an outstanding non-Soviet source, on which I rely heavily, John N. Hazard, *Settling Disputes in Soviet Society: The Formative Years of Legal Institutions* (New York: Columbia University Press, 1960), pp. 1–175, are sources for the system of justice up to 1921, except where otherwise indicated.

21. Hazard, *Settling Disputes in Soviet Society*, pp. 1–3.

22. Aleksandr Solzhenitsyn, *Arkhipelag Gulag, 1918–1956: Opyt khudozhestvennogo issledovaniya Parts I–II;* (Paris: YMCA Press, 1973), pp. 309–311.

23. The code of 1903 was partially applied in 1906, 1909, and 1911. Samuel Kucherov, *Courts, Lawyers, and Trials under the Last Three Tsars* (New York: Frederick A. Praeger, 1953), pp. 70–71.

24. Smirnov and Shargorodskii, "Ugolovnoe pravo," pp. 477, 517; A.A. Gertsenzon, *Ugolovnoe pravo i sotsiologiya (Problemy sotsiologii ugolovnogo prava i ugolovnoi politiki)* (Moscow: "Yuridicheskaya literatura," 1970), pp. 217, 220, 247; Ivanov, "Organizatsiya suda i prokuratury," pp. 562–563.

25. Ibid., pp. 568–575; Hazard, *Settling Disputes in Soviet Society*, pp. 9–63.

26. Ibid., pp. 34–175, 182–183; Ivanov, "Organizatsiya suda i prokuratury," 575–580.

27. Ibid., pp. 568–569, 571.

28. Hazard, *Settling Disputes in Soviet Society*, p. 17.

29. See note 22.

30. Hazard, *Settling Disputes in Soviet Society*, pp. 40–42, 218–226; Ivanov, "Organizatsiya suda i prokuratury," pp. 580–583.

31. Portnov and Slavin, "Nekotorye voprosy istorii sovetskoi militsii (1917–1918g.)," pp. 85–90.

32. This account of the Cheka is based on Simon Wolin and Robert M. Slusser (eds.), *The Soviet Secret Police* (New York: Frederick A. Praeger, 1957), pp. 3–13, 31–39; Robert Conquest, *The Great Terror: Stalin's Purge of the Thirties* (New York: Macmillan, 1968), pp. 542–545, except where noted.

33. Gertsenzon, *Ugolovnoe pravo i sotsiologiya*, pp. 211–215, 259–264; Smirnov and Shargorodskii, "Ugolovnoe pravo," pp. 505–511; I.N. Steinberg, *In the Workshop of the Revolution* (New York: Rinehart, 1953), pp. 57–106, 225, 226.

34. Alexander Dallin and George W. Breslauer, *Political Terror in Communist Systems* (Stanford, Calif.: Stanford University Press, 1970), pp. 10, 13, 21–22.

35. Gertsenzon, *Ugolovnoe pravo i sotsiologiya,* pp. 267–268.

36. Dallin and Breslauer, *Political Terror in Communist Systems,* p. 22, note 10.

37. Merle Fainsod, *How Russia Is Ruled* (2nd ed.; Cambridge: Harvard University Press, 1963), p. 425.

38. Conquest, *Great Terror,* p. 545.

39. Will Adams, "Capital Punishment in Soviet Criminal Legislation, 1922–1965: A Code Content Analysis and Graphic Representation," in Roger E. Kanet and Ivan Volgyes (ed.), *On the Road to Communism: Essays on Soviet Domestic and Foreign Politics* (Lawrence: University Press of Kansas, 1972), p. 81.

40. This account of capital punishment in Russia and the USSR is based on ibid., pp. 79–121.

41. Ibid., p. 115, note 34.

42. Solzhenitsyn, *Arkhipelag Gulag,* pp. 306–307, 434–435.

43. *SU RSFSR,* 1919, No. 66, item 590.

44. Smirnov and Shargorodskii, "Ugolovnoe pravo," p. 511.

45. *Kommunisticheskaya partiya sovetskogo soyuza v resolyutsiyakh i resheniyakh s"ezdov, konferentsii i plenumov TsK (1898–1970)* (8th enl. and rev. ed.; Moscow: Izd. pol. lit., 1970) vol. 2, pp. 47–48.

46. E.V. Boldyrev, *Mery preduprezhdeniya pravonarushenii nesovershennoletnikh v SSSR* (Moscow: Izd. "Nauka," 1964), pp. 12–14.

47. Ibid., pp. 14–21; V.I. Kufaev, *Yunie pravonarushiteli* (2nd ed.; Moscow: "Novaya Moskva," 1925), pp. 26–76; P.I. Lyublinskii, "Okhrana detstva i bor'ba s besprizornost'yu za 10 let," *Pravo i zhizn',* No. 8 (1927), p. 31; G.M. Min'kovskii, "Osnovnye etapi razvitiya sovetskoi sistemy mer bor'by s prestupnost'yu nesovershennoletnikh," *Voprosy bor'by s prestupnost'yu,* No. 6 (1967), p. 45.

48. Sheila Fitzpatrick, *The Commissariat of Enlightenment: Soviet Organization of Education and the Arts under Lunacharsky October 1917–1921* (Cambridge, Eng.: Cambridge University Press, 1970), pp. 228–233; Gernet in Kufaev, *Yunie pravonarushiteli,* p. 10; Lyublinskii, "Okhrana detstva," p. 29.

49. V. Zenzinov, *Besprizornye* (Paris: Izd. "Sovremennyya zapiski," 1929), pp. 72–94.

50. Frank Lorimer, *The Population of the Soviet Union: History and Prospects* (Geneva: League of Nations, 1946), pp. 41–43.

51. My basis for the figure of seven million waifs and more information on conditions in children's homes and on the streets are contained in my forthcoming study, *The Soviet Experience with Delinquency.*

52. Robert A. Lewis and Richard H. Rowland, "Urbanization in Russia and the USSR: 1897–1966," unpublished, mimeograph, Columbia University; B. Ts. Urlanis, *Rost naseleniya v SSSR* (Moscow: Statistika, 1966), p. 28; I. Yu. Pisarev, *Naselenie i trud v SSSR* (Moscow: "Ekonomika," 1966), p. 76; P.I. Lyublinskii, in Introduction to L.M. Vasilevskii, *Detskaya Prestupnost' i*

detskii sud (Tver': "Oktyabr," 1923), pp. iv–v; Vserossiiskaya tsentral'naya komissiya pomoshchi golodayushchim V.Ts.I.K., *Itogi bor'by s golodom v 1921–1922 gg.* (Moscow: Izd. Ts.K. Pomgol., 1922), p. 34.

53. Gertsenzon, *Ugolovnoe pravo i sotsiologiya,* pp. 265–266.

54. D.I. Kurskii, "Chetyrekhletie moskovskogo narodnogo suda," *Ezhenedel'nik sovetskal yustitsii,* No. 1 (January 1, 1922), p. 9, quoted in Hazard, *Settling Disputes in Soviet Society,* p. 148.

55. P.I. Stuchka (ed.), *Entsiklopediya gosudarstva i prava,* vol. 3 (Moscow, 1927), p. 1594, quoted in Harold J. Breman, *Justice in the USSR: An Interpretation of Soviet Law* (rev. ed., enl.; New York: Vintage Books, 1963), p. 26.

56. Ibid., pp. 26–28, 389–390, note 9; E.B. Pashukanis, *The General Theory of Law and Marxism* (3rd ed.; Moscow, 1927); Babb and Hazard, *Soviet Legal Philosophy,* pp. 111–225; Robert Sharlet, "Pashukanis and the Rise of Soviet Marxist Jurisprudence, 1924–1930," *Soviet Union,* vol. 1 No. 2 (1974), pp. 103–121.

57. V.I. Lenin, "O dvoinom podchinenii i zakonnosti: Tovarishchu Stalinu dlya Politburo" (May 20, 1922), *Pol. sobr. soch.,* vol. 45, pp. 197–201.

58. V.I. Lenin, "Luchshe men'she da luchshe" (March 2, 1923), *Pol. sobr. soch.,* vol. 45, pp. 389–406; "Pis'mo k s'ezdu" (December 23, 24, 25, 26, 1922, and January 4, 1923), ibid., pp. 343–348.

59. Hazard, *Settling Disputes in Soviet Society,* pp. 230–246.

60. Galkin, *Organizatsiya suda i prokuratury v SSSR,* pp. 76–81; Ivanov, "Organizatsiya suda i prokuratury," pp. 580–590; Hazard, *Settling Disputes in Soviet Society,* pp. 176–395.

61. Smirnov and Sharogorodskii, "Ugolovnoe pravo," pp. 488–491. About eliminating terms like "punishment" and "crime," Prof. Pashukanis said: "While such a terminological change has undoubtedly a certain declarative importance, declarations do not essentially solve the problem . . . so long as the forms of court proceeding and of material criminal codes are preserved, a change of terminology will be merely a reform in words." Babb and Hazard, *Soviet Legal Philosophy,* pp. 222–223.

62. David Dallin and Boris I., Nicolaevsky, *Forced Labor in Soviet Russia* (New Haven: Yale University Press, 1947), pp. 166–167.

63. Lapenna, *Soviet Penal Policy,* p. 39; Smirnov and Shargorodskii, "Ugolovnoe Pravo," pp. 481–488.

64. Ibid., pp. 520–556.

65. For distinctions between conviction and actual crime rates, see A. Shlyapochnikov, "Likvidatsiya bezrabotnitsy v SSSR i prestupleniya," *Sovetskoe gosudarstvo,* Nos. 9–10 (1932), pp. 148–149; Yu. P. Kasatkin, "Ocherk istorii izuchenii prestupnosti v SSSR," *Problemy iskoreniya prestupnosti,* No. 1 (1965), pp. 194–197. Changes in criminal law in 1925–1926 lowered penalties for moonshining and wood poaching, treating them as infractions, not crimes; an amnesty in 1927 may have lowered conviction rates that year and caused an increase the next. A drive on hooliganism was mounted in 1925–1926. *Kriminologiya,*

p. 111; N.F. Kuznetsova, *Prestuplenie i prestupnost'* (Moscow: Izd. Moskovskogo universiteta, 1969), p. 187; Gernet, *Prestupnost' za granitsei i v SSSR* (Moscow: "Sovetskoe zakonodatel'stvo," 1931), p. 107.

66. Here are some of the data problems encountered. G.M. Min'kovskii, "Osnovnye etapi razvitiya sovetskoi sistemy mer bor'by s prestupnost'yu nesovershennoletnikh," in *Voprosy bor'by s prestupnost'yu,* No. 6 (1967), p. 48, puts juvenile court convictions at 18,500 in 1923 and 27,300 in 1925, both figures unaccountably low. That the 1925 figure was 4.6 percent of all convictions checks roughly with the figure of 4.7 given in A.A. Gertsenozn, *Sovetskaya ugolovnaya statistika* (2nd ed.; Moscow: Yuridicheskaya izd. NKYu SSSR, 1937), p. 174. But Min'kovskii's figure would mean total convictions, adult and juvenile, of only 593,000, about one third of any other, figure available (see Table 2–2.

Large discrepencies appear between conviction data of Kuznetsova, *Prestuplenie i prestupnost',* p. 185 and *Kriminologiya,* p. 111. That latter source lists 869,035 convictions for the RSFSR in 1926. But Gernet's complete table, *Prestupnost' za granitsei,* p. 79, lists that figure, 869,035 convictions, for 1925, not 1926. Various sources give conflicting and loosely worded conclusions as to whether crime increased or decreased during NEP. Discerning a long-term diminution: Gertsenzon, *Sovetskaya ugolovnaya statistika* (2nd ed.; Moscow: Yurid. izd. NKYu SSSR, 1937), pp. 173–174; *Kriminologiya,* p. 111; discerning an upward tendency, Gertsenzon, "Osnovnye tendentsii dinamiki prestupnosti za destyat' let," p. 19.

67. See my forthcoming *The Soviet Experience with Delinquency.*

68. Dallin and Nicolaevsky, *Forced Labor in Soviet Russia,* pp. 160–161.

69. Sources for Table 2–2 are as follows:

(1) A. Shlyapochnikov (then director, Institute of Criminal Policy), "Likvidatsiya bezrabotnitsy v SSSR i prestupleniya," *Sovetskoe gosudarstvo,* Nos. 9–10 (1932), p. 149.

(2) Calculated from (1) and: Population of the RSFSR, December 17, 1926, was 100,891,244; Frank Lorimer, *The Population of the Soviet Union: History and Prospects* (Geneva: League of Nations, 1946), p. 67. Natural increase of population per 1,000 = 23.7 in 1926, 21 in 1928. *Narodnoye khozyaistvo SSSR v 1968g.* (Moscow: Izd. "Statistika," 1969), p. 36. Population for RSFSR estimated midyear as 102,110,000 for 1927, 106,200,000 for 1929, and 97,400,000 for 1925. Figure for 1928 estimated from 1929 figures, and index for 1929, 131. A. Shlyapochnikov, "Prestupnost' i repressiya v SSSR (Kratkii obzor)," *Problemy ugolovnoi politiki,* vol. 1 (1935), p. 78. Figure for 1926 is estimated, so as to be consistent, as follows: A.A. Gertsenzon gives 953,715 convictions in 1928 and 881,895 convictions for 1926, RSFSR. But he indicates that these were incomplete reporting. The ratio of his figures, 1928/-1926 = 1.09. A.A. Gertsenzon, *Prestupnost' i alkogolizm v RSFSR* (Moscow: Izd. Mosoblispolkoma, 1930), p. 48. M.N. Gernet for the same years gives figures correcting for underreporting: 975,105 convictions in 1926, 1,046,352 convictions in 1928, or a ratio of 1,072. This ratio I have used to estimate the 1926 convictions total on the same basis as Shlyapochnikov, for consistent

figures, giving approximately 1,030,000 convictions. Gernet, *Prestupnost' za granitsei,* p. 79.

(3) Estimated from (2) $\times \frac{\text{Population of USSR}}{\text{Population of RSFSR}}$ or 1.46.

That this is a reasonable assumption, at least approximately correct, is seen from statistics of M.N. Gernet. For 1927 he shows 1,026,084 RSFSR convictions, 1,507,360 USSR convictions, a USSR/RSFSR ratio of 1.468. His total is 4 percent less than mine for the USSR, 7 percent less for the RSFSR. I have used later statistics of Shlyapochnikov, so as to have more comparable data for trend analysis in the late 1920s, early 1930s. Gernet's figures are estimates, anyway, because of court underreporting. Gernet *Prestupnost' za granitzei i v SSSR,* p. 79.

70. Hazard, *Settling Disputes in Soviet Society,* pp. 163–165.

71. Yu. P. Kasatkin, "Ocherk istorii izucheniya prestupnosti v SSSR," *Problemy iskoreniya prestupnosti* (1965), pp. 187–197.

72. Ibid., pp. 197–212; E.G. Shirvindt, "K istorii voprosa ob izuchenii prestupnosti i mer bor'by s nei," *SGP,* No. 5 (1958), pp. 137–142; N. Spasokukotskii, "Organizatsiya i pervye shagi deyatel'nosti Gosduarstvennogo Instituta po izucheniyu prestupnosti i prestupnika pri NKVD," *Problemy Prestupnosti,* vol. 1 (1926), pp. 269–275: N.N. Spasokukotskii, "Deyatel'nost' Gosudarstvennogo Instituta po izucheniyu prestupnosti i prestupnika," *Problemy prestupnosti,* vol. 3 (1928), pp. 299–312; *Kriminologiya,* pp. 71–83. Walter Connor has a useful account of Soviet crime studies in his *Deviance in Soviet Society: Crime, Delinquency and Alcoholism* (New York: Columbia University Press, 1972), pp. 27–34, 93–113, 161–189.

73. E.K. Krasnushkin, "K psikhologii nishchenstva," in E.K. Krasnushkin et al, *Nishchenstvo i besprizornost'* (Moscow: Izd. Moszravotdela, 1929), pp. 264–277; A.S. Griboedov (director, Child Research Institute, State Psychological Academy), *Na puti k prestupleniyu (trudnovospituemye deti)* (Leningrad, 1928); P.G. Bel'skii, *Issledovanie emotsional'noi sfery nesovershennoletnikh, otklonyayushchikhsya ot normy v svoem povedenii* (Moscow: Yuridicheskoe izd. narkomyusta, 1924), especially pp. 8–15. See also the work of the jurist S.V. Poznyshev, *Kriminal'naya psykhologiya: Prestupnye tipy* (Leningrad: Gos. izd., 1926).

One must allow for a hostility to biopsychological theories in recent Soviet commentary. This causes them to exaggerate the gulf between sociologists and psychiatrists, some of whom were combining defectological and sociological theories. Soviet commentary includes A.A. Gertszenzon, "Protiv biologicheskikh teorii prichin prestupnosti (ocherk vtoroi)," *Voprosy bor'by s prestupnost'yu,* No. 5 (1967), pp. 28–38; Kasatkin, "Ocherk istorii," pp. 211–212; *Kriminologiya,* pp. 71–83. Much of their critique of "biologizing" explanations of crime has parallels in Western criminology.

74. Radzinowicz, *Ideology and Crime,* p. 58; along with Radzinowicz, two outstanding studies of criminology are Sutherland and Cressey, *Principles of Criminology,* and Hermann Mannheim, *Comparative Criminology* (2 vols.; London: Routledge and Kegan Paul, 1965).

75. E. Shirvindt, "O metode izucheniya prestupnosti i mer bor'by s nei v SSSR," *Problemy prestupnosti,* vol. 2 (1927), p. 4.

76. Ibid., pp. 11–13; E. Shirvindt, "O problemakh prestupnosti (tseli i zadachi Gosudarstvennogo instituta)," *Problemy prestupnosti,* vol. 1 (1926), pp. 5, 10.

77. Lapenna, *Soviet Penal Policy,* pp. 35–37.

78. M.N. Gernet, *Istoriya tsarskoi tyur'my* (3rd ed.; 5 vols.; Moscow: Gosudarstvennoe izd. yuridicheskoi literatury, 1960–1963), p. 23; Conquest, *Great Terror,* p. 335; Dallin and Nicolaevsky, *Forced Labor in Soviet Russia,* pp. 52, 168–188.

79. Aleksandr I. Solzhenitsyn, *The Gulag Archipelago 1918–1956: An Experiment in Literary Investigation, III IV* (New York: Harper and Row, 1975), deepens our knowledge of Soviet camps. I have not changed what I have written, but it understates in comparison. On the origins of Soviet labor camps see also James Bunyan, *The Origin of Forced Labor in the Soviet State, 1917–1921: Documents and Materials* (Baltimore: Johns Hopkins University Press, 1967).

80. Dallin and Nicolaevsky, *Forced Labor,* p. 163.

81. A.G. Beloborodov discussed the "prison crisis" when addressing the Institute for the Study of Crime and the Criminal, as quoted by N.N. Spasokukotskii, "Deyatel'nost' Gosudarstvennogo Instituta po izucheniyu prestupnosti i prestupnika," *Problemy prestupnosti,* vol. 3 (1928), p. 301; see also Gertsenzon, *Bor'ba s prestupnost'yu v RSFSR,* pp. 20, 103.

82. Dallin and Nicolaevsky, *Forced Labor in Soviet Russia,* pp. 161–162. Percentages of sentences to compulsory labor without loss of liberty fell from 38 in 1922 to 13.9 percent of all sentences in 1926. But it seems not so that sentencing "all but disappeared" until revived in 1940. Apparently, as the job market improved during the plan period, the practice of compulsory labor without loss of liberty revived, making up 22 percent of sentences in 1928, 56.9 percent in 1934, 43.7 in the first half of 1938. B. Man'kovskii, "Voprosy ugolovnogo prava v period perekhoda ot sotsializma k komommunizmu," *SGP,* No. 3 (1939), p. 94.

83. William Henry Chamberlin, *The Russian Revolution, 1917–1921* (2 vols.; New York: Macmillan, 1951); A.G. Kharchev, *Brak i sem'ya v SSSR: opyt sotsialisticheskogo issledovaniya* (Moscow: Izd. "Mysl'," 1964), p. 139.

84. Crane Brinton, *The Anatomy of Revolution* (rev. and expanded ed.; New York: Vintage Books, 1965), pp. 121–264.

Chapter 3

1. See Chapter 2, note 51.

2. N.N. Sukhanov, *The Russian Revolution 1917: A Personal Record,* ed., abridged, and transl. by Joel Carmichael (New York: Oxford University Press, 1955), p. 230.

3. J.V. Stalin, "The Results of the First Five-Year Plan: Report Delivered at the Joint Plenum of the Central Committee and the Central Control Commission of the CPSU (B.), January 7, 1933," *Problems of Leninism* (11th ed.,; Moscow: Foreign Languages Publishing House, 1953), p. 516.

4. *History of the Communist Party of the Soviet Union: Short Course* (New York: International Publishers, 1939), p. 305.

5. Stalin's rationale appeared in his speeches; e.g., "On the Grain Front: Excerpt from a Talk to Students of the Institute of Red Professors, the Communist Academy, and Sverdlov University, on May 28, 1928," *Problems of Leninism,* pp. 247–259; "The Right Deviation in the CPSU (B.): Speech Delivered at the Plenum of the Central Committee and Central Control Commission of the CPSU (B.), April 1929," ibid., pp. 286–373; "The Tasks of Business Executives: Speech Delivered at the First All-Union Conference of Managers of Socialist Industry, February 4, 1931," *Ibid.,* pp. 448–458; and in the Stalin-sponsored *History of the Communist Party of the Soviet Union: Short Course*. Quite another Soviet view comes through in Roy A. Medvedev, *Let History Judge: The Origins and Consequences of Stalinism,* transl. by Colleen Taylor, ed. by David Joravsky and Georges Haupt (New York: Alfred A. Knopf, 1971).

6. Donald W. Treadgold, *Twentieth Century Russia* (Chicago: Rand McNally, 1959), pp. 341–342, 350–351; *VKP (b) v resolyutsiyakh i resheniyakh s"ezdov, konferentsii i plenumov, 1898–1933* (2 vols.; Moscow: Partiinoe izd., 1933), vol. 2, p. 467; *SZ SSSR,* 1930, No. 6, item 65; No. 8, item 102; No. 38, items 411, 412; No. 35, item 384. For Stalin on the need of a working class intelligentsia, but warning to stop persecuting the "old intelligentsia," see *Problems of Leninism,* pp. 378, 471. On increase of percent of workers in higher technical schools from 38.3 in 1928 to 61.9 in 1931, see *Kul'turnoe stroitel'stvo SSSR* (Moscow: V/O Soyuzorguchet, 1935), p. 43.

7. On full urban employment by 1930's end, see A.A. Piontkovskii et al., *Kurs sovetskogo ugolovnogo pravo* (6 vols.; Moscow: Izd. "Nauka," 1970), vol. 2, p. 79. Stalin, *Problems of Leninism,* p. 620; *The School in the USSR* (Moscow: V/O VOKS, 1933), p. 451; Fannina W. Halle, *Woman in Soviet Russia* (New York: Viking Press, 1933), pp. 394–395, *passim.*

8. Stalin, "Tasks of Business Executives," pp. 456–458. "At least within the Party and Komsomol or Young Communist circles, the outpouring of enthusiasm was genuine and impressive. It was accompanied by a temporary reaffirmation of proletarian orthodoxes." Merle Fainsod, *How Russia Is Ruled* (2nd ed.; Cambridge: Harvard University Press, 1963), p. 103.

9. "A revitalization movement is defined as a deliberate, organized, conscious effort by members of a society to construct a more satisfying culture. . . . The Communist Revolution of 1917 in Russia was almost typical in structure of religious revitalization movements." Anthony F.C. Wallace, "Revitalization Movements," *American Anthropologist,* vol. 58 (April 1956), pp. 264–281, reprinted in Barry McLaughlin, *Studies in Social Movements: A Social Psychological Perspective* (New York: Free Press, 1969), pp. 31–32, 48.

10. W.H. Chamberlin, *Russia's Iron Age* (London: Gerald Duckworth, 1935), pp. 109–116, 269–277.

11. Ibid., pp. 52–53, 103, 173–174, 372–373.

12. Sidney and Beatrice Webb, *Soviet Communism: A New Civilization* (3rd ed.; London: Longmans Green, 1941), pp. 563–750, 862–864. The 1936 edition of their book had a question mark in the title.

13. Frankwood E. Williams, *Russia, Youth, and the Present-Day World: Further Studies in Mental Hygiene* (New York: Farrar and Rinehart, 1934), p. 140.

14. Mary Stevenson Calcott, *Russian Justice* (New York: Macmillan, 1935), pp. vii, 1–8, 45, 235–238.

15. I deal with the liquidation of the labor communes and the possible reasons for this in my forthcoming study, *The Soviet Experience with Delinquency*.

16. Chamberlin, *Russia's Iron Age,* pp. 52–53, 103, 173–174, 372–373.

17. John Scott, *Behind the Urals* (Bloomington: Indiana University Press, 1973), pp. 5–6.

18. See Chapter 1, note 2.

19. Stalin, "Results of First Five-Year Plan," pp. 535–536; Chamberlin, *Russia's Iron Age,* p. 155; Robert Conquest, *Great Terror: Stalin's Purge of the Thirties* (New York: Macmillan, 1968), pp. 549–556.

20. On alternate courses for Russia proposed by Bukharin and Stalin's break with him, see Stephen F. Cohen, *Bukharin and the Bolshevik Revolution: A Political Biography 1888–1938* (New York: Alfred A. Knopf, 1973).

21. J. Stalin, "Political Report of the Central Committee," *Works* (Moscow: Foreign Languages Publishing House, 1955), vol. 10, pp. 277, 291–296, 341.

22. J. Stalin, "Work of the April Joint Plenum of the Central Committee and Central Control Commission" (April 13, 1928), *Works,* vol. 11, pp. 57–68.

23. See, e.g., ibid., pp. 42–57, note 4.

24. J. Stalin, "Industrialization and the Grain Problem. Speech Delivered on July 9, 1928," *Works,* vol. 11, p. 180.

25. J.V. Stalin, "Political Report of the Central Committee to the XVI Congress of the CPSU (B.), June 27, 1930," *Works,* vol. 12, pp. 380–381.

26. I.V. Stalin, during interview with H.G. Wells, July 23, 1934, *Sochineniya,* ed. by Robert H. McNeal (vols. 14–16; Stanford, Calif.: Hoover Insittution of War, Revolution, and Peace, Stanford University, 1967), vol. 14, No. 1, pp. 23, 32.

27. On the radical clampdown, see, e.g., Loren R. Graham, *The Soviet Academy of Sciences and the Communist Party, 1927–1932* (Princeton, N.J.: Princeton University Press, 1967), pp. 30–37; Edward J. Brown, *The Proletarian Episode in Soviet Literature, 1928–1937* (New York: Columbia University Press, 1953).

28. See Chapter 2, notes 55, 56.

29. Quoted in E.G. Shirvindt, "K istorii voprosa ob izuchenii prestupnosti i mer bor'by s nei," *SGP,* No. 5 (1958), pp. 140–141; Gertsenzon, "Protiv biologicheskikh teorii prichin prestupnosti (ocherk vtoroi) (1965)," p. 40.

30. S. Ya. Bulatov, "Vozrozhdenie lombrozo v sovetskoi kriminologii," *Revolyutsiya prava,* No. 1 (1929), pp. 42–61; citing A.A. Gertsenzon, "K metodike individual'no-sotsiologichesko izucheniya pravonarvshitelei," *Prestupnik i prestupnost',* vol. 2 (1928), p. 152. The decline and fall of criminology is described in Walter D. Connor, *Deviance in Soviet Society* (New York: Columbia University Press, 1972), pp. 27–32.

31. Yu. P. Kasatkin put it: "Mistakes in the work of Institute crime study offices and individual scholars were taken advantage of by persons making policy in the period of the cult of personality. Research on crime and its causes was curtailed." Yu. P. Kasatkin, "Ocherk istorii isucheniya prestupnosti v SSSR," *Problemy iskoreniya prestupnosti,* vol. 1 (1965), p. 215.

32. "Disput k voprosu ob izuchenii prestupnosti v SSSR: V sektsii prava i gosudarstva," *Revolyutsiya prava,* No. 3 (1929), pp. 47–78. On the 1929 discussion, see also Peter H. Solomon, Jr., "Soviet Criminology: Its Demise and Rebirth, 1928–1963, Soviet Union," vol. 1, No. 2 (1974), pp. 124–127.

33. Hugh W. Babb and John N. Hazard (eds.), *Soviet Legal Philosophy* (Cambridge: Harvard University Press, 1951), p. 27; Harold J. Berman, *Justice in the USSR* (rev. and enl. ed.; New York: Vintage Books, 1963), pp. 26–29; Robert Sharlet, "Pashukanis and the Rise of Soviet Marxist Jurisprudence, 1924–1930," *Soviet Union,* vol. 1, No. 2 (1974), pp. 112–119; Solomon, "Soviet Criminology" pp. 124–125.

34. Shirvindt, "O problemakh prestupnosti," pp. 3–13.

35. Solomon, "Soviet Criminology," pp. 127–128.

36. Kasatkin, "Ocherk istorii," p. 215.

37. Shirvindt, "O problemakh prestupnosti," pp. 4–12, and "O metode izucheniya," p. 8.

38. A. Shlyapochnikov, "Likvidatsiya bezrabotnitsy v SSSR i prestupleniya," *Sovetskoe gosudarstvo,* Nos. 9–10 (1932), pp. 145–155.

39. Kasatkin, "Ocherk istorii," pp. 215–216; Solomon, "Soviet Criminology," pp. 128–130, note 55, p. 133.

40. Shlyapochnikov, "Likvidatsiya bezrabotnitsy," and G. Volkov, "Ugolovnaya statistika v svyazi s ugolovnoi politiki," *Problemy ugolovnoi politiki,* I (1935), pp. 118–130.

41. Kasatkin, "Ocherk istorii," pp. 216–217.

42. R. Beerman, "Study of the Soviet Criminal," *Soviet Studies,* No. 1 (1962), p. 86.

43. Peter H. Solomon, Jr., *Soviet Criminology: A Selective Bibliography* (Cambridge, Eng.: Institute of Criminology, University of Cambridge, Bibliographical Series No. 4, 1969), p. ii; Solomon, "Soviet Criminology," p. 131.

44. On theological explanations of crime and *ancien régime* justice, see Edward H. Sutherland and Donald R. Cressey, *Principles of Criminology*

17th ed.; New York: J. B. Lippincott, 1966), p. 53; Leon Radzinowicz, *Ideology and Crime* (New York: Columbia University Press, 1966), pp. 1–4.

45. That year the age of criminal liability went down from fourteen to twelve, mitigation for age, and the CJA's went, and drastic steps were taken against waifs. E.V. Boldyrev, *Mery preduprezhdeniya pravonarushenii nesovershennoletnikh v SSSR,* p. 29, and my forthcoming *The Soviet Experience with Delinquency.*

46. Lecture by Prof. Brusilovsky (Deputy Director, Institute of Criminal Policy), quoted in Calcott, *Russian Justice,* p. 23; ibid., p. 100, note 1; Piontkovskii et al. (eds.), *Kurs sovetskogo ugolovnogo prava,* vol. 1 (1970), pp. 36–37.

47. *Pyatnadtsatyi s"ezd VKP(b). dekabr' 1927 goda: Stenograficheskii otchet* (2 vols.; Moscow: Gos. izd. politicheskoi literatury, 1961), vol. 1, pp. 425–426.

48. J.V. Stalin, "Grain Procurement and the Prospects for the Development of Agriculture. From Statements Made in Various Parts of Siberia in January, 1928 (Brief Record)," *Works,* vol. 11, pp. 5–9.

49. Between 1929 and 1952, 638 billion rubles were invested in heavy industry, 72 billion in light industry, and 94 billion in agriculture. P. Mstislavskii, "Narodnoe blagosostoyanie," *Novyi mir,* No. 11 (1953), p. 178, cited in Edith Belle Rogovin, "*Novyi mir:* A Case Study in the Politics of Literature, 1956–1958" (Ph.D. dissertation, Columbia University, 1974).

50. Chamberlin, *Russia's Iron Age,* p. 366.

51. Sharlet, "Pashukanis," pp. 108–115.

52. Piontkovskii et al., *Kurs sovetskogo ugolovnogo prava,* vol. 1, p. 120. V.G. Smirnov and M.D. Shargorodskii, "Ugolovnoe pravo," in O.S. Ioffe, et al. (eds.), *Sorok let Sovetskogo pravo, 1917–1957* (2 vols.; Leningrad: Izd. Leningradskogo universiteta, 1957), vol. 1, p. 519; Shlyapochnikov, "Prestupnost' i repressiya v SSSR (kratkii obzor)," p. 94; *SZ,* No. 9 (1966), p. 17.

53. David Dallin and Boris I. Nicolaevsky, *Forced Labor in Soviet Russia* (New Haven: Yale University Press, 1947), pp. 206–207.

54. V.A. Ivanov, "Organizatsiya suda i prokuratury," in Ioffe, et al. (eds.), *Sorok let Sovetskogo Prava, 1917–1957* pp. 590–591, 597–598; Conquest, *Great Terror,* p. 75. Sentences to confinement jumped from 9.6 percent in 1930 (partly due to transfer of petty cases) to 29 percent in 1933 and 44.6 percent by 1937. Man'kovskii, "Voprosy ugolovnogo prava v period perekhoda ot sotsializmu k kommunizmu," p. 94.

55. B. Utevskii, "Novye formy i metody bor'by s prestupnost'yu i lichnost' prestupnika," *SZ,* No. 2 (1960), p. 18.

56. Simon Wolin and Robert M. Slusser (eds.), *The Soviet Secret Police* (New York: Frederick A. Praeger, 1957), p. 13. "The Soviet government answered kulak terror with harsh repression which was carried out both through the court and through the OGPU Board, which continued the glorious traditions of the Vecheka in the struggle with counterrevolution." Ivanov, "Organizatsiya suda i prokuratury," p. 594.

57. On the Procuracy's vigil against kulak tax evasions and judges' treating kulaks too leniently or nonkulaks too harshly, see Merle Fainsod, *Smolensk Under Soviet Rule* (Cambridge: Harvard University Press, 1956), pp. 179–185.

58. Ivanov, "Organizatsiya suda i prokuratury," p. 594.

59. Fainsod, *Smolensk Under Soviet Rule,* p. 245.

60. Shlyapochnikov, "Prestupnost' i repressiya v SSSR (kratkii obzor)," p. 91. In the RSFSR alone in 1932, 91,000 comrades' courts operated, though how often they met is not stated. Ivanov, "Organizatsiya suda i prokuratury," p. 593.

61. Stalin, "Results of the First Five-Year Plan," p. 537; Smirnov and Shargorodskii, *Ugolovnoe pravo,* p. 557.

62. Calcott, *Russian Justice,* p. 32; Smirnov and Shargorodskii, "Ugolovnoe pravo," in Ioffe, *Sorok let sovetskogo prava,* vol. 2, p. 485.

63. Solzhenitsyn, *Arkhipelag gulag,* p. 69.

64. Chamberlin, *Russia's Iron Age,* pp. 200–205.

65. *Kriminologiya,* p. 114.

> A woman cook failed to salt the dinner. She was prosecuted under Par. 111 [Par. 111 deals with "failure to perform official duties" and with exceeding one's authority]. A kolkhoz worker took a horse and went about his business; the horse was stolen; the kolkhoz worker was prosecuted under Par. 111, although it would have been much fairer and simpler to have him make up for the value of the horse. . . . A kolkhoz worker was prosecuted for reducing the sowing norm, even though the harvest turned out to be good; he was tried and convicted. The manager of a farm had pity on two calves and brought them indoors out of the frost. The calves' ears froze up, and the man was tried and convicted under Par. 111.

Andrei Vyshinskii, quoted in Dallin and Nicolaevsky, *Forced Labor in Soviet Russia,* p. 239.

66. Fainsod, *Smolensk Under Soviet Rule,* pp. 185–186.

67. J.V. Stalin, "Results of the July Plenum of the CC, CPSU (B.). Report to a Meeting of the Active of the Leningrad Organization of the CPSU (B.), July 13, 1928," *Works,* vol. 11, p. 220; Deutscher, *Stalin: A Political Biography* (2nd ed.; New York: Oxford University Press, 1967), pp. 319–320.

68. J.V. Stalin, "First Results of the Procurement Campaign and the Further Tasks of the Party. To All Organizations of the CPSU (B.), *Works,* vol. 11, pp. 20–21; "Lenin and the Question of the Alliance with the Middle Peasant. Reply to Comrades," *Works,* vol. 11, p. 110; Cohen *Bukharin,* pp. 276–291.

69. *Pyatnadtsatyi s"ezd,* pp. 63–64; J. Stalin, "Lenin and the Question of the Alliance with the Middle Peasants," *Works,* vol. 11, pp. 107–110.

70. J.V. Stalin, "Industrialization and the Grain Problem," *Works,* vol. 11, p. 172.

71. J.V. Stalin, "A Year of Great Change," *Works,* vol. 12, p. 124.

72. J.V. Stalin, "Lenin and Question of Alliance with Middle Peasant," vol. 11, p. 111.

73. J.V. Stalin, "Concerning Question of Agrarian Policy in the U.S.S.R. Speech Delivered at a Conference of Marxist Students of Agrarian Questions, December 27, 1929, *Works,* vol. 12, p. 173.

74. Already loose, the definition of "kulak" stretched even more during collectivization. As formulated by the Council of People's Commissars at the beginning of the collectivization drive in the fall of 1929, kulaks were taken to be farmers fulfilling any of the following criteria: regularly hiring wage labor; possessing power or wind-driven industrial undertaking (e.g., a mill); hiring out, permanently, complex powered agricultural machinery; renting out a house or other premises; or having members of the family earning nonlabor income from usury, commerce, priesthood. Peasant households having a member on active military service were exempted from dekulakization, in theory. Moshé Lewin, *Russian Peasants and Soviet Power: A Study of Collectivization* (London: George Allen and Unwin, 1968), pp. 491, 482–513. On the brunt borne by middle peasants, see also Fainsod, *Smolensk Under Soviet Rule,* p. 180; J. Stalin, "Reply to Collective Farm Comrades," *Problems of Leninism,* pp. 427–430.

75. Fainsod, *How Russia Is Ruled,* p. 531; Stalin, *Problems of Leninism,* p. 609; Conquest, *Great Terror,* p. 20, note 41.

76. J. Stalin, "On the Grain Front," *Problems of Leninism,* pp. 246–253; Deutscher, *Stalin,* pp. 322–323. Graphic first-hand tales of collectivization and peasants' reaction are summarized and excerpted in Fainsod, *Smolensk Under Soviet Rule,* pp. 238–264.

77. Lewin, *Russian Peasants and Soviet Power,* pp. 496–498; Fainsod, *Smolensk Under Soviet Rule,* pp. 243, 245.

78. Chamberlin, *Russia's Iron Age,* pp. 36–37, 144; Victor Kravchenko, *I Chose Freedom: The Personal and Political Life of a Soviet Official* (New York: Scribner, 1946).

79. Dallin and Nicolaevsky, *Forced Labor in Soviet Russia,* p. 44; Lewin, *Russian Peasants and Soviet Power,* p. 506. For a fictionalized recollection of a family's death after being dumped in the naked tundra, see Alexander Solzhenitsyn, *The Love-Girl and the Innocent,* a play transl. by Nicholas Bethell and David Burg (New York: Farrar, Straus, and Giroux, 1969), p. 104.

80. Lewin, *Russian Peasants and Soviet Power,* pp. 499, 501–505.

81. Jonathan Schell, *The Village of Ben Suc* (New York: Alfred A. Knopf, 1967), and *The Military Half: An Account of Destruction in Quang Ngai and Quang Tin* (New York: Alfred A. Knopf, 1968); Seymour M. Hersh, *My Lai 4* (New York: Random House, 1970); U.S. Senate. Ninety-First Congress. Second Session, Subcommittee to Investigate Problems Connected with Refugees and Escapees of the Committee on the Judiciary of the United States

Senate. *Refugee and Civilian War Casualty Problems in Laos and Cambodia* (Washington, D.C.: U.S. Government Printing Office, 1970); *Ibid., Refugee and Civilian War Casualty Problems in Vietnam* (Washington, D.C.: U.S. Government Printing Office, 1971). "My Lai had happened in every war. It's not an isolated incident, even in Vietnam." Lieut. William L. Calley, Jr., quoted in *New York Times,* March 30, 1971; "Colonel Says Every Large Combat Unit in Vietnam Has a My Lai," *Ibid.,* May 25, 1971. On the bombings, shellings, and terrorization of the peasants, see also Neil Sheehan, "Should We Have War Crimes Trials?" *New York Times Book Review,* March 28, 1971, pp. 1–3, 30–34.

82. Conquest, *Great Terror,* p. 26.

83. Wolin and Slusser, *Soviet Secret Police,* p. 13. "The Soviet government answered kulak terror with harsh repression which was carried out both through the court and through the OGPU Board, which continued the glorious traditions of the Vecheka in the struggle with counterrevolution." Ivanov, "Organizatsiya suda i prokuratury," p. 594.

84. Chamberlin, *Russia's Iron Age,* p. 152.

85. Fainsod, *Smolensk Under Soviet Rule,* p. 245.

86. From a speech of November 23, 1961, cited in Zbigniew Brzezinski, *Between Two Ages: America's Role in the Technetronic Era* (New York: Viking Press, 1971), p. 130.

87. Chamberlin, *Russia's Iron Age,* pp. 255, 79, 252–266.

88. Dana G. Dalrymple, "The Soviet Famine of 1932–1934," *Soviet Studies,* vol. 15, No. 3 (January 1964), pp. 250–277; Conquest, *Great Terror,* p. 22. Both call the famine "man-made" and blame it on Stalin, but Dalrymple gives a broader picture of causes. One high official is quoted as saying to a fellow Communist who later defected: "It took a famine to show them who is master here. It has cost millions of lives, but the collective farm system is here to stay. We have won the war." Conquest, *Great Terror,* p. 24. See also Chamberlin, *Russia's Iron Age,* pp. 67, 88–89. Stalin told Churchill collectivization involved a more difficult struggle for him than World War II and indicated ten million casualties. Winston Churchill, *The Second World War: The Hinge of Fate* (5 vols.; Boston: Houghton Mifflin, 1948–1951), vol. 4 (1950), p. 498.

89. Solzhenitsyn, *Arkhipelag gulag,* p. 66.

90. A. Afinogenev, *Fear,* transl. from the Russian by Nikander Strelsky et al. Acting versions by Hallie Flanagan (Poughkeepsie, N.Y.: Experimental Theatre of Vassar College, 1934), p. 52, about the USSR of 1930.

91. Dallin and Nicolaevsky, *Forced Labor in Soviet Russia,* pp. 50–58, 212–213; Conquest, *Great Terror,* p. 335. J. Stalin, "Results of the First Five-Year Plan," p. 529; chapters 1, 2.

92. Dallin and Nicolaevsky, *Forced Labor in Soviet Russia,* pp. 197–201. The first of a series of government orders to effect savings by using prison labor appeared March 26, 1928. Ibid., p. 206.

93. Ibid., p. 232; Conquest, *Great Terror,* p. 335.

94. Fainsod, *Smolensk Under Soviet Rule,* pp. 196–206.

95. Cyril E. Black, "Soviet Society: A Comparative View," in Allen Kassof (ed.), *Prospects for Soviet Society* (New York: Frederick A. Praeger, 1968), p. 32. Some of this urbanization was to labor camp and deportee settlements; but camps were no less lawless and certainly less secure than cities. Dallin and Nicolaevsky, *Forced Labor in Soviet Russia,* pp. 50–51.

96. The urban population of the USSR increased in 1926–1929 by 29.8 million, from 26.3 to 56.1 million. *Itogi vsesoyuznoi perepisi naseleniya 1959 goda: SSSR (svodnyi tom)* (Moscow: Gosstatizdat TsSU SSSR, 1962), p. 13. Soviet demographers and Frank Lorimer differ on how they count into calculations of net in-migration the reported population of rural areas reclassified as urban areas between 1926 and 1939. After comparing their methods, I assume that the net in-migration amounted to between twenty and twenty-three million persons in twelve years. This does not take into account the extraordinarily high rate of shifting from job to job and place to place within the urban sector. On urbanization, see, for a start, Frank Lorimer, *The Population of the Soviet Union: History and Prospects* (Geneva: League of Nations, 1946), pp. 149–150; B. Ts. Urlanis, *Rost naseleniya y SSSR* (Moscow: Statistika, 1966), pp. 66, 68; I. Yu. Pisarev, *Narodonaseleniya SSSR* (Moscow: Izd. Sotsial'no-ekonmicheskoi literatury, 1962), pp. 62, 66–69, 97–98.

97. Shlyapochnikov, "Likvidatsiya bezrabotnitsy," pp. 150–153. (On homeless waifs, see my study on juvenile delinquency.)

98. Ibid., p. 154.

99. Raymond A. Bauer, *The New Man in Soviet Psychology* (Cambridge: Harvard University Press, 1959), pp. 41–42.

100. Shlyapochnikov, "Likvidatsiya bezrabotnitsi," p. 151.

101. Shlyapochnikov, "Prestupnost' i repressiya," pp. 92–93.

102. "O merakh bor'by s khuliganstvom," Decree of Central Executive Committee and Council of People's Commissars of USSR, publ. March 30, 1935, repr. in *SYu,* No. 11 (1935), p. 11.

103. "O resul'tatakh obsledovaniya raboty narsudov g. Moskvy i Moskovskogo gorodskogo suda po delam o khuliganstve (Post. Prezidiuma Verkhsuda RSFSR 14/II 1935 g.)," ibid., pp. 11–12.

104. Nicholas Sergeyevich Timasheff, *The Great Retreat* (New York: E.P. Dutton, 1946).

105. See section, "Breaking Peasant Resistance," and Glenn C. Morgan, *Soviet Administrative Legality: The Role of the Attorney General's Office* (Stanford, Calif.: Stanford University Press, 1962), pp. 86–89.

106. P. Yudin, "Protiv putanitsy, poshlosti i revizionizma," reprinted from *Pravda,* January 20, 1937, in *SYu,* No. 5 (1937), pp. 1–2; A. Vyshinskii, "20 let proletarskoi diktatury i Stalinskaya konstitutsiya," *Sovetskoe gosudarstvo,* No. 12 (1937), pp. 10–43; Berman, *Justice in USSR,* pp. 57–65; Robert Conquest (ed.), *Justice and the Legal System in the USSR* (New York: Frederick A. Praeger, 1968), p. 16.

107. J.V. Stalin, addressing 18th Party Congress, March 10, 1939, *Sochineniya,* vol. 14, No. 1, p. 395.

108. Descriptions of court system structure, unless otherwise noted, are based on Ivanov, Organizatsiya suda i prokuratury, in Ioffe, et al. (eds.), *Sorok let Sovetskogo pravo,* vol. 2, pp. 560–583.

109. Ibid., p. 564.

110. Conquest, *Great Terror,* rev. ed., pp. 230, 369.

111. B.A. Galkin (ed.), *Organizatsiya suda i prokuratury v SSSR* (Moscow: Izd. "Yuridicheskaya literatura," 1967), p. 83.

112. Nikita S. Khrushchev, *The Crimes of the Stalin Era,* annotated by Boris I. Nicolaevsky (New York: New Leader, n.d.), p. 22.

113. *Sbornik dokumentov po istorii ugolovnogo zakonodatel'stvo SSSR i RSFSR 1917–1952* (Moscow: Gos. izd. yurid. lit., 1953), pp. 347, 396.

114. Ibid., pp. 382, 389–392, 407–408, 412, 495.

115. Piontkovskii et al., *Kurs sovetskogo ugolovnogo pravo,* vol. 1, pp. 125–127; *Sbornik dokumentov,* pp. 392–393, 396.

116. Ibid., pp. 405–408, 412.

117. Ibid., pp. 414–418, 423–425.

118. Ibid., pp. 426–427.

119. Ibid., pp. 429–430, 435.

120. Michael Solomon, *Magadan* (Princeton, N.Y.: Vertex Books, 1971), p. 187; Conquest, *Great Terror,* pp. 494, 531–532; Joseph Schmolmer, *Vorkuta* (London: Weidenfeld and Nicolson, 1954), pp. 55, 202–204.

121. Harold J. Berman, "Soviet Legal Reform—Dateline Moscow 1957," *Yale Law Journal,* vol. 66 (1957), p. 1202.

122. John N. Hazard, "Trends in the Soviet Treatment of Crime," *American Sociological Review,* No. 4 (1940), pp. 566–576, and the record reviewed here.

123. Text of 1926 Criminal Code of RSFSR, November 22, 1926, effective January 1, 1927, *Sbornik dokumentov,* Article 162, p. 284.

124. Ibid., pp. 430–435.

125. Raymond A. Bauer, *New Man in Soviet Psychology,* p. 123.

126. "Postanovlenie TsK KPSS o preodolenii kul'ta lichnosti i ego posledstvii, 30 iyunya 1956 g.," *Kommunisticheskaya partiya sovetskogo soyuza v resolyutsiyakh i resheniyakh s"ezdov, konferentsii i plenumov TsK (1898–1971),* vol. 7 (1971), p. 208.

127. Berman, *Justice in USSR,* pp. 52–65; I.V. Stalin, "O nedostatkakh partiinoi raboty i merakh likvidatsii trotsiskikh i inykh dvurushnikov" (March 31, 1937), *Sochineniya,* vol. 14, No. 1, pp. 213–214; Khrushchev, *Crimes of Stalin Era,* p. 24.

128. Solzhenitsyn, *Arkhipelag gulag,* p. 69.

129. Khrushchev, *Crimes of Stalin Era,* pp. 13–16, 20–21, 34, 45–46, 60–61; Conquest, *Great Terror,* rev. ed., pp. 65–96.

130. Khrushchev, *Crimes of Stalin Era,* p. 15.

131. Article 58, RSFSR Criminal Code, given exegesis in Solzhenitsyn, *Arkhipelag gulag,* pp. 71–79, and transl. in Conquest, *Great Terror.*

132. On the killing of the foreman, see Anatoly Marchenko, *My Testimony,* transl. by Michael Scammell (New York: E.P. Dutton, 1969), pp. 144–146.

133. Solzhenitsyn, *Arkhipelag gulag,* pp. 25–26, 46–47, 69–83, 90; Khrushchev, *Crimes of Stalin Era,* pp. 44–50; Robert Conquest, *Power and Policy in the USSR: The Study of Soviet Dynasties* (New York: St. Martin's Press, 1961), pp. 79–191.

134. Wolin and Slusser, *Soviet Secret Police,* pp. 16–29; Dallin and Nicolaevsky, *Forced Labor in Soviet Russia,* pp. 249–261; Leonard Schapiro, *The Communist Party of the Soviet Union* (2nd ed., rev. and enl.; New York: Vintage Books, 1971), pp. 390–434, 534–535. Khrushchev, *Crimes of Stalin Era,* pp. 27–30, 34–35; Medvedev, *Let History Judge;* Alexander Solzhenitsyn, *One Day in the Life of Alexander Denisovich,* transl. by Max Hayward and Ronald Hingley (New York: Bantam Books, 1963); F. Beck and W. Godin, *Russian Purge and the Extraction of Confession,* transl. by Eric Mosbacher and David Porter (New York, Viking Press, 1951); Alexander Weissberg, *The Accused* (New York: Simon and Schuster, 1952); Conquest, *Great Terror,* rev. ed., pp. 194–210, 450–495. The special board was set up by decree of November 5, 1934. Ivanov, "Organizatsiya suda i prokuratury," Ioffe, "Sorok let Sovetskogo prava," vol. 2, p. 583.

135. Conquest gives a total casualty figure of at least 20 million for the period 1936–1950; 12 million died in camps (no more than 10 percent came out), 1 million were executed. According to him, 3.5 million dekulakized peasants died in camps, and about the same amount during collectivization including the famine and epidemics. But he himself cites a figure elsewhere of 5.5 million famine deaths. Hence, even a total of 23 million Stalinist victims killed between 1929 and 1950 alone is an understatement (Conquest, *Great Terror,* pp. 23, 533). Conquest estimates 9 million in camp and prison in late 1938, not including criminals, another 2 million, at least (rev. ed., 1973, p. 709). Robert Conquest discusses party casualties in "The Great Terror Revised," *Survey,* No. 1 (Winter 1971), p. 93, and the total casualty figures appear again. For party membership figures and summary of the purges, see Fainsod, *How Russia Is Ruled,* pp. 49–87. Andrei D. Sakharov mentioned 20 million victims of Gulag by 1948. *My Country and the World* (New York: Vintage, 1975), p. 4.

136. Dallin and Nicolaevsky, *Forced Labor in Soviet Russia,* pp. 84–87, report estimates of from five to twenty-five million: they say eight to twelve million, eighty to ninety-five percent males. They reach an estimate of at least 16 percent of adult males in camp, but based on an estimated population loss of seven million, when we know that actual losses reached at least twenty million, owing to the war. Conquest, in *Great Terror,* p. 533, estimates an average of camp inmates at eight million, 1936–1950, nine million in camps and prisons in late 1938. Solzhenitsyn in *Arkhipelag gulag,* p. 587, says there were never more than twelve million together at one time in the camps.

137. Dallin and Nicolaevsky, *Forced Labor in Soviet Russia,* pp. 4, 237–238.

138. Solzhenitsyn, *Arkhipelag gulag,* p. 501.

139. Ibid., pp. 502–509, 538–540, 552–555; Solzhenitsyn, *Gulag Archipelago,* vol. 2, pp. 425–446.

140. Aleksandr Solzhenitsyn, *V kruge pervom* (New York: Harper and Row, 1968), p. 324.

141. Table 3–1 and Table 5–1.

142. The Special Board of the NKVD "created in direct violation of the Constitution, had the right to use criminal punishment." A.M. Yakovlev, "Ob izuchenii lichnosti presutpnika," *SGP,* No. 11 (1962), p. 108.

143. My *Soviet Experience with Delinquency,* Chapter 4; see, e.g., from just one newspaper, *Komsomolskaya pravda,* 1952, for one month: "Melochi zhizni," December 1; "Pochemu zabita ulitsa," December 9; A. Alekseev, "Ne proshchat' nedostatkov," December 16; S. Garbuzov and A. David'yants, "Do sleduyushchego proisshestviya," December 11; "Iz zala suda: Khuligany poluchili po zaslugam," December 11; note 145.

144. Edward Crankshaw, quoted from *Khrushchev Remembers,* transl. and ed. by Strobe Talbott (Boston: Little, Brown, 1970), p. 228. See also Khrushchev's purported reminiscence, pp. 229, 232–235; Conquest, *Great Terror,* p. 494.

145. John N. Hazard, *Law and Social Change in the USSR* (Toronto, 1953), pp. 108–110; Roy A. Medvedev, *Let History Judge: The Origins and Consequences of Stalinism* (New York, 1971), p. 521; Mark G. Field, "Alcoholism, Crime, and Delinquency in Soviet Society," *Social Problems,* vol. 3 (1955), pp. 100–109; note 144.

146. V.M. Chkhivadze et al. (eds.), *Entsiklopedicheskii slovar' pravovykh znanii (sovetskoe pravo)* (Moscow: Izd. "Sovetskaya entsiklopediya," 1965), p. 431.

147. Opinion of a U.S. federal court cited by Tom Wicker, "The Federal Lawbreaker," *New York Times,* June 1, 1971, p. 39.

148. Smirnov and Shargorodskii, "Ugolovnoe pravo," vol. 2, pp. 498–499; Chapter 4.

Chapter 4

1. Police chief Lavrenti Beria—told the populace in his speech at Stalin's funeral service—March 9, 1953—that they "could work calmly and confidently, knowing that the Soviet government will solicitously and untiringly guard their rights, which are recorded in the Stalin Constitution." Soon the MVD moved to repudiate the false "doctors' plot" charges and the "Stalin Constitution" became the "USSR Constitution." Leo Gruliow (ed.), *Current Soviet Policies: The Documentary Record of the 19th Party Congress and the Reorganization after Stalin's Death* (New York: Frederick A. Praeger, 1953),

pp. 251–260. On deterrorization and its limits, see Harold J. Berman, "Soviet Legal Reform—Dateline Moscow 1957," *Yale Law Journal,* vol. 66 (1957), pp. 1192–1215; Simon Wolin and Robert M. Slusser (eds.), *The Soviet Secret Police* (New York: Frederick A. Praeger, 1957), pp. 27–31; Merle Fainsod, *How Russia Is Ruled* (2nd ed.; Cambridge: Harvard University Press, 1963), pp. 448–452. For a history and analysis of the Soviet court system, criminal procedure, and the legal profession from the viewpoint of the departure of "socialist legality" from the rule of law, see Samuel Kucherov, *Organs of Soviet Administration of Justice: Their History and Operation,* with foreward by John N. Hazard (Leiden: E.J. Brill, 1970). Ironically, the report of Beria's trial recalled the illegal forced confession and purge trial atmosphere of the 1930s, as Kucherov wrote, pp. 701–702. But whether Beria actually was tried and actually confessed any "serious crimes against the state" is still not clear.

2. Robert Conquest, *The Great Terror: Stalin's Purge of the Thirties,* (New York: Macmillan, 1968), p. 514.

3. Nikita S. Khrushchev, *The Crimes of the Stalin Era,* annotated by Boris I. Nicolaevsky (New York: New Leader, n.d.), p. 24.

4. Berman, *Justice in the USSR* (rev. and enl. ed.; New York: Vintage Books, 1963), pp. 66–96, describes post-Stalin legal reforms in terms of tendencies up to 1963.

5. M.D. Shargorodskii, "Prognoz i pravovaya nauka," *Pravovedenie,* No. 1 (1971), p. 47, cited in Yu. A. Tikhomirov and V.P. Kazimirchuk, *Pravo i sotsiologiya* (Moscow: Izd. "Nauka," 1973), p. 101.

6. B.S. Nikiforov, "Otvet serdiytm oponentam," *Literaturnaya gazeta,* No. 47, November 20, 1968.

7. *UK* (1957), pp. 135–137. *UK* (1957) stands for Criminal Code of RSFSR, 1957 edition: *Ugolovnyi kodeks RSFSR: Ofitsial'nyi tekst s izmeneniyami na i marta 1957 g.* (Moscow: Gos. izd. yurid. lit., 1957).

8. Criminal sanctions ended against peasants failing to work the required minimum on collective farm fields (1954); women having nontherapeutic abortions (1954); doctors giving abortions under approved conditions (1955); persons riding freight trains or pulling the emergency cord without valid reason (1955); managers selling or exchanging surplus equipment (1955); leaving a job or being absent without permission (1956). Criminal sanctions were reduced for juveniles who could get parole after serving one-third time, adults after two-thirds (1954); first petty hooliganism (1956) and petty speculation (1961), both becoming administrative infractions. *UK* (1957), pp. 123–128, 134–135, 180–181; *UK* (1970), p. 202. *UK* (1970) stands for *Ugolovnyi kodeks RSFSR: Ofitsial'nyi tekst s izmeneniyami i dopolneniyami na 21 maya 1970 g.* (Moscow: "Yuridicheskaya literatura," 1970).

9. *UK* (1957), p. 109 (Edict of January 10, 1955).

10. *Sbornik zakonov SSSR i ukazov prezidiuma Verkhovnogo Soveta SSSR 1938–1967* (2 vols.; Moscow: Izd. "Izvestiya Sovetov deputatov trudyashchikhsya SSSR," 1968), vol. 2, pp. 627–628, 633–635.

11. *Zasedaniya Verkhovnogo Soveta SSSR. Chetvertogo sozyva. Shestaya*

sessiya (5–12 fevralya 1957 g.). Stenograficheskii otchet (Moscow: Izd. Verkhovnogo Soveta SSSR, 1957), p. 752; *Sbornik zakonov,* vol. 2, p. 572. Repeal of the summary procedures introduced in 1934 and 1937 was by edict of April 19, 1956. *Sbornik zakonov,* vol. 2, p. 572.

12. Experts and officials "showed overcautiousness, feared all that was new, feared their own shadows and began to show less initiative in their work," Khrushchev, *Crimes of Stalin Era,* p. 57.

On jurists' fears that innovations would get them labeled "wreckers" in law or "bourgeois deviationists" see V.A. Ivanov, "Organizatsiya suda i prokuratura," in O.S. Ioffe, et al. (eds.), *Sorok let sovetskogo prava, 1917–1957* (2 vols.; Leningrad: Izd. Leningradskogo universiteta, 1957), vol. 2, pp. 589–590. See also Conquest, *Justice and Legal System in USSR* (New York: Frederick A. Praeger, 1968), pp. 136–137.

13. Harold J. Berman, "Law Reform in the Soviet Union," *The American Slavic and East European Review,* No. 15 (April 1956), pp. 185–188; Donald D. Barry and Harold J. Berman, "The Jurists," in H. Gordon Skilling and Franklyn Griffiths (eds.), *Interest Groups in Soviet Politics* (Princeton, N.J.: Princeton University Press, 1971), p. 322.

14. V. Nikolaev, "Preodolenie nepravil'nykh teorii v ugolovnom prave—vazhnoe uslovie ukrepleniya sotsialisticheskoi zakonnosti," *Kommunist,* No. 14 (1956), pp. 47–60; John N. Hazard, "Soviet Law and Justice," in John W. Strong (ed.), *The Soviet System under Brezhnev and Kosygin* (New York: Van Nostrand–Reinhold, 1971), pp. 96–97.

15. A law of February 11, 1957, turned over to the Union republics responsibility for codifying criminal law and procedure and the law on the court system as well as codes of civil law and procedure. The republics draft codes within the guidelines set by a series of fundamental laws, such as Fundamentals of Criminal Procedure of the USSR and Union Republics and Fundamentals of Criminal Legislation of the USSR and Union Republics. *Zasedaniya* (1957), p. 735; *Zasedaniya* (1958) (see note twenty-four), pp. 619–635, 671–688. Also on December 25, 1958, other fundamental guidelines were passed: A Law Ending Deprivation of Electoral Rights by Court Sentence, a Law on Responsibility for State Crimes; Fundamentals of Legislation on the Court System of the USSR and Union and Autonomous Republics, a Law Changing Procedures for Electing People's Court Judges, and a Law on Military Tribunals.

Presumption of the accused's innocence is implied in the Fundamentals of Criminal Law, Article 14, ordering court, prosecutor, investigator, and person conducting the inquest to assure legally a thorough, complete, and objective investigation of the facts of the case, to ascertain circumstances that incriminate and those that vindicate the accused, as well as the circumstances aggravating and mitigating his or her guilt if convicted. Article 14 states, moreover, that court, prosecutor, investigator, and person conducting the inquest "have no right to transfer to the accused the obligation of proof." Article 17 tells court, prosecutor, investigator, and person conducting the inquest that no evidence "shall have pre-established weight" for them but that they shall weigh the evidence "in accordance with their inner convictions, based on a complete, objective consideration of all circumstances of the case." Similar provisions and more are in the republic criminal codes; e.g., *Ugolovno-protsessual'nyi kodeks RSFSR: offitsial'nyi tekst s izmeneniyami na 10 dekabrya 1972 g.* (Moscow: "Yuridicheskaya literatura," 1973), henceforward *UPK* (1973), Articles 20, 33, 77, etc.; Harold J. Berman and James W. Spindler, *Soviet Criminal Law and Procedure: The RSFSR Codes* (2nd ed.; Cambridge: Harvard University Press, 1972), pp. 57–62.

16. Fundamentals of Criminal Procedure, Article 22. *Zakonodatel'stvo ob ugolovnom sudoproizvodstve Soyuza SSR i soyuznykh respublik* (2 vols.; Moscow: Gos. izd. yurid. lit., 1963), permits comparison of 1958 reforms in criminal procedure and republic codes of criminal procedure based on them; *UPK* (1973), Article 47.

17. *UPK* (1973), Articles 90, 97, 133; Fundamentals of Criminal Procedure, Article 33, 34; Berman and Spindler, *Soviet Criminal Law and Procedure,* pp. 51–52.

18. Abraham Brumberg, *In Quest of Justice: Dissent and Protest in the Soviet Union Today* (New York, Frederick A. Praeger, 1970), p. 41; Kucherov, *Organs of Soviet Administration of Justice,* p. 711.

19. Roy A. Medvedev, *On Socialist Democracy,* transl. and ed. by Ellen de Kadt (New York: Alfred A. Knopf, 1975), pp. 149–150; a non-*samizdat* complaint with similar import was published in the Soviet press, one of several over the years: N. Chetunova, "The Right to Defend," *Literaturnaya gazeta,* September 20, 1966, transl. in *Current Digest of the Soviet Press* (hereinafter, *CDSP,* vol. 18, No. 38 (1966), pp. 18–19.

A detailed review of the legal formulations on rights and duties of defense lawyers and the rights of defendants appears, with legal historical background, in Christopher Osakwe, "Due Process of Law under Contemporary Soviet Criminal Procedure, *Tulane Law Review,* vol. 50, No. 2 (1976), pp. 266–317.

20. Fundamentals of Criminal Law omits the old analogy clause. Article 3 reads: "Only a person guilty of committing a crime, that is who intentionally or through negligence has committed a socially dangerous act specified by the criminal law, is deemed liable to criminal responsibility and punishment." On analogy, see Lapenna, *Soviet Penal Policy* (London: The Bodley Head, 1968), pp. 31–37, 59. Union republics contain some differences, e.g., on penalties for murder or on the definition of malice in "malicious hooliganism." Berman and Spindler, *Soviet Criminal Law and Procedure,* pp. 14–16. Fundamentals and republic codes are collected in *Ugolovnoe zakonodatel'stvo Soyuza SSSR i soyuznykh respublik* (Moscow: Gos. izd. yurid. lit., 1963). See also Berman, "Soviet Legal Reform—Dateline Moscow 1957," *Yale Law Journal,* vol. 66 (1957, pp. 1203–1204; V.D. Men'shagin (ed.), *Osobennosti ugolovnykh kodeksov soyuznykh respublik* (Moscow: Izd. "Yurid. lit.," 1963).

21. Lapenna, *Soviet Penal Policy,* pp. 47–135; Barry and Berman, "The Jurists," pp. 329–330, note 130.

22. Fundamentals of Criminal Law, Articles 33, 34; *Ugolovnyi kodeks RSFSR s izmeneniyami a dopolneniyami na 1 yanvarya 1975 goda* (Moscow: "Yuridicheskaya literatura," 1975), hereinafter *UK* (1975), Articles 37–57,

64–88, 152–169 and "official crimes," 170–175; section below, "comparisons and conclusions;" UK (1957), Part I, chapters 4–6, and Part II, chapters 1–5; I.S. Noi, *Sushchnost' i funktsii ugolovnogo nakazaniya v sovetskom gosudarstve* (Saratov: Izd. Sar. univ., 1973), pp. 6–18; M.D. Shargorodskii, *Nakazanie: Ego tseli i effektivnost'* (Leningrad: Izd. Leningradskogo universiteta, 1973), pp. 5–12; Berman and Spindler, *Soviet Criminal Law and Procedure,* pp. 20–46, 120–121.

23. Anatoly Marchenko, *My Testimony,* transl. by Michael Scammell (New York: E.P. Dutton, 1969), pp. 144–146, 220–234; Law on State Crimes of December 25, 1958, Articles 3, 6, *Zasedaniya Verkhovnogo Soveta SSSR. Pyatogo sozyva. Vtoraya sessiya (22–25 dekabrya 1958 g.)* (Moscow: Izd. Verkhovnogo Soveta SSSR, 1959) (abbr. *Zasedanie* [1958]), pp. 637–638.

24. *Zasedaniya* (1958), p. 487.

25. Fundamentals of Criminal Procedure, Article 2; *UPK* (1973), Article 321. "Preduprezhdenie prestuplenii—glavnoe napravlenie bor'by s prestupnost'yu na sovremennom eatpe," *SYu,* No. 6 (1972), pp. 1–3; "Effectivnost' chastnykh opredelenii po ugolovnym delam," SYu, No. 22 (1972), pp. 1–2. Directive, USSR Supreme Court, October 14, 1964, on supplementary findings in criminal cases, *Byulleten' Verkhovnogo Suda SSSR,* hereinafter *BVS SSSR,* No. 6 (1964), pp. 9–10; A. Merkushov, "Bol'shoe vnimanie chastnym opredeleniyam," *SYu,* No. 10 (1972), pp. 5–7. S. Pulatkhodzhaev and A. Mikhailants, "Rabota sudov po preduprezhdeniyu prestuplenii," *SZ,* No. 8 (1971), pp. 18–21. On popularization of justice, see A.N. Vasil'ev (ed.), *Razvitie sovetskoi demokratii i ukreplenie pravoporyadka na sovremennom etape* (Moscow: Izd. Moskovskogo universiteta, 1970), pp. 253–294.

26. V. Mel'nikov and S. Yudushkin, "Kontrol' za isoplneniem chastnykh opredelenii," *SYu,* No. 7 (1974), p. 2.

27. Svetlana Pochivalova, "Mesyats v sude: Iz zapisok narodnogo zasedatelya," *Literaturnaya gazeta,* January 20, 1971; V. Pokhmelkin, "O putiakh povysheniya akitvnosti narodnykh zasedatelei," *SYu,* No. 14 (1969), pp. 11–12. People's assessors may be uninformed on the law or believe that "the question of guilt is predetermined by the pre-trial investigation and the main job of the court is to pick the proper form of punishment." "Narodnyi sud'ya i narodnye zasedateli," *SYu,* No. 13 (1970), p. 1. On the German equivalent, *Schöffen,* and their passive role, see Samuel Kucherov, *Courts, Lawyers, and Trials under the Last Three Tsars* (New York: Frederick A. Praeger, 1953), pp. 29, 53–57, 75. On people's assessors elsewhere in Europe, their relatively active part in verdicts and sentencing in Poland and the "eclipse" of the jury system in Europe generally, see Stanislaw Pomorski, "Comment: Law Judges in the Polish Criminal Courts: A Legal and Empirical Description," *Case Western Reserve Journal of International Law,* vol. 7 (1975), pp. 198–209, and footnotes.

28. A. Likas, "Usuzhden uslovno," *Pravda,* March 25, 1973; A. Mozhaev, "Rabota sovetov narodnykh zasedatelei," *SYu,* No. 8 (1971), pp. 19–20; N. Radutnaya, "Sovety narodnykh zasedatelei i puti uluchsheniya ikh deyatel'nosti," *SYu,* No. 23 (1969), pp. 8–9.

29. Public accusers participated in 9.3 percent of USSR criminal trials in 1960–1974 and public defenders in 5.6 percent. P.P. Yakimov, "Effektivnost'

obshchestvennogo obvineniya i zashchity, *SGP,* No. 12 (1975), p. 70. See also, ibid., p. 74, on visiting session participation, and A. Orlov, "Sovershenstvovat'-deyatel'nost' sudebnykh organov," *SYu,* No. 1 (1974), p. 3; R.D. Rakhunov, *Vyezdnaya sessiya suda* (Moscow: Izd. Yuridicheskoi literatury, 1968); provisions on social defenders and social accusers in *UPK* (1973), Articles 47, 49, 50, 228, 250; A. Radontsev, "Obshchestvennye obviniteli i zashchitniki," *SZ,* No. 7 (1971), pp. 69–71; Lapenna, *Soviet Penal Policy,* p. 126; A. Gorkin, "Pyatidesyatiletie sovetskoi vlasti i sotsialisticheskoe pravosudie," *SZ,* No. 11 (1967), p. 18.

30. Peter H. Juviler, "Mass Education and Justice in Soviet Courts: The Visiting Sessions," *Soviet Studies,* vol. 18 (1967), pp. 449–510; "Zadachi organov yustitsii i sudov v svete reshenii dekabr'skogo (1973 g.) plenuma TsK KPSS," *SYu,* No. 6 (1974), pp. 1–3.

31. Petty hooligans were more likely in 1966–1967 to face administrative sanctions—fines or fifteen days in jail, than they were to be handed over to the collective for reeducation. "Rasshirennoe zasedanie kolegii Prokuratury SSSR," *SZ,* No. 7 (1968), p. 77.

32. *XX S"ezd Kommunisticheskoi partii sovetskogo soyuza. 14–25 fevralya 1956 goda. Stenografichekii otchet* (Moscow: Gos izd. polit. lit., 1956), p. 95; Jan Vinokur, "The Anti-Parasite Laws, 1957–1972" (Senior Essay, Barnard College, 1972), effectively discusses the work ethic; and see note 34.

33. Edict of October 5, 1956, "O priobshchenii k trudu tsygan, zanimayushchikhsya brodyazhnichestvom," *Sbornik zakonov,* vol. 2, p. 187.

34. Marianne Armstrong, "The Campaign against Parasites," in Peter H. Juviler and Henry W. Morton (eds.), *Soviet Policy-Making: Studies of Communism in Transition* (New York: Frederick A. Praeger, 1967), pp. 163–182. R. Beerman, "The Parasites Law," *Soviet Studies,* vol. 13 (1961), pp. 191–205, and "Soviet and Russian Anti-Parasite Laws," ibid., vol. 15 (1964), pp. 420–429. Beerman treats, in the first article, aspects of the anti-parasite laws as martialing public opinion against disapproved ways of obtaining unearned income; in the second, he draws some fascinating parallels with prerevolutionary Russian laws on deportation of undesirables and relates them to times of social stress.

35. Andrei Amalrik, *Involuntary Journey to Siberia,* transl. by Mania Harari and Max Hayward (New York: Harcourt Brace Jovanovich, 1970), pp. 130–132.

36. Armstrong, "Campaign against Parasites," pp. 179–180.

37. The remaining antiparasite penalties of exile guarded against communitarian abuse. But, as a Moscow University jurist wrote, they retained an anomalous situation wherein the penalty of exile remained for vaguely defined offenses and was stiffer as an administrative penalty than were many of the penalties for the supposedly more serious and more severely punished violations listed in the criminal codes. N.F. Kuznetsova, *Prestuplenie i prestupnost'* (Moscow: Izd. Moskovskogo universiteta, 1969), pp. 130–131. The penalties returned in effect to punishment for a noncrime which Stalin achieved through

the principle of "analogy" or the secret police special boards. Hazard, "Soviet Law and Justice," pp. 103–104.

38. *Vneocherednoi XXI S"ezd Kommunisticheskoi partii sovetskogo soyuza. 27 yanvaria–5 fevralya 1959 goda. Stenograficheskii otchet* (Moscow: Gos. izd. polit. lit., 1959), vol. 1, pp. 103–104.

39. Ibid.

40. Ibid., p. 105.

41. F. Nikitinskii and A. Dosugov, "Obshchestvo uchastvuet v preduprezhdenii pravonarushenii," *SZ,* No. 7 (1971), pp. 8–12. This article gives some idea of the role of the Administrative Organs Department of a party committee, a department in a network specially set up to oversee the courts, Procuracy, and police as well as all activities of the legal profession under the direction of superior departments of administrative organs up to the level of the Central Committee of the CPSU. Leonard Schapiro, *The Government and Politics of the Soviet Union* (rev. ed.; New York: Vintage Books, 1965), p. 65; John S. Reshetar, Jr., *The Soviet Polity: Government and Politics in the USSR* (New York: Dodd Mead, 1971), pp. 160, 229; N. Mironov, "Persuasion and Compulsion in Combating Anti-Social Acts," *Soviet Review,* vol. 2 (1961), pp. 56–57. Mironov was then head of the Department of Administrative Organs.

42. Vernon V. Aspaturian, "The Soviet Military-Industrial Complex—Does It Exist?" *Journal of International Affairs,* No. 1 (1972), p. 25.

43. John N. Hazard, Isaac Schapiro, and Peter B. Maggs, *The Soviet Legal System: Contemporary Documentation and Historical Commentary* (Dobbs Ferry, N.Y.: Oceana Publications, 1969), pp. 14–15; A. Vlasov, "Sud strogii, sud tovaricheskii," *Pravda,* October 3, 1973.

44. A. Vasil'ev, "V interesakh ukrepleniya sotsialisticheskoi zakonnosti," *SYu,* No. 14 (1971), pp. 17–18. Vasil'ev, *Razvitie sovetskoi demokratii,* pp. 166–167.

45. A. Bezmat'ev, "Deputaty na strazhe sotsialisitcheskoi zakonnosti," *SZ,* No. 7 (1971), pp. 67–68; B.N. Gabrichidze and A.K. Konev, *Ulichnye komitety* (Moscow: Izd. "Yuridicheskaya literatura," 1965); Vasil'ev, *Razvitie,* p. 64; Nikitinskii and Dosugov, "Obshchestvo uchastvuet," p. 9.

46. V.S. Osnovin et al. (eds.), *Mestnye sovety i zakonnost'* (Moscow: "Yuridicheskaya literatura," 1970), pp. 64–65; Robert G. Wesson, "Volunteers and Soviets," *Soviet Studies,* vol. 15 (1964), pp. 231–239; Lapenna, *Soviet Penal Policy,* pp. 99–100, 136–138; "People's Control," in F.J.M. Feldbrugge (ed.), *Encyclopedia of Soviet Law* (2 vols.; Dobbs Ferry, N.Y.: Oceana and Leiden, Neth.: A.W. Sijthoff, 1973), vol. 2, pp. 503–506.

47. A.I. Bogachev, "Voprosy organizatsii raboty dobrovol'nykh druzhin i ikh pravovoe polozhenie," *Voprosy bor'by s prestupnost'yu,* No. 14 (1971), pp. 66–74; A. Sozykin, "Narodnye druzhiny: kak oni sozdayutsya i deistvuyut," *Sovety deputatov trudyashchikhsya,* No. 7 (1971), pp. 95–99; M. Portyanko, "Obyazannosti i prava druzhinika," ibid., No. 8 (1971, pp. 86–90; T. Aleksandrova, "Druzhiniku o zakonodatel'stve," ibid., No. 9 (1971), pp. 90–94. On the background, legal implications, and first years of the people's detachments see Dennis M. O'Connor, "Soviet People's Guards: An Experiment with

Civic Police," *New York University Law Review,* vol. 39 (1964), pp. 579–614. People's detachments operate under a general directive of the CPSU Central Committee and the USSR Council of Ministers of March 2, 1959, "On the Participation of Working People in the Maintenance of Public Order," and under republic statutes, e.g., the Russian Republic Statute of March 30, 1960.

48. Edict of May 20, 1974, *Ved,* No. 22, item 326, Articles 3, 10.

49. A. Berezkin, "Druzhiniki sel'skogo raiona," *Chelovek i zakon,* No. 11 (1975), pp. 58–64; notes 47, 50.

50. Ibid., Article 5.

51. Bogachev, "Voprosy organizatsii raboty dobrovol'nykh druzhin," p. 73.

52. Sozykin, "Narodnye druzhiny," p. 96.

53. Portyanko, "Obyazannosti i prava druzhinika," p. 87.

54. Steven Laine Goldstein, "Volunteer Foot Patrol Fights Crime on W. 105th Street," *Manhattan Park West,* September 23, 1971; "Editorial: A Call to Action," *Amsterdam News,* September 30, 1972; Ira Breskin, "Civilians Augment Police Protection," *Columbia Spectator,* October 4, 1972.

55. Note 47.

56. Edict of May 20, 1974, Article 4.

57. D. Novopolyansky, "Behind the Mask of a People's Volunteer," *Komsomolskaya pravda,* October 6, 1960, transl. in *CDSP,* vol. 12, No. 45 (1960), pp. 24–25; "Follow-up on a *Komsomolskaya Pravda* Report: 'Behind the Mask of a People's Volunteer,'" ibid., May 5, 1961, transl. in *CDSP,* vol. 13, No. 19 (1961), p. 23; D. Novopolyanski, "The Trial Is On!" ibid., May 30, 1961, transl. in *CDSP,* vol. 13, No. 23 (1961), pp. 22–23; "Protectors of Criminals," *Izvestiya,* June 23, 1961, transl. in *CDSP,* vol. 13, No. 25 (1961), pp. 29–30; "Follow-up on *Izvestia* Report: 'Protectors of Criminals,'" *Izvestiya,* July 21, 1961, transl. in *CDSP,* vol. 13, No. 29 (1961), pp. 31–32.

58. Portyanko, "Obyazannosti i prava," pp. 88–89.

59. R. Iskenderov and V. Sukharev, "What Kind of Volunteer Militia Aides Should We Have?" *Pravda,* April 27, 1971, transl. in *CDSP,* vol. 23 (1971), pp. 45–46.

60. V. Yegorov, "The Reader Continues the Discussion: If You Are a Volunteer Militia Aide," *Pravda,* July 16, 1971, transl. in *CDSP,* vol. 23, (1971), p. 20.

61. Bogachev, "Voprosy organizatsii"; Sozykin, "Narodnye druzhiny."

62. S. Ostroumov et al., "Uchet i statistika pravonarushenii v svete leninskikh ukazanii," *SZ,* No. 4 (1969), p. 13.

63. *Polozhenie o tovaricheskikh sudakh. Utverzhdeno ukazom Prezidiuma Verkhovnogo Soveta RSFSR ot 3 iyulya 1961 g. s izmeneniyami* (Moscow: "Yuridicheskaya literatura," 1970).

64. Ibid., Article 15.

65. A. Bedernikov, "Tovaricheskie sudy v bor'be za ukreplenie ditsipliny truda," *SYu,* No. 9 (1972), pp. 25–26. For graphic impressions of comrades'

and regular courts see George Feifer, *Justice in Moscow* (New York: Simon and Schuster, 1964).

66. A. Tazetdinov, "Rabota s tovaricheskimi sudami v avtonomnoi respublike," *SYu,* No. 20 (1975), pp. 8–9.

67. "The Public and Law and Order," *Izvestiya,* December 28, 1971, excerpted in *CDSP,* vol. 23, No. 52 (1972), pp. 20–21. For a useful history and carefully balanced survey of Soviet and Western interpretations of the comrades' courts, see Kucherov, *Organs of Soviet Administration of Justice,* pp. 154–180. Mr. Yuri Luryi, an eminent Soviet defense attorney and member of the Leningrad bar, who emigrated in 1974, wrote to me in 1975:

> Given a cultural tradition going back to the period of serfdom and Stalinist terror, the level of legal consciousness of the broad masses of the population is exceedingly low. Members of the Soviet liberal intelligentsia have often pointed this out. Under these conditions, giving a certain part of the population authority over the rest of the population leads inevitably to violations of the most elementary forms of legality, abuses of authority and such. Creating the People's detachments brought on a sharp increase in specific crimes committed by the *druzhiniki* themselves, such as exceeding authority, using an official position for one's own purposes, and similar offenses. The occurrence of fear of *druzhiniki* among masses of the Soviet populace has not yet been described in the literature as far as I know. A number of big trials of leaders and members of People's Detachments in the 1960's indicated the danger of such a 'popularization.' For this reason the real role today of people's detachments, especially in the large cities, has been reduced to a minimum. The small part played by people's detachments and comrades' courts in maintaining order in factories is explained mainly by their ineffectuality and the danger of using them under present conditions.

Pointing out that union and party officials have "other options available for handling cases of work discipline," Prof. Peter H. Solomon, Jr., wrote me, also in 1975, "My impression is that . . . in factories, comrades' courts seem to be used less often."

68. Khrushchev's espousal of community suasion grew not only out of an ideological competition with China by 1969, but out of preferences for popularizing justice going back at least to 1956 (*XX S"ezd,* p. 95), even 1948 (Armstrong, "Campaign Against Parasites," p. 165). Opposition to the antiparasite laws has been mentioned. M.A. Suslov of the Party Presidium, speaking at the 21st Congress in 1959, took a more reserved position than Khrushchev, outlining not just a residual role for regular law enforcement but a major one alongside community agencies. *XXI S'ezd,* p. 361. By 1961 N.R. Mironov, head of the Department of Administrative Organs, was warning against treating criminals too leniently ("Persuasion and Compulsion," pp. 60–63). Khrushchev and legal commentators had adopted Suslov's kind of emphasis.

69. For Khrushchev's and Party Program's formulations at Twenty-second Congress, see *XXII S"ezd kommunisticheskoi partii sovetskogo soyuza.*

17–31 oktyabrya 1961 goda. Stenograficheskii otchet (Moscow: Gos. izd. politicheskoi literatury, 1962), vol. 1, p. 212, and vol. 3, p. 307. Darrell P. Hammer gives a thoughtful coverage of Khrushchev's policies in "Law Enforcement, Social Control, and the Withering of the State: Recent Soviet Experience," *Soviet Studies,* vol. 14 (1963), pp. 379–397. See also O'Connor, "Soviet People's Guards," p. 588.

70. B.S. Nikiforov and A.S. Shlyapochnikov, "Nekotorie problemy dal'neishego razvitiya sovetskogo ugolovnogo prava v svete programmy KPSS," *SGP,* No. 2 (1962), p. 61.

71. On popularization interpreted as state withering without withering of coercion, see Herbert Ritvo, "Totalitarianism without Coercion?" *Problems of Communism,* vol. 9 (November–December 1960), pp. 19–29; Jeremy R. Azrael, "Is Coercion Withering Away?" ibid., vol. 11 (November–December 1962), pp. 9–17; Leon Lipson, "Hosts and Pests: The Fight against Parasites," ibid., vol. 14 (March–April 1965), pp. 72–82.

72. New crimes included: not informing on the preparation or commission of serious state crimes including banditry—up to three years' confinement; concealing any of a longer list of state crimes—up to five years; first time petty theft of state or public property—up to six months' confinement (previously a crime only if twice repeated or offender already had been subjected to "social influence" with up to one year's confinement the penalty) or up to two years' confinement for persons already convicted of this offense; criminal negligence causing damage to farm machinery—up to one year's confinement; false reporting of plan fulfillment—up to three years'.

The government cracked down (on paper) on noncommercial moonshining by increasing maximum penalty from one year correctional work at liberty to one year corrective labor (confinement); extended criminal liability for timber poaching; lowered maximum penalty for simple receiving of stolen property from five to two years' confinement; and increased maximum for receiving stolen property with the intention of selling it or selling it as a business or in especially large amounts to seven years' confinement with five years' exile and confiscation of property or without them. Attempts on the life and rights of citizens under the guise of carrying out religious ceremonies always entailed three years' maximum penalty, now this penalty was extended from the leaders and organizers to any participants in the crime, making the whole congregation liable to prosecution and conviction.

These changes and the death penalty extensions, 1961–1962, (detailed in the next paragraph), are listed in *UK* (1970), Articles 23, 24, 53, 88^{-1}, 96, 99^{-1}, 152^{-1}, 158, 169, 208, 224, 227; *Ugolovnoe zakonodatel'stvo Soyuza SSSR i soyuznikh respublik* (2 vols.; Moscow: Gos. izd. Yuridicheskoi literatury, 1963); *Sbornik zakonov,* vol. 2, pp. 449–450, 473–474, 475–477.

The original edicts adding the supreme measure of death by shooting to other penalties in 1961–1962 and the crimes entailing this extension of capital punishment were:

(1) Edict of May 5, 1961 (*Ved.,* No. 19, item 207)—for theft of state or social property in especially large amounts, for making for sale or selling coun-

terfeit currency and securities as a business; terrorizing, in prisons or labor camps, prisoners who have taken the path of reform or atttacking the administration or organizing criminal groups for that purpose or actively participating in such groups [giving correctional authorities and courts virtual complete arbitrary power of life and death over defiant prisoners], if committed by especially dangerous recidivists or persons convicted for serious crimes—but not for persons under 18 when committing these crimes or other capital offenses or for women pregnant when committing the crime or at time of sentencing. And the death sentence may not be carried out against women pregnant at the time scheduled for execution.

(2) Edict of July 1, 1961 (*Ved.*, No. 27, item 291)—for speculation in foreign currencies or in securities as a business or in large amounts, and violation of currency regulations by persons already convicted of this offense.

(3) Edict of February 15, 1962 (*Ved.*, No. 8, item 83)—for attempts on the life of a people's guard or militiaman acting in line of duty, under aggravating circumstances.

(4) Edict of February 15, 1962 (*Ved.*, No. 8, item 84)—for rape by a group, a specially dangerous recidivist, or entailing especially grave consequences or rape of a minor.

(5) Edict of February 20, 1962 (*Ved.*, No. 8, item 85)—for accepting bribes for committing or failing to commit acts possible or required in line of duty, by an official in a responsible position, earlier convicted for bribery, who has received bribes several times, or who used extortion to get the bribe under especially aggravating circumstances.

In several cases these edicts added offenses to the criminal code or increased penalties, other than death penalties, for offenses already listed as crimes.

73. I. Shatunovsky, "The Vultures—Band of Currency Hunters to be Brought to Trial," *Komsomolskaya Pravda,* May 19, 1961, transl. in *CDSP,* vol. 13, No. 20 (1961), p. 17. See also in ibid., pp. 17–18, the joint KGB–USSR procuracy release outlining the currency speculation charges against Rokotov, Faibishenko, and seven others: "In the State Security Committee and the USSR Prosecutor's Office," *Pravda, Izvestiya,* and *Komsomolskaya Pravda,* May 19, 1961; Yuri Brokhin, *Hustling on Gorky Street: Sex and Crime in Russia Today* (New York: Dial Press, 1975), pp. 37–43. Brokhin's background color is plausible, but some of his dates are incorrect. Rokotov and Faibishenko went to trial May 31–June 15, sentenced to fifteen years (their accomplices received eight years), the maximum specified by the edict of March 25, 1961 (*Ved.*, No. 13, item 137). But their crimes occurred before that edict appeared, when the maximum penalty was eight years' confinement (Fundamentals of Criminal Law, Article 25, as reaffirmed in the edict of February 24, 1961, in *Ved.*, No. 9, item 91). The fifteen-year sentences violated Aritcle 6 of Fundamentals of Criminal Law: "Whether an act is criminal and the punishment for it are defined by the law in effect at the time the act was committed." The second retroactive violation came in that part of the sentence denying all the convicted gang members the possibility of later change to a lighter sentence, or parole. But this was based on an even later edict, that of May 5, 1961, *Ved.*, No. 19, item 207.

74. The retroactive death penalty for Rokotov and Faibishenko upon their retrial by the RSFSR Supreme Court, July 18–19, 1961, was illegal by the same token, that is, because it applied new legislation retroactively—in this case the edict of July 1, 1961, adding a possible death penalty for currency speculations, listed in note 72. A secret edict authorizing this application of the death penalty to Rokotov and Faibishenko in indictment and sentencing if the court found necessary and also dated July 1, 1961—in effect, a bill of attainder—was shown to Harold J. Berman by a member of the USSR Supreme Court in September 1961. Berman, *Justice in USSR,* p. 403, note 43; "V Verkhovnom sude RSFSR," *Pravda, Izvestiya,* July 21, 1961. On Khrushchev's manifestations of anti-Semitism, see *Encyclopedia Judaica* (17 vols.; New York: Macmillan, 1971), pp. 3, 150.

75. V. Ponomarev, "From the Courtroom: The End of the Gang of Bursak and Co.," *Sovetskaya Belorussia,* June 23, 1961; "Currency Speculators Sentenced to Death by Shooting," *Pravda Ukrainy,* June 12, 1961, transl. in *CDSP,* vol. 14, No. 25 (1961), p. 23.

76. Andrei D. Sakharov, *My Country and the World,* transl. by Guy V. Daniels (New York: Vintage Books, 1975), p. 43. The death penalty may not be applied to juveniles (under eighteen). So one is unlikely to read what one may about the United States where it is possible to pass sentence of death on a 15-year-old. *Amnesty International Annual Report 1974/1975* (London: Amnesty International Publications, 1975), p. 79.

77. Hazard, "Soviet Law and Justice," p. 93.

78. Compare, e.g., V. I. Lenin, "Gosudarstvo i revolyutsiya," and "Uderzhat li bolsheviki gosudarstvennuyu vlast'?" *Pol. sohr. Soch.,* vol. 33, pp. 88–91, and vol. 34, p. 348.

79. See *Vechernyaya moskva,* March 19, 1964, on party sponsored meeting addressed by Brezhnev.

80. See note 83, and N. Egorychev, "Vospitanie molodezhi delo partiinoe," *Kommunist,* No. 3 (1965), p. 16; L. Smirnov, "XXII S"ezd i zadachi sudebnykh organov v bor'be s prestupnost'yu," *SYu,* No. 14 (1966), p. 2.

81. Bernard Weinraub, "Crime in London Shows an Increase: 'Permissive Society' Partly to Blame, Police Say," *New York Times,* August 27, 1971.

82. V. Tikunov, "Sniskhozhdeniya khuliganam ne budet," *Izvestiya,* April 21, 1966; note 94.

83. A good summary on alcohol problems and alcoholism is in Walter D. Connor, *Deviance in Soviet Society: Crime, Delinquency, and Alcoholism,* pp. 34–79.

84. "We all know, for example, that recently sanctions for hooliganism were increased. This means that science had not succeeded up to then in giving sufficiently weighty recommendations, had not taken into account the demands of our Soviet social life." N. Zhogin, "Zakon i pravovaya nauka," *Izvestiya,* June 18, 1968.

85. *SZ,* No. 4 (1966), pp. 9–16; No. 7 (1966), p. 1; V. Kulikov, "Za uprochenie sotsialisticheskoi zakonnosti," ibid., 10–14, 23–24; *SZ,* No. 8 (1966), pp. 5–18.

86. V. Andreev, "How Was the Sentence Executed?" *Izvestiya,* November 16, 1965, transl. in *CDSP,* vol. 17, No. 46 (1965), pp. 24–25; V. Kudryavtsev, *Izvestiya,* November 25, 1965.

87. "V Tsk KPSS, Prezidiume Verkhovnogo Soveta SSSR i Sovete Ministrov SSSR," *Pravda,* July 27, 1966.

88. Edicts of July 26, 1966, *Ved,* No. 30; "Ob obrazovanii soyuznorespublikanskogo Ministerstvo okhrany obschestvennogo poryadka SSR" (item 594); "Ob usilenii otvetstvennosti za khuliganstvo" (item 595); "O poryadke primeneniya Ukaza Prezidiuma Verkhovnogo Soveta SSSR ot 26 iyulya 1966 goda 'Ob usilenii otvetstvennosti za khuliganstvo' " (item 596); "Ob administrativom nadzore organov militsii za litsami, osvobozhdennymi iz mest lisheniya svobody" (item 597).

89. "Po vole nardoda," *Izvestiya,* July 29, 1966.

90. Compare *op. cit.,* notes 120, 121, with edicts of July 26, 1966.

91. "Ob obrazovanii", notes 193, 194.

92. *Ugolovnyi kodeks RSFSR: Ofitsial'nyi tekst s izmeneniyami na 1 dekabrya 1963 g.* (Moscow: Izd. "Yuridicheskaya literatura" (1964), hereinafter *UK* (1964), Article 206; *Ved. SSSR,* No. 30 (1966), item 595.

93. *Uk* (1970), Article 10.

94. Hazard, "Soviet Law and Justice," p. 94.

95. V. Chkhikvadze (then director, Institute of State and Law), paraphrased in *SZ,* No. 7 (1966), p. 30.

96. Smirnov, "XXIII S" ezd i zadachi," p. 1.

97. On the atmosphere and special emissaries sent out by the Procuracy to speed up the drive and local party activities, see *Pravda,* July 27–28, 1966, *passim.; Izvestiya,* July 27–29, 1966, passim; *SZ,* No. 9 (1966), pp. 3–10; ibid., No. 10 (1966), pp. 3–10; and especially ibid., No. 11 (1966), pp. 7–21, 31–35.

98. Amalrik, *Involuntary Journey to Siberia,* pp. 227–279.

99. Convictions in 1966 were 33 percent higher than in 1965. The drive began during the last five months of 1966, hence the conviction rate then was roughly 12/5 x 33 percent or 80 percent higher than previously. See Table5–1.

100. "Unfounded sentencing to deprivation of freedom . . . causes persons to end up in places of confinement when neither their characters nor the social danger of their crimes in any way requires their being there. Sentencing to flagrantly excessive terms of confinement can lead to extreme overcrowding of places of confinement." A. A. Piontkovskii, "Puti ukrepleniya sotsialisticheskogo pravoporyadka," *SGP,* No. 1 (1967), p. 37.

101. Edict of October 31, 1967, "On Amnesty in Connection with the 50th Anniversary of the Great October Social Revolution," *Ved.,* No. 44 (1967), item 595.

102. M. P. Malyarov, "Za dal'naishee ukreplenie zakonnosti v bor'be s khuliganstvom," *SGP,* No. 9 (1967), pp. 50–58; *Byulleten' Verkhovnogo Suda RSFSR,* hereinafter *BVS RSFSR* No. 1 (1967), pp. 1–2; *BVS SSSR,* No. 6 (1966), pp. 7–8; V. Reznikov, "Nechhist'," *Komosomolskaya pravda,* June 5,

1966; I. Tyazhkova, "Voprosy otvetstvennosti za khuliganstvo," *SZ,* No. 3 (1967), pp. 29–34; *BVS RSFSR,* No. 12 (1968), p. 10; A. Chuvilev, "Protesessual'nye garantii po delam o khuliganstve bez otyagayushchikh obstoyatel'stv," *SZ,* No. 1 (1967), pp. 16–18.

103. Malyarov, "Za dal'naishee," p. 57, wrote that there were no cases of citizens' abusing their rights to defend themselves or others attacked by hooligans. The evidence of Soviet court reports, including the case of a homicide, indicates otherwise. See, e.g., *BVS RSFSR,* No. 9 (1967), pp. 7–8.

104. I. Perlov, "Protsessual'nye voprosy predvaritel'nogo rassledovaniya del o khuliganstve," *SYu,* No. 24 (1966), pp. 19–20; G. Anashkin, "Diagnoz prestupnika," *Izvestiya,* March 14, 1965; G. Anashkin, "Pravosudie. Nakazanie. Spravedlivost'," *Literaturnaya gazeta,* May 29, 1968; G. Z. Anashkin, "O zadachakh i tendentsiyakh razvitiya sotsialisticheskogo pravosudiya," *Vestnik moskovskogo universiteta,* No. 4 (1966), pp. 3–15; and by him in ibid., June 13, 1965, "Lichnost', obstolatel'stvo i otvetstvennost'." This article capped off a debate in *Literaturnaya gazeta* over crime and punishment in issues of May 27 and 30, June 3, 10, and 13, 1965; *BVS SSSR,* No. 5 (1966), pp. 11–12, 14.

105. "Sovershenstvovat' organizatsiyu raboty prokuratury v bor'be s prestupnost'yu," *SZ,* No. 11 (1968), p. 3.

106. "Sovmestnoe zasedanie kollegii Prokuratury SSSR i Ministerstva okhrany obshchestvennogo poryadka SSSR," *SZ,* No. 10 (1968), pp. 28–30.

107. Ibid.

108. A. Rekunov and V. Rozenfeld, "Ukreplenie ditsipliny truda—trebovanie zakona," *SZ,* No. 11 (1968), pp. 15–16. See also, e.g., N. Emelin, "Khuliganstvu—boi shirokim frontom," *Sovetskaya Moldaviya,* January 14, 1967.

109. *SZ,* No. 11 (1968), pp. 5–6; V. Kulikov, "Za uprochenie sotsialisticheskoi zakonnosti," *SZ,* No. 7 (1967), pp. 15–22.

110. David E. Powell, "Alcoholism in the USSR," *Survey* No. 1 (1971), p. 123; a good overview also in Connor, *Deviance in Soviet Society,* pp. 59–79.

111. My observations in the USSR, 1958–1959; writer Atarov and psychiatrist Zemskov in *Literaturnaya gazeta,* January 11 and 20, 1966.

112. *Literaturnaya gazeta,* February 3, 1966.

113. *SSSR v tsifrakh v 1967 godu* (Moscow: Izd. "Statistika," 1968), p. 144; *SSSR v tsifrakh v 1973 godu* (Moscow: Izd. "Statistika," 1974), p. 187. N. Khodakov, "Drunkenness through a Doctor's Eyes," *Literaturnaya gazeta,* July 10, 1974, cond. in *CDSP,* vol. 26 (August 14, 1974), pp. 8–9.

114. Up to then, drunkenness was an aggravating circumstance only if crime was committed using means constituting a public menace. *UK* (1964), Article 39, Part X, *Ved.* (1966), item 595.

115. Edict of April 8, 1967. *Ved. RSFSR,* No. 15, item 333, transl. in *CDSP,* vol. XIX 19 (1967), p. 11.

116. It resembled punishment for crime in that penalties for attempted escape en route under guard or from institution applied here. *UK* (1970), Article 186. Also, pay was docked for maintenance, hence hurting the family; the

culprit was subject to dismissal without severance pay (but, unlike for criminal sanctions, culprit did not lose in the count of years toward retirement; also penalty did not apply to men over sixty years old or women over fifty-five or mentally deficient persons).

117. Powell, "Alcoholism in USSR," p. 134.

118. "In the CPSU Central Committee: On Measures for Intensifying the Struggle Against Alcoholism and Drunkenness," *Pravda* and *Izvestiya,* June 13, 1972, transl. in *CDSP,* vol. 24, No. 24 (1972), p. 19; "In the USSR Council of Ministers: On Measures for Intensifying the Struggle Against Drunkenness and Alcoholism," ibid., pp. 19–20.

119. "The Citizen and the Law, Street without Incidents," *Pravda,* September 28, 1972, excerpted in *CDSP,* vol. 24, No. 39 (1972), p. 26.

120. Compare, for example, penalties for home brew violators as raised in 1961 *Kommentarii k ugolovnomu kodeksu RSFSR 1960 g.* (Leningrad: Izd. Leningradskogo universiteta, 1962), pp. 289–292; *UK* (1964), pp. 199–201, with the new penalties; changes in RSFSR Criminal Code, November 30, 1972, *SZ,* No. 3 (1973), pp. 81–82. On the limits of coercion and need to treat alcoholism as a disease, see A. Sergeev, "A Crucial Topic: On the Trail of a Great Killer," *Literaturnaya Rossiya,* No. 6 (1964), cond. in *CDSP,* vol. 26, No. 6 (1974), p. 6.

121. *UK* (1964), Article 158; *Kommentarii k ugolovnomu kodeksu RSFSR* (Moscow: "Yuridicheskaya literatura," 1971), pp. 473–474, gives a Soviet definition of narcotics.

122. Directive of Plenum of USSR Supreme Court, February 25, 1966, *Sbornik postanovlenii Plenuma Verkhovnogo Suda SSSR, 1924–1970* (Moscow: "Yuridicheskaya literatura," 1970), pp. 494–498: A. Aimamedov, "Sudebnaya praktika bor-by s narkomaniei," *SZ,* No. 7 (1962), pp. 21–22. On the way drugs are spread, see Hedrick Smith, *The Russians* (New York, Quadrangle, 1976) p. 179.

123. Revision of July 3, 1965. Compare *UK* (1964), Article 210, and (1970), ibid.

124. Edict of RSFSR of August 25, 1972, transl. in *CDSP,* vol. 24, No. 37 (1972), p. 7.

125. A. Fedorov and B. Polonskii, "Premenenie prinuditel'nykh mer meditsinskogo kharaktera k alkogolikom i narkomanam," *SZ,* No. 5 (1974), pp. 28–31.

126. V. Korchyagin, "Praktika primeneniya sudami mer meditsinskogo kharaktera k alkogolikam i narkomanam," *SZ,* No. 11 (1973), pp. 63–64.

127. *Ved.,* No. 18 (1974), item 275. G. Levitskii, "Okvetsvennost' za nezakonnoe izgotovlenie, priobretenie, khranenie, perevozki ili sbyt narkoticheskikh veshehestv," *SYu,* No. 13 (1976), pp. 22–24. A followup order came from the USSR Supreme Court to the trial courts for more firm and searching justice in drug cases. Decree No. 7, September 25, 1975, *SYu,* No. 22 (1975), pp. 29–30.

128. "O merakh po usileniyu bor'by protiv p'yanstva i alkogolizma," Edict of RSFSR, June 19, 1972, *SYu,* No. 14 (1972), pp. 24–25. New crimes other than those created by the measures listed in notes 90 and 121 and this edict are listed in *UK* (1970), Articles 124^{-1}, 142, 154^{-1},, 156, 186, 189, 190, 190^{-1}, 190^{-2}, 190^{-3}, 205^{-1}, 209, 209^{-1}, 210, 211, 211^{-1}, 211^{-2}, 212^{-1}, 213^{-1}, 217, 223, 225; "Ob usilenii otvetstvennosti za rasprostranenie venericheskikh zabolevanii," Edict of October 1, 1971, *Ved.* No. 40 (1971), item 392. On increased penalties, see *UK* (1970), Articles 93, 96, 198^{-1}, 206, sections 1 and 2 and antialcohol measures listed above. For minor elimination of crimes, see Articles 189, 212.

129. For changes making it harder to get parole and easier to be classified as an "especially dangerous recidivist," an aggravating circumstance of special seriousness, see Law of July 11, 1969, *Izvestiya,* July 12, 1969, and *Pravda,* July 13, 1969, transl. in *CDSP,* vol. 21, No. 30 (1969), pp. 3–4; see also directives of Plenum of USSR Supreme Court, March 18, 1970, *BVS SSSR,* No. 3 pp. 14–20.

130. Edict of RSFSR Supreme Soviet of December 15, 1972, *SZ,* No. 3 (1973), pp. 83–84.

131. Edict of February 11, 1974, *Ved.,* No. 7 (1974), item 11.

132. Edict of January 3, 1973, *SZ,* No. 3 (1973), p. 81.

133. Edict of February 26, 1974, *Ved.,* No. 10, item 161.

134. Fred P. Graham, "A Vagrancy Law in Florida Upset by Supreme Court," *New York Times,* February 25, 1972; John J. Phillips, Civil Liberties Trip in Thoreau's Town," *WIN,* April 1, 1976, p. 17.

135. Decree of Central Committe of CPSU and USSR Council of Ministers, February 23, 1970, *SYu,* No. 10 (1970), pp. 23–25. See also *UK* (1970), Articles 209, 209^{-1}, pp. 205–206. Such legislation first appeared in Estonia in 1966. Albert Boiter, "The Parasite Law Rides Again," *Radio Liberty Dispatch,* April 20, 1970.

136. *Kommentarii k ugolovnomu kodeksu RSFSR,* p. 447; *Sbornik postanovlenii plenuma Verkhovnogo Suda SSSR 1924–1973* (Moscow: Izd. "Izvestiya sovetov deputatov trudyashchikhsya SSSR," 1974), p. 567; I. Malandin and V. Shankov, "Bor'ba s tuneyadstvom i ee trudnosti," *SZ,* No. 3 (1974), p. 54; S. Sal'nov and V. Pavlinov, "Bor'ba s tuneyadstvom vo Vladimirskoi oblasti," *SZ,* No. 12 (1973), p. 29; earlier discussion on parasites.

137. Jon Lukomnik, "Soviets Charge Rubin with Treason," *Columbia Spectator,* August 1, 1974; Kucherov, *Organs of Soviet Administration of Justice,* pp. 213–241.

138. *Vedomosti Verkhovnogo Soveta RSFSR,* No. 33 (1975), items 698, 699. Item 698 revised Articles 209 and 209^{-1} to read: "Article 209. Systematic vagrancy or begging. Systematic vagrancy or begging *and also leading any other parasitic way of life for a prolonged period of time*—is punishable by deprivation of freedom for a period of up to one year or correctional labor for the period. The same acts committed by persons previously convicted under part one of this article—are punishable by deprivation of freedom for a period of up to two years." See also *UK* (1975), Articles 209, 209^{-1}. In the Russian republic

criminal code, effective January 1, 1961, there was just an Article 209 making "systematic vagrancy or begging after repeated warning" a crime punishable by up to one year's deprivation of freedom. *Kommentarii k ugolovnomu kodeksu 1960 g,* pp. 355–357. The penalties were increased when parasitism entered the code via a separate new article 209-1 to two years—or four years if repeated—and the phrase "after repeated warnings" dropped. *Vedomosti Verkhovnogo Soveta RSFSR,* No. 14 (1970), items 225, 256. See also ibid. No. 18, (1961), item 273; No. 38 (1965), item 932. Since item 699 repealed the anti-parasite legislation of 1961, 1965 and 1970, the italicized phrase is all that is left of anti-parasite legislation in the RSFSR and, possibly, other parts of the USSR.

139. Malandin and Shvankov, "Bor'ba s tuneyadstvom," p. 52; E. Khudyakov, "Otvetstvennost' za uklonenie ot obshchestvenno-poleznogo truda i vedenie paraziticheskogo obraza zhizni," *SYu,* No. 4 (1974), pp. 7–8; Sal'nov and Pavlinov, "Borba s tuneyadstvom," p. 30.

140. Ibid., p. 30.

141. H. Jack Griswold, Mike Misenheimer, Art Powers, and Ed Tromanhauser, *An Eye for an Eye* (New York: Pocket Books, 1971), p. 213; and also, e.g., Fred Ferretti, "Job Crisis Afflicts Ex-Convicts," *New York Times,* May 28, 1971.

142. Piontkovskii, "Puti ukrepleniya sotsialisticheskogo pravoporyadka," p. 37.

143. B. Nikiforov, "Otvet serditym oponentam," *Liternaturnaya Gazeta,* November 20, 1968.

144. "Ob uslovnom osuzhdenii k lisheniyu svobody s obyazatel'nym privlecheniem osuzhdennogo k trudu," edict of June 12, 1970, *Ved.* (1970), No. 24, item 204; "O poryadke premeneniya Ukaza Prezidiuma Verghovnogo Soveta SSSR ot 12 iyunya 1970 goda," "Ob uslovnom osuzhdenii k lisheniyu svobody s obyazatel'nym privlecheniem osuzhdennogo k trudu," edict of June 12, 1970, ibid., item 205.

145. I. I. Karpets, *Nakazanie: Sotsial'nye, pravovye i kriminologicheskie problemy* (Moscow: "Yuridicheskaya literatura," 1973), p. 236.

146. Ibid., pp. 234–237.

147. See my forthcoming study of juvenile lawbreaking and Connor, *Deviance in Soviet Society,* pp. 206–229.

148. V. Kolosova, "Praktika primeneniya sudami uslovnogo osuzhdeniya s obyasatel'nym privlecheniem k trudu," *SYu,* No. 18 (1973), p. 19; see note 189.

149. Kolosova, "Praktika primeneniya," pp. 19–21: "Plenum Verkhovnogo Suda SSSR," *BVS SSSR,* No. 3 (1972), p. 6; Supreme Court Decree No. 2, April 11, 1972, ibid., pp. 12–14; Decree of USSR Supreme Soviet on disciplinary rules and residence when applying the work-release measure of June 12, 1970, March 10, 1975, *BVS SSSR* No. 4 (1975), p. 48.

150. P.F. Pashkevich, "Kontrol" nad uslovno osuzhdennymi i uslovno-dosrochno osvobozhdennymi," *SGP,* No. 10 (1975), p. 75.

151. "Prinuditel'nyi sel'skokhozyaistvennyi trud v SSSR," *Kronika zashchity prav v SSSR,* No. 8 (March-April, 1974), pp. 32–33.

152. A. Ya. Sukharev, "Pravovoe vospitanie i yuridicheskaya nauka," *SGP,* No. 2 (1974), pp. 3–11; L.I. Brezhnev, "Otchetnyi doklad Tsentral'nogo Komiteta KPSS XXIV S'ezdu Kommunisticheskoi partii Sovetskogo Soyuza," *Pravda,* March 31, 1971; "Zasedanie Komissii zakonodatel'nykh predpolozhenii Soveta Soyuza i Soveta Natsional'nostei Verkhovnogo Soveta SSSR," *Ved. SSSR,* (1972), No. 39 p. 597; N. A. Shchelokov, "Pravovoe vospitanie na sovremennom etape," *SGP,* No. 1 (1972), pp. 11–19; B. Nifontov, "Deistvennost' raboty po pravomu vospitaniyu," *SYu,* No. 16 (1972), pp. 18–19. See also above, notes 24–31, and Harold J. Berman, "The Educational Role of Soviet Criminal Law and Civil Procedure" in Donald D. Barry, William E. Butler and George Ginsburgs (eds.), *Contemporary Soviet Law: Essay in Honor of John N. Hazard* (The Hague: Martinus Nijhoff, 1974), pp. 1–16.

153. Minister of Justice V. Terebilov, "Ukreplenie zakonnosti-obshchaya zadacha organov yustitsii, suda i prokuratury," p. 19.

154. Sukharev, "Pravovoe vospitanie," p. 3.

155. Ibid., p. 20; "Polozhenie o Ministerstve yustitsii RSFSR," Article 5 (q).

156. Sukharev, "Pravovoe vospitanie," p. 3.

157. Note 197; N. Yablokov, "Fakul'tet komandirov dobrovol'nykh narodnykh druzhin universiteta pravovykh znanii," *SYu,* No. 9 (1974), pp. 16–17.

158. V. Soroko, "Pravovaya propaganda na zavode," *SYu,* No. 2 (1974), pp. 30–31: On Leningrad's effort, see V. Afonina and Yu. Naumov, "Deistvennye formy pravovogo vospitaniya trudyashchikhsya," *SYu,* No. 21 (1975), pp. 3–4,

159. Sukharev, "Pravovoe vospitanie," p. 5.

160. A. Kozhevnikova (deputy head, Department of Justice, Executive Committee, Moscow City Soviet, chairperson of Coordinating and Methodological Council on Legal Propaganda) and A. Medvedev (member of Scientific and Methodological Council, Moscow City Organization of Znanie), "Vneshkol'nye formy pravovogo vospitaniya uchashchikhsya," *SYu,* No. 8 (1974), pp. 11–12.

161. Sukharev, "Pravovoe vospitanie," pp. 4, 8–9.

162. G. Dashkov and N. Sokolov, "Znachenie pravovogo vospitaniya v bor'be s prestupleniyami protiv sotsialisticheskoi sobstevennosti," *SYu,* No. 9 (1974), pp. 3–5.

163. Likas, "Osuzhden uslovno."

164. Evgenii Voronov, "Kollektiv nachinaetsya s ditsiplinoi," *Pravda,* October 29, 1973, p. 151.

165. Sukharev, "Pravovoe vospitanie . . .," pp. 6–7.

166. V. Sesin (head of department, Bondarskii District Party Committee, Tambov Province, and chairman, Coordinating and Methodological Council on Legal Propaganda) and V. Papshin (deputy head, Department of Justice of

Executive Committee, Tambov Province soviet), "Raionnyi koordinatsionno-metodologicheskii soviet po pravomu propagande," *SYu,* No. 4 (1974), p. 6.

167. Personal communication from Mr. Yuri Luryi, 1975

168. "Narodom izbrannye," *Byulleten' Verkhovnogo suda SSSR,* hereafter *Byulleten',* No. 1 (1970), p. 3.

169. *UPK* (1972), Articles 36–38; Rivlin, *Organizatsiya suda i prokuratury v SSSR,* pp. 66–70, 123–124, 170–171; Lapenna, *Soviet Penal Policy,* pp. 105–107; Berman, "Soviet Legal Reform—Dateline Moscow 1957," p. 1205; Ivanov, "Organizatsiya suda i prokuratury," vol. 2, p. 591; note 15.

170. Rivlin, *Organizatsiya suda i prokuratury,* pp. 71–93; Fund. on Ct. Syst., Articles 5–8, 30; USSR Constitution, Articles 103–112.

171. Kircheimer, "Political Justice," Theodore Becker (ed.), *Political Trials* (Indianapolis and New York: Bobbs-Merrill, 1971).

172. Rivlin, *Organizatsiya, suda,* pp. 83–84.

173. "Partiinye organizatsii sudov i ukreplenie sotsialistichesoi zakonnosti," *SYu,* No. 6 (1971), p. 3.

174. S. Radzhabov, "Partiinaya organizatsiya administrativnykh organov nashego raiona v bor'be za ukreplenie sotsialisticheskoi zakonnosti," *SYu,* No. 8 (1970), pp. 26–27.

175. "Partiinye organizatiya sudov," p. 5; "Narodom izhrannye," p. 4.

176. Prof. L.E. Vladimirov, *Sud prisyazhnykh i metod razrabotki dokazatel'stv* (Kharkov, 1873), quoted in Kucherov, *Courts, Lawyers, and Trials under Last Three Tsars,* p. 84.

177. Conquest, *Justice and Legal System in USSR,* pp. 112–113.

178. Berman, "Law Reform in Soviet Union," p. 183.

179. *UPK* (1973), Article 126; and of note 201.

180. M.P. Malyarov (ed.), *Prokuratorskii nadzor v SSSR* (3rd rev. and enl. ed.; Moscow: "Yuridicheskaya literatura," 1973), pp. 3–50.

181. Glen C. Morgan, *Soviet Administrative Legality: The Role of the Attorney General's Office,* (Stanford, Stanford University Press, 1962), pp. 10–21.

182. Amalrik, *Involuntary Journey to Siberia.*

183. Rivlin, *Organizatsiya suda,* p. 142.

184. *Sudebnyi protsess po ugolovnomu delu amerikanskogo letchika-shpiona Frensis G. Pauersa, 17–19 avgusta 1960 goda* (Moscow: Gos. izd. polit. lit., 1960).

185. Michel Tatu, *Power in Kremlin: From Khruschev to Kosygin,* transl. by Helen Katel (New York, Viking Press, 1968), p. 325.

186. L.N. Smirnov et al. (eds.), *Verkhovnyi Sud SSSR* (Moscow: "Yuridicheskaya literatura," 1974), pp. 22–23.

187. Statute of USSR Supreme Court, February 12, 1957, *Sbornik zakonov,* vol. 2, pp. 513–518.

188. *Sbornik postanovlenii plenuma Verkhovnoko Suda, 1924–1973,* pp. 269–279. Quote is from p. 270.

189. Plenum decree of December 23, 1970, with subsequent revisions in 1972 and 1973, *Sbornik postanovlenii, 1924–1973,* pp. 401–411.

190. See Chapter 5.

191. Plenum decree of December 4, 1969, *Sbornik postanovlenii 1924–1973,* pp. 356–363; P. Pashkevich, "Sluchai na platforme," *Izvestiya,* February 13, 1974, P. Pashkevich, "Esli na puti-khuligan," *Izvestiya,* May 15, 1974. Donald D. Barry and Carol Barner-Barry "The USSR Supreme Court and Guiding Explanations on Civil Law, 1962–1971," in Barry, Butler, and Ginsburgs (eds.), *Contemporary Soviet Law,* pp. 69–83.

192. *BVS SSSR,* No. 6 (1973).

193. "V tsentral'nom komitete KPSS i sovete ministrov SSSR," *Pravda,* November 29, 1968.

194. L. Kornilov and T. Fetisov, "Into Service in the Militia," *Nedelya,* No. 13 (March 23–29, 1970), excerpted in *Current Abstracts of the Soviet Press,* No. 2 (June 1970), pp. 20–21; Gogolev, "Shield of Order," p. 25. On shortcomings of the militia during the antihooliganism drive, which may have prompted the 1968 reforms, see Malyarov, "Za dal'naishee," p. 55; *SZ,* No. 7 (1968), p. 77.

195. Connor, *Deviance in Soviet Society,* pp. 193–194.

196. *UPK* (1972), Article 125.

197. Ray Vicker, "Soviet Setback: Lagging Economy Puts Leaders, Workers Alike on the Spot in Russia," *Wall Street Journal,* April 10, 1970; *Narodnoe khozyaistvo SSSR v 1970 godu* (Moscow, 1971). Page 59, lists Soviet industrial growth at 7.1 percent in 1969, lower than that for the year 1964, following the bad harvest of 1963, when growth was just slightly higher, 7.3 percent. See also "O zadachakh sudebnykh organov v svyazi s resheniyami dekabr'skogo (1969g) plenuma TsK KPSS," directive of plenum of USSR Supreme Court, March 18, 1970. *BVS SSSR,* No. 3 (1970), pp. 11–14; "Plenary Session of the Central Council of Trade Unions," *Trud,* January 28, 1970, transl. in *CDSP,* vol. 22 (1970), p. 9; N.G. Aleksandrov, *Ekonomicheskaya Politika KPSS, trud i pravo: Voprosy trudovogo prava v svete reshenii XXIV S"ezda KPSS* (Moscow: Izd. Moskovskogo Universiteta, 1973), pp. 90–116.

198. See, e.g., *SZ,* No. 5 1970), pp. 77–78.

199. Edict of June 8, 1973, *Ved.* No. 24 (1973), item 309.

200. Jerry Hough, "The Soviet Elite: Groups and Individuals," *Problems of Communism,* vol. 16 January–February 1967), p. 29; "The USSR's New Police Chief," *Radio Free Europe Research Report,* September 19, 1966; "The USSR's New Police Chief—II" ibid., March 9, 1967. The power and prestige of the MVD was signaled, apart from anticrime measures involving the MVD, by the promotion of its head, Shchelokov, from candidate to full membership on the Central Committee on April 10, 1968, joining Procurator General Rudenko there. *Pravda,* April 11, 1968.

201. M. Kizikov and E. Okushev, "Nepravilnaya praktika," *SZ,* No. 7 (1970), pp. 35–36. Andrei Amalrik's being freed on pornography charges at the insistence of the police investigator, the latter's conflicts with the judge who sentenced Amalrik to exile as a parasite, and the roles of the KGB, the prosecutors who had Amalrik released upon protest to the RSFSR Supreme Court, and Amalrik's lawyer who fought to obtain his freedom provide fine examples of interservice disagreement, belying any concept of Soviet law enforcement as an absolute monolith. Amalrik, *Involuntary Journey to Siberia.* On signs of militia-KGB rivalry in 1963, see Tatu, *Power in Kremlin,* pp. 326–327. In the early 1960s the MVD gained concurrent jurisdiction with the Procuracy for lesser crimes and the KGB gained concurrent jurisdiction for an increased number of serious state crimes. Note 177, Berman and Spindler, *Soviet Criminal Law and Procedure,* p. 84.

202. F.J.M. Feldbrugge, "Ministry of Justice," in F.J.M. Feldbrugge (ed.), *Encyclopedia of Soviet Law* (2 vols.; Dobbs Ferry, N.Y.: Oceana and Leiden, Neth.: A.W. Sijthoff, 1973), vol. 2, pp. 453–454; note 258; Chapter 5, note 11.

203. Edict of September 30, 1967, *Sbornik zakonov,* vol. 2, pp. 513–518.

204. "Za dal'neishee povyshenie urovnya sudebnoi deyatel'nosti." *BVS SSSR,* No. 6 (1970), p. 4.

205. "V tsentral'nom komitete KPSS I Sovete ministrov SSSR," *BVS SSSR,* No. 5 (1970), pp. 3–4; V. Terebilov (USSR Minister of Justice), "Ukreplenie zakonnosti—obshchaya zadacha organov yustitsii, suda i prokuratury," *SZ,* No. 5 (1972), pp. 15–20; "Polozhenie o ministerstve yustitsii RSFSR," *SYu,* No. 16 (1972), pp. 3–6; V. Blinov (RSFSR Minister of Justice), "Sovershenstvovat' deyatel'nost'organov yustitsii," *Ibid.,* pp. 1–3.

206. Statute on Labor Colonies for Juveniles of USSR MVD, June 3, 1968, *Ved.,* No. 23 (1968), item 189, reprinted in M.P. Evteev and V.A. Kirin, *Zakonodatel'stvo ob otevetsvennosti nesovershennoletnikh,* pp. 92–111; Connor, *Deviance in Soviet Society,* pp. 143–145; Amnesty International, *Prisoners of Conscience in the USSR: Their Treatment and Conditions* (London: Amnesty International Publications, 1975), pp. 45–47; V.M. Blinov (ed.), *Kommentarii k ispravnitel'no-trudovomu kodeks RSFSR* (Moscow: "Yuridicheskaya literatura," 1973): N.A. Belyaev and M.I. Fedorov (ed.), *Ispravitel'no—trudovoe pravo* (Moscow: "Yuridicheskaya literatura," 1971).

207. On numbers of political prisoners, see Chapter 5, note 87. Uruguay's population is 2.5 million, about 1/100th the population of the USSR. But its extraordinarily high political prisoner count is of the same order of magnitude as the Soviet political prisoner count: 6,000 for Uruguay, according to Amnesty International. Jeri Laber, "Torture and Death in Uruguay," *New York Times,* March 10, 1976.

208. E.V. Boldyrev, "Ob izuchenii i preduprezhdenii prestuplenii nesovershennoletnikh," *SGP,* No. 12 (1960), pp. 96–100; Z.A. Astemirov, *Trudovaya koloniya dlya nesovershennoletnikh* (Moscow: "Yuridicheskaya literatura," 1969); note 206. On conditions in labor colonies, see below.

209. Fundamentals of Corrective Labor Legislation of USSR and Union

Republics," July 11, 1969, in effect November 1, 1969, *SYu,* No. 16 (1969), pp. 3–11; Statute on Preliminary Detention, July 11, 1969, in effect November 1, 1969, ibid., pp. 12–14; Corrective Labor Code of RSFSR is in Blinov, *Kommentarii k ispravitel'nomu-trudovomu kodeks RSFSR*. The best recent summary of corrections as it concerns political prisoners is in Amnesty International, *Prisoners of Conscience in USSR*.

209. *Khronika tekushchikh sobytii,* the famous *Chronicle of Current Events,* began appearing in *samizdat* in April 1968. Reprints are widely available from such sources as Khronika Press, New York, and Amnesty International London. Material on corrections and criminal justice appears also in such publications as Khronika Press' *Khronika zashchity prav v SSSR,* published in New York in Russian and English six times annually since 1972. Walter Connor compiled considerable information on camp countercultures and conditions from Soviet sources in *Deviance in Soviet Society,* pp. 206–235. A much quoted camp and prisoner memoir is Marchenko. *My Testimony*. Much material on camps in recent years, up to 1972, is in Peter Reddaway (ed. and transl.), *Uncensored Russia: Protest and Dissent in the Soviet Union: The Unofficial Moscow Journal Chronicle of Current Events* (New York: American Heritage Press, 1972). See also note 206, 211–223. This list is far from complete as to sources of *samizdat* or writings based on it.

211. Amnesty International, *Prisoners of Conscience in USSR*, pp. 36–39, 54–63; Vyacheslav Chornovil and Boris Penson, *Daily Life in a Correction Colony in Soviet Mordovia* (*in Russian*) (Jerusalem: Soviet and East European Research Center, Hebrew University of Jerusalem, Soviet Institutions Series, Paper No. 3, October 1975), pp. 11–13.

212. Amnesty International, *Prisoners of Conscience in USSR,* p. 63.

213. Chornovil and Penson, *Daily Life in Correction Colony,* pp. 16–19; Amnesty International, *Prisoners of Conscience in USSR,* pp. 64–68.

214. Marchenko, *My Testimony,* pp. 3, 47, 114, etc.; Amnesty International, *Prisoners of Conscience in USSR,* pp. 42–47, 82–94.

215. Ibid., p. 84.

216. Ibid., pp. 85–87.

217. Quote on prisoner volunteer guinea pigs is from Larry Gara, "Prison Notes," *Win,* February 26, 1976, p. 19. On use of prisoners in drug testing and/or on prisons conditions and policies see also Jessica Mitford, *Kind and Unusual Punishment* (New York: Alfred A. Knopf, 1973); Erik Olin Wright, *The Politics of Punishment: A Critical Analysis of Prisons in America* (New York: Harper and Row, 1973), pp. 3–261; U.S. Department of Justice, *National Jail Census 1970,* pp. 2–19; U.S. Department of Justice, Law Enforcement Assistance Administration, National Institute of Law Enforcement and Criminal Justice, *Homosexuality in Prisons* (Washington, D.C.: U.S. Government Printing Office, 1972); Leon Radzinowicz and Marvin E. Wolfgang, *Crime and Justice,* vol. 3, *The Criminal in Confinement* (New York: Basic Books, 1971); Walter Rugaber, "The West Virginia Penitentiary: A Center for Shakedowns, Robberies, and Violence," *New York Times,* July 12, 1971. For prisoner's

writings, see, e.g., H. Jack Griswold, Mike Misenheimer, Art Powers, and Ed Tromanhauser, *An Eye for an Eye* (New York: Holt, Rinehart, and Winston, 1970); Robert J. Minton, Jr. (ed.), *Inside: Prison American Style* (New York: Random House, 1971); Lester Douglas Johnson, *The Devil's Front Porch* (Lawrence: University of Kansas Press, 1970); Eve Pell and members of the Prison Law Project (eds.), *Maximum Security: Letters from California's Prisons* (New York: E. P. Dutton, 1972); Cynthia Owen Philip, *Imprisoned in America: Prison Communications: 1776 to Attica* (New York: Harper and Row, 1973). On U.S. court intervention, see Brian Glick, "Change through the Courts," in Wright, *Politics of Punishment*, pp. 281–312, and National Advisory Commission on Criminal Justice Standards and Goals, *Corrections* (Washington, D.C.: U.S. Government Printing Office, 1973), pp. 17–72. On the first comprehensive U.S. court order to reform a state's entire prison system (in Alabama), see "Landmark Prison Reforms Won," *Poverty Law Reporter*, No. 2 (March 1976), pp. 1–2.

218. Quoted in Chornovil and Penson, *Daily Life in Correction Colony*, p. 43. According to T.H. Friedgut in his introduction, the quote "inertia of style" is from a 1960 poem by Naum Korzhavin, who now lives in America.

219. Medvedev, *On Socialist Democracy*, p. 155.

220. *Amnesty International Annual Report 1974/1975*, pp 78–79; James A. Wechsler, "For Martin Sostre," *New York Post*, December 9, 1975. On the local use of criminal punishment to reinforce community power relationships, see Ray Jenkins, "And You Land in Jail," *New York Times*, January 26, 1976.

221. Amnesty International, *Amnesty International Report on Torture* (New York: Farrar, Straus, and Giroux, 1975), p. 193; *Win*, February 19, 1976, p. 117; David Vidal, "A Freed Dissident Sees No Change," *New York Times*, February 15, 1976.

222. *Amnesty International Report 1974/1975*, pp. 10–11. See also, e.g., on the case of human rights activist, Moscow biologist Sergei Kovalev, sentenced December 12, 1975, *Khronika zashchity prav v SSSR*, No. 18 (December, 1975), pp. 5–7; *On Trial: The Soviet State versus "Abram Tertz" and "Nikolai Arzhak,"* transl. and ed. by Max Hayward (rev. and enl. ed.; New York: Harper and Row, 1967); *The Trial of the Four: A Collection of Materials in the Case of Galanskov, Ginzburg, Dobrovolsky, and Laskova 1967–1968*, comp. by Pavel Litvinov (New York: Viking Press, 1972); Berman and Spindler, *Soviet Criminal Law and Procedure*, pp. 87–89; note 194, etc.

223. *UK* (1975), "Article 64. *Betrayal of the Motherland* . . . flight abroad or refusal to return from abroad to the USSR . . . is punished by deprivation of freedom for 10 to 15 years with confiscation of property, with or without two to five years exile, or the death penalty with confiscation of property. . . . Article 70. *Anti-Soviet Agitation and Propaganda.* Agitation or propaganda carried on with the intent of subverting or weakening the Soviet regime or circulating or keeping slanderous literature for that purpose . . . Article 72. *Organizational Activity Directed Toward Committing Especially Dangerous State Crimes, As Well As Participation in Anti-Soviet Organizations* . . . Arti-

cle 142. *Violation of the Law on the Separation of Church from State and School from Church* . . . Article 190-¹, *Disseminating Fabrications Known to Be False Which Defame the Soviet State and Social System* . . . Article 190-². *Desecration of the State Emblem or Flag* . . . Article 190-³. *Organizing or Active Participation in Group Acts Violating Public Order* . . . Article 227. *Infringement of the Person and Rights of Citizens under the Guise of Carrying Out Religious Ceremonies.* Medvedev, *On Socialist Democracy*, pp. 153–184.

224. "Excerpts From the Nobel Lecture by Andrei Sakharov on Human Rights Issues," *New York Times,* December 13, 1975.

225. James F. Clarity, "A Freed Dissident Says Soviet Doctors Sought to Break His Political Beliefs," *New York Times,* February 4, 1976, and "Paris Red Charges Soviet Repression," *New York Times,* February 5. 1976; Andre Fontaine, "Superpower Rivalry—There's No Alternative to Detente," *The Guardian,* January 25, 1976. I. Aleksandrov (a pseudonym indicating article reflects a party leadership position), "O svobodakh podlinnykh i mnimykh," *Pravda,* February 20, 1976; "Soviet Rebuffs Criticisms of Human Rights Stand," *New York Times,* February 21, 1976.

226. Sakharov, *My Country and the World, p. 12;* P.G. Grigorenko, cited in Reddaway, *Uncensored Russia,* p. 236.

227. *Amnesty International Report on Torture, passim;* Bruce Enmi, *Prisoners of Psychiatry: Mental Patients, Psychiatrists, and the Law* (New York: Harcourt, Brace Jovanovich, 1972).

228. Mitford, *Kind and Unusual Punishment,* pp. 104–150.

229. "The 1961 Directives: Directives on the Immediate Hospitalization of Persons Mentally Ill Who Are a Source of Danger," October 10, 1961, reprinted in *Survey,* No. 81 (1971), pp. 114–117; Medvedev, *On Socialist Democracy,* pp. 157–159; V. Bukovskii and S. Gluzman, "Posobie po psikhiatrii dlya inakomyslyashchikh," *Khronika zashchity prav v SSSR,* No. 13 (January-February 1975), pp. 36–61, transl. in *A Chronicle of Human Rights in the USSR,* No. 13, English version, and in *Survey,* No. 94/95 (1975), pp. 180–199.

230. Article 2, 1961 directives.

231. "Documents: Soviet Mental Prisoners: II," *Survey,* No. 81 (1971), pp. 111–133, and an example of civil commitment and release after pressure on the authorities in Zhores Medvedev and Roy Medvedev, *A Question of Madness,* transl. by Ellen de Kadt (New York: Vintage Books, 1971).

232. *Survey,* No. 81 (1971), pp. 115–116.

233. P.G. Grigorenko, quoted from *Chronicle of Current Events,* December, 1969, in Reddaway, *Uncensored Russia,* p. 227.

234. Bukovskii and Gluzman, *Posobie,* p. 36.

235. Russian authorities under Nicholas I declared Pyotr I. Chaadayev insane for his "Philosophical Letter" of 1836 comparing Russian culture unfavorably with the West and the Catholic Church. He was put under medical surveillance but not locked away. "Political" psychiatric commitments did not occur regularly under the tsars. Reddaway, *Uncensored Russia,* pp. 228, 231–

232; Philip Pomper, *The Russian Revolutionary Intelligentsia* (New York: Thomas Y. Crowell, 1970), pp. 35–37.

236. A biography of the protesting official, Sergei Petrovich Pisarev, and his letter of April 20, 1970, to the Presidium of the USSR Academy of Medical Sciences are in *Survey,* No. 77 (1970), pp. 175–180.

237. Ibid., pp. 178–179; *Amnesty International Report on Torture,* p. 188; Bukovskii and Gluzman, *Posobie,* p. 185.

238. *UK* (1958), Article 148.

239. Medvedev, *On Socialist Democracy,* pp. 156–157.

240. Reddaway, *Uncensored Russia,* p. 235.

241. Valeriy Tarsis, *Ward 7,* transl. by Katya Brown (New York: E.P. Dutton, 1966).

242. Tarsis, *Ward 7,* p. 24, on 1966 setup; Special Order No. 345/209, May 15, 1969. "Measures for the Prevention of Socially Dangerous Actions by Mentally Ill Persons," signed by Minister of Health B. Petrovskii and Minister of Internal Affairs P. [*sic*] Shchelokov; Medvedev, *On Social Democracy,* pp. 158–159.

243. *UK* (1975), Articles 58, 59, 60; "Instruktsiya o poryadke primeneniya prinuditel'nogo lecheniya i drugikh mer meditsinskogo kharaktera v otnoshenii psikhicheski bol'nykh, sovershivshikh obshchestvenno opasnye deyaniya," February 14, 1967. Approved by Deputy Minister of Health of USSR, A. Serenko, in collaboration with USSR Supreme Court, USSR Procuracy, USSR Ministry for Preservation of Public Order (since 1968, MVD). *BVS SSSR, No. 7* (1967), pp. 37–39.

244. Medvedev, *On Socialist Democracy,* p. 78; "Grigorenko's Prison Diary," *Survey,* No. 77 (1970), pp. 182–183.

245. Amnesty International, *Prisoners of Conscience in USSR,* p. 69.

246. Chornovil and Penson, *Daily Life in Correction Colony,* pp. 28–29.

247. Amnesty International, *Prisoners of Conscience in USSR,* pp. 101–137. On the much publicized case of Leonid Plyushch, mathematician and human rights activist released February 8, 1976, and allowed to emigrate, see Tat'yana Khodorovich (ed.), *Istoriya bolezny Leonida Plyushcha,* (Amsterdam: Fond imeni Gertsena, 1974); *Khronika zashchity prav v SSSR,* No. 7 (January–February 1974), pp. 28–29; No. 8 (March–April 1974), pp. 19–20; No. 15 (May–June 1975), p. 16. For British psychiatrists' protest on Bukovskii, Gluzman, and Plyushch, see *Khronika zashchity prav v SSSR,* No. 16 (July–September 1975), pp. 20–21.

248. *UK* (1975), Article 70.

249. Bukovskii and Gluzman, *Posobie,* p. 40.

250. Transl. note, Medvedev, *On Socialist Democracy,* p. 80; "Grigorenko's Prison Diary," and "The Fate of Pyotr Grigorevich Grigorenko," *Survey,* No. 77 (1970), pp. 181–187; *Khronika zashchity prav v SSSR,* No. 9 (May–June 1974), pp. 31–37.

251. Bukovskii and Gluzman, *Posobie,* pp. 42–47.

252. "Grigorenko's Prison Diary," p. 184.

253. *Khronika zashchity prav v SSSR,* No. 12 (November-December 1974), pp. 24–30; Reddaway, *Uncensored Russia,* pp. 244–247.

254. Notes 231, 247; case of P.G. Grigorenko, above.

255. Reddaway, *Uncensored Russia,* p. 461, note 34; Khodorovich, *Istoriya bolezni,* pp. 187–190. Smith, *The Russians,* pp. 455–459.

256. Sakharov, *My Country and the World,* pp. 41–42.

257. Marchenko, *My Testimony,* p. 2; Chornovil and Penson, *Daily Life in Correction Colony,* p. 43; *Amnesty International Annual Report 1974/1975,* p. 119.

258. Chapter 5, note 11; Donald D. Barry and Harold J. Berman, "The Soviet Legal Profession," *Harvard Law Review,* vol. 82, No. 1 (1968), p. 15.

259. N. Chetunova, "The Right to Defend" (last in a series of three articles), *Literaturnaya gazeta,* September 22, 1966, excerpted in *CDSP,* vol. 18, No. 38 (1968), p. 19. I am indebted to Wayne Stuart Miller for bringing this article to my attention in his paper, "The Soviet Defense Lawyer: His Dual Commitments in a Dichotomous System of Justice," December 1, 1975.

260. Amnesty International, *Prisoners of Conscience in USSR,* pp. 30–31; Yuri Luryi, "Dopusk advokata v sovetskom ugolovnom protsesse: Ponyatie, zakon, praktika," Unpublished paper, July 14, 1975, pp. 1–3.

261. Ibid., pp. 14–18.

262. Ibid., pp. 12–13; *UPK* (1973), Article 377.

263. Luryi, "Dopusk advokata," p. 6; *UPK* (1973), Articles 47–3, 120, 126; *UK* (1975), Articles 96, 97, 112, 130, 131, 154, 158, 162, 163, 166, 168, 169, 197, 197^{-1}, 198, 198^{-1}, 198^{-2}, 199, 200, 201, 206, 209, 209^{-1}.

264. *UPK* (1973), Article 126.

265. (1) and (2) were introduced in 1970. (3) originally gave right to defense lawyer before the pretrial investigation to such foreign language speaking persons, until the 1972 retraction. Edict of August 31, 1970, *BVS SSSR,* No. 5 (1970), pp. 5–6; Edict of February 3, 1972, ibid., No. 3 (1972), p. 47; Berman and Spindler, *Soviet Criminal Law and Procedure,* pp. 84–86. On participation of defense lawyer in pretrial investigations, see A. Grun, "Sovetskoi adovkature 50 let," *SYu,* No. 10 (1972), pp. 1–2; A. Boikov and L. Karneeva, "Ob uchastii zashchitnika na predvarital'nom sledstvii," *SYu,* No. 18 (1970), p. 19.

266. "In USSR Prosecutor's Office," *SZ,* No. 8 (1960), transl. in *CDSP,* vol. 12, No. 42 (160), p. 24.

267. B.A. Protchenko, "Uchastie zashchitnika na predvaritel'nom sledstvii," *Problemy sovershenstvovaniya sovetskogo zakonodatel'stva,* vol. 3, (1975), pp. 127–137; Luryi, "Dopusk advokata," pp. 9–10.

268. Berman and Spindler, *Soviet Criminal Law and Procedure,* p. 47.

269. Miller, "The Soviet Defense Lawyer," p. 10; "Last year a New Orleans judge sentenced 16-year-old Johnny Ross to die in the electric chair. Johnny,

who is black, had met with his lawyer only once, briefly, before the trial. The trial lasted one day. The jury took 90 minutes to find him guilty of raping a white woman." Southern Poverty Law Center letter signed by Julian Bond of February 9, 1976. See also Jerold S. Auerbach, *Unequal Justice: Lawyers and Social Change in Modern America* (New York: Oxford University Press, 1976), *passim,* but especially pp. 12, 289, 291.

270. Berman and Spindler, *Soviet Criminal Law and Procedure,* p. 67.

271. Berman, *Justice in USSR,* pp. 299–308; Note 151.

272. BPCP, Article 10; *UPK* (1973), Article 16.

273. Talk by Yuri Luryi, Columbia University, October 22, 1975.

274. Donald D. Barry and Harold J. Berman, "The Soviet Legal Profession," *Harvard Law Review,* vol. 82, No. 1 (1968), p. 22.

275. Medvedev, *On Socialist Democracy,* p. 149.

276. Ibid., pp. 161–162.

277. Talk by Yuri Luryi, International League for the Rights of Man, October 23, 1975.

278. Medvedev, *On Socialist Democracy,* p. 151.

279. Valery Chalidze, *To Defend These Rights: Human Rights and the Soviet Union,* transl. by Guy Daniels (New York: Random House, 1974), pp. 27–30, 66; Amnesty International, *Prisoners of Conscience in USSR,* p. 32; Medvedev,*On Socialist Democracy, pp. 151–152; The Trial of the Four: A Collection of Materials on the Case of Galanskov, Ginzburg, Dobrovolsky, and Lashkova 1967–1968* (New York: Viking Press, 1972); Sakharov, *My Country and the World,* p. 44; note 73 and Yu. Feofanov, "Firma terpit krakh," *Izvestiya,* May 19, 1961, about a press conference on Rokotov, Faibishenko, and Co. even before the trial depicting them as guilty.

280. Berman, *Justice in USSR,* p. 68.

Chapter 5

1. L.N. Smirnov, "50 let verkhovnogo Suda SSSR," in L.N. Smirnov, V.V. Kulikov, and B.S. Nikiforov (eds.), *Verkhovnyi Sud SSSR* (Moscow: "Yuridicheskaya literatura," 1974), p. 16.

2. *Kriminologiya,* pp. 181–182, 185; L. Remnev, "Organizuyushchaya rol' partiinogo komiteta," *SZ,* No. 5 (1972), pp. 27–32.

3. On the full Politburo membership of KGB head Yuri Andropov, see *Pravda,* April 28, 1973. A.N. Shelepin, Politburo member, 1964–1975, was KGB chairman, 1958–1961, and A.Y. Pelshe, Politburo member since 1966, served in the police *apparat.* John Barron, *KGB: The Secret Work of Soviet Agents* (New York: Readers Digest Press, 1974), p. 73. Shelepin resigned from the Politburo in 1975. For more details and documentation on jurists' posts and access see Peter Juviler, "Crime and Its Study," in Henry W. Morton and Rudolf L. Tökés (eds.), *Soviet Politics and Society in the 1970s* (New York: Free Press, 1974), pp. 202–203, 223; Donald D. Barry and Harold J. Berman,

"The Jurists," in H. Gordon Skilling and Franklyn Griffiths (eds.), *Interest Groups in Soviet Politics* (Princeton: Princeton University Press, 1971), pp. 291–333.

4. Gordon Skilling has pointed out that loose groupings of individuals are more likely to propose innovations to the leadership than are organized groups. H. Gordon Skilling, "Groups in Soviet Politics: Some Hypotheses," in Skilling, and Griffiths, *Interest Groups in Soviet Politics,* p. 30.

5. Barry and Berman, "The Jurists," pp. 297–301; V.V. Kulikov and Kh. B. Sheinin, "Verkhovnyi Sud SSSR i yuridicheskaya nauka," in Smirnov et al., *Verkhovnyi Sud SSSR,* p. 201.

6. Barry and Berman, "The Jurists," p. 298; *Narodnoe khozyaistvo SSSR v 1973 godu* (Moscow: "Statistika," 1974), p. 592; M. Vyshinskii, "Nasushchnye nuzhdy podgotovki yuristov," *SZ,* No. 9 (1973), p. 37. 127,000 working jurists as of Nov. 15, 1973 had higher legal education and 26,000 had secondary legal education.

7. "Yuridicheskaya nauka: nekotorye itogi i perspektivy," *SGP,* No. 12 (1973), pp. 3–5.

8. A. Sukharev, "Nasushchnye problemy podgotovki yuridicheskikh kadrov," *SZ,* No. 2 (1974), p. 3.

9. Ibid., pp. 3–8; Vyshinskii, "Nasushchnye nuzhdy podgotovki yuristov," pp. 37–39; "Konferentsiya rekomenduet," *SZ,* No. 2 (1974), pp. 9–10; *Narodnoe khozyaistro SSSR v 1973,* p. 592.

10. *Narodnoe khozyaistvo SSSR v 1970 godu* (Moscow: "Statistika," 1971), pp. 523, 657; Barry and Berman, "The Jurists," pp. 301, 305–306, 308, 311.

11. M.S. Strogovich et al. (eds.), *Advokatura v SSSR* (Moscow: "Yuridicheskaya literatura," 1971). Statute of the Advocacy of the RSFSR, law of July 25, 1962, *Ved. Verkh. Sov. RSFSR,* No. 29 (1962), item 450.

12. Prof. Peter H. Solomon, Jr., is completing a study of the role of criminologists in policy making. See also his "Soviet Criminology: Its Demise and Rebirth", 1928–1963, Soviet Union, vol. 1, No. 2 (1974), pp. 122–140; James O'Neill of Queens College is doing a doctoral study on the 1958 legal reforms.

13. Andrei D. Sakharov, *Progress, Coexistence, and Intellectual Freedom,* Introd., Afterword, and Notes by Harrison E. Salisbury (New York: W.W. Norton, 1968), pp. 56–57, 125–126.

14. "Yuridicheskaya nauka," p. 4

15. See Chapter 4 and Barry and Berman, "The Jurists," p. 315.

16. Frederick C. Barghoorn, "The Security Police," in Skilling and Griffiths, *Interest Groups in Soviet Politics,* p. 117.

17. Ibid., p. 118; *XXIII s"ezd Kommunisticheskoi Partii Sovetskogo Soyuza. 29 marta–8 aprelya 1966 g. Stenograficheskii otchet* (Moscow: Gos. izd. politicheskoi literatury, 1966), vol. 2, p. 551; *Deputaty Verkhovnogo Soveta SSSR. Vos'moi sozyv* (Moscow: Izd. "Izvestiya sovetov deputatov trudyashchikhsya SSSR," 1970), which on p. 380 has short biography of Savinkin.

18. E.g., Savinkin was present at the All-Union Conference on Problems of Improving the Activities of Internal Affairs Agencies in Strengthening Socialist Legality and Law and Order, hosted by the MVD in October 1970. *Pravda,* October 7, 1970. The above-cited conference of November 1973 on improving legal education was attended by V. Gladyshev, deputy head, Administrative Organs Department, Central Committee, CPSU. "Konferentsiya rekomenduet," p. 9.

19. *Zasedaniya Verkhovnogo Soveta SSSR. Pyatogo sozyva. Vtoraya sessiya (22–25 dekabrya 1958 g.). Stenograficheskii otchet.* (Moscow: Izd. Verkhovnogo Soveta SSSR, 1959), pp. 494–496; Harold J. Berman, "Law Reform in the Soviet Union," *American Slavic and East European Review,* vol. 15 (April 1956), pp. 179–189; Barry and Berman, "The Jurists," pp. 297–299, 316–331; Skilling, "Groups in Soviet Politics," pp. 34, 40–43; H. Gordon Skilling, "Group Conflicts in Soviet Politics: Some Conclusions," in Skilling and Griffiths, *Interest Groups in Soviet Politics,* p. 381; Franklin Griffiths, "A Tendency Analysis of Soviet Policy-Making," ibid., pp. 373–375.

20. Milton C. Lodge, *Soviet Elite Attitudes Since Stalin* (Columbus, Ohio: Charles E. Merrill, 1969), pp. 11–30; Barry and Berman, "The Jurists."

21. Amnesty of March 23, 1953, Article 8, reprinted in *Sbornik zakonov,* vol. 2, p. 628; Chapter 4.

22. Smirnov, "50 let Verkhovnogo Suda SSSR," p. 15.

23. Max Hayward (ed.), *On Trial: The Soviet State versus "Abram Tertz" and "Nikolai Arzhak"* (rev. and enl. ed.; New York: Harper and Row, 1967).

24. Barron, *KGB,* p. 11.

25. Unless otherwise noted, this description of the ties of jurists with the USSR Supreme Court is based on S. Bannikov (deputy chairman, USSR Supreme Court), "Zakonodatel'naya initsiativa Verkhovnogo Suda SSSR," *SGP,* No. 3 (1974), pp. 12–18; S.G. Bannikov, "Verkhovnyi Sud SSSR i sovershenstvovanie sovetskogo zakondodatel'stva," in Smirnov, Kulikov and Nikiforov, *Verkhovnyi Sud SSSR,* pp. 47–70; V.V. Kulikov (deputy chairman, USSR Supreme Court), "Vzaimnootnosheniya Verkhovnogo Suda SSSR s Verkhovnymi sudami soyuznykh respublik," ibid., pp. 31, 40–41; Kulikov and Sheinin, "Verkhovnyi sud SSSR i yuridicheskaya nauka," ibid., pp. 194–204.

26. Bannikov, "Verkhovnyi Sud SSSR," pp. 67–69.

27. Vyshinskii, "Nasushchnye nuzhdy," p. 37.

28. "Yuridicheskaya nauka," p. 4.

29. "Akademiya nauk SSSR otechestvennoe pravovdednie," *SGP,* No. 5 (1974), p. 9.

30. Sections of the Scientific Council in the area of crime prevention are described in Peter H. Solomon's Ph.D. dissertation, cited in Chapter 1, note 6.

31. There are law research centers affiliated with the 14 Union republics outside the Russian republic (there is no Russian republic Academy of Sciences, but a branch in Leningrad, the former home of the USSR Academy of Sciences) the Institute of State and Law of the Academy of Sciences of the Ukrainian

SSR (Soviet Socialist Republic); the Institutes of Philosophy and Law of the Academies of Science of the Azerbaidjhan, Armenian, Belorussian, Kazakh, Kirgiz, and Uzbek SSRs; the Departments of Philosophy and Law of the Academies of Science and the Moldavian and Turkmen SSRs; the Department of Philosophy, Law, and Sociology of the Academy of Sciences of the Lithuanian SSR; the Institute of Economy and Law of the Georgian SSR; and the Section of Law of the Institute of Economics of the Academy of Sciences of the Estonian SSR. "Adademiya nauk SSSR," pp. 9–10.

32. IGPAN's and criminology's reorganization since 1960 are mentioned here and the directions of MVD research are summarized in a personal communications from Peter H. Solomon, Jr.

33. Barry and Berman, in "The Jurists," pp. 292–297; indicate that jurists constitute " a profession," with felt common interests and attitudes. In practice, however, there may be sharp disunity on specific issues of criminal policy, as opposed to relative unity now on the need for jurists, professional law enforcement, etc.

34. The program of the conference, November 17–72, 1958, attended by this writer, while in his first year of research residence at the Moscow University Law Faculty, was issued as *Mezhvuzovskoe nauchnoe soveshchanie na temu: dal'neishee razvitie sovetskoi demokratii i ukreplenie sotsialisticheskoi zakonnosti. Noyabr' 1958 g.* (Moscow: Izd. MGU, 1958).

35. P.S. Romashkin, "Razvitie funktsii sovetskogo gosudarstva v protsese perekhoda k kommunizmu," in K.V. Ostrovityanov (ed.), *Voprosy stroitel'stva kommunizma v SSSR. Materialy nauchnoi sessii otdelenii obshchestvennykh nauk Akademii nauk SSSR* (Moscow: Izd. Akad, Nauk SSSR, 1959), p. 122.

36. Shirvindt, "K istorii voprosa ob izuchenii prestupnosti i mer bor'by s nei," p. 142.

37. A.A. Gertsenzon, "Ob izuchenii i preduprezhdeii prestupnosti," *SGP,* No. 7 (1960), pp. 80–81; Walter D. Connor, *Deviance in Soviet Society* (New York: Columbia University Press, 1972), pp. 33–34; V. Nikolaev, "Preodolenie nepravil'nykh teorii v ugolovnom prave—vazhnoe uslovie ukrepleniya sotsialisticheskoi zakonnosti," *Kommunist,* No. 14 (1956), p. 50; *Kriminologiya,* pp. 80–83; Solomon, "Soviet Criminology," pp. 131–140.

38. N. Solov'ev et al., *Problemy byta, braki i sem'i* (Vilna: Izd. "Mintis," 1970); the periodical collections, *Chelovek i obshchestov,* published on the average twice yearly since 1967 under the auspices of Leningrad University and the Institute of Complex Social Research, USSR Academy of Sciences, in Leningrad; *Sotsial'nye issledovaniya,* issued annually since 1965 under the auspices of this institute as well as the Soviet Sociological Association and the Scientific Council on Problems of Concrete Social Research; M.A. Alemaskin (of Institute of Psychology, USSR Academy of Pedagogical Sciences), "Problemy vospitaniya 'trudnykh' podrostkov," *Sovetskaya pedagogika,* No. 10 (1966), pp. 26–33; A.G. Kharchev, *Brak i sem'ya v SSSR: Opyt sotsiologicheskogo issledovaniya* (Moscow: "Mysl'," 1964); Y.A. Yadov and V.I. Dobrynin (eds.), *Molodezh i trud: Vsesoyuznaya konferentsiya' Sotsializma i molodezh'* (Moscow: Izd.

TSK VLKSM "Molodaya gvardiya," 1970); Arkadii Adamov, "Pozhnesh' sud' bu . . . : 'Trudnyi podrostok i ego druz'ya," *Komsomlskaya pravda,* October 14, 1967 (report on a meeting on the upbringing of youth participated in by researchers and "practical workers" from the USSR Ministry of Public Order, sponsor of the meeting, and criminologists, doctors, teachers, philosophers, sociologists, school principals, artists, party officials, Komsomol officials. The meeting was devoted mainly to problems of juvenile lawbreaking); "Nauchnaya zhizn': Problemy iskoreniya pravonarushenii v SSSR," *SGP,* No. 6 (1972), pp. 134–140, and No. 7 (1972), pp. 129–136 (summarizes a conference on eliminating crime in the USSR held at the end of 1971, organized by the Institute of State and Law of the USSR Academy of Sciences, the All-Union Research Institute of Soviet Legislation, the Institute of Crime Study and Prevention, the All-Union Research Institute of the USSR MVD—the top research institutes in law—and attended by over 400 scholars and "practical workers" from many Soviet cities).

39. As the Lithuanian republic prosecutor sees it, "Criminological centers coordinate their research projects only to the extent that it is considered desirable by their leaders or the leaders of the agencies of higher educational institutions under which they operate." The Lithuanian prosecutor had been trying to get transferred to the Procuracy by the Department of Studying the Causes of and Working Out Means of Preventing Crime, run in Lithuania by the republic's Ministry of Justice. According to the prosecutor, the department was an "alien entity" with low priority in the Ministry of Justice's Research Institute of Criminal Expertise. He wanted it moved to the Lithuanian Procuracy, and given support and guidance by the USSR Procuracy's Institute of Crime Study and Prevention in Moscow. That institute apparently has no regular ties with criminological sections in the universities of the other Union republics or the department of criminology of the Ministry of Justice in the Lithuanian republic. A. Kairlyalis (Prosecutor, Latvian SSR), "Kakoi dolzhna byt' sistema kriminologicheskikh uchrezhdenii?" *SZ,* No. 11 (1973), pp. 25–28. On the loose coordinating function which does exist through coordinating bureaus of the institute of criminology, see Peter H. Solomon's Ph.D. dissertation, cited in Chapter 1, note 6.

40. R.A. Rudenko, "Zadachi dal'neishego ukrepleniya sotsialisticheskoi zakonnosti v reshenii XX s'ezda KPSS," *SGP,* No. 3 (1956), pp. 20–21; A.A. Gertsenzon, *Vvdenie v sovestkuyu kriminologiyu* (Moscow: "Yuridicheskaya literatura," 1965), pp. 91, 95; S.S. Ostroumov, "Znachenie ugolovnoi statistiki dlya issledovaniya prestupnosti," *SGP,* No. 10 (1962), pp. 88–95; V. Kudryavtsev, "Aktual'nye problemy sovetskoi kriminologii," *SYu,* No. 20 (1965), pp. 6–9; S.S. Ostroumov, "Statisticheskie metody v kriminologii," *SGP,* No. 7 (1967), pp. 68–75.

41. S.S. Ostroumov, *Sovetskaya sudebnaya statistika* (Moscow: Izd. Moskovskogo universiteta, 1970), pp. 4, 31–36, 49–50, 54–59, 67–77, 80–90.

42. On reasons U.S. statistics exaggerate increases in crime, see *Challenge of Crime,* pp. 20–27, 35. The President's Commission was inclined to credit the Uniform Crime Reports (compiled by the FBI) with information on broad

trends, despite needs to qualify. Ibid., p. 31. Peter P. Lejins wrote the only article I found aside from this which was even mildly favorable to the reports. Peter P. Lejins, "Uniform Crime Reports," *Michigan Law Review,* vol. 64 (April 1966), pp. 1011–1030. Lejins' was the only mildly favorable article on the *UCR* found also by Eugene Doleschal (assistant director, Information Center, National Commission on Crime and Delinquency) in "Criminal Statistics," *Information Review on Crime and Delinquency,* vol. 1, No. 8 (August 1969), p. 5. Doleschal gives a useful annotated list of articles on criminal statistics, and a comparative survey of European statistical methods, pp. 11–28. See also his excellent survey, *Criminal Statistics* (Washington, D.C.: U.S. Department of Health, Education, and Welfare, National Institute of Mental Health, Center for Studies of Crime and Delinquency, 1972), pp. 11–27.

For critical opinion on the Uniform Crime Reports and debunking views on the seriousness of crime, see, e.g., The President's Commission on Law Enforcement and the Administration of Justice, *Task Force Report: Crime and Its Impact,* p. 87; Thorsten Sellin and Marvin Wolfgang, *The Measurement of Delinquency* (New York: John Wiley and Sons, 1964), pp. 78–86; Albert K. Cohen and James F. Short, Jr., "Juvenile Delinquency," in Robert K. Merton and Robert A. Nisbet (eds.), *Contemporary Social Problems* (2nd ed.; New York: Harcourt Brace and World, 1966), pp. 84–135; Sophia M. Robison, "Measuring Juvenile Delinquency," in Frank J. Cohen (ed.), *Youth and Crime: Proceedings of the Law Enforcement Institute Held at New York University* (New York: International Universities Press, 1957), pp. 10–16, and "Juvenile Delinquency," *Current History* (June 1967), pp. 341–348.

43. V. Somin, "Analiticheskaya deyatel'nost' organov yustitsii i sudov po bor'be s prestupnost'yu," *SYu,* No. 24 (1973), pp. 10–11.

44. See note 40.

45. For some plausible estimates of USSR defense expenditures, see William T. Lee, "The 'Politico-Military-Industrial Complex' of the USSR," *Journal of International Affairs,* vol. 26, No. 1 (1972), pp. 83–85.

46. Ostroumov, *Sovetskaya sudebnaya statistika,* p. 48.

47. Sources for Table 5–1 are as follows:

Column (1) 1928 Convictions per 100,000 inhabitants, RSFSR, 1929, were 1,363. A. Shlyapochnikov, "Likvidatsiya bezrabotnitsy v SSSR i prestupleniya," *Sovetskoe gosudarstvo,* Nos. 9–10 (1932), p. 149. For total convictions, RSFSR, 1929, derive population as follows: population of RSFSR was 100,891,244 on December 17, 1926. Frank Lorimer, *The Population of the Soviet Union: History and Prospects* (Geneva: League of Nations, 1946), p. 67. Natural increase of population per 1,000 in USSR was 21 in 1928. *Nardnoe khozyaistvo SSSR v 1968 g.* (Moscow: Izd. "Statistika," 1969), p. 36. Population for RSFSR midyear, then, is estimated at 106,200,000 for 1929, and convictions at 1,450,000 (106,200,000 × 0.01363). But these convictions were 131 percent higher than the convictions in 1928. A. Shlyapochnikov, "Prestupnost' i repressiya v SSSR (Kratkii obzor)," *Problemy ugolovnoi politiki,* vol. 1 (1935), p. 78. Convictions for 1928, RSFSR = 1,145,000/1.31 = 1,106,000. Convictions for USSR in 1928, then, are estimated as 1,106,000 × (population of USSR ÷ population of

RSFSR) = 1.46 × 1,106,000 = 1,610,000. A check exists on this important figure for the table: M.N. Gernet shows for *1927* 1,026,084 RSFSR convictions and 1,507,360 USSR convictions, for a ratio of 1,468 between convictions in USSR and RSFSR, meaning a difference of about one half of 1 percent in the ratios. *Prestupnost' za granitsei i v SSSR* (Moscow: "Sovetskoe zakonodatel'stvo," 1931), p. 79.

1940, 1963, 1964, 1965 "Analysis of court statistics for the country as a whole shows that the number of convictions is decreasing. For example, the number of convictions in 1965 was 7.6 percent less than in 1964, 16.7 less than in 1963. The number of convictions per 100,000 population in 1964 diminished in comparison with the prewar period (1940) more than twice, with 1928, more than 3 times. The number of convictions in 1963–1965 was the smallest in thirty years." G.Z. Anashkin (chairman, Criminal Collegium, USSR Supreme Court), "O zadachakh i tendentsiyakh razvitiya sotsialisticheskogo pravosudiya," *Vestnik Moskovskogo universiteta,* No. 4 (1966), pp. 6–7.

1958, 1962 "Numbers of convictions have decreased by 7.6 percent in 1965 as compared with 1964, by 30.3 as compared with 1962, and by 47 percent as compared with 1958." V. Kulikov (first deputy chairmen, USSR Supreme Court), "Za uprochenie sotsialisticheskoi zakonnosti," *SYu,* No. 7 (1966), p. 16.

1959, 1960 The number of convictions was "nearly 20 percent less" in 1959 than it was in 1958; convictions in 1960 were "more than one-third less." N. R. Mironov (head, Department of Administrative Organs, Central Committee, CPSR), "O nekotorykh voprosakh preduprezhdeniya prestupnosti i drugikh antiobshchestvennykh yavlenii i bor'by s nimi v sovremennykh usloviyakh," SGP, No. 5 (1961), pp. 4–5.

1967 "During the last 40 years . . . crime has decreased more than 3.5 times. The number of persons convicted per thousand population in 1967 decreased almost to a half, compared with 1940, and to less than a third compared with 1928." G. Anashkin, "Pravosudie. Nakazanie. Spravedlivost'," *Literaturnaya gazeta,* May 29, 1968, p. 11.

1946 "The number of persons per 100,000 inhabitants found to have committed crimes decreased more than two times in 1967 as compared to 1946." Vsesoyuznyi institut po izucheniyu prichin i razrabotke mer preduprezhdeniya prestupnosti, *Kriminologiya,* p. 116. The average population of the USSR in 1946 I estimate at about 172 million.

1961 "Between 1961 and 1967, crime rates per capita decreased over 7 percent." *Kriminologiya,* p. 117.

1966 "Numbers of convictions in the USSR last year in comparison with those in 1968, when earlier criminal legislation was in effect, decreased as a whole by 29.8 percent." A. Gorkin (Chairman, USSR Supreme Court), "Pyatidesyatiletie sovetskoi vlasti i sotsialisticheskoe pravosudie, *SZ,* No. 11 (1967), p. 20.

1955, 1968 "If the number of persons convicted in the USSR in 1928 is taken as 100, then in 1955 it declined to 63 . . . the number of persons convicted in 1968 as compared with 1958 fall by 35 percent." Ostroumov, *Sovetskaya sudebnaya statistika,* p. 246.

1971 "as compared with the postwar year of 1946, the crime index (i.e., the number of persons committing crimes per 100,000 population) had dropped by 50 percent as of last year." M. P. Malyarov (USSR First Deputy Prosecutor General), "The Reader Asks to Be Told: With the Full Severity of the Law," *Pravda,* July 11, 1972, transl. in *CDSP,* vol. 24, No. 28 (1972), p. 5.

Sources for Column (3): Estimated midyear population figures for USSR used here are in millions: 1928—150; 1940—195.6; 1955—194.4; 1948—204.9; 1959—210.6; 1960—214.3; 1961—218; 1962—221.5; 1963—224.8; 1964—227.9; 1965—231.1; 1966—233.2; 1967—235.6; 1968—238.4. See population for December 17, 1926 (147 million). *Narodnoe khozyaistvo SSSR v 1958 godu* (Moscow: Gos. statisticheskoe izd., 1959), p. 7 Populations for 1950–1968 are listed in *Narodnoe khozyaistvo SSR v 1970 g.,* p. 7, and relevant natural increases for computing midyear populations in 1928 and 1940, approximately, are found in *Narodnoe khozyaistvo SSR v 1967 g.* (Moscow: Statistika, 1968), p. 36.

48. Personal communication from Mr. Yuri Luryi, formerly of the Leningrad bar, 1975.

49. G. Bulatov, "Problemy sovershenstvovaniya sudebnoi statistiki," *SYu,* No. 11 (1971), p. 18.

50. S.S. Ostroumov, *Prestupnost' i ee prichiny v dorevolyutsionnoi Rossii* (Moscow: Izd. Moskovskogo universiteta, 1960), pp. 4, 233.

51. V. Korshunova, "Analiz statisticheskikh dannykh v otdele yustitsii i v narodnykh sudakh," *SYu,* No. 5 (1974), p. 15.

52. V. Popkov, "Sudebnaya statistika v organakh yustitsii i sudakh," *SYu,* No. 1 (1974), pp. 18–19.

53. G.A. Zlobin, "O kharaktere i zadachakh moral'noi statistiki," *Vsesoyuznyi nauchno-issledovatel'skii institut sovetskogo zakonodatel'stva, Uchenie zapiski,* No. 28 (1973), p. 35.

54. Ibid., Somin, "Analiticheskaya deyatel'nost' " pp. 11–12.

55. Ostroumov, *Sovetskaya sudebnaya statistika,* pp. 45–49.

56. *Kriminologiya,* pp. 117, 170.

57. *Narodnoe khozyaistvo SSSR v 1973 godu,* p. 48.

58. S. Ostroumov, S. Panchenko, and A. Shlyapochnikov, "Uchet i statistika pravonarushenii v svete leninskikh ukazanii," *SZ,* No. 4 (1969), p. 13.

59. Zlobin, "O kharaktere," *Vsesoyuznyi nauchno-issledovatel'skii institut sovetskogo zakonodatel'stva, Uchenie zapiski,* No. 28 (1973), p. 38.

60. L. Smirnov, "XII S'ezd KPSS i zadachi sudebnykh organov v bor'be s prestupnost'yu," *SYu,* No. 14 (1966) p. 1.

61. "Sovershenstvovat' organizatsiyu raboty Prokuratury v bor'be s prestupnost'yu," *SZ,* No. 11 (1968), pp. 7, 9; V. Tikunov, "Sniskhozhdeniya khuliganam ne budet," *Izestiya,* April 21, 1966; G. Grebennikov and K. Raspevin, "Sotsialisticheskaya ditsiplina nezyblema," *Pravda,* April 25, 1966.

62. Zlobin, "O kharaktere," p. 37.

63. Only 4.6 percent of cases going to criminal investigation in 1967 originated in private citizens' complaints as compared with 16.2 percent in 1958.

S. S. Ostroumov and S. N. Panchenko, "Aktual'nye zadachi ugolovnoi statistiki i preduprezhdenie prestupnosti," *SGP,* No. 8 (1968), p. 110.

64. *Kriminologiya,* pp. 15, 119, 181–182; *SZ,* No. 7 (1966), p. 27.

65. V. I. Lenin, *Pol. sobr. soch.* vol. 17, p. 119, quoted in Ostroumov, *Sovetskaya sudebnaya statistika,* p. 3.

66. See note 59.

67. Connor, *Deviance in Soviet Society,* p. 34.

68. N. Kuznetsova, "Sravnitel'noe kriminologicheskoe issledovaniya prestupnosti v Moskve (1923–1968/69 gg.)," *SZ,* No. 6 (1971), pp. 22–27; and the document, "for staff use," on which this article was based: Yuridicheskii fakul'tet. Problemnaya sotsiologicheskaya gruppa. *Sravnitel'noe kriminologicheskoe issledovanie prestupnosti v Moskve v 1923 i 1968–1969 g* (Moscow: Izd. Mosk. univ., 1971).

69. Bernard Gwertzman, "Soviet Awareness of Crime Problems Rising," *New York Times,* September 8, 1969.

70. I provide details in my forthcoming study on Soviet juvenile delinquency.

71. *Narodnoe khozyaistvo SSSR v 1970 g.,* pp. 35, 41.

72. A. Gramotkina, "Gorod khochet spokoistvo," *Komsomolskaya pravda,* September 12, 1971.

73. James Reston, *New York Times,* November 20, 1968.

74. V. Lyashenko, "Amnistiya—ostryi vopros," *Komsomolskaya pravda,* December 1, 1967. For text of amnesty see *Ved.,* No. 44 (1967), item 595.

75. Sergei Ostroumov, "Crime and Its Causes," *Soviet Life,* No. 4 (April 1969), p. 60; Case of Alexander Bazhenov, heard by this writer, Moscow City Court, November 10, 1958. The proprietor of an orchard cited by Ostroumov used an electrified fence. Bazhenov stalked his trespassers with a shotgun and had also more provocation. See also E. Grafov, "At Life's Crossroads: An Oasis for One," *Izvestiya,* August 13, 1970, excerpted in *CDSP,* vol. 22, No. 32 (1970), p. 14.

76. S. Pulatkhodzhaev and A. Mikhailants, "Raboty sudov po presuprezhdeniyu prestuplenii," *SZ,* No. 8 (1971), p. 18; Andrei Amalrik, *Involuntary Journey to Siberia,* transl. by Mania Harari and Max Hayward (New York: Harcourt Brace Jovanovich, 1970), pp. 187, 190, 277.

77. *Narodnoe khozyaistvo SSSR v 1970 godu,* p. 43.

78. V. Kozak, "Shto znayut grazhdane o neobkhodimoi oborone," *SYu,* No. 18 (1968), pp. 12–13. On hooliganism, see UK (1975), Article 206; G.Z. Anashkin, I.I. Karpets and B.S. Nikiforov (eds.), *Kommentarii k ugolovnomu Kodeksu RSFSR* (Moscow: "Yuridicheskaya Literatura," 1971), pp. 437–442.

79. K. Cherniavskii and B. Kleiner, "Usilit' bor'bu s khuliganstvom," *SZ,* No. 4 (1952), pp. 36–38; Gablin, "Usilit' bor'bu s khuliganstvom," *SZ,* No. 8 (1952), pp. 36–38; F. Kudrin, "Reshitel'no usilit' bor'bu s khuliganstvom," *SZ,* No. 10 (1952), pp. 30–34; A.V. Kuznetsov, *Khuliganstvo i bor'ba s nim*

(Moscow: Gos. Izd. Yuridicheskoi literatury, 1962); A. Sol'ts, "O khuliganstve," *SGP*, No. 10 (1937), pp. 62–63; note 78.

80. Ostroumov, *Sovetskaya sudebnaya statistika,* p. 148.

81. See notes 71 and 76.

82. Smirnov, "50 let Verkhovnogo Suda SSSR," p. 17; "Nash zakon i ego garantii. Na voprosy chitatelei 'Truda' otvechaet Ministr Yustitsii SSSR Vladimir Ivanovich Terebilov," *Trud,* March 2, 1970.

83. *Kriminologiya,* pp. 117–118.

84. See Chapter 4.

85. See notes 24–28, Chapter 6; Chapter 4.

86. More data for Table 5–2 are as follows:

Types of Crimes	*Percent*
Stealing state and public property	17
Hooliganism	24
Crimes against personal property	16
Crimes against persons	17
Economic crimes	5
Malfeasance in office	4
Motor vehicle crimes	5
Crimes against justice	1.5
Crimes against the administrative order	4
Others	6.5

Source: Ostroumov, Sovetskaya sudebnaya statistika (1970), p. 248. Ostroumov attributes these data to *Kriminologiya,* pp. 118–119. But data there are slightly different (and I estimate my Table 5–2 from both Ostroumov and *Kriminologiya*).

Types of Crimes	*Percent*
Persons convicted for crimes against socialist property "in recent years"	15–18
Persons convicted for crimes against personal property (1967) (incl. about 30 percent snatching and robbery)	16
Persons convicted for crimes against persons "fluctuated at about 15 percent in recent years"	
Persons convicted for crimes against public safety, order, health, of which the major share are persons convicted for hooliganism ("more than one third")	
Persons convicted for malfeasance in office (1967)	2.3
Persons convicted for economic crimes	5.0
Persons convicted for crimes against political and labor rights of citizens "currently"	0.5
Persons convicted for crimes against justice	1.5
Persons convicted for crimes that are survivals of the past	0.4

Source: Kriminologiya, pp. 118–119.

87. On types of labor colonies, see Chapter 4.

88. "From the Courtroom: He Saved a Minute," *Pravda,* July 5, 1974, abstracted in *CDSP,* vol. 26, No. 27 (1974), p. 23.

89. *Kriminologiya,* pp. 117–118. There was an apparent attempt on the life of Brezhnev as he drove into the Kremlin with cosmonauts in 1969.

90. Andrei D. Sakharov, *My Country and the World,* transl. by Guy V. Daniels (New York: Vintage Books, 1975) pp. 12, 31; Amnesty International, *Prisoners of Conscience in USSR: Their Treatment and Conditions* (London: Amnesty International Publications, 1975) pp. 51–53.

91. *UK* (1975), Articles 142, 143, 227 on religious crimes; Chapter 4.

92. P. Andreyev, "From the Courtroom: Crime by a Campfire," *Pravda,* November 14, 1970, transl. in *CDSP,* vol. 22, No. 46 (1970), p. 29; Chapter 6.

93. B. Kostin, " 'Firmachi'i rotozei," *Komsomolskaya pravda,* March 1, 1973.

94. Roy A. Medvedev, *On Socialist Democracy,* transl. and ed. by Ellen de Kadt (New York: Alfred A. Knopf, 1975) p. 339, note 21.

95. Ibid., p. 25.

96. Sakharov, *My Country and the World,* p. 25.

97. Medvedev, *On Socialist Democracy,* p. 25.

Chapter 6

1. Both quotations are from the paraphrase of a speech by Dr. V.M. Chkhikvadze (then director of the Institute of State and Law), "Nauchnaya zhizn': Problemy iskoreniya pravonarushenii v SSSR," *SGP,* No. 6 (1972), p. 134.

2. Mitchell Wilson writes of the Academic City science center in Siberia that its successes and existence "are possible only in a society that allows for ambitious and daring long-range planning, its failures are due to precisely the same constricting forces that demanded its creation in the first place." "The Siberian Jewel," *World,* February 27, 1973, p. 30.

3. I. Kalmanovich, "O prostom slove 'nel'zya'," *Literaturnaya gazeta,* July 24, 1968.

4. "Teoreticheskaya konferentsiya. Antiobshchestvennye yavleniya, ikh prichiny i sredstva bor'by s nimi," *Kommunist,* No. 12 (1966), pp. 58–68.

5. Peter H. Solomon, Jr., "Specialists in Soviet Policy-Making: Criminologists and Criminal Policy in the 1960s" (Ph.D. dissertation, Faculty of Political Science, Columbia University, 1973).

6. Nikita S. Khrushchev, *The Crimes of the Stalin Era,* annotated by Boris I. Nicolaevsky (New York: New Leader, n.d.), p. 24.

7. Shirvindt, "K istorii voprosa ob izuchenii prestupnosti," p. 142; *SGP,*

No. 4 (1956), p. 128; *SGP,* No. 5 (1964), pp. 11–20; *Kommunist,* No. 16 (1963), pp. 33–34. Brezhnev did change his phraseology from "survivals of the past" (*perezhitki proshlogo*) in 1971 to "heritage of the past" (*unasledovanie ot proshlogo*) in 1972. "O pyatidesyatiletii Soyuza Sotsialisticheskikh Respublik: Doklad General'nogo sekretarya TsK KPSS tovarishcha L.I. Brezhneva," *Pravda,* December 22, 1972.

8. On the many meanings given "ideology" see Robert E. Lane, *Political Ideology: Why the American Common Man Believes What He Does* (New York: Free Press, 1967), pp. 13–16; Willard A. Mullins, "On the Concept of Ideology in Political Science," *American Political Science Review,* vol. 66 (June 1972), pp. 498–510. On the controversy about ideology see, e.g., Chaim I. Waxman (ed.), *The End of Ideology Debate* (New York: Funk and Wagnalls, 1968). On the USSR see Daniel Bell, "The End of Ideology in the Soviet Union," in Milorad M. Drachkovich *Marxist Ideology in the Contemporary World: Its Appeals and Paradoxes* (ed.), (New York: Frederick A. Praeger, 1966), pp. 76–112.

9. B. Mel'nikova, "Burzhuaznaya kriminologiya o vliyanii ekonomicheskogo progressa na prestupnost' molodezhi," *SGP,* No. 5 (1967), pp. 142–145; F.M. Reshetnikov, *Sovremennaya amerikanskaya kriminologiya* (Moscow: Izd. "Yuridicheskaya literatura," 1965), pp. 4–5, 95.

10. N.A. Struchkov, "Izuchenie obstoitel'stv obuslovlivayushchikh prestupnost' v SSSR," *SGP,* No. 12 (1971), p. 100.

11. A.A. Piontkovskii, "Puti ukrepleniya sotsialisticheskogo pravoporyadka," *SGP,* No. 1 (1967), p. 37.

12. *Kriminologiya,* pp. 121–165; V. Somin, "Analiticheskaya deyatel'nost' organov yustitsii i sudov po bor'be s prestupnost yu," *SYu,* No. 24 (1973)," p. 10; V.N. Kudryavtsev, *Prichinnost' v kriminologii* (Moscow: "Yuridicheskaya literatura," 1968).

13. Piontkovskii, "Puti ukrepleniya," p. 33; Walter D. Connor, *Deviance in Soviet Society: Crime, Delinquency and Alcoholism* (New York: Columbia University Press, 1972), pp. 170–127; my forthcoming study on juvenile delinquency, Chapter 5.

14. A.N. Ezerskaya, "O nekotorykh merakh preduprezhdeniya khishchenii na avtomobil'nom transporte pri perevozke gruzov," *Voprosy bor'by s prestupnost'yu,* No. 17 (1972), pp. 32–40.

15. James Q. Wilson, "Crime and Criminologists," *Commentary,* No. 1 (July 1974) p. 50.

16. V.P. Ryabtsov, "Bor'ba s latentnymi khischeniyami na zheleznodorozhom transporte," *Voprosy bor'by s prestupnost'yu,* No. 15 (1972), pp. 126–134. On ways to steal from farms, see E. Titov, "Usloviya sposobstvuyushchie khishceniyam v sel'skom khozvaistve, i ikh osobennosti," *SZ,* No. 5 (1974), pp. 54–56.

17. *Kriminologiya,* p. 410.

18. V.S. Minskaya, "Kriminologicheskoe i ugolovnopravovoe znachenie povedeniya poterpevshikh," *Voprosy bor'by s prestupnost'yu,* No. 16 (1972), pp. 9–26. I received a communication about this article from Mr. Michel Meyer,

who is preparing a study on Soviet criminology under the direction of Mr. Meillan of the Institute of Criminology in Paris.

19. V.S. Minskaya, "Opyt viktimologicheskogo izucheniya iznasilovaniya," *Voprosy bor'by s prestupnost'yu,* No. 17 (1972), pp. 21–31.

20. A. Yakovlev, "Sotsiologiya pravonarushenii," *SYu,* No. 22 (1972), pp. 5–7.

21. Edwin H. Sutherland and Donald R. Cressey, *Principles of Criminology* (7th ed.; New York: J.B. Lippincott, 1966), pp. 77–98.

22. Connor, *Deviance in Soviet Society,* pp. 80–113, 219–225.

23. Yuridicheskii fakul'tet, Problemnaya sotsiologicheskaya gruppa. *Sravnitel'noe kriminologicheskoe issledovanie prestupnosti v Moskve v 1923 i 1968–1969 g* (Moscow: Fzd. Mosk. univ., 1971), p. 24; D.O. Khan-Magomedov, "Metody izucheniya effektivnost' ugolovnogo zakonodatel'stva," in A.P. Shlyakhov and V.N. Kudryavtsev, *Pravovaya kibernetika* (Moscow: Izd. "Nauka," 1973), p. 71.

24. "Nash zakon i ego garantii: Na voprosy chitatelei 'Truda' otvechaet ministr yustitsii SSSR Vladimir Ivanovich Terebilov," *Trud,* March 2, 1970.

25. Summary of report of National Institute on Alcohol Abuse and Alcoholism, in Harold M. Schmeck, Jr., "U.S. Report Says Top Drug Problem Is Alcohol Abuse," *New York Times,* February 19, 1972.

26. Chapter 4; Connor, *Deviance in Soviet Society,* pp. 35–79.

27. Study A is by USSR Procuracy, "Usilim bor'bu protiv p'yanstva i alkogolizma", *SZ,* No. 9 (1972), p. 9. Study B is by RSFSR Ministry of Justice and Supreme Court, "Zadachi sudov v bor'be protiv p'yanstva i alkogolizma," *SYu,* No. 17 (1972).

28. Connor, *Deviance in Soviet Society,* p. 43.

29. Kondrashkov, "Issledovanie statisticheskikh dannykh o prestupnosti i merakh bor'by s neyu v soyuznom respublike," *Voprosy bor'by s prestupnost'yu,"* No. 10 (1969), p. 11.

30. V.G. Tanasevich, A.D. Berenzon, and A.P. Syrov, "Rol'proizvodstvennogo kollektiva v preduprezhdenii khishchenii sotsialisticheskogo imushchestva," in V.N. Kudryavtsev (ed.), *Bor'ba s khishcheniem gosudarstvennogo i obshchestvennogo imushchestva* (Moscow: "Yuridicheskaya literatura," 1971), pp. 12, 14, 19, 21–22, 30.

32. Ibid., pp. 15–16.

32. "Nash zakon i ego garantii," *Trud,* March 2, 1970.

33. Connor, *Deviance in Soviet Society,* pp. 151–152.

34. Tanasevich, et al., "Rol' proizvodstvennogo kollekriva," pp. 17, 24–28.

35. Yuridicheskii fakul'tet, *Sravnitel'noe,* pp. 167–170.

36. Ibid., pp. 22, 160, 170–171; Larisa Kuznetsova, " 'Po semeinym obstoyatel'stvam,' " *Literaturnaya gazeta,* May 29, 1974.

37. V.A. Serebryakova, "Kriminologicheskaya kharakteristika zhenshchin-pretupnits (po materialam izucheniya lits soderzhashchikhsya v ITK)," *Voprosy bor'by s prestupnost'yu,* No. 14 (1971), pp. 3–16; Ostroumov, *Sovetskaya sude-*

bnaya statisitika, pp. 254–255, except where otherwise indicated; Yu. Feofanov, "The Fourth Dimension," *Izvestiya,* July 8, 1970, excerpted in *CDSP,* vol. 22, No. 27 (1970), p. 27.

38. "Yuridicheskii fakul'tet," *Sravnitel'noe,* pp. 161–162.

39. Ibid., pp. 20, 96–100.

40. *Kriminologiya,* pp. 320, 428–431.

41. Chapters 5 and 6, of my forthcoming study on juvenile delinquency.

42. V. Tsepkov, "Return to Life," *Izvestiya,* March 27, 1973, excerpted in *CDSP,* vol. 25, No. 13 (1973), pp. 23–24.

43. K. Sharmazyan, "Dangerous Industry," *Zarya vostoka,* June 24, 1972, abstr. in *CDSP,* vol. 24, No. 51 (1972), p. 23.

44. "From the Courtroom: Retribution," *Pravda,* July 3, 1974, transl. in *CDSP,* vol. 26, No. 27 (1974), p. 23.

45. Natal'ya Kuznetsova, "Khishchniki," *SYu,* Nos. 9, 10, 11 (1969), pp. 30–31, 28–30, and 24–26, respectively.

46. See note 37.

47. Hedrick Smith, *The Russians* (New York: Quadrangle Books, 1976), pp. 81–101.

48. Edgar Spirit, "Under Cover of Secrecy," *Pravda,* March 31, 1973, in *CDSP,* vol. 25, No. 13 (1973), p. 24; John N. Hazard, *The Soviet System of Government* (4th ed.; Chicago: University of Chicago Press, 1968), p. 207.

49. V.G. Tanasevich, I.L. Shraga, and V.B. Yastrebov, "Zadachi bor'by s khishcheniem na sovremennom etape," *SGP,* No. 2 (1970), p. 72.

50. A.G. Kharchev, *Brak i sem'ya v SSSR: Opyt sotsiologichiskogo issledovaniya* (Moscow: Mysl' 1964), pp. 243–245; Natalia Dashkevich, "I Want to Rent a Dacha," *Sovetskaya kul'utra,* March 30, 1973, abstr. in *CDSP,* vol. 25, No. 19 (1973), p. 18.

51. T. Arshba, "Load the Tangerines into the Boxes," *Pravda,* January 10, 1974, abstr. in *CDSP,* vol. 26, No. 2 (1974), p. 10.

52. S. Solovyov, "Prosecutor's Notes: Golden Hairpins," *Izvestiya,* January 3, 1974, abstr. in *CDSP,* vol. 26, No. 1 (1974), pp. 18–19.

53. A. Lykov, "The Law Is Binding on Everyone: A Shot on the Steppe," *Trud,* September 12, 1973, abstr. in *CDSP,* vol. 26, No. 19 (1974), pp. 23–24.

54. I. Kiryanov, "The Case Is Heard: Shot in the Back," *Pravda,* February 11, 1972, in *CDSP,* vol. 24, No. 6 (1972), p. 10; note 98.

55. A.I. Alekseev and V.M. Burykin, "Resul'taty izucheniya spekulyatsii (opyt konkretnogo sotsiologicheskogo issledovaniya)," *Voprosy bor'by s prestupnost'yu,* No. 15 (1972), pp. 115–125.

56. Ibid., pp. 123–125.

57. Sutherland and Cressey, *Principles of Criminology,* p. 45.

58. On a ring of thieves, bribe takers, and speculators trading in scarce rugs, woolen kerchiefs, and haberdashery, see P. Barashev, "A Case Is Heard: Not Subject to Appeal!" *Pravda,* February 18, 1972, cond. in *CDSP,* vol. 24, No. 7 (1972), p. 15, repr. in Jan S. Adams, George Demko, and Warren W.

Eason (eds.), *The USSR Today: Current Readings from the Soviet Press* (2nd ed.; Columbus, Ohio: AAASS, 1973), p. 95; note 52; V. Tychnin, "After Izvestiya Spoke Out," *Izvestiya,* May 20, 1973, transl. in *CDSP,* vol. 25, No. 20 (illegal sale of cement); on report padding and unearned bonuses, see V. Kulikov, "Tol'ko pravdu," *Pravda,* February 18, 1973; V. Komov, "From the Courtroom: Embezzlers Are Punished," *Izvestiya,* May 16, 1973, transl. in *CDSP,* vol. 25, No. 20 (1973), p. 20, and M. Pankov, "From the Courtroom: Exaggerated 'Successes,'" *Pravda,* June 28, 1974, transl. in *CDSP,* vol. 26, No. 26 (1974), p. 29. On bribes for apartments, see L. Tairov, "From the Courtroom: Bribe-Takers Uncovered," *Pravda,* May 19, 1973, cond. in *CDSP,* vol. 25, No. 20 (1973), p. 20.

59. M. Malyarov, "Accountable in Rubles," *Izvestiya,* June 11, 1974, cond. in *CDSP,* vol. 26, No. 23 (1974), pp. 27–38.

60. "Personnel Changes in Georgia," transl. and excerpts from *Zarya vostoka,* May 30, June 6, July 26, July 30, August 18, August 23, 1972, in *CDSP,* vol. 24, No. 34 (1972), p. 9; "Communique of the Plenary Session of the Georgian Communist Party Central Committee," *Zarya vostoka,* November 2, 1972, cond. in *CDSP,* vol. 24, No. 45 (1972), p. 8; "Plenary Session of the Georgian Communist Party Central Committee," *Zarya vostoka,* September 30, 1972, transl. in *CDSP,* vol. 24, No. 39 (1972), p. 10. As this was going to press, Hedrick Smith published a succinct account of the Georgian Scandal in *The Russians,* pp. 97–98, and bombing reports were coming out of Georgia.

61. "Bring the Organizational and Political Work of the Capital's Party Organizations Up to the Level of Today's Tasks—Speech by Comrade E.A. Shevardnadze, First Secretary of the Georgian Communist Party Central Committee," *Zarya vostoka,* February 8, 1974, abstr. in *CDSP,* vol. 26, No. 8 (1974), pp. 1–5. See also "Communique on the Plenary Session of the Georgian Communist Party Central Committee," *Zarya vostoka,* October 30, 1973, cond. in *CDSP,* vol. 25, No. 44 (1973), p. 1, and "Plenary Session of the Georgian Communist Party Central Committee," ibid., November 3, 1973, excerpted in ibid., pp. 1–5; "Consolidate Successes and Eliminate Shortcomings in the Development of Agriculture," *Zarya vostoka,* November 25, 1972, excerpted in *CDSP,* vol. 24, No. 50 (1972), pp. 5–8; E. Shevardnadze, "Criteria of Responsibility," *Izvestiya,* April 6, 1974, cond. in *CDSP,* vol. 26, No. 14 (1974), pp. 8–9; "After Criticism: Punished for Illegal Construction," *Pravda,* July 5, 1974, transl. in *CDSP,* vol. 26, No. 27 (1974), pp. 22–23.

62. Steven J. Staats, "Corruption in the Soviet System," *Problems of Communism,* vol 21 (January-February 1972), pp. 43–44.

63. *Challenge of Crime,* p. 50; Sutherland and Cressey, *Principles of Criminology,* p. 43.

64. Ezerskaya, "O nekotorykh merakh preduprezhdeniya khishchenii," p. 23.

65. Note 36; A.B. Sakharov, *O lichnosti prestupnika i prichinakh prestupnosti v SSSR* (Moscow: Gos. izd. yuridicheskoi literatury, 1961), dealing with the criminal personality, was the first major criminological work published in the USSR after Stalin.

66. Connor sums up the dispute well in *Deviance in Soviet Society,* pp. 176–182. See also A.A. Gertsenzon, "Protiv biologicheskikh teorii prichin prestupnosti," *Voprosy preduprezhdeniya prestupnosti,* No. 4 (1966), pp. 3–4, and *Voprosy bor'by s prestupnost'yu* (new title), No. 5 (1967), pp. 3–53; Gertsenzon's attacks on the researches into *x-y-y* chromosomes' link with crime in "novye popytki vozrozhdeniya lombrozyanstvo v zarubezhnoi kriminologii," *SZ,* No. 8 (1970), pp. 26–28; V. Kudryavtsev, "Dano li pri rozhdenii?" and N. Struchkov and B. Utevskii (penologists believing in need to consider biological causation), "Ne tak vse prosto," *Literaturnaya gazeta,* November 29, 1967; I. Karpets, V. Kudryavtsev, A. Leont'ev, and N. Felinskaya, "Priroda pravonarushenii," *Izvestiya,* July 8, 1968; O.E. Freierov, "O tak nazyvaemom biologicheskom aspekte problemy prestupnosti," *SGP,* No. 10 (1966), pp. 108–113, and "Motivizatsiya obshchestvennogo opasnykh deistvii psikhicheski nepolnotsennykh lits," *SGP,* No. 4 (1969), pp. 96–101; A.B. Sakharov, "Ob antisotsial'nykh chertakh lichnosti prestupnika," *SGP,* No. 10 (1970), pp. 110–116.

67. Struchkov, "Izuchenie obstoyatel'stva obuslovlivayushchikh prestupnost' v SSSR," pp. 103–105.

68. *Kriminologiya,* p. 135.

69. A.A. Gertsenzon wanted criminology kept in criminal law. *Ugolovnoe pravo i sotsiologiya,* pp. 5–6, 39–54.

70. Struchkov, "Izuchenie obstoyatel'stva," p. 105.

71. Lapenna, *Soviet Penal Policy,* p. 143.

72. V. Kudryavtsev, "Bor'ba s prestupnost'yu i zadachi kriminologicheskoi nauki," *SZ,* No. 2 (1973), pp.17–19; V. Klochkov, "Osnovnye napravleniya nauchnykh issledovanii po problemam bor'by s prestupnost'yu," *SZ,* No. 2 (1974), p. 48.

73. The Institute of Crime Study and Prevention has these sections: general methodology of studying crime; research on juvenile crime; infringements on socialist property; infringements on persons and public order; problems of procuratorial supervision; problems of pretrial investigation and court trials; criminal law and procedure; criminalistic techniques; forensic psychology (dealing with problems like combating perjury and extracting the truth, but it could one day deal with the psychopathology of crime); legal education; organizing, introducing, and implementing scientific recommendations; criminal statistics; and the applications of computers. "Interv'yu," p. 48.

74. A. Sakharov, "Lichnost' prestupnika i tipologii prestupnikov," *SZ,* No. 3 (1973), pp. 19–24.

75. Klochkov, "Osnovnye napravleniya nauchnykh issledovanii," p. 13.

76. Kudryavtsev, "Bor'ba s prestupnost'yu," pp. 17–18.

77. As their work is viewed by a critic, see V.V. Orekhov, *Sotsial'noe planirovanie i voprosy bor'by s prestupnost'yu* (Leningrad: Izd. Leningradskogo universiteta, 1972), pp. 16–25. As their work is viewed by a major lawyer proponent, see I.S. Noi, *Sushchnost' i funktsii ugolovnogo nakazaniya v sovetskom gosudarstve* (Saratov: Izd. Saratovskogo universiteta, 1973), pp. 105–113.

He cites with approval reports on work in the Serbskii Institute of Criminal Psychiatry, pointing to extra high rates of psychopathology among criminals, and dismisses adversaries' opposite conclusions that only social factors play a part in the probability of crime. Ibid., pp. 188–190.

78. Yuridicheskii fakul'tet, *Sravnitel'noe,* pp. 4–17, 175–196. Quote is from p. 17.

79. A. Shlyapochnikov and A. Dolgova, "O sozdanii eksperimental'nykh uchrezhdenii dlya izucheniya lichnosti prestupnika," *SZ,* No. 12 (1974), pp. 58–59.

80. Yu. M. Antonyan, "Sisetmnyi podkhod k isucheniyu lichnosti prestupnika," *SGP,* No. 4 (1974), p. 89.

81. A.B. Sakharov, "Sotsial'naya sistema presuprezhdeniya prestuplenii," *SGP,* No. 11 (1972), p. 69.

82. Kudryavtsev, "Bor'ba s prestupnost'yu," p. 20.

83. M.M. Babaev, "Kriminologicheskie issledovaniya problem migratsii naseleniya," *SGP,* No. 3 (1968), pp. 86–90; M. Babaev, "Sotsiologicheskie issledovaniya i bor'ba s prestupnost'yu," *SYu,* No. 19 (1969), p. 10; M.M. Babaev, "Kriminologicheskaya otsenka sotsial'no-ekonomicheskikh i demograficheskihk faktorov," *SGP,* No. 6 (1972), pp. 97–102.

84. Popkov, "Sudebanaya statistika," pp. 18–19; Korshunova, "Analiz statisticheskikh dannykh," p. 15; note 66.

85. Kudryavtsev, "Bor'ba s prestupnost'yu," p. 20.

86. "Kriminologicheskie issledovaniya i preduprezhdenie prestupleniya," *SYu,* No. 2 (1974), p. 2; V. Zvirbul', "Perspectivy sozdaniya ASU v sfere okhrany zakonnosti i bor'by s prestupnost'yu," *SZ,* No. 4 (1974), p. 40; notes 96, 98.

87. Norbert Wiener, *Cybernetics: Or Control and Communications in the Animal and the Machine* (New York: John Wiley and Sons, 1948), pp. 7–22. W. Ross Ashby, *An Introduction to Cybernetics* (New York: Barnes and Noble, 1956).

88. Felice D. Gaer, "A Cybernetic Reform Model for the Soviet Union," in Andrew W. Cordier (ed.), *Columbia Essays in International Affairs: The Dean's Papers, 1971* (New York: Columbia University Press, 1972), pp. 90–113; Loren Graham, "Cybernetics," in George Fischer (ed.), *Science and Ideology in the Soviet Union* (New York: Atherton Press, 1967), pp. 88–91; K.A. Bagranovskii, *Modeli i metody ekonomicheskoi kibernetiki* (Moscow: Izd. Ekonomika, 1973), pp. 3–9; Viktor Pekelis, *Kiberneticheskaya smes'* (2nd ed.; Moscow: Izd. "Znanie," 1973).

89. "Systems Analysis:" Anatol Rappoport, "General Systems Theory," Talcott Parsons, "Social Systems," William C. Mitchell, "Political Systems," Morton A. Kaplan, "International Systems." David S. Gochman, "Psychological Systems," in David L. Sills (ed.), *International Encyclopedia of the Social Sciences* (New York: Macmillan and Free Press, 1968), vol. 15; D.M. Gvishiani, *Organizatsiya i upravlenie* (2nd ed.; Moscow: Izd. "Nauka," 1972), pp. 380–518.

90. Yu. A. Dmitriev, "Razvitie XXIV s"ezdom KPSS leninskikh printsipov upravleniya," *Chelovek i obshchestvo,* No. 11 (1972), pp. 3–10; V.G. Klyuev, "Rol' partiinoi organizatsii v sovershenstvovanii upravleniya proizvodstvom," in N.P. Fedorenko, D.M. Gvishiani, V.G. Afanas'ev et al., (eds.), *Organizatsiya upravleniya* (Moscow: Izd.. "Ekonomika," 1973), p. 27.

91. I.A. Kruchinin, "Proektnaya i fakticheskaya effektivnost' ASU," ibid., pp. 74–85; I.A. Kruchinin, "Voprosy effektivnosti sozdaniya ASU," in D.M. Gvishiani and S.E. Kamenitser (eds.), *Problemy nauchnoi organizatsii upravleniya sotsialisticheskoi promyshlennost'yu (po materialam Vtoroi Vsesoyuznoi nauchnotekhnicheskoi konferentsii)* (Moscow: Izd. "Ekonomika," 1974), pp. 569–578; V.A. Myasnikov and V.D. Knyazev, "Problemy sozdaniya avtomatizirovannykh sistem upravleniya," in Fedorenko et al., *Organizatsiya upravleniya,* pp. 64–74; V. Glushkov, "At the Crossroads of Opinion: Remove Departmental Barriers to Automated Management Systems," *Izvestiya,* March 8, 1974, transl. in *CDSP,* vol. 26, No. 10 (1974), pp. 1–3.

92. Quote is from A. Berg, B. Biryukov, and I. Novik, "Metodologicheskie aspekty kibernetiki," *Kommunist,* No. 18 (1971). See also Gvishiani and Kamenitser, *Problemy nauchnoi organizatsii upravleniya,* a major compendium and guide to the Soviet universe of economic cybernetic experts and their organizations. The problems they were considering are summarized by D.M. Gvishiani, G. Kh. Popov, A.I. Mikhailov, and S.I. Kozlov, in Gvishiani and Kamenitser, *Problemy nauchnoi organizatsii upravleniya,* pp. 7–28, 61–80, 517–533; Fedorenko, et al., *Organizatsiya upravleniya,* especially V.G. Afanas'ev, "Upravlenie i sistema sotsial'noi informatsii," pp. 37–49, and "Razvitie kompleksnogo podkhoda k analyzu upravleniya sotsialisticheskogo proizvodstva," pp. 50–63; A.K. Semenov, *Metody sistemnogo analyza struktury narodnogo khozyaistva* (Moscow: Izd. Nauka, 1974), pp. 3–4, 11–67; Yu. Tikhomirov, "Science of Management: Paths for the Optimization of Decisions," *Pravda,* March 9, 1974, cond. in *CDSP,* vol. 26, No. 10 (1974), pp. 3–4.

93. *XXIV s"ezd Kommunisticheskoi partii Sovetskogo Soyuza, Stenograficheskii otchet* (Moscow: Izd. politicheskoi literatury, 1971), vol. 1, p. 91.

94. Gaer, "Cybernetic Reform Model," p. 190.

95. Yu. A. Tikhomirov and V.P. Kazimirchuk, *Pravo i sotsiologiya* (Moscow: Izd. "Nauka," 1973), pp. 95–130; "Kriminologicheskie issledovaniya," pp. 2–3.

96. G.A. Avanesov and S.E. Vitsin, *Prognozirovanie i organizatsiya bor'by s prestupnost'yu* (Moscow: Izd. "Znanie," 1972), pp. 20–22.

97. V.N. Kudryavtsev, "Struktura prestupnosti i sotsial'nye izmeneniya," *SGP,* No. 6 (1971), pp. 108–109, and his *Prichinnost' v kriminologii,* especially pp. 151–170.

98. "Dostizheniya nauki—v praktiku bor'by s prestupnost'yu," *SYu,* No. 17 (1972), pp. 1–2.

99. Tikhomirov and Kazimirchuk, *Pravo i sotsiologiya,* p. 103.

100. G.A. Avanesov, "Organizatsiya kriminologicheskogo prognozirovaniya i planirovaniya," *SGP,* No. 1 (1972), pp. 110–114. Avanesov and Vitsin, *Prognozirovanie,* p. 28, give a summary differing in some details.

101. V.N. Kudryavtsev, "Sotsiologiya, pravo i kriminologiya," *SGP,* No. 2 (1969), p. 68.

102. L. Il'ina, "Seminar o prognozirovanii prestupnosti," *SZ,* No. 7 (1971), p. 66.

103. V. Kudryavtsev, "G. Avanesov, *Osnovy kriminologicheskogo prognozirovaniya* M., Izd. VSh MVD SSSR, 1970, 52 c.," *SZ,* No. 6 (1971), pp. 95–96.

104. N.A. Shchelokov, "Leninskie printsipy—v osnovu upravleniya," *SGP,* No. 10 (1970), p. 14; Klochkov, "Osnovnye napravleniya," pp. 12–13; "Interv'yu s professorom V. Zvirbulem," p. 49.

105. See note 73.

106. See note 96.

107. Yu. Feofanov, "The Fourth Dimension," *Izvestiya,* July 8, 1970, excerpted in *CDSP,* vol. 22, No. 27 (1970), p. 27.

108. M. Rassolov, "Ob osnovakh pravovoi kibernetiki," *SYu,* No. 9 (1974), p. 28.

109. Graham, "Cybernetics," p. 94.

110. D.A. Kerimov, *Svoboda, pravo i zakonnost' v sotialisticheskom obshchestve* (Moscow: Gos. izd. yuridicheskoi literatury, 1960), pp. 206–222 (I am grateful to Felice Gaer for showing and lending me this book); A.R. Shlyakhov and L.G. Edzhubov, "Sovremennoe sostoyanie i nekotorye problemy ispol'zovaniya kibernetiki v prave," *SGP,* No. 6 (1960), pp. 83–92.

111. Kh. A. Randalu, "Opyt ispol'zovaniya perfokart," *SGP,* No. 9 (1966), pp. 127–133; his "Organizatsiya pravovoi informatsionnoi sluzhby," *SGP,* No. 3 (1967), pp. 124–127; his "Obrabotka dannykh statisticheskikh kartotek na podsudimykh," *SGP,* No. 10 (1968), pp. 87–93; his "Informatsionno-poiskovye sistemy dlya isucheniya prestupnosti nesovershennoletnikh," *SGP,* No. 10 (1971), pp. 120–123; his "Primenenie EVM v deyatel'nosti komissii po delam nesovershennoletnikh," *SGP,* No. 11 (1973), pp. 75–80. His articles describe work at the Sector of Law, Institute of Economics, Estonian Academy of Sciences. Work on a legal ASU at the Law Faculty, Tartu University, in cooperation with the Estonian Ministry of Justice, is described in, e.g., V. Yu. Raudsalu, I.A. Rebane, and I. Ya. Sil'dmyae, "O sozdanii avtomatizirovannoi sistemy yuridicheskoi informatsii," *SGP,* No. 5 (1974), pp. 28–36; I.G. Kull', I. Ya. Sil'dmyae, A.K. Khelemyae, and Kh. Ya. Yiim, "O razrabotke tesaurusa yuridicheskikh terminov dlya informatsionno-poiskovoi sistemy," in A.P. Shlyakhov and V.N. Kudryavtsev (eds.), *Pravovaya kikernetika* (Moscow: Izd. "Nauka," 1973), pp. 54–62. Neither Randalu nor the group at Tartu University and the Estonian Ministry of Justice cite the others' work. I am grateful to Felice Gaer for drawing my attention to Randalu's work and *Pravovaya kibernetika.*

112. Raudsalu, et al., "O sozdanii avtomatizirovannoi," p. 28; "Interv'yu s professorom V. Zvirbulem," p. 49; Rassolov, "Ob osnovakh pravovoi kibernetiki," pp. 28–29.

113. K.E. Kolibab, "Izdanie Sobraniya deistvuyushchego zakonodatel'stva SSSR," *SGP,* No. 8 (1974), pp. 3–9; S.S. Moskvin, "Problemy issledovanii v oblasti ispol'zovaniya vychislitel'noi tekhniki dlya organizatsii IPS normativnykh

materialov," in Shlyakhov and Kudryavtsev, *Pravovaya kibernetika,* pp. 39–40.

114. Zvirbul', "Perspektivy sozdaniya ASU," pp. 40–41.

115. Moskvin, "Problemy issledovani," p. 36. See also A.R. Shlyakhov and S.S. Moskvin, "Aktual'nye voprosy sovershenstvovaniya ucheta i poiska normaitvnykh materialov," in Shlyakhov and Kurdryavtsev, *Pravovaya kibernetika,* pp. 23–34; I.N. Gafinova, L.O. Litvinova, S.S. Moskvin, and I.V. Trofimova, "Rezhim i poryadok raboty IPS 'Pravo-l'," ibid., pp. 43–54; S.N. Yusupov, "Osobennosti otbora klyuchevykh slov iz pravovogo dokumenta," ibid., pp. 63–67; E.A. Pranishnikov, "Semiotika i zakon," ibid., pp. 91–97.

116. A. Shlyakhov, "Problemy razvitiya pravovoi kibernetiki," *SZ,* No. 3 (1976), pp. 27–31; note 111 and Zvirbul', "Perspektivy sozdaniya ASU," pp. 40–41.

117. Ibid. Quote is from p. 41.

118. See note 99.

119. A. Yakovlev, "G.A. Avenasov, Teoriya i metodologiya kriminologicheskogo prognozirovaniya (izd-o 'Yuridicheskaya literatura,' 1972, 436 str.)," *SYu,* No. 5 (1972), p. 31.

120. Conversation with Felice Gaer.

121. Zvirbul', "Perspektivy sozdaniya ASU," pp. 41–43; N. Polevoi, "Electronics Serve the Law," *Izvestiya,* January 10, 1974, cond. in *CDSP,* vol. 26, No. 2 (1974), pp. 17–18.

122. Rassolov, "Ob osnovakh pravovoi kibernetiki," p. 28; note 116.

123. Zvirbul', "Perspekivy sozdaniya ASU," p. 43; I.S. Samoshchenko and A.B. Vengerov, "Yuridicheskaya otvetstvennost' i ASU," *SGP,* No. 3 (1974), pp. 31–39; A.B. Vengerov, "Problemy pravovogo regulirovaniya ASU," *VNII Sovetskogo zakonodatel'stva, Uchenie zapiski,* No. 28 (1973), pp. 3–21.

124. This expression is used by Kudryavtsev in "Bor'ba s prestupnost'yu," p. 20.

125. It is hard to stereotype Soviet works on "the management of social processes" because of the range of emphasis from order, discipline, and productivity to a truly totalist vision, but one so vaguely linked to practical reality as to be simply ideological "boiler plate." As a starter, see, e.g., V.G. Afanas'ev (ed.), *Nauchnoe upravlenie obshchestvom,* (Moscow: Izd. "Mysl'," 1970), No. 4 of a series; *Sotsial'nye issledovaniya,* No. 4 (1970), devoted to "Problems of Work and the Personality"; *Chelovek i obshchestvo,* No. 11 (1973), devoted to "Social Problems of Management"; and A.I. Afanas'ev and A.A. Nurullaev, *Kollektiv i lichnost'* (Moscow: Izd. "Mysl'," 1965). For more totalist but much vaguer works see, e.g., V.D. Parygins, *Sotsial'naya psikhologiya kak nauka* (Leningrad: Lenizdat, 1967), pp. 232–269 ("Forming the New Man as a Practical Problem of Social Psychology"); A.K. Belykh (ed.), *Kommunizm i upravlenie obshchestvenymi protsessami* (Leningrad: Izd. Leningradskogo universiteta, 1972), vol. 1; Kh. P. Pulatov, *Kommunizm, gosudarstvo, kul'tura, lichnost': Stroitel'stvo kommunizma i problemy kul'turno-vospitatel'noi funktsii obshchenarodnogo sotsialisticheskogo gosudarstva* (Tashkent: Izd. "Uzbekistan,"

1971); F.V. Konstantinov (ed.), *Stroitel'stvo kommunizma i razvitie obshchestvennykh otnoshenii* (Moscow: Izd. "Nauka," 1966).

126. Zvirbul', "Perspektivy sozdaniya ASU," p. 40; Kull' et al., "O razrabotke tezauriusa," p. 62; A.V. Dmitriev, "Rol' strukturnogo funkstionalizma v Amerikanskoi politologii," *Chelovek i Obshchestvo,* No. 11 (1973), pp. 90–99. Compare Soviet sources with Western ones like Sutherland and Cressey, *Principles of Criminology.* It mentions one Russian prerevolutionary and misspells his name, p. 58.

127. Kudryavtsev, "Bor'ba s prestupnost'yu," pp. 15–16; I. Karpets, "Kontseptsii burzhuaznogo pravovedeniya—orudie ideologicheskoi bor'by," *Kommunist,* No. 3 (1974), pp. 103–112; Avanesov and Vitsin, *Prognozirovanie,* p. 15.

128. Belykh, *Kommunizm i upravlenie obshchestvennymi protsessami,* pp. 104–167.

129. David Easton, *The Political System: An Inquiry into the State of Political Science* (New York: Alfred R. Knopf, 1953), p. 223; his "The Current Meaning of Behavioralism," in James C. Charlesworth (ed.), *Contemporary Political Analysis* (New York: Free Press, 1967), pp. 11–31; and his *A Framework for Political Analysis* (Englewood Cliffs, N.J.: Prentice-Hall, 1965), pp. ix–xii, 1–45; Robert A. Dahl, "The Behavioral Approach in Political Science: Epitaph for a Monument to a Successful Protest," *American Political Science Review,* No. 55 (1961), pp. 770–771; Richard C. Snyder, "Experimental Techniques and Political Analysis: Some Reflections in the Context of Concern over Behavioral Approaches," in James C. Charlesworth (ed), *The Limits of Behavioralism in Political Science* (Philadelphia: American Academy of Political and Social Science, 1962), pp. 94–123.

130. V.G. Afanase'ev, "Eshche raz o problemakh nauchnogo upravelniya obshchestvom," in V.G. Afanas'ev (ed.), *Nauchnoe upravlenie obshchestvom* (Moscow: Izd. "Mysl'," 1969), vol. 3, pp. 19–21; A.V. Kireev, "Nauchnyi kharakter politiki KPSS," in V.G. Afanas'ev, *Nauchnoe upravlenie obshchestvom: opyt sistemnogo issledovaniya* (Moscow: Izd. Polit. lit., 1968), pp. 30–31.

131. Mulford Q. Sibley, "The Limits of Behavioralism," in Charlesworth, *Contemporary Political Analysis,* pp. 59–71; L.N. Moskvichev, "Kritika kontseptsii 'deideologizatsii' nauki i problema partiinosti sotsial'nogo poznaniya," in D.I. Chesnokov (ed.), *Problemy poznaniya sotsial'nykh yavlenii* (Moscow: Izd. "Mysl'," 1968), pp. 94–129.

132. Herbert J. Spiro, "An Evaluation of Systems Theory," in Charlesworth, *Contemporary Political Analysis,* p .165.

133. Easton, "Current Meaning of Behavioralism," p. 24.

134. Antonyan, "Sistemnyi podkhod," pp. 88–89.

135. Orekhov, *Sotsial'noe planirovanie,* pp. 16–17.

136. V.N. Kudryavtsev, "Ugolovnaya yustitsiya kak sistema," in Shlyakhov and Kudryavtsev, *Pravovaya kibernetika,* pp. 8–21; S.S. Alekseev, "Sovetskoe pravo kak sistema: Metodologicheskie printsipy issledovaniya," *SGP,* No. 7 (1974), pp. 11–18; A.F. Cherdantsev, "Sistemoobrazuyushchie svyazi prava,"

SGP, No. 8 (1974), pp. 10–17; A.A. Zvorykin, "Sotsial'nye aspekty upravleniya," *Chelovek i obshchestva,* vol. 11 (1973), pp. 17–19; Avanesov and Vitsin, *Prognozirovanie,* p. 18; Tikhomirov and Kazimirchuk, *Pravo i sotsiologiya,* pp. 5, 253–290:

137. Dmitriev, "Razvitie XXIV s"ezdom," p. 8.

138. Erik P. Hoffmann, "Soviet Metapolicy: Information Processing in the Communist Party of the Soviet Union," *Journal of Comparative Administration,* vol. 5, No. 2 (1973), p. 281.

139. "Clearly Khrushchev's populist variant of rationalizing totalitarianism has given way to a new and different model, which in its leviathan-like design is awesome." Paul Cocks, "The Rationalization of Party Control," in Chalmers Johnson (ed.), *Change in Communist Systems* (Stanford, Calif.: Stanford University Press, 1970), p. 183. See also pp. 181–182. Already by 1960 Khrushchev's administration appears to have decided to push ahead rapidly the development and economic applications of cybernetics. S. Olgin, "Soviet Ideology and Cybernetics," *Bulletin of the Institute for the Study of the USSR,* vol. 9, No. 2 (February 1962), pp. 12–14. But Khrushchev was forced out before administrative (economic and legal cybernetics got beyond the project stage. Administrative and crime prevention policy still reflected Khruschev the embattled and erratic visionary no less than Khrushchev the rationalizer. Edward Crankshaw, *Khrushchev: A Career* (New York: Viking Press, 1966), pp. 270–278.

140. Dmitriev, "Razvitie XXIV s'ezdom," p. 9; G. Dobrov and L. Smirnov, "School of Economic Management: To See the Future," *Izvestiya,* December 19, 1970, cond. in *CDSP,* vol. 22, No. 51 (1970), pp. 8–9; on health services, I encountered a project for an ASU of republic health services at Public Health Exhibition, Moscow, Summer 1971.

141. L.N. Kogan, *Sotsial'noe planirovanie: rabota, obrazovanie byt* (Moscow: Izd. politicheskoi literatury, 1970), p. 9.

142. Graham, "Cybernetics," pp. 84–85, 88.

143. See page note at beginning of chapter.

144. Wiener, *Cybernetics,* p. 34.

145. Ibid., pp. 155–191.

146. Roman Kolkowitz, "Strategic Elites and Politics of the Superpowers," *Journal of International Affairs,* vol. 26, No. 1 (1972), p. 58; note 2.

147. Herbert J. Spiro, *Politics as the Master Science: from Plato to Mao* (New York: Harper and Row, 1970), pp. 108–109.

148. V.I. Laputin, "KPSS ob ukreplenii zakonnosti na sovremennom etape," in R.A. Dudenko and N.V. Zhogin (eds.), *Na strazhe sovetskikh zakonov* (Moscow: "Yuridicheskaya literatura," 1972), p. 47.

Chapter 7

1. Ralf Dahrendorf, *Society and Democracy in Germany* (Garden City, N.Y.: Anchor Books, Doubleday, 1969), p. 43; Walter A. Lunden, *Crimes and Criminals* (Ames: Iowa State University Press, 1967), pp. 75–76.

2. Remarks here on juvenile crime incorporate the results of findings in a separate study referred to during the course of this book.

3. Lunden, *Crimes and Criminals,* p. 77.

4. Paul Frolich, *Rosa Luxemburg: Her Life and Work,* transl. by Johanna Hoornweg (New York: Monthly Review Press, 1972), pp. 297–300; Michael Solomon, *Magadan* (New York: Vertex Books, 1971), pp. 183–186; Joseph Schmolmer, *Vorkuta,* transl. by Robert Kee (London: Weidenfeld and Nicolson, 1954), pp. 225–228; *Attica: The Official Report of the New York State Special Committee on Attica* (New York: Bantam Books, 1972); *The Report of the President's Commission on Campus Unrest* (Washington, D.C.: U.S. Government Printing Office, 1970); Peter Davies, *The Truth About Kent State: A Challenge to the American Conscience* (New York: Farrar, Straus and Giroux, 1973); IDOC/North America, *Chile Under Military Rule: A Dossier of Documents* (New York: IDOC/North America, 1974), Chapter 3.

5. On America's "losing battle against crime," see *Crime and the Law* (Washington, D.C.: Congressional Quarterly Service, 1971), p. 1. On crime "steadily diminishing", see, e.g., N.A. Shchelokov, "The Citizen, the Militia, the Law," *Ogonek,* No. 44 (1970), transl. in *Reprints from the Soviet Press,* No. 11 (1970), p. 38; chapters 5, 6; on European rates see Lunden, *Crimes and Criminals,* pp. 49–63.

6. N. Shchelokov, "Glavnoe—Preduprezhdenie pravonarushenii," *SZ,* No. 8 (1967), p. 7; "Nash zakon i ego garantii: Na voprosy chitatelei 'Truda' otvechaet Ministr yustitsii SSSR Vladimir Ivanovich Terebilov," *Trud,* March 2, 1970; note 7.

7. M.P. Malyarov quoted in "With the Full Severity of the Law," *Pravda,* July 11, 1972, transl. in *CDSP,* vol. 24, No. 28 (1972), pp. 5–6; Theodore Shabad, "Sakharov: A Warning Defied," *New York Times,* August 26, 1973, section 4.

8. Walter D. Connor, *Deviance in Soviet Society: Crime, Delinquency and Alcoholism* (New York: Columbia University Press, 1972), p. 251.

9. V. Zvirbul', "Razvitie form i metodov preduprezhdeniya prestupnosti v SSSR," *SZ,* No. 5 (1973), p. 20.

10. Leon Radzinowicz, *Ideology and Crime* (New York: Columbia University Press, 1966), p. 53.

11. Peter H. Solomon, Jr., "Specialists in Soviet Policy-Making; Criminologists and Criminal Policy in the 1960s" (Ph.D. dissertation, Faculty of Political Science, Columbia University, 1973), pp. 72–75.

12. "Each young energetic sovereign has attempted to inaugurate a new epoch by thoroughly remodelling the administration according to the most approved foreign political philosophy of the time." Donald Makenzie Wallace, *Russia on the Eve of War and Revolution,* ed. with intro. by Cyril E. Black (New York: Vintage Books, 1961), p. 47.

13. V.M. Chkhikvadze et al., (eds.), *Entsiklopedicheskii slovar' pravovikh znanii,* (Moscow: Izd. Sovetskaya entsiklopedia, 1965), p. 431; A.I. Denisov, *Teoriya gosudarstva i prava* (Moscow: Izd. Moskovskogo universiteta, 1967), p. 324.

14. Teresa Rakowska-Harmstone, "The Dilemma of Nationalism in the Soviet Union," in John W. Strong, *The Soviet Union*, pp. 115–134; Jerry F. Hough, "The Party *Apparatchiki*," in H. Gordan Skilling and Franklyn Griffiths (eds.), *Interest Groups in Soviet Politics* (Princeton: Princeton University Press, 1971), pp. 47–92.

15. Robert V. Daniels writes about "participatory democracy" in "Soviet Politics Since Khrushchev," in Strong, *Soviet Union*, pp. 16–25. Analyses made before the fall of Khrushchev were less likely to point out pluralistic sides of Soviet policy making. See *e.g.*, Donald W. Treadgold (ed.), *The Development of the USSR: An Exchange of Views* (Seattle: University of Washington Press, 1964), pp. 3–40. But Carl Linden saw "time is running out" for Khrushchev in the face of opposition from his critics in "Khrushchev and the Party Battle," *Problems of Communism*, vol. 12 (September-October 1963), pp. 27–35.

16. Carl A. Linden, *Khrushchev and the Soviet Leadership 1957–1964* (Baltimore: Johns Hopkins Press, 1966).

17. John Osborne, "The Nixon Watch: The Pressure of Fear," *New Republic*, June 3, 1972, pp. 13–15.

18. Jerry F. Hough, "The Soviet Union: Petrifaction or Pluralism?" *Problems of Communism*, No. 2 (March-April 1972), p. 31.

Selective Bibliography

The many footnote references in this book provide a topical research bibliography. What follows here is meant to be a short, usable listing of sources I have found valuable for reading and research about law, justice, and crime in the Soviet Union, the United States, and beyond.

Bibliographies, References, and Specialized Periodicals in English

ABSEES. *Soviet and East European Abstract Series* (University of Glasgow).

BUTLER, WILLIAM E. "Checklist of Soviet Normative Acts Available in English Translation," *American Journal of Comparative Law,* vol. 33 (1975), pp. 530–549.

Bulletin on Current Research in Soviet and East European Law (Prof. Will Adams, William Jewel College, Liberty, Mo. 64068).

FELDBRUGGE, F.J.M. (ed.). *Encyclopedia of Soviet Law.* 2 vols.; Dobbs Ferry, N.Y.: Oceana, and Leiden, Neth.: A.W. Sijthoff, 1973. Includes "Bibliography (of Soviet Law)," vol. 1, pp. 77–80.

SOLOMON, PETER H., JR. *Soviet Criminology: A Selective Bibliography.* University of Cambridge, Bibliographical Series No. 4. Cambridge, Eng.: Institute of Criminology, 1969.

Soviet Law and Government. Published quarterly since 1961 by the International Arts and Sciences Press. Unabridged translations.

Soviet Statutes and Decisions. Published annually since 1964 by the International Arts and Science Press.

SZIRMAI, Z., and F.J.M. FELDBRUGGE (general eds.). *Law in Eastern Europe,* 19 vols. so far, 1958–1975. Leiden, Neth.: A.W. Sijthoff.

Imperial Russia, 1864–1917

In English

KENNAN, GEORGE. *Siberia and the Exile System,* 2nd abridged ed.; Chicago: University of Chicago Press, 1958.

KUCHEROV, SAMUEL. *Courts, Lawyers, and Trials under the Last Three Tsars.* New York: Frederick A. Praeger, 1953.

LEROY-BEAULIEU, ANATOLE. *The Empire of the Tsars and the Russians.* 3 vols.; New York and London: G.P. Putnam's Sons, 1894, vol. 2, pp. 252–425.

WALLACE, SIR HAROLD MACKENZIE. *Russia on the Eve of War and Revolution,* ed. by Cyril E. Black. New York: Vintage, 1961.

In Russian

DAVYDOV, N.V., and N.N. POLYANSKII (eds.). *Sudebnaya reforma.* 2 vols., Moscow: "Ob"edinenie," 1915.

GERNET, M.N. *Istoriya tsarskoi tyurm'my,* 3rd ed., 5 vols.; Moscow: "Yurid. lit," 1962, 1963.

ROSIN, N.N. *Ugolovnoe sudoproizvodstvo.* 2nd. ed., St. Petersburg: "Pravo," 1914.

VLADIMIRSKI-BUDANOV, M.F. *Obzor istorii russkogo prava.* 6th ed.; St. Petersburg, Kiev: N. Ya. Ogloblin, 1909. Reproduced. The Hague, 1966.

Soviet Russia

In English

AMNESTY INTERNATIONAL. *Prisoners of Conscience in the USSR: Their Treatment and Conditions.* London: Amnesty International Publications, 1975.

BABB, HUGH W., and JOHN N. HAZARD (eds.). *Soviet Legal Philosophy.* Cambridge: Harvard University Press, 1951.

BERMAN, HAROLD J. *Justice in the USSR.* Rev. and enl. ed.; New York: Vintage, 1963.

——, and JAMES W. SPINDLER. *Soviet Criminal Law and Procedure: The RSFSR Codes.* 2nd ed.; Cambridge: Harvard University Press, 1972.

BRUMBERG, ABRAHAM. *In Quest of Justice: Protest and Dissent in the Soviet Union Today.* New York: Frederick A. Praeger, 1970.

CHALIDZE, VALERY. *To Defend These Rights: Human Rights and the Soviet Union,* transl. by Guy Daniels. New York: Random House, 1974.

CHAMBERLIN, W.H. *Russia's Iron Age.* London: Gerald Duckworth, 1935.

CONNOR, WALTER D. *Deviance in Soviet Society.* New York: Columbia University Press, 1972.

CONQUEST, ROBERT. *The Great Terror: Stalin's Purge of the Thirties.* Rev. ed.; New York: Collier Books, 1973.

FAINSOD, MERLE. *How Russia Is Ruled.* 2nd ed.; Cambridge: Harvard University Press, 1963. A new posthumous edition of this standard work is being prepared by Jerry F. Hough.

FEIFER, GEORGE. *Justice in Moscow*. New York: Simon and Schuster, 1964.

HAZARD, JOHN N. *Communists and Their Law: A Search for the Common Core of the Legal Systems of the Marxian Socialist States*. Chicago: University of Chicago Press, 1969.

———. *Law and Social Change in the USSR*. Toronto: Carswell, 1953.

———, ISAAC SHAPIRO, and PETER B. MAGGS. *The Soviet Legal System: Contemporary Documentation and Historical Commentary*. Dobbs Ferry, N.Y.: Oceana, 1969.

HOLLANDER, PAUL. *Soviet and American Society: A Comparison*. New York: Oxford University Press, 1973.

KUCHEROV, SAMUEL. *The Organs of Soviet Administration of Justice: Their History and Operation*. Leiden, Neth.; Brill, 1970.

LAPENNA, IVO. *Soviet Penal Policy*. London: Bodley Head, 1968.

OSAKWE, CHRISTOPHER. "Due Process of Law under Contemporary Soviet Criminal Procedure," *Tulane Law Review*, vol. 50, No. 2 (1976), pp. 266–317.

REDDAWAY, PETER (ed.). *Uncensored Russia: Protest and Dissent in the Soviet Union; The Unofficial Moscow Journal A Chronicle of Current Events*. New York: American Heritage Press, 1972.

SKILLING, H. GORDON, and FRANKLYN GRIFFITHS (eds.). *Interest Groups in Soviet Politics*. Princeton, N.J.: Princeton University Press, 1971, espec. Frederick C. Barghoorn, "The Security Police," pp. 93–129, and Donald D. Barry and Harold J. Berman, "The Jurists," pp. 291–333.

SOLOMON, PETER H., JR. "Soviet Criminology: Its Demise and Rebirth, 1928–1963," *Soviet Union*, vol. 1, No. 2 (1974), pp. 122–140.

SOLZHENITSYN, ALEKSANDR I. *The Gulag Archipelago 1918–1956: An Experiment in Literary Investigation*, vol. 1–2. New York: Harper and Row, 1974. *Ibid.*, vol. 3–4. New York: Harper and Row, 1975.

In Russian

ANASHKIN, G.Z. et al. (eds.). *Kommentarii k ugolovnomu kodeksu RSFSR*. Moscow: "Yurid. lit.," 1971.

BELYAEV, N.A., and M.I. FEDOROV (eds.). *Ispravitel'no–trudovoe pravo*. Moscow: "Yurid. lit.," 1971.

BLINOV, B.M. (ed.). *Kommentarii k ispravitel'no-trudovomu Kodeksu RSFSR*. Moscow: "Yurid. lit.," 1973.

GERNET, M.N. *Prestupnost' za granitsei i v SSSR*. Moscow: "Sov. zakonodatel'stvo," 1931.

GERTSENZON, A.A. et al. (eds.). *Kriminologiya*. 2nd ed.; Moscow: Yurid. lit., 1968.

GOLYAKOV, I.T. *Sbornik dokumentov po istorii ugolovnogo zakonodatel'stvo SSSR i RSFSR 1917–1952*. Moscow: Gos. izd. yurid. lit., 1953.

GORKIN, A.F., V.V. KULIKOV, N.V. RADUTNAYA, I.D. PERLOV. *Nastol'naya kniga sud'i*. Moscow: "Yurid. lit.," 1972.

IOFFE, O.S. et al. (eds.). *Sorok let sovetskogo prava: 1917–1957*. 2 vols.; Leningrad: Izd. Leningradskogo U., 1957.

MENSHAGIN, V.D. (ed.). *Osobennosti ugolovnykh kodeksov soyuznykh respublik*. Moscow: "Yurid lit.," 1963.

PIONTKOVSKII, A.A., P.S. ROMASHKIN, and V.M. CHKHIKVADZE (eds.). *Kurs sovetskogo ugolovnogo prava*. 6 vols.; Moscow: "Nauka," 1970–1971.

MINISTERSTVO YUSTITSII *RSFSR*. *Ugolovnyi kodeks RSFSR*. Moscow: "Yurid. lit.," 1975.

——. *Ugolovno-protsessual'nyi kodeks RSFSR*. Moscow: "Yurid, lit.," 1973.

General: Crime and Penology

BECKER, HOWARD S. *Outsiders: Studies in the Sociology of Deviance*. New York: Free Press, 1963.

KIRCHEIMER, OTTO. *Political Justice: The Use of Legal Procedures for Political Purposes*. Princeton, N.J.: Princeton University Press. 1961.

MANNHEIM, HERMANN. *Comparative Criminology*. 2 vols.; London: Routledge and Kegan Paul, 1965.

MITFORD, JESSICA. *Kind and Uusual Punishment: The Prison Business*. New York: Alfred A. Knopf, 1973.

PHILIP, CYNTHIA OWEN. *Imprisoned in America: Prison Communications 1776 to Attica*. New York: Harper and Row, 1973.

PRESIDENT'S COMMISSION ON LAW ENFORCEMENT AND ADMINISTRATION OF JUSTICE. *The Challenge of Crime in a Free Society*. Washington, D.C.: U.S. Government Printing Office, 1967.

RADZINOWICZ, LEON. *Ideology and Crime*. New York: Columbia University

——, and MARVIN E. WOLFGANG (eds.), *Crime and Justice*. 3 vols.; New York: Basic Books, 1971.

SUTHERLAND, EDWIN H., and DONALD R. CRESSEY. *Principles of Criminology*. 9th ed.; New York: Lippincott, 1974.

Index